CHURCH ON FIRE

Church on Fire

The Story of Anglican Evangelicals

Roger Steer

Hodder & Stoughton

LONDON SYDNEY AUCKLAND

British Library Cataloguing in Publication Data
A record for this book is available from the British Library

ISBN 0 340 64193 2

Typeset by Avon Dataset Ltd, Bidford-on-Avon, Warks

Printed and bound in Great Britain by
Clays Ltd, St Ives plc

Hodder & Stoughton Ltd
A division of Hodder Headline PLC
338 Euston Road
London NW1 3BH

Contents

Acknowledgments

I want to thank all those who helped make writing this book enjoyable despite the magnitude of the task.

I came across my first book by John Stott in the early 1960s and since then have read nearly every book he has written as it has been published. But, although I had heard him preach on a number of occasions, I had never met him until we spent an afternoon together in May 1997 talking about his hopes and fears for Anglican Evangelicals and his recollections of the All Souls years. On a visit to Oxford I talked to the past and present holders of the Regius Chair of Hebrew at that University, James Barr and Hugh Williamson.

The Archbishop of Canterbury, Dr George Carey, agreed to answer a series of questions I put to him and I would like to thank him and his staff at Lambeth Palace for taking an interest in this project despite so many demands on their time. Canon Michael Saward talked to me on the phone and pointed me in the direction of some useful material. My thanks go as well to a whole number of people, too many to mention individually, who talked to me at the 1995 and 1997 Anglican Evangelical Assemblies and also delegates to the Evangelical Anglican Leaders' Westminster Conference 1996, and conferences in June of the same years arranged by Reform and the Proclamation Trust. Sarah Finch has kindly kept me in touch with the Trust's activities.

My old friend Colin Spivey, himself a former Rector of Haworth, talked to me about his famous predecessor, William Grimshaw, and passed on to me some valuable source material. Arthur Scotchmer introduced me to the TESM story and lent me his copy of Majory's biography of her late husband, Alf Stanway.

During a visit to the USA in May 1996, John and Margaret Nicholas entertained me in their home in Ambridge, Pennsylvania. Robert Munday and David Mills helped in all sorts of ways in making the arrangements for my visit to Trinity Episcopal School for Ministry (TESM) and answered my questions during my stay. Philip Wainwright welcomed me to the Episcopal Evangelical Assembly and many delegates helped me to build up a picture of Anglican Evangelicalism in America past and present. Stephen Noll took time to talk to me about the history of Evangelicalism in the Episcopal Church and the situation today. Many of the people I met on this visit to the Pittsburgh area have become friends and it is good to keep in touch with them regularly by e-mail, as it is with Gillis Harp, Richard Kew, Charles Flinn and Bubber Cockrell, all of whom have made helpful suggestions and answered my queries. Gillis Harp also made available to me some of his work on Phillips Brooks.

When I travelled north-west to Wheaton College, Mark Noll gave me the benefit of his extensive work on Evangelicalism, and talked to me from the perspective of a non-Anglican as did his colleague Bud Kellstedt who, with his wife Charmaine, took me to visit the massive Willow Creek Community Church. Phil Harrold devoted a day to showing me Seabury-Western Anglican Theological Seminary and the University of Chicago and talked to me then and since by e-mail about Anglican history on which he lectures. So that my time in the Chicago area should not be all work and no play, Janet Bein treated me to a breathtaking river-boat tour providing a never-to-be-forgotten view of the incredible Chicago skyscrapers. We ascended the 1,454 feet to the top of the Sears Tower, a memorable experience for a simple Devon boy.

I owe a great deal to the members of 'List Anglican', a lively Internet discussion list, who since 1995 have helped me understand how Anglicans from all over the world and every tradition think. They have also impressed me with their prayerfulness, amused me with their wit and, at times, dismayed me with their prickliness. Discussions on similar lists run by the Church of England and American Episcopalians (known as 'White Horse Tavern') have been rather more staid on the whole, but no less instructive and enjoyable.

Cynthia McFarland, archivist and historian for the Diocese of

Central New York, sent me a number of books and unpublished material for which I am most grateful. Tom Rightmyer, who works for the Episcopal Church's Ordinations Examinations Board, recommended some important source material to me and gave me the benefit of his historical knowledge and wisdom.

All the published (and some unpublished) sources I consulted are listed in the bibliography. I am particularly grateful to the following living authors whose books I referred to many times (in alphabetical order): James Barr, Diana Butler, Michael Hinton, Kenneth Hylson-Smith, Diarmaid MacCulloch, Alister McGrath, Jim Packer, Anthony Russell, Marjory Stanway, John Stott, Tom Wright and all the contributors to *Has Keele Failed?*

My wife, Sheila, read every word of the manuscript before I made my final revision, and made countless suggestions for improvements as well as spotting errors. Hannah Wolstenholme kindly translated a Latin prayer in the Sarum Breviary so that I could compare the result with Cranmer's version. James Catford from Hodder and Stoughton conceived the idea of this book in the first place, established me on the project and then moved to pastures new. His successor, Judith Longman, took over and was understanding when I failed to meet several deadlines, encouraging me at every stage. Julie Ambrose helped me as well as assisting Judith. Bryony Bénier did a splendid copy-editing job and Patrick Knowles designed an eye-catching cover. The faults which remain are the result of my stubbornness. My warm thanks to you all. I hope and pray that you like the result.

Roger Steer
Copplestone, Devon

Introduction

Nearly eleven weeks after the world focused its shocked attention on Westminster Abbey for the funeral of Diana, Princess of Wales, another service marked an altogether happier occasion. On 20 November 1997 a large congregation joined Queen Elizabeth II and Prince Philip in the Abbey to celebrate their golden wedding anniversary. Two of the hymns they sang, 'Love Divine' and 'O Thou Who Camest from Above', were born in the eighteenth-century Evangelical revival. Their author, Charles Wesley, like his brother John, never left the Church of England and all his life Charles opposed any moves within Methodism which tended towards separation from the Church in which he had been brought up.

Although Anglican Evangelicals trace their pedigree to the Lollards, the Reformers and the Puritans, their existence *as a party* is normally dated from the Evangelical revival in the eighteenth century, of which Wesley's fine hymns are but one manifestation. This is the first book to tell the story of Anglican Evangelicals on both sides of the Atlantic, but it does not attempt to chart the contribution Evangelicals in other parts of the world have made to Anglican history. I hope it will not be too long before someone attempts that task in more detail, because the influence of Anglican Evangelicals today is overwhelmingly in what westerners often call the Third World. Their *history*, however, is a narrative which unfolds in Britain and North America.

I imagine that members of the royal family and congregation gathered in the Abbey on that November Thursday took the words of the second of the two Wesley hymns on their lips with varying degrees of conviction. They sang of 'pure celestial fire' and asked God to 'kindle a flame of sacred love on the mean altar' of their hearts.

> There let it for thy glory burn
>   With inextinguishable blaze
> And trembling to its source return,
>   In humble prayer and fervent praise.

This is the story of a brand of Christianity which, at its best, has burned with the fire both of holiness and evangelism. I chose the title because I think it captures the zeal, commitment and burning spirituality which have characterised the best manifestations of Anglican Evangelicalism from the days of Wycliffe and the Lollards to the era when the present Archbishop of Canterbury found Christ in an Evangelical parish church. 'Fire' also reminds us of the tensions (sometimes, but not always, creative) which a commitment to Evangelicalism has produced in individual lives, within Anglican Evangelicalism itself, and in the wider Anglican Communion.

Who do Anglican Evangelicals think they are?

Why do people attend Anglican Evangelical churches? Some go because they feel they want to go to church, and the nearest happens to be Anglican Evangelical. They may have only a vague idea what 'Evangelical' or even 'Anglican' means, but they like it there. Others may be more in the know, owning copies of books by John Stott, Jim Packer, Michael Green, Alister McGrath, supplemented these days – particularly if the church has run an Alpha course – by one or two by Nicky Gumbel. A few may be members of Diocesan Evangelical Fellowships and one or two may attend the annual Anglican Evangelical Assembly or conferences organised by Reform.

Even those Anglican Evangelicals most aware of their heritage, however, will not hold identical beliefs or attach the same emphasis to all aspects of doctrine. Traditionally, Anglican Evangelicals have had antennae which are finely tuned to sense that which is 'sound' and 'unsound', but this is probably less true these days, particularly since most Evangelical churches have been influenced to some degree by the Charismatic movement (or 'renewal') which is less concerned with doctrinal issues. And throughout the history of Anglican Evangelicalism, there have always been some mavericks at all levels who have taken minority positions in some matters of belief and practice.

Perhaps the twentieth century's most influential Anglican Evangelical, John Stott (see pages 268–76), said in the 1980s that he thought of himself first and foremost as a Christian seeking to follow Jesus Christ; second, as an Evangelical Christian, because of his conviction that Evangelical principles were integral to authentic Christianity; and third, as an Anglican Evangelical Christian, since the Church of England was the particular historical tradition to which he belonged. So he preferred the term Anglican Evangelical (with Evangelical as the noun and Anglican as the adjective) to Evangelical Anglican (where Anglican is the noun and Evangelical the adjective). Other prominent players in the movement, like Canon Michael Saward, who are rather more 'churchy', prefer the term 'Evangelical Anglican'.

John Stott has pointed out that the word 'Evangelical' has a theological meaning and is not the same as 'evangelistic'. 'Evangelical' describes a theology which the apostle Paul called 'the truth of the gospel' (Gal. 2:5, 14). Ideally the two words 'Evangelical' and 'evangelistic' belong to each other since they both contain the 'evangel', the gospel.

The word 'Evangelical' first came into common use at the time of the Reformation, when Luther and the Reformers liked to describe themselves in Latin as *evangelici* (short for *evangelici viri*, 'evangelical men'), or in German as *die Evangelischen*. I begin my story of Anglican Evangelicals with John Wycliffe who was named, in Latin, the *doctor evangelicus* at the time of his death in 1384.

Hensley Henson, Bishop of Durham in the 1920s and '30s, defined Anglican Evangelicals as 'an army of illiterates generalled by octogenarians'! More seriously, and more accurately, the most prolific author among the current generation of Anglican Evangelicals, Alister McGrath, gives the following working definition of Evangelicalism:

- a focus, both devotional and theological, on the person of Jesus Christ, especially his death on the cross;

- the identification of Scripture as the ultimate authority in matters of spirituality, doctrine and ethics;
- an emphasis upon conversion or a 'new birth' as a life-changing religious experience;
- a concern for sharing faith, especially through evangelism.[1]

Who do Anglicans think they are?

The word 'Anglicanism' was coined in the nineteenth century from the much older term 'Anglican'. It denotes the system of doctrine and practice of those Christians who are in communion with the Archbishop of Canterbury. Today there are nearly seventy million members of the Anglican Communion in thirty-six self-governing Member Churches or Provinces in more than one hundred and sixty countries.

The Archbishop of Canterbury is regarded as a unique focus of Anglican unity. He calls the once-a-decade Lambeth Conference, chairs the meeting of Primates, and is President of the Anglican Consultative Council. The 103rd Archbishop in the succession of St Augustine is Dr George Carey, enthroned in April 1991.

Dr Carey found Christ in Dagenham Parish Church at the age of seventeen (see pages 324–30). The church was thoroughly Evangelical, although the young Carey did not know what that word meant when he joined it. More recently, when I asked him what were the distinctive treasures of the Anglican Communion, Dr Carey told me that

- the Anglican tradition is a significant Reformation tradition within worldwide Christianity;
- its *via media* approach to truth – holding the tension between 'Catholic' and 'Low Church' – is a gift of God to the world (not all Anglicans have thought of the *via media* in this sense, as we shall see);
- its tradition of tolerance and comprehensiveness is a sign of hope;
- its loose federation of churches avoids the extremes of hierarchism on the one hand and the problems of Nonconformism on the other;

- it ensures we keep our eyes looking outwards to the needy of God's world;
- it provides a richness of liturgy;
- it has a strong tradition of linking love of God to love of neighbour in practical service.

The story of Anglican Evangelicals

'What is truth?' asked Pontius Pilate, governor of Judea from AD 26 to 36 (John 18:38). You could argue that this question makes Pilate a postmodernist ahead of his time, but it is more sensible to see it as an understandable question from someone used to spending long hours sitting in his palace listening to charges and countercharges. He might, had he lived two thousand years later, have asked the same question about this history of Anglican Evangelicals. What do we really know of the thoughts and motives of the players in the story which follows? How many of the stalwarts of faith whose portraits I have painted had inner doubts which have gone unrecorded?

I have done the best I could with the available evidence. The result is a series of accounts, in the cases where I have drawn on source material written in the first person, at least of what people wanted others to believe they were trying to achieve or, in the case of source material in the third person, of how others saw them. As a historian, it has been my business to be accurate, in the sense that I have tried to maintain a scrupulous respect for fact. However, a history may contain nothing but accurate statements of fact and yet be as a whole misleading and untrue. Inevitably I have had to select my facts: some facts tell us more about reality than others, and it is with those facts that I have particularly tried to concern myself. It has not been possible to tell the story of every Anglican Evangelical who ever lived. I have, however, selected what I believe to be a representative series of people who played a significant role in the unfolding drama. I have tried to maintain balance and objectivity while also attempting to make the narrative readable.

I hope that in the course of telling the story I have given enough objective facts for you to make up your own mind about motives and, if you are so inclined, to enable you to act as a detective on the lookout for signs of doubt and insecurity. We may never know and probably do not need to know all about another person's motives, whether he (or she) is an evangelist, a Bible translator, a reformer, a bishop, an author or a philanthropist. We may have our suspicions but we can never be sure. Even when motives are mixed, good may result. When he wrote his letter to 'all the saints in Christ Jesus at Philippi', the apostle Paul told them that he suspected that 'some preach Christ out of envy and rivalry, but others out of good will'. The former preached Christ out of 'selfish ambition', the latter did so 'in love'. 'But what does it matter?' he asked. 'The important thing is that in every way, whether from false motives or true, Christ is preached. And because of this I rejoice' (Phil. 1:1, 15–18).

At every stage contemporaries observed the characters in our story. In 1407 Archbishop Arundel examined William Thorpe for heresy and asked him from whom he had taken his information. Thorpe's answer was that he had been guided by John Wycliffe whom he described as 'the most virtuous and goodly wise man that I heard or knew'. So much so that 'a great many communed often with him, and loved so much his learning that they wrote it, and busily enforced themselves to be guided according to his learning'. The attractive goodness of his character guaranteed him an audience for his reforming ideas and ensured him a following after his death.

A friend who is inclined to be unsympathetic towards Evangelicals wrote to me suggesting that I might find it difficult to 'separate the teachers with vision and conviction from the charlatans'. I do not think I have come across any obvious charlatans in the story. There are some whose thinking strikes me as somewhat confused or distorted and some whose actions were misguided. Overall, however, the story which has emerged – expressing it in human terms – is of a chain of men and women, overwhelmingly men as far as leadership for much of the period is concerned, who have taken biblical Christianity intensely seriously. That seriousness by no means made them all unhappy people – sometimes quite the reverse.

In the pages which follow, we look in Part One at England from the birth of Wycliffe in the fourteenth century until the time of the glorious revolution under William and Mary at the end of the seventeenth century. It is a story in which we meet the Lollards, William Tyndale, Thomas Cranmer, Hugh Latimer, Nicholas Ridley, Richard Hooker, George Herbert and Richard Baxter. This part of the narrative also takes us into the courts of kings and queens as the story of the establishment of the reformed Church of England gets entangled with Henry VIII's divorce and remarriage, Mary's Catholicism, Elizabeth's love of compromise, disestablishment during the Civil War and Interregnum, and restoration under Charles II.

Part Two brings us to eighteenth-century England in a story dominated not only by John Wesley and George Whitefield but also by revival within the Church of England itself under the leadership of Fletcher of Madeley, John Newton, Thomas Scott and Charles Simeon. We pay special attention to the colourful figure of William Grimshaw, who helped to establish Anglican Evangelicalism in the north of England. Wesley said of Grimshaw, 'It is not easy to ascribe such unwearied diligence, chiefly among the poor, to any motive but the real one.'

Part Three takes us to the New World across the Atlantic. We begin in the young British colony of Virginia, where we see how George Whitefield and the American revival known as the Great Awakening affected the Church of England. We follow the story of Devereux Jarratt's conversion, his visit to England to be ordained and subsequent energetic work in Virginia, only to be frustrated, in his eyes, by the coming of the Baptists and Methodists. We see how the American Episcopal Church (ECUSA) got off the ground following the achievement of independence by the former British colonies. During the golden years of Anglican Evangelicalism in mid-nineteenth-century America we are introduced to Joseph Pilmore, Alexander Griswold, Charles McIlvaine and Manton Eastburn. These were the years which witnessed the foundation of the Virginia Theological Seminary and the Episcopal Theological School, and saw Phillips Brooks abandon the Evangelicalism of his youth for broad-church Liberalism.

In Part Four we return to England in the nineteenth century to meet the Clapham Sect and watch as William Wilberforce worked patiently to abolish the slave trade in the British Empire. These years saw the foundation of the Church Missionary Society, the

Bible Society, the Church Pastoral Aid Society and the Keswick Convention. It was the era of Shaftesbury's industrial and social reforms, and a period when Evangelicalism came under attack from the former Evangelical John Henry Newman and the leaders of the Oxford Movement. This was the century when some major Evangelical figures became bishops, notably Daniel Wilson and J. C. Ryle, the latter going some way to answering Tractarian attacks on Evangelicalism and distancing himself from Keswick teaching.

Part Five introduces us to two of the best-known Anglican Evangelicals of this century, John Stott and Jim Packer. We witness one of the most dramatic moments in the whole story, when Martyn Lloyd-Jones publicly appealed to Evangelicals to leave their denominations and stand together. We hear John Stott's response and see how decisions made at the National Evangelical Anglican Congress at Keele in 1967 were almost totally contrary to what Dr Jones had pleaded with Anglican Evangelicals to do. We discover some of the reasons why Jim Packer left England for Canada.

Part Five also examines James Barr's major attack on 'Fundamentalism' and, over twenty years later, Barr gives his current assessment of Evangelicalism. We consider how justified Evangelicals are in seeing 'Liberals' as 'the enemy'. We notice Archbishop Carey's verdict on Evangelicals and their assessment of him. We look at the Charismatic movement, David Watson, the ordination of women and Reform.

In Part Six, we discover how, after sixty years when Evangelicalism virtually disappeared from the Episcopal Church, it was reborn in the 1960s and 1970s and how, inspired by one man's faith and prayer, an Evangelical seminary was successfully established. We gain an insight into American perspectives on Anglicanism and examine why some Evangelicals are becoming Episcopalians while others are leaving ECUSA.

Part Seven examines the Evangelical approach to homosexual partnerships and describes how the Church has been set on fire over this issue in America, Britain and the wider Anglican communion as the 1998 Lambeth Conference of Anglican bishops approaches.

We reflect on the strengths and weaknesses of Anglican Evangelicalism, the pros and cons of loyalty to the doctrines and ethos of a single strand within Christianity, and consider how Anglican Evangelicals might set about tackling the main task facing them in the new millennium.

PART ONE

Church on fire
with reforming zeal

England, 1330–1700

For he will be like a refiner's fire.
(Malachi 3:2b)

JOHN WYCLIFFE

Today, the Parish Church of St Mary, Lutterworth, has an Evangelical feel: they use *Mission Praise Combined*; there are Bibles on the pews; there is a bookstall with volumes by John Stott; colourful banners hang from the pillars.

The church where John Wycliffe (*c*. 1330–84) was rector between 1374 and 1384 has become something of a place of pilgrimage, particularly for those interested in the history of Evangelicalism. The present building dates from the very early thirteenth or late twelfth century, and every Sunday for eight hundred years Christians have worshipped in this church while the story told in the pages which follow has unfolded. On the south side of the church is 'Wycliffe's door', so called because Wycliffe was carried through it to his death after he suffered a severe stroke while leading worship on 31 December 1384.

John Wycliffe was born nearly two hundred years before Luther posted his ninety-five theses on indulgences to the door of the castle church at Wittenberg. Although a document condemning the Lollards at the end of the fourteenth century referred to him (in Latin) as the 'Evangelical doctor', Wycliffe would have looked blank if you had spoken to him about either Anglicanism or Evangelicalism. Nevertheless, it is remarkable how many of his ideas anticipated those of the Reformation. He reminds us, too, that severe tensions between the English government and the authorities of the Church of Rome go back two hundred years before Henry VIII.

Wycliffe was born near Richmond in Yorkshire somewhere around 1330. He was Master of Balliol in the early 1360s and probably Warden of Canterbury Hall, Oxford (later to become a part of Christ Church), for a while after that.

Although Wycliffe was rector of Fillingham in the 1360s, and of Ludgershall and Lutterworth in the 1370s and 1380s, until 1381 he lived most of the time in Oxford. At a period in English history when

13

there was no clear separation between the sacred and secular, he served both the Black Prince and John of Gaunt (the Duke of Lancaster). The government sent him to Bruges as an ambassador to conduct negotiations with papal representatives in Ghent over a series of disputes between the English authorities and Pope Gregory XI. His handling of these negotiations won him support among the English nobility and informed citizens of London. When the Roman Church began to censure him for what they saw as his increasingly heretical views, both John of Gaunt and the Black Prince's widow protected him.

Wycliffe was a popular teacher at Oxford and earned his early reputation as a philosopher. However, when he argued that a secular government had a right to control the clergy, this annoyed the bishops who summoned him to appear before the Archbishop of Canterbury at a council in the old St Paul's Cathedral on 19 February 1377.

Wycliffe arrived at the cathedral accompanied by John of Gaunt, Lord Henry Percy, the Lord Marshal of England, and four friars. They found that a huge crowd had already gathered, making it difficult for them to make their way to the Lady Chapel where the court was sitting. The Lord Marshal had to make a passageway for the accused by force.

The Bishop of London addressed Lord Percy, 'If I had known before what authority he would have assumed in the church, I would have stopped him from coming here.'

'He will keep that authority whether you like it or not,' intervened John of Gaunt.

At last they arrived at the Lady Chapel to find two archbishops and a number of bishops sitting with an assortment of dukes and barons. According to custom, Wycliffe stood to face them waiting to discover what precisely was the charge against him.

'Will you not sit down?' asked Lord Percy.

'He shall not sit here,' said the Bishop of London. 'It would not be fitting for him to sit while he is hearing the charge.' From that time, it was said, Lord Percy and the bishop hated each other.

Then a most undignified quarrel erupted between the Bishop of London and John of Gaunt. The crowd began to take sides between the duke and the bishop and the council broke up in scenes of uproar. The proceedings were never concluded and no charges were brought against Wycliffe.

Wycliffe was no mere Oxford don writing papers to be read only in academic circles. He was himself an energetic preacher in Latin and in English. His sermons show that at this stage the main thrust of his ideas was not doctrinal but vigorous complaints against the Church of Rome which, he maintained, was not the head of all churches; Peter had no more power given him than any other apostle; the Pope has no more keys of the Church than any other person in the order of priesthood; the state may deprive unworthy and offending churchmen of their possessions; the gospel is a *rule* sufficient of itself to rule the life of every Christian; and all other rules which govern the lives of monks and nuns add nothing to the gospel.

For this sort of preaching and his many writings, Pope Gregory XI instructed King Richard II, the bishops and the University of Oxford to imprison Wycliffe and make him answer before the archbishop and himself. The Pope sharply rebuked the university for allowing Wycliffe to hold such doctrines for so long without censure. But when proceedings were undertaken against Wycliffe at Lambeth in 1378, the prosecution had little effect on Wycliffe's position.

In the same year the Roman Church was shaken by the election of rival popes, Urban VI and Clement VII. Warming to his task, Wycliffe now began to assert strongly that everyone had a right to read the Bible for themselves. He argued that the Bible, as the eternal 'exemplar' of the Christian religion, was the sole criterion of doctrine, to which no church authority could lawfully add. He said that Scripture offered no backing for the authority of the Pope. Wycliffe's reverence for the Bible is seen in his innumerable references to it in his writings and sermons.

Until then, he had written his works in Latin, but from this time on he started to appeal to the people in their own language and in the process of issuing popular tracts he became a leading English prose writer – perhaps the first Evangelical populist in the country.

Wycliffe organised a body of travelling preachers, his 'poor priests', later known as Lollards, who spread his teachings all over England. He began a translation of the Bible, of which there was then no complete English version. He did the work quickly, assisted by a team of followers, and they circulated sections widely as they completed them.

From 1380 his writing became more doctrinal. In his *De Eucharista* he said that the doctrine of transubstantiation was philosophically unsound and encouraged superstitious attitudes. Transubstantiation is the doctrine which teaches that at the Eucharist (Holy Communion) the whole substance of bread and wine is converted into the whole substance of the body and blood of Christ: only the appearances (or 'accidents') of bread and wine remain. Wycliffe tried to stop people thinking of the Eucharist as something magical and encouraged them to think instead of its moral and spiritual effects.

In 1382 Archbishop Courtenay called a council and condemned Wycliffe's views. They arrested his followers and compelled them to recant. Curiously, however, they did not arrest Wycliffe himself. He left Oxford for the quiet Leicestershire town of Lutterworth and continued his unremitting work of writing books and pamphlets, and directing the completion of a translation of the Bible by his team of linguists. Proudly on display in the church in Lutterworth today is an edition of Wycliffe's Bible, presented to the church by the British and Foreign Bible Society.

His output over the next two years in Lutterworth was remarkable: uncompromising in tone and consistently powerful. Moreover, what Wycliffe wrote is attractive when we read it today. His theme was to insist that inward religion – faith and practice which touched the heart – was more important than mere formalism. He laid heavy stress on moral character as the mark of a true Christian. He even argued that a priest was not needed to administer Holy Communion.

Wycliffe impressed his contemporaries with his integrity, and his followers spread his teachings throughout England. Although the authorities tried to suppress them, the influence of his ideas continued until the Reformation in the sixteenth century when many Reformers quoted his writings. John Huss (*c.* 1372–1415), the Bohemian Reformer, was his most famous disciple spreading his ideas in Europe.

The Lollards

People began, derisively at first, to call Wycliffe's supporters 'Lollards' (from a Dutch word meaning 'mumblers'). The Lollards foreshadowed many of the emphases and methods which have been dear to the hearts of Evangelicals ever since. The focus of their preaching and their tracts was personal faith in and obedience to Christ and the Bible. The Scriptures, they said, were the sole authority in religion and ordinary people had a right to read them for themselves.

The Lollards attacked clerical celibacy, compulsory confession to a priest, and the practice of indulgences (by which professional 'pardoners' sold remission of sins on behalf of the Church). They criticised pilgrimages as having become idolatrous, and were remarkably sceptical about the whole idea of priesthood.

The Lollards spread their teaching by preaching, books and tracts. A favourite Lollard tract *The Lantern of Light* shows that its writer shared Wycliffe's preference for heart religion above outward form. The author of the tract was a Latin scholar, for he apparently made his own translations of passages from the Scriptures to illustrate his arguments and quoted a good deal from the writings of the early Church fathers. He repeatedly draws a contrast between the heartfelt devotion of God's Church, founded on the gospel, and the formality and corruption of the 'devil's church'.

For a number of years at the end of the fourteenth century the Lollards enjoyed a measure of academic support, and some knights in Richard II's court supported them. But after the accession of Henry IV in 1399 they were rigorously persecuted and their numbers declined. From the 1430s they worked mainly underground but revived again towards the end of the fifteenth century. At the time of the early Tudors, there were still some Lollards in the Chilterns, Cotswolds, London, Kent, Essex, Coventry and parts of the north of England. The Lollards were never strong enough to achieve major reform on their own, but they contributed to the English Reformation by preparing hearts and minds.

WILLIAM TYNDALE

Overlooking North Nibley, Gloucestershire, on the edge of the Cotswold escarpment, stands the 111-foot-high Tyndale Monument commemorating one of the greatest Bible translators. William Tyndale (*c.* 1494–1536) was probably born at Slimbridge, a mile or so from today's monument – an area where the Lollards had once been strong. There is also a fine statue of him in the Victoria Embankment Gardens in London. He studied at Magdalen Hall, Oxford, and later at Cambridge where he was one of the famous White Horse Tavern Group (see page 22) in the early 1520s.

Tyndale was at Cambridge, and in and out of the famous Tavern, in those heady five years immediately after Martin Luther had, in 1517, drawn up his list of ninety-five theses on indulgences and nailed them to the church door at Wittenberg.

Bibles for ploughboys, weavers and travellers

Tyndale translated Erasmus's *Enchiridion Militus Christiani* ('The Christian Soldier's Handbook') which the Dutch scholar had written in 1502. In this book, Erasmus insisted on the duty of studying the New Testament and making it the court of appeal in questions of life and doctrine. Tyndale grew convinced that the root cause of much confusion in people's minds on matters then being debated was ignorance of Scripture. This ignorance was not confined to the laity: it was shared by many of the clergy. If this ignorance could be corrected the eyes of all would be opened and the truth understood. 'I defy the Pope and all his laws,' Tyndale told an educated man. 'If God spare my life, ere many years I will cause a boy that driveth the plough shall know more of the Scripture than thou dost.'

An echo of Erasmus's words in the preface to his Greek New Testament of 1516 must surely have been in Tyndale's mind. Erasmus had expressed his total disagreement with those who were unwilling that the Scriptures, translated into the language of the people, should be read by the uneducated:

Christ desires his mysteries to be published abroad as widely as possible. I could wish that even all women should read the Gospel and St Paul's Epistles, and I would that they were translated into all the languages of all Christian people, that they might be read and known not merely by the Scots and the Irish but even by the Turks and the Saracens. I wish that the farm worker might sing parts of them at the plough, that the weaver might hum them at the shuttle, and that the traveller might beguile the weariness of the way by reciting them.[1]

Almost certainly, the knowledge that Luther had given his countrymen the German New Testament in 1522 encouraged Tyndale in his objectives. He travelled from Gloucestershire to London in the summer of 1523 to find out whether the new Bishop of London, Cuthbert Tunstall (1474–1559), would offer him a residential chaplaincy in his palace which would allow him to translate the Bible into English. After Tunstall declined to offer him a suitable position, Tyndale decided he would have to leave England to carry out his task.

So in April or May 1524, Tyndale sailed for the continent of Europe, never to return to England. He finished his first translation of the New Testament into English in 1525 at Worms. When the translation arrived in England the following year, Archbishop Warham, Cuthbert Tunstall and Thomas More bitterly attacked it. More denounced Tyndale as 'hell-bound' and Bishop Tunstall burnt all the copies he could collect.

Tyndale spent most of his remaining years in Antwerp where he revised his New Testament. He also translated parts of the Old Testament and his straightforward, vigorous English remained the basis of both the Authorised and Revised versions of the Bible.

Like Luther, he insisted on the authority of the Bible, but in the course of his translation work he moved away from Luther's teaching on justification by faith alone towards the idea of justification by faith *and* works.

Although Antwerp was a free city, the surrounding territory was controlled by Charles V, Holy Roman Emperor. Tyndale's enemies could take no legal action against him in Antwerp, but in the area around they could easily proceed against him for heresy. On 21 May

1535, they kidnapped Tyndale, took him out of Antwerp and imprisoned him in the fortress of Vilvorde six miles north of Brussels. From England, Henry VIII's powerful Secretary of State Thomas Cromwell made an energetic attempt to procure Tyndale's release, and the King himself made some efforts on his behalf.

Since Henry had recently divorced Charles V's aunt Catherine of Aragon the Emperor was in no mood to respond to overtures from England and allowed the law against heretics to take its tedious and barbaric course. In August 1536 the authorities found Tyndale guilty of heresy. On 6 October they brought him out of Vilvorde Castle and tied him to a stake.

'Lord, open the King of England's eyes,' he shouted.

A hangman then strangled Tyndale, before they lit the flames which leapt around his dead body. Sadly and ironically, Tyndale probably did not know that some months earlier, King Henry had given permission for 'Coverdale's Bible' of 1535, which drew heavily on the martyr's work, to be circulated in England. In the sense which Tyndale intended, the King of England's eyes were already opening.

In November 1996 curators in a Stuttgart museum found a copy of the second edition of Tyndale's English translation of the New Testament – only the third known to be in existence. It was undisturbed in its original sixteenth century binding, with a title page which neither of the other two existing copies (one in the British Library and the other in the library of St Paul's Cathedral) has. The title page reads: 'The newe Testament as it was written and caused to be written by them which herde yt. To whom also our saveour Christ Jesus commaunded that they shulde preache it unto al creatures.'[2]

REFORM UNDER HENRY VIII: ORIGINS OF THE CHURCH OF ENGLAND

Henry VIII began his reign (1509–47) as a devout Catholic receiving from Pope Leo X the title 'Defender of the Faith' for a book which he co-authored (published in 1521) taking issue with Luther on the sacraments. Elizabeth II is apparently still proud to bear the title.

Some historians of the Church of England argue that it was not a new church which began at the Reformation, like some other churches in Europe. They point out that the church in England began a thousand years earlier as part of the Western Church under the control of the Pope in Rome. There were English bishops at the Council of Arles (now France) in 314 so there must have been an organised church in England then.

In 597 Augustine had landed in Kent with orders from Pope Gregory to preach the gospel to the English. It was a successful mission and Augustine became the first Archbishop of Canterbury. Dr George Carey is therefore the last name on a list headed by Augustine (not to be confused with the famous writer and Bishop of Hippo).

In this sense, some Anglicans do not think of themselves as members of a Protestant church. But, in another sense, the Church of England did of course protest at what it saw as the errors and corruption of the Church of Rome.

THOMAS CRANMER

Thomas Cranmer (1489–1556) was born at Aslockton, Nottinghamshire, educated at Jesus College, Cambridge, and ordained when he became a Fellow there in 1523. Cranmer is one of the big names in English history, whose role in the establishment of the Church of England is much debated. There were attractive, as well as unattractive, strands to his personality. Apart from his skill in compiling liturgy in a masterly English style as seen in the *Book of Common Prayer*, Anglicanism surely owes Cranmer a debt of gratitude for the essentially scriptural spirituality which characterised at least the first four hundred years of its history.

Cranmer's 'Evangelicalism'

Diarmaid MacCulloch's major biography of Thomas Cranmer was published in 1996. It is likely to be many years (if ever) before a more important biography of the man who did so much to influence the birth of the reformed Church of England is written. Of interest for historians of Anglican Evangelicalism is the fact that MacCulloch uses the word 'Evangelical' to describe the religious Reformation which developed in England during the 1520s and 1530s.

MacCulloch decided not to use terms like 'Protestant' or 'Lutheran' which he believes are inappropriate at this stage of the English Reformation. The word 'Protestant' was not used much in England until the reign of Mary, after 1553. The term 'Lutheran', MacCulloch argues, unacceptably narrows the spread of reformist views in Henry VIII's England.

For MacCulloch 'Evangelicalism' is the religious outlook which makes the primary point of Christian reference the good news of the *euangelion*, or the text of Scripture generally. He regards it as a convenient word which can be applied across the board, except to a small number of English reformers who went in a more radical direction. In the eighteenth century, the word began to be used in the English-speaking world to describe a party within Protestantism and within the Church of England, but MacCulloch has argued that the word 'Evangelical' can do a useful job in describing the religious history of Tudor England.

MacCulloch sees the struggles over religion from the beginning of the 1520s up to the death of Cranmer as a series of events in which an 'old world of devotion' struggled to conserve and maintain its identity against a new religious outlook which aimed to destroy it and replace it with something 'reformed'.

The White Horse Tavern, Cambridge

'There was at Cambridge', wrote Merle d'Aubigné about the 1520s, 'a house called the White Horse, so situated as to permit the most timid members of King's, Queen's, and St John's Colleges, to enter at the rear without being perceived.'[3]

Members of those colleges used to meet at the White Horse Tavern to read the Bible and the works of the German Reformers. The priests named the pub 'Little Germany'. 'There are the Germans going to Germany,' they would say. But actually their opinions were not slavishly Lutheran. According to John Foxe those who formed this group included Thomas Bilney, Thomas Cranmer, William Tyndale, George Joye, William Roy, Robert Barnes, John Frith, Nicholas Ridley, Rowland Taylor, Thomas Arthur, Matthew Parker and Hugh Latimer.

Henry: man and theologian

Henry VIII has a well-justified reputation in English history for cruelty to his wives who either failed to produce male heirs or displeased him in other ways. He was, however, popular with his people and seems to have inspired the devoted affection of those in immediate contact with him.

He certainly did not spend all his time living like an idle playboy. He took his religion seriously and worked hard at it. When a new theological book was published, he would put copies out to a team of theologians of differing viewpoints, read the book himself, and then take a view on it after studying the detailed comments he received. He wrote a number of theological books himself besides his attack on Luther's doctrine of the sacraments.

Cranmer was among the first to be asked for comments on the King's and others' writings, and spent long hours providing pages and pages of commentary, even to the extent of correcting Henry's grammar and English style. Since the King respected and admired him, Cranmer kept his head.

In 1527 Henry VIII first asked the Pope to annul his marriage to Catherine of Aragon. All her children, except Mary Tudor, had died in infancy and Henry decided that he saw in this God's judgment on an unnatural alliance – Catherine was his brother Prince Arthur's widow. He thought that any doubt about Mary's legitimacy might lead to a renewal of civil wars. What is more, he had fallen in love with Anne Boleyn, a niece of Thomas Howard, Duke of Norfolk.

In 1529 Cranmer met John Foxe and Stephen Gardiner. John Foxe

(1516–87) was to become a Fellow of Magdalene College, Oxford, and later his name became associated for ever with his *Book of Martyrs* (1563) which recounted in vivid detail the stories and sufferings of Protestant victims of papal punishment. Stephen Gardiner (*c*. 1481–1555) had been Thomas Wolsey's secretary since 1525 and would be made Bishop of Winchester in 1531. Although he supported the supremacy of King over Pope, he opposed doctrinal reformation.

Cranmer discussed Henry VIII's proposed divorce from Catherine of Aragon with Foxe and Gardiner. He suggested that they should appeal to European universities on the question of whether Henry had broken God's law by marrying his brother's widow. Cranmer worked hard to influence academic opinion in Europe on behalf of the King. This pleased Henry and Cranmer became a royal chaplain and Archdeacon of Taunton. He was by this time attached to the household of Anne Boleyn's father (Anne was by now Henry's mistress).

In 1531 English clergy, by 'the Submission of the Clergy', agreed to acknowledge Henry as their 'supreme lord'. And so the English church was no longer a potential obstacle in the progress of the breach with Rome.

The King now sent Cranmer on an unsuccessful diplomatic mission to Emperor Charles V in Germany, and in Nuremberg he met and secretly married Margaret Osiander, the niece of a Reformation theologian. Then a royal summons reached Cranmer to return as Archbishop of Canterbury in succession to Warham. He sent his wife secretly to England and followed himself.

Archbishop Cranmer

Cranmer was consecrated Archbishop on 30 March 1533 and when he took the oath of allegiance to the Pope, he protested that he did it 'for form's sake'.

Although Cranmer had accepted the post of Archbishop reluctantly, it was soon clear that he was to be Henry's chief instrument in overthrowing the Pope's rule in England. In May he pronounced Catherine's marriage null and void and the private marriage to Anne Boleyn four months earlier valid. The Pope promptly excommunicated Henry. In September the King made Cranmer godfather to Anne's daughter Elizabeth. The Act of Supremacy, passed by Parliament the following year, sealed England's break with Rome.

Cranmer seems to have been kindly and humane by nature. All through his life he was blessed, or as some would say cursed, with the ability to see his opponent's point of view, an attribute in short supply during the Reformation. However, despite Cranmer's natural humanity, just over three months into his time as Archbishop, John Frith was burned at Smithfield on 4 July 1533 for denying that purgatory and transubstantiation were necessary dogmas. It was not Cranmer who called for the sentence; but he did not apparently intervene to prevent it. At this time he still held to a belief in transubstantiation himself, but later came to believe that Christ was only spiritually present in the bread and wine.

Evidence of Cranmer's changing views came when in 1534 he made Hugh Latimer royal chaplain. Latimer (c. 1485–1555) had been dramatically converted to Evangelical doctrines in 1524, influenced by Thomas Bilney. His preaching style was direct and uncomplicated. He had a good understanding of human character and a homely style.

In February 1535 Cranmer issued an interesting new set of instructions for use at Worcester Cathedral Priory. The first item told the monks to organise and attend a Scripture reading for an hour daily throughout the year and to cover the whole of the Bible from start to finish. He ordered that the Scripture should be expounded in English 'according at least to the literal sense'. Cranmer had recently advised Latimer to preach 'according to the pure sense and meaning' of the text.

In the same year Thomas More, formerly Lord Chancellor and the most eloquent Catholic opponent of the English Reformation, was executed for treason. Cranmer later asserted that he had opposed More's execution.

In January 1536 Catherine of Aragon died and Cranmer annulled Henry's marriage to Anne Boleyn. She was executed and Henry married Jane Seymour. The following year, Jane gave birth to a son, Edward (the future King), and then died.

Cranmer, the King and justification

Although the two men respected each other, the King and his Archbishop by no means always agreed. Cranmer had now become enthusiastically Evangelical in many of his views and wrote extended essays for the King about Lutheranism.

Two opposing schemes of salvation were now doing battle in Europe. On the one hand was Luther's view of fallen humanity, helpless and totally under condemnation until given the grace of God through faith; on the other was the late-medieval view of a Christian life in which the contrite human spirit was capable of co-operating with God towards his or her salvation by performing good works.

Henry could never bring himself fully to embrace Luther's theology. Repeatedly the King indicated his preference for the medieval view of the co-operation of the human will with God. Where he found a written statement of belief that a human was 'right inheritor' of the kingdom of God, he wanted to add to it 'as long as I persevere in his precepts and laws'.

Cranmer would have none of this. He insisted to the King that whatever good works one performed, they were good only because they proceeded from the once-for-all gift from God of 'very pure Christian faith and hope'. True Christian faith should not, of course, be confused with mere intellectual assent to the propositions of Christianity, which he pointed out was a faith available to 'all devils and wicked Christian people'. For Cranmer, from pure faith flowed the compulsion to do good works, but they were an *effect* and never a *cause* of that transforming act of God: justification. All was the work of God, and it could neither be reversed nor improved upon by human effort.

In his marginal notes to the King's writings, Cranmer clearly expounded his view of the once-for-all character of justification by faith. Yet Cranmer never (except perhaps at the King's deathbed) persuaded Henry to abandon his view of human life as progress towards God through the steady performance of duty in obedience to his commands.

One of Henry's objections to Luther's view of justification was that the Evangelical emphasis on justification by faith alone through grace undermined the whole principle of human morality. By removing the value of good works, it endangered the peace of a godly country. Cranmer thought this worry was removed by a suitable doctrine of repentance. He defined repentance as 'a pure conversion of the sinner in heart and mind from his sins unto God'. For Cranmer, repentance was the one authentic mark of a right will, and a right will was the only qualification for repentance; a right will was the free gift of God. Repentance naturally resulted in good works, so believers ought always to scrutinise their lives anxiously for good deeds.

The Great Bible

In July 1539 the 'Great Bible' appeared in English. Cromwell had entrusted this work to Miles Coverdale, who had already been responsible for a translation drawing on Tyndale's work. By 1541 the Great Bible had run into seven editions. Coverdale (1488–1568), a native of York and a Cambridge graduate who later became Bishop of Exeter, had a good ear for phrases and sentences which read well and sounded pleasant. Coverdale was not, however, as reliable a scholar as Tyndale and his Bible contained a number of flaws due to his enthusiasm at times to use his translation as a vehicle to put across his Protestant views.

In the same year, Cranmer opposed the Six Articles which aimed to impose a uniform dogma on the English church at a time of theological change. One of the Articles made the marriages of priests punishable by death. Cranmer did what he dared to argue against them and sent his wife away to Germany, not recalling her until 1548.

In 1540 Cranmer conducted the wedding of Henry to Anne of Cleves, but soon also arranged their divorce. Henry then married Katherine Howard. To his dismay Cranmer discovered that Katherine was enjoying herself conducting sexual adventures with a series of lovers behind the King's back. As the rumours multiplied in chattering circles, Cranmer took the risk of breaking the story to the authorities. Eventually he wrote a letter to the King about it. Henry's reaction was one of stunned disbelief. Cranmer tried to coax

Katherine into confessing her premarital affairs as well as the ones she had entered into since marrying the King. In 1542 she was executed and Henry married Catherine Parr.

First officially authorised service in English

On 27 May 1544 Cranmer issued the text of the first church service to be officially authorised in English. It was the processional service of intercession known as the litany. A litany is a form of prayer which consists of a series of petitions or biddings which are sung or said in church by a deacon, a priest or lead singers, and to which the congregation make fixed responses.

Cranmer's litanies were for use in the procession ordered by Henry at a time when England was at war with Scotland and France. They were not especially edifying, enlisting God's help against England's enemies. But they are the first surviving specimens of Cranmer's liturgical craftsmanship in English; with only minor modifications they survive as the litany which follows the Athanasian Creed in the 1662 version of the *Book of Common Prayer*. Its wonderfully sonorous language conceals the fact that, like all Cranmer's compositions, it is an ingenious effort with scissors and paste using previous texts.

A squeeze of the hand

Towards the end of 1546 Henry's health began to deteriorate. When Sir Anthony Denny, Chief Gentleman of the Privy Chamber, persuaded Henry that he must face death, the King asked specifically for Archbishop Cranmer to be with him. By the time that Cranmer reached him in the small hours of the morning of 28 January 1547, Henry was unable to speak, but reached out to his old friend.

'Put your trust in Christ,' said Cranmer, 'and call upon his mercy. You cannot speak, but I beg your Grace to give me some token with your eyes or with your hand that you trust the Lord.' Then the King, who was already holding the Archbishop's hand, wrung it as hard as he could.

So Cranmer quietly did his duty as Evangelical chaplain to the King. He may even have thought that he had won a final victory in his years of argument with the King on justification. Notwithstanding Henry's slow moves towards Protestantism, and Cranmer's major moves in that direction, however, the Archbishop sang the mass of requiem for the King's soul.

There is no doubt that Cranmer mourned the dead King. They said that he demonstrated his grief for the rest of his life by growing a beard.

EDWARD VI

Edward VI was only nine years old and sickly when he became King in 1547. Henry had ensured that Edward's uncle the Duke of Somerset would head the Council of Regency which ruled the country. Cranmer also sat on the Council but actually meddled little with affairs of state. The Duke of Somerset was a Reformer and during Edward's reign many traditional furnishings and images began to be removed from England's parish churches.

In 1547 the theologically Catholic Six Articles were repealed. During the summer of that year Cranmer issued a collection of homilies. His aim was to remedy the shortage of reliable preachers in the church. Cranmer wrote four of the twelve homilies himself, including the opening 'Exhortation to the Reading of the Holy Scripture', a theme apparently dear to his heart. He also reserved to himself the subjects which he felt important to get right if the English Church were to be preserved from what he regarded as popish error – salvation, faith and good works.

In the homilies Cranmer was keen to establish the nature of salvation as God's free gift of grace by faith, while demonstrating to the person in the pew that this should not result in the collapse of morality. In composing the homilies Cranmer made it clear that although justification was by faith, good works were still an important part of the Christian life. The sermons have an emphasis on the way daily life should be lived as well as references to human helplessness and God's mercy.

Sensibly, the homilies avoid technical theological terms and are sparing in classical allusions, recognising that these would not go down well in most English parish churches. Cranmer was designing a collection of sermons to stand the test of time, so the homilies avoided anecdotes or any passages which might entertain at first hearing but would become embarrassing on repetition.

Cranmer's first Prayer Book

Cranmer, and the other English reformers, wanted to simplify and condense the Latin services of the medieval Church and to produce in English a single, convenient and comprehensive volume to guide priest and people. In 1548 Cranmer discussed a draft he had produced with a conference of scholars. He had drawn on the Roman Catholic Sarum Breviary (a liturgical book in Latin) of 1543 and the English litany.

He was impressed with the breviary, liking its uniformity, continuous reading of Scripture and its recitation of the whole Psalter during a given period. Following the breviary, Cranmer was able to condense the richness and complexity of the monastic offices into the two services of Morning and Evening Prayer. By doing so he preserved something of the monastic tradition in a new form.

On 2 June 1549, the Sunday after Ascension, congregations in English churches worshipped according to the medieval Latin service books for the last time. Seven days later, on Whitsunday, they were introduced to the *Book of Common Prayer*, the product of Cranmer's liturgical skill and scholarship. The liturgical reading and the Psalms came from Coverdale's 'Great Bible'.

King Edward's Act of Uniformity made the use of Cranmer's first Prayer Book compulsory. The book was a compromise between Catholicism and Protestantism, with concessions to Catholicism especially regarding ceremonies, which greatly disappointed the Evangelicals. Stephen Gardiner was able to give the book an orthodox Catholic reading. You could call Gardiner the first 'Anglo-Catholic'; Cranmer labelled him and his sympathisers 'English Papists'. Typically though, Cranmer believed that you should make haste slowly when introducing changes.

Cranmer had been tireless in his efforts to seek out good phrases from many sources and he did not mind capturing words from the Church of Rome and putting them to good use. He must take credit for the overall job of editorship and the structure of the 1549 book. We owe Cranmer the present form of the sequence of eighty-four seasonal collects and other features of the 1549 book. Many see his prayers as one of the glories of the Anglican liturgical tradition.

Cranmer found in the Sarum Breviary a prayer which had been said in the monastic services at the 'Lauds of the Blessed Virgin' ('Lauds' indicates that they were morning prayers). The Latin prayer read:

> *Deus auctor pacis et amator, quem nosse vivere, cui servire regnare est: protege ab omnibus impugnationibus supplices tuos: ut qui in defensione tua confidimus, nullius hostilitatis arma timeamus.*[4]

A literal Latin translation of this prayer reads:

> God, author and lover of peace, whom to know is to live, whom it is commanded we should serve: protect your supplicants from all attacks so that we, who trust in your defence, may never fear the weapons of enemies.

Cranmer, however, took hold of the Latin and produced the following prayer which has been said and loved by English-speaking people for centuries.

> O God, who art the author of peace and lover of concord, in knowledge of whom standeth our eternal life, whose service is perfect freedom: Defend us thy humble servants in all assaults of our enemies; that we, surely trusting in thy defence, may not fear the power of any adversaries.

This prayer, the Second Collect for Peace, is familiar as part of the Order for Morning Prayer and was of course retained in the 1662 *Book of Common Prayer*. It well illustrates how Cranmer often succeeded in improving on the original sources he used. The magnificent paradoxical phrase 'whose service is perfect freedom' is not in the original Latin, although the thought is thoroughly biblical.

In the service for the 'solemnisation of matrimony', marriage vows had always been in the vernacular for obvious reasons. Cranmer removed the wife's promise to be 'bonner and buxom in bed and at the board' – perhaps the phrase was a little racy for some, although, as MacCulloch has commented, 'its retention might have stemmed the slide of the word "buxom" down the scale of respectability. Cranmer added the promise by the groom to "love and to cherish" and by the wife to "love, cherish and obey" . . .'

In 1549 Cranmer invited the German Reformer Martin Bucer (1491–1551) to come to England as Regius Professor of Theology at Cambridge. Bucer had earlier recorded his thanks to God for providing England with a model archbishop in Cranmer, 'a Primate extraordinary as a man in holiness of life, in doctrine, perseverance, and zeal for the government of the church'. Bucer declared himself well pleased with the underlying principles of English reform. Everything in the churches was read and sung in English; the doctrine of justification was purely and soundly taught; the Eucharist was correctly administered; private masses had been abolished.

In the same year, the English clergy were allowed to marry, and Cranmer publicly acknowledged the existence of his wife. Margaret could now begin to work out her role as clerical wife in her husband's palaces. It is no doubt unfair to judge Cranmer by today's standards, but it must be said that he was one of the few English bishops still living like a great magnate, with a lifestyle structured round his five well-kept palaces at Lambeth, Croydon, Canterbury, Ford and Bekesbourne.

In 1550 the diocese of London came into Evangelical hands under Bishop Nicholas Ridley (c. 1500–55). Ridley had studied at Cambridge (where he had been one of the White Horse Tavern group), the Sorbonne and Louvain. He had been a major influence in shifting Cranmer away from a 'real presence' view of the Eucharist to a 'spiritual presence' view and had helped him compile the 1549 Prayer Book.

Cranmer's 1552 Prayer Book

During the winter of 1551–2 Cranmer revised his 1549 Prayer Book and presented it to Parliament for authorisation in a new Act of Uniformity, passed in April 1552. The revised Prayer Book acknowledged many of the Evangelical objections to the first one. It added the introduction to Morning and Evening Prayer which is retained in today's *Book of Common Prayer*, excluded all prayers for the dead, ordered the use of the surplice instead of other vestments, and omitted all references to 'Mass' and 'Altar'. Cranmer tried to omit everything which he could not defend as scriptural. Even his most Protestant critics could now be sure that the mass had really been abolished in England.

Congregations all over England would have been most aware of the replacement of the altar by the Communion table in a more accessible position in the chancel or nave for a celebration of the Lord's Supper, rather than as an altar of sacrifice. Traditional vestments were out; a plain surplice was in. The more perceptive members of congregations would notice that the structure of the Communion service had been radically changed and the canon had been redesigned to give emphasis to the congregational or communal features of the service.

One important change in the new Prayer Book was that at the administration of Communion the clergyman would now say those beautiful words that would become loved by English-speaking men and women for four hundred years:

Take and eat this, in remembrance that Christ died for thee, and feed on him in thy heart by faith with thanksgiving.

Although this form of words did not deny belief in a real presence, it could be interpreted in a way which was acceptable to the most radical Swiss Reformers who believed that Communion was nothing more than a memorial of Christ's death.

· Everyone is encouraged to go to church

The preface to the 1552 book positively encouraged the laity to attend the services of the church. In the 1549 preface, by contrast, the emphasis had been on the fact that there was no compulsion on anyone to attend the offices apart from those with the cure of souls or specific duties in cathedrals and the greater churches. Now not only were 'all priests and deacons' specifically ordered to say the offices daily, but the parish clergyman was told to say the service openly in church, and to 'toll a bell thereto, a convenient time before he begin, that such as be disposed may come to hear God's word and pray with him'.

Up and down England the bells were indeed tolled and the people arrived at their newly whitewashed churches. From this sprang a characteristic pattern of Sunday worship in the Church of England – morning and evening prayer. This dominated the mainstream of devotional life in the Church of England from the reign of the first Elizabeth until well into the reign of the second, until the modern emphasis on restoring the central place of the Eucharist changed the shape of worship once more.

Cranmer's Forty-two Articles

On 19 June 1553 Cranmer issued his Forty-two Articles of Religion. He had done most of the drafting. However, an event occurred which meant that these Articles were never enforced, although they formed the basis of the later Thirty-nine Articles. King Edward's health was finally giving way as his tuberculosis took hold. The diagnosis was now fatal. His successor under the terms of Henry's will was the King's half-sister, Mary. There could be no doubt that she would restore the old religion and it would be a devastating blow for the Evangelical revolution.

Won over by the dying King's pleading, Cranmer reluctantly signed the documents aimed at diverting the succession from Mary to Lady Jane Grey. The Duke of Northumberland, who had been Edward's chief minister, had Lady Jane proclaimed Queen in an attempt to save Protestantism in England. But Northumberland was disliked and the people rallied to Mary. After only nine days, Queen Jane's reign ended and she was beheaded in 1554. The Duke of Northumberland was also executed.

QUEEN MARY

To his credit, Cranmer made no attempt to flee the country. He is sometimes criticised for his timidity, but the significance of his behaviour during the late summer and early autumn of 1553 should not be forgotten. In this time he could have done what so many other Protestants did: slip away to the continent, living to fight another day.

Yet he did not desert his post. He cannot have been under much illusion about Mary's attitude towards him, the man who had humiliated her mother, ruined her own life and played his part in destroying the religion she loved.

The beginning of the end for Cranmer

In September 1553 the inevitable happened. Cranmer was ordered to appear before the Council of the Star Chamber. On Wednesday 13 September he managed to carry on the conduct of his normal responsibilities as Archbishop of Canterbury, including making arrangements for the installation of a new rector in the vicarage of Croydon.

On the Thursday he had a final dinner with Peter Martyr (1499–1562), an Italian Reformer who had been Regius Professor of Divinity at Oxford since 1548 and who had helped Cranmer in the drafting of the 1552 Prayer Book. After the meal Cranmer called his friend to his private rooms.

'A trial is now inevitable,' Cranmer said. 'We shall never meet again. If you cannot get a passport straight away, you must escape from England.' He was recommending to his friend an option he had denied himself over the previous month and a half.

The next morning Cranmer crossed the River Thames and went to the Court of the Star Chamber. His treason in trying to bring about the succession of Queen Jane ensured that he was now sent straight to the Tower, to join Nicholas Ridley who was already there. Soon the two men were joined by Hugh Latimer, who later recalled what a happy chance it was: 'There did we together read over the New Testament with great deliberation and painful study.'

As Cranmer had predicted to Peter Martyr, he would never again be a free man. On 13 November he was charged with treason and, pleading guilty, was condemned to die. Queen Mary, however, intervened to spare his life at this stage. In her eyes, he had committed an even more serious crime than treason: he had led the whole country into heresy. He must die for that, but only after a trial.

In July 1554 Philip II of Spain, to whom Mary was betrothed, landed in England. Their marriage was a failure and unpopular with English people.

As the burning of Protestants began, the Queen was supported in her resolve by Edmund Bonner, Bishop of London, and Stephen Gardiner, Bishop of Winchester, who had crowned her. The number of Protestant burnings was not great compared with what happened in the Netherlands, but it was traumatic for England which had never seen anything like it before. As an attempt to destroy Protestantism it failed.

Latimer and Ridley are burned

Cranmer, Latimer and Ridley were eventually moved to Oxford to be tried for heresy. After ceremonies on 15 October 1555 to remove Latimer and Ridley from the priesthood, the two men were sentenced to be burnt the next day outside the city gate in Broad Street, in front of Balliol College.

As they were led to the stake past the prison where Cranmer was being held, they hoped they would catch a glimpse of him and be able to shout a greeting. But it was not until the proceedings at the stake were under way that Cranmer was brought to a tower of the gatehouse to watch what was happening. One historian says that a major aim of the authorities was to frighten him out of his defiance, and that as many eyes in the crowd were on him as on the two victims at the stake. According to a Catholic commentator, Cranmer was traumatised by the awful sight of his two friends at the stake. He tore off his cap, fell to his knees and cried out in anguish.

Meanwhile Hugh Latimer made his famous observation to his fellow bishop. 'Be of good comfort, Master Ridley, and play the man. We shall this day light such a candle, by God's grace in England, as I trust shall never be put out.' Cranmer would not have been able to hear these words, and it may be that they were never reported to him in his hour of need.

They allowed Cranmer to eat well in his Oxford prison: boiled meat, roast beef, rabbit, fresh salmon and fruit. They gave him beer to drink during the day and even allowed him a personal servant. It did little to relieve his anguish.

Cranmer is sentenced to death

Cranmer was sentenced to death for heresy and in 1556 formally stripped of the title 'Archbishop'. At one stage during the long process of question and answer Villagarcia, his Spanish Roman Catholic interrogator, put a sarcastic question to him about his abandonment of the doctrine of transubstantiation: 'Will all the saints who disagreed with your eucharistic theology perish because they were ignorant of your new faith?'

Cranmer was too worn out to try to correct the suggestion that his views were novel (his argument was that transubstantiation had itself been a relatively recent papal innovation). 'Indeed I think that you can attain salvation through your faith,' he meekly replied, 'likewise I can in mine.'

'So,' said Villagarcia triumphantly, 'the matter of corporeal presence is not a question of the essence of the faith! What, then, of Paul's claim in 1 Corinthians 11 that his narrative of the Eucharist was "received from the Lord"?'

Cranmer made no attempt to expound what he understood by 'This is my body'. He seemed disturbed and tugged at his beard in his distress. 'I have no answer,' he said.[5]

Cranmer's recantations

Under duress and acutely depressed, Cranmer signed six recantations of his Protestant faith in rapid succession. Catholic reports spoke of a man 'trembling in every limb'. It is unlikely that Cranmer wrote his recantations himself. Even the Catholic account merely says that he was ordered to sign them. One of his recantations reads:

I, Thomas Cranmer, late Archbishop of Canterbury, do renounce, abhor, and detest all manner of heresies and errors of Luther and Zwingli, and all other teachings which are contrary to sound and true doctrine. And I believe most constantly in my heart, and with my mouth I confess, one holy and Catholic church visible, without which there is no salvation; and thereof I acknowledge the Bishop of Rome to be the supreme head on earth; whom I acknowledge to the highest bishop and pope, and Christ's vicar, unto whom all Christian people ought to be subject.

And as concerning the sacraments, I believe and worship in the sacrament of the altar, the very body and blood of Christ being contained most truly under the forms of bread and wine; the bread through the mighty power of God being turned into the body of our Saviour Jesus Christ, and the wine into his blood . . .

Finally, in all things I profess, that I do not otherwise believe than the Catholic Church and Church of Rome teaches. I am sorry that ever I held or thought otherwise. And I beseech Almighty God that of his mercy he will vouchsafe to forgive me, whatsoever I have offended against God or his church, and I also desire and beseech all Christian people to pray for me . . .

And to conclude, as I submit myself to the Catholic Church of Christ, and to the supreme head thereof, so I submit myself unto the most excellent majesties of Philip and Mary, King and Queen of this realm of England, etc., and to all other laws and ordinances, being ready always as a faithful subject ever to obey them. And as God is my witness that I have not done this for favour or fear of any person, but willingly and of mine own mind, as well as the discharge of mine own conscience, as to the instruction of others.

The Roman authorities had the recantations printed and widely circulated including a copy to Mary. This time the Queen did not intervene to prevent the sentence of death taking its course. Instead, she instructed Dr Henry Cole, the Provost of Eton, to visit Cranmer in prison and inform him of his impending death.

At first Cranmer took the news calmly. 'I have never been afraid of dying,' he told Cole, 'but feel oppressed by the weight of all my sins. Please ensure that the personal estates left to me by the King are passed on to my son Thomas.'

At the thought of his son, Cranmer broke down in tears. Cole was not sympathetic. 'You ought to be concentrating your thoughts on loyalty to the Catholic cause,' he told Cranmer and left the prisoner in a state of nervous collapse.

Cranmer's last full day on earth was 20 March 1556. He spent it planning how he would present himself on the day of his burning, particularly at the service at St Mary's Church which would precede his execution. He composed a final address.

His last recorded menu for his evening meal was appropriate for a Friday in Lent: spice cakes and bread, fruit and nuts and a dish of stewed prunes. With wine and ale at the table, he prolonged conversation with his companions into the night before getting some sound sleep.

That evening he gave a small coin to a servant-girl. 'Pray for me,' he said to her. 'I think more of the prayers of a good layperson than those of a bad priest.'

In the morning he made some edifying remarks to the assembled prison staff, recited the litany and signed some fourteen additional copies of his sixth recantation with minor alterations. Still acting as a devout Catholic, he asked Nicholas Woodson to arrange special prayers for him in the cathedral. Just before he was taken to St Mary's he told Woodson: 'God will finish what he has begun.' The statement could be taken two ways.

Drama at St Mary's

Then a procession made its way from the prison to St Mary's. Large crowds had gathered in the rain to watch the events. At the head of the procession was the mayor, followed by Oxford's aldermen. Then came Cranmer flanked by Villagarcia and Pedro de Soto, a Spanish theologian who had been involved in the attempts to persuade Cranmer to return to the Roman Catholic faith.

They led Cranmer to a specially prepared stand in a packed and excited church. You can still see the marks in one of the pillars of St Mary's where they constructed the stand. The former Archbishop, primate of all England, the King's privy councillor, now stood in a bare and ragged gown, with an old square cap on his head. He lifted his hands and prayed once or twice.

Dr Henry Cole began to preach a sermon which the Queen had asked him to prepare some weeks earlier. He had the job of explaining why a repentant sinner should be burnt at the stake for heresy. He spoke of God's mercy, but also of his justice. He reproved Cranmer for once having been 'endued with the favour and feeling of wholesome Catholic doctrine but then falling into the contrary opinion of pernicious error'. He accused him of being a traitor for dissolving the lawful marriage between the King and Catherine of Aragon, and of being a heretic. Addressing the congregation, Cole warned them that God's vengeance is equally directed against all men and spares none. Therefore they should beware. Before them was a man who had fallen from a position of the highest dignity into great misery. Cranmer listened quietly, at times with tears on his cheeks.

Towards the end of his sermon, Cole turned to Cranmer again with some words intended to comfort him. He encouraged him to take his death well. He quoted many portions of Scripture, including Christ's words to the dying thief, 'This day shalt thou be with me in paradise.' He urged him to trust in God. He gave glory to God for Cranmer's reconversion to the Catholic faith. He told him that immediately after his death there would be dirges, masses and funerals conducted for him in all the churches of Oxford. Cole asked all the priests present to pray for Cranmer.

As soon as he had finished his sermon, Henry Cole addressed the congregation and Cranmer with a note of expectancy in his voice. 'Brethren,' said Cole, 'lest any man should doubt of this man's earnest conversion and repentance, you shall hear him speak before you; and therefore I pray you, Master Cranmer, that you will now perform what you promised long ago; namely that you will openly express the true and undoubted profession of your faith, that you may take away all suspicion from men, and that all men may understand that you are a Catholic indeed.'

'I will do it,' said Cranmer, 'and that with a good will. I desire you, well-beloved brethren in the Lord, that you will pray to God for me, to forgive me my sins, which above all men, both in number and greatness I have committed. But among all the rest, there is one offence which most of all at this time doth vex and trouble me, whereof in process of my talk, you shall hear more in its proper place.'

Cranmer rested his hand on his chest and continued addressing the congregation calling them 'good Christian people, my dearly beloved brethren and sisters in Christ'. He asked them to pray that God would forgive his sins referring again to one thing which 'grieved his conscience more than all the rest' which he would speak about later. In the meantime he knelt down and prayed for God's mercy followed by the Lord's Prayer.

Cranmer then stood up again and asked God to give him the grace to 'speak something at this my departing whereby God may be glorified and you edified'. He proceeded to deliver a series of exhortations, first describing his grief that 'so many folk' doted on the love of this false world while caring so little for the love of God and the world to come. Second, he exhorted them to obey the King and Queen (Philip and Mary) willingly and without murmuring: resisting them would be 'to resist the ordinance of God'. Third, he exhorted them to love one another, saying how sad it was when Christians treated each other as strangers and enemies rather than as brothers and sisters. Fourth, he warned them of the danger of riches – turning their attention to a series of Scriptures which warned how difficult it is for the rich to enter the Kingdom of Heaven.

Then Cranmer embarked on a passage of his address which first surprised and then alarmed the authorities. Cranmer had given them a text of what he would say and they expected him to read his recantations. What he was saying now was not in the script.

'And now,' he continued, 'forasmuch as I am come to the last end of my life, whereupon hangeth all my life past, and all my life to come, either to live with my master Christ for ever in joy, or else to be in pain for ever with wicked devils in hell, and I see before mine

41

eyes presently either heaven ready to receive me, or else hell ready to swallow me up. I shall therefore declare unto you my very faith how I believe, without any colour of dissimulation, for now is no time to dissemble, whatsoever I have said or written in times past.

'First, I believe in God the Father Almighty, maker of heaven and earth, etc. And I believe every article of the Catholic faith, every word and sentence taught by our Saviour Jesus Christ, his apostles and prophets, in the New and Old Testaments.

'And now I come to the great thing, which so troubleth my conscience, more than anything that ever I did or said in my whole life, and that is the setting abroad of a writing contrary to the truth, which now here I renounce and refuse, as things written with my hand contrary to the truth which I thought in my heart and written for fear of death and to save my life if it might be. I refer to all the bills and papers which I have written or signed with my hand since my degradation, wherein I have written many things which are untrue. And forasmuch as my hand offendeth, writing contrary to my heart, my hand shall be first punished for it; for when I come to the fire it shall be first burned . . .'

A mixture of joy and noisy anger was breaking out in the church. Through the hubbub, Cranmer persevered in shouting; it was vital to get his message across. He was deadly pale, but a surge of energy had taken away the tears.

'And as for the Pope,' Cranmer went on, 'I refute him as Christ's enemy, and Antichrist, with all his false doctrine. As for the sacrament, I believe as I have taught in my book against the Bishop of Winchester, which book teacheth so true a doctrine of the sacrament that it shall stand at the last day of judgment of God, where the papistical doctrine shall be ashamed to show her face . . .' Here the enraged officials tried to stop him.

'Ah, my masters, do not take it so,' Cranmer said to them. 'Always since I lived hitherto, I have been a hater of falsehood, and a lover of simplicity, and never before the time of my recantation have I dissembled . . .' Then he broke down again in tears.

'Stop the heretic's mouth,' shouted Dr Cole, 'and take him away.'

The officials pulled him from his stage, hurried him out into the street and led him towards the stake.

'What madness', the friars asked him, 'has brought you again into this error by which you shall draw innumerable souls with you into hell?'

Cranmer made no reply to this, but turned to address a noisy member of the crowd. 'Go home,' he said. 'Apply yourself to your books and ask God, through reading, to give you knowledge.'

The crowd arrived at the place where Latimer and Ridley had suffered five months earlier.

'This unworthy hand'

Cranmer knelt down and prayed briefly. Then he took off all his clothes except a long shirt which reached to his now bare feet. His head was completely bald, his beard long and thick. It is said that both his friends and enemies in the crowd were moved by the composure and serenity of the expression on his face.

They tied an iron chain around him and lit the wood. As the flames began to leap around him, he kept the promise he had made in his last words in the church.

'Forasmuch as my hand offended,' he shouted, looking up to heaven, 'writing contrary to my heart, my hand shall be punished there for.' He stretched out his hand into the heat of the fire, for all the spectators to see. He repeated while he could, 'This unworthy right hand, this hand hath offended. Oh this unworthy hand!' And also while he could, the dying words of the first martyr, Stephen, 'Lord Jesus receive my spirit.'

According to the accounts, he died quickly. It was said that in the ashes of the fire his heart was found unburnt.

The effect of Cranmer's behaviour in his final hours was to make maximum use for the Evangelical cause of a piece of theatre which had been designed to show off the Catholic Church's most important prize since 1553 – perhaps the most important reconversion of the whole European Reformation so far. If Cranmer had made it clear beforehand that he was going to the stake with the defiance of a Ridley or a Latimer, then he would not have been given such a unique chance to make his final position clear.

Cranmer is a key figure in the story of early Anglican Evangelicalism. His was a remarkable life. Brought up in the world of the late medieval Church, his views underwent profound change in the later 1520s and early 1530s. It was a remarkable step for a temperamentally cautious man to take in middle life.

From 1529 the major influence in his life had been King Henry, the man whose scorn he dreaded. It seems strange that anyone could have so loved and respected such a monster. But Cranmer really came to believe that the Supreme Headship as exercised by this tyrant expressed God's will better than the traditional headship of the Western Church.

Like most of the great Reformers, Cranmer was a reformed Catholic in the sense that he wanted to rebuild the Catholic Church on the same foundations of Bible, creeds and the great councils of the early Church. Rather than the later notion of an Anglican Church walking between extremes, listening out in many directions for good ideas, Cranmer had tried to guide the Church of England to a renewal of Catholicity, avoiding the errors of Rome on the one hand and Anabaptism on the other, both of which were 'sects' in his eyes.

Perhaps the greatest tribute to Cranmer's life and work is to be found in the twin achievements of launching the Anglican Church with a liturgy which was thoroughly biblical and his contribution to the English language. Cranmer could not know in 1552 that he was providing a text and ethos for worship which would remain almost unchanged for four hundred years. Yet it was a happy accident that this career churchman, propelled into high office by the twists and turns of affairs of state, had a natural feel for English prose – how it sounds and how sentences should be constructed.

Certainly, what we think of as Cranmer's Prayer Book English is in fact a patchwork of adaptations from medieval sources and other writers. His motive was not sinister, however, and his alterations of existing texts were usually improvements.

Millions who have never heard of Cranmer or read the story of his death have echoes of his words in their minds. The Prayer Book played a key role in deciding what was good English: it was destined to be one of the most frequently printed and heard texts in the language. Cranmer stands with a select company of Tudor writers, from Tyndale to Shakespeare, who set English on its future course.

Queen Mary died on 17 November 1558 and was succeeded by her sister Elizabeth. Mary's reign had seen a return to Catholic worship in the Roman style, often without compulsion, and to the delight of many people. But, according to Kenneth Hylson-Smith, there occurred 'a certain recasting of Catholicism in the Marian era, in conformity to a European-wide redirection in the Counter-Reformation, whereby there was a more self-conscious emphasis on the cross and redemption'.[6]

ELIZABETH I

On 23 November 1558 the daughter of Henry VIII and Anne Boleyn rode into London.

The new Queen's collection of private prayers suggests that she was genuinely attached to the Protestant faith. Elizabeth disliked the Roman Catholic mass but was fond of the pomp and splendour of the old religion. She immediately appointed Protestant preachers for public occasions.

The majority of men in her Council and Administration were firmly attached to Cranmer's moderate Protestantism. In throwing off the yoke of Rome, Parliament had no intention of introducing religious tolerance, and the Act of Uniformity authorised a certain form of public worship which prohibited all others. The Act revived the use of the 1552 Prayer Book with certain modifications, and instructed that it should be used throughout the kingdom.

Elizabeth's Act of Supremacy

The Act of Supremacy of 1559 initially pleased Evangelicals who welcomed the Prayer Book as substituting a purer form of worship for the breviary and the mass; and it was conservative enough not to alarm traditionalists unduly.

There were three significant concessions to conservative opinion in the 1559 settlement. First, the Queen was to be 'Supreme Governor' not 'Supreme Head'; second, the settlement allowed many of the old vestments in services and was silent about destroying other familiar items of the liturgy; third, the 1552 Communion service was modified to add the words of administration of the 1549 book: 'The body of our Lord Jesus Christ, which was given for thee, preserve thy body and soul unto everlasting life . . .' (followed by the invitation to 'feed on him in thy heart by faith with thanksgiving') and this form of words was later retained in the 1662 book. The new Prayer Book also retained the word 'priest' and specifically sanctioned the priestly power of absolution.

Two bodies of critics opposed the Elizabethan settlement. Many among the ordinary ranks of the clergy and the laity retained a preference for the ways of the pre-Reformation Church. On the other side a considerable volume of Evangelical opinion regarded the Prayer Book, Articles and the whole idea of bishops as only a halfway house to a fuller and better Reformation.

Almost all the churchmen who took this view remained within the Church of England, striving for changes from within, and controversy ranged over a wide area from the wearing of the surplice to the reform of the Prayer Book and even getting rid of bishops in favour of Presbyterianism.

The Thirty-nine Articles

The Thirty-nine Articles were enacted in 1563. Based on the Forty-two Articles of 1553, each of the Articles deals with some point raised in the controversies of the Reformation (or sometimes medieval) period and lays down in general terms the Anglican view. Although the Articles had their origin in a time of debate and turmoil, there is nevertheless a warmth of language which has the capacity to touch the heart.

Although it would not be correct to describe the Articles as vague, they avoid unnecessarily narrow definition. Over the centuries which have followed, a variety of interpretations has been put on them, often without unduly straining the text. (In 1841, in his famous Tract 90, J. H. Newman attempted to show that much of the language of the Articles was not directed against the Church of Rome.) Almost certainly, a degree of licence was deliberately intended by the framers of the Articles.

The first five Articles deal with the *substance of faith*, beginning with a strong assertion of the existence of God and going on to lay down a Trinitarian foundation to what follows. There is 'but one living and true God' who is 'everlasting, without body, parts or passions; of infinite power, wisdom, and goodness'. He is the 'Maker, and Preserver of all things both visible and invisible' (Article 1). In the Word or Son of God 'Godhead and Manhood were joined together in one Person, never to be divided'. Jesus Christ 'truly suffered, was crucified, dead and buried, to reconcile his Father to us, and to be a sacrifice, not only for original guilt, but also for all actual sins of men' (2).

Christ 'did truly rise again from death, and took again his body, with flesh, bones, and all things appertaining to the perfection of man's nature; wherewith he ascended into Heaven, and there sitteth, until he return to judge all Men at the last day' (4). The Holy Ghost 'proceeding from the Father and the Son, is of one substance, majesty, and glory, with the Father and the Son, very and eternal God' (5).

Articles 6 and 7 speak of *Holy Scripture* which 'containeth all things necessary to salvation: so that whatsoever is not read therein, nor may be proved thereby, is not to be required of any man, that is should be believed as an article of Faith, or be thought requisite or necessary to salvation' (6). The Old Testament 'is not contrary to the New: for both in the Old and New Testament everlasting life is offered to Mankind by Christ, who is the only Mediator between God and Man' (7).

The final sentence of Article 7 is an important statement of the *Christian's relationship to the law*. It deals with an issue which is relevant to contemporary debates about sin and morality (including human sexuality): 'Although the Law given from God by Moses, as touching Ceremonies and Rites, do not bind Christian men, nor the Civil precepts thereof ought of necessity to be received in any commonwealth; yet notwithstanding, no Christian man whatsoever is free from the obedience of the Commandments which are called Moral'.

Article 8 says that the three creeds, *Nicene, Athanasius's*, and 'that which is commonly called the *Apostles'* Creed ought 'thoroughly to be received and believed: for they may be proved by most certain warrants of holy Scripture'.

Articles 9 to 18 all deal with the life of faith, or personal religion. Article 9 asserts the doctrine of *original or birth-sin*, pointing out that every person born into this world has to battle with a flesh which 'lusteth always contrary to the spirit' and therefore 'deserveth God's wrath and damnation'. This infection of nature remains even 'in them that are regenerated' although 'there is no condemnation for them that believe and are baptised'.

Article 10, which deals with the much debated question of *free will*, reads as if it has gone through many drafts in committee, and is not easy to understand on first reading. Its central thought, however, is that 'we have no power to do good works pleasant and acceptable to God, without the grace of God by Christ'.

Articles 11 to 16 refer to *justification*, *good works* and *sin*. The framers of the Articles had no doubt that 'we are accounted righteous before God only for the merit of our Lord and Saviour Jesus Christ by Faith, and not for our own works or deservings: Wherefore, that we are justified by Faith only is a most wholesome Doctrine, and very full of comfort' (11). Good works are 'the fruits of Faith, and follow after Justification'. Although they 'cannot put away our sins, and endure the severity of God's Judgement', nevertheless they 'are pleasing and acceptable to God in Christ, and do spring out necessarily of a true and lively Faith'. By good works 'a lively Faith may be evidently known as a tree discerned by the fruit' (12).

Medieval and Reformation theologians had devoted much energy to debating the value of good works done 'before justification'. Article 13 announced that 'works done before the grace of Christ, and the Inspiration of his Spirit, are not pleasant to God, forasmuch as they spring not of faith in Jesus Christ, neither do they make men meet to receive grace, or (as the School-authors say) deserve grace of congruity'.

Christ never sinned. He offered a perfect sacrifice to take away the sins of the world. 'But all the rest, although baptised, and born again in Christ, yet offend in many things; and if we say we have no sin, we deceive ourselves, and the truth is not in us' (15). Those people 'are to be condemned, which say, they can no more sin as long as they live here, or deny the place of forgiveness to such as truly repent' (16).

Article 17 deals with *predestination and election*, a key element of Calvin's thought. The Article has been described as a masterpiece of ambiguity, and it is certainly vaguer than the Presbyterian Westminster Confession (see page 82), but it has a certain warmth of tone. The Article states that 'Predestination to Life is the everlasting purpose of God'. Consideration of this truth, coupled with the idea of our Election in Christ (chosen before the foundation of the world) is 'full of sweet, pleasant, and unspeakable comfort to godly persons, and such as feel in themselves the working of the Spirit of Christ, mortifying the works of the flesh, and their earthly members, and drawing up their mind to high and heavenly things'. Reflecting on these truths and acting upon them kindles our love towards God. On the other hand, if 'curious and carnal persons, lacking the Spirit of Christ' have 'continually before their eyes the sentence of God's Predestination' the result is that 'the Devil doth thrust them either into desperation, or into wretchlessness [*sic*] of most unclean living'.

Article 18 denies that we may be saved by the Law. Holy Scripture teaches that it is 'only the Name of Jesus Christ, whereby men must be saved'.

Articles 19 to 22 all deal with the Church, defining the visible Church of Christ as 'a congregation of faithful men, in which the pure Word of God is preached, and the Sacraments be duly ministered according to Christ's ordinance in all those things that of necessity are requisite to the same'. Just as the Churches of *Jerusalem*, *Alexandria* and *Antioch* have erred, so also the Church of *Rome* has erred 'not only in their living and manner of Ceremonies, but also in matters of Faith' (19).

Referring to the *authority of the Church*, Article 20 says that although the Church has power to decree Rites and Ceremonies, and authority in Controversies of Faith, yet 'it is not lawful for the Church to ordain any thing that is contrary to God's Word written, neither may it so expound one place of Scripture, that it be repugnant to another'. Certainly the Church is 'a witness and a keeper of holy Writ', but it should never 'enforce anything to be believed for necessity of Salvation'.

Article 21 says that General Councils 'may err, and sometimes have erred, even in things pertaining unto God'.

Article 22 sharply rebukes the 'Romish Doctrine concerning Purgatory' and a series of related practices all of which not only have no scriptural warrant but are actually 'repugnant to the Word of God'.

Articles 23 and 24, dealing with the Church's ministry, state that it is not lawful for any man to take the office of preacher, or to minister the sacraments in the congregation, unless he is lawfully called (23). Article 24 says that it is unscriptural, and against the custom of the ancient Church, for anyone to speak to the congregation in a language which they cannot understand.

Articles 25 to 31 deal with the *sacraments*, which are 'certain sure witnesses, and effectual signs of grace, and God's good will towards us, by which he doth work invisibly in us, and doth not only quicken, but also strengthen and confirm our Faith in him'. It speaks of two sacraments only which are ordained of Christ in the gospel, 'Baptism and the Supper of the Lord'. The so-called sacraments of 'Confirmation, Penance, Orders, Matrimony, and Extreme Unction' are 'not to be counted for Sacraments of the Gospel'. Furthermore, the sacraments 'were not ordained of Christ to be gazed upon, or to be carried about' whereas 'in such only as worthily receive the same they have a wholesome effect or operation' (25).

Article 27 describes *Baptism* as 'not only a sign of profession and mark of difference, whereby Christian men are discerned from others that be not christened, but it is also *a sign of Regeneration or new Birth*, whereby, as by an instrument, they that receive Baptism rightly are grafted into the Church; the promises of forgiveness of sin, and of our adoption to be the sons of God by the Holy Ghost, are visibly signed and sealed; Faith is confirmed, and Grace increased by virtue of prayer unto God. The Baptism of young children is in any wise to be retained in the Church, as most agreeable with the institution of Christ'.

Articles 28 to 31 cover the *Supper of our Lord* which is 'not only a sign of the love that Christians ought to have among themselves one to another; but rather is a Sacrament of our Redemption by Christ's death . . . to such as rightly, worthily, and with faith, receive' the bread and wine. *Transubstantiation*, which the Article briefly defines in parenthesis as 'the change of the substance of Bread and Wine', 'cannot be proved by holy Writ; but is repugnant to the plain words of Scripture, overthroweth the nature of a Sacrament, and hath given occasion to many superstitions'. Instead, the line taken in the Article is that the 'Body of Christ is given, taken, and eaten, in the Supper, only after an heavenly and spiritual manner. And the mean whereby the Body of Christ is received and eaten in the Supper is Faith'. The Article says that Christ never intended that the sacrament of the Lord's Supper should be 'reserved, carried about, lifted up, or worshipped'.

The medieval practice in the Church of Rome had been only to give Communion to the laity in 'one kind' (just the bread), although the Council of Trent (1545–63) had attempted unsuccessfully to reverse this. Article 30 says that the wine should not be denied to laypeople.

Article 31 rebukes in vivid language the Roman practice of sacrificial masses. Having established that the offering of Christ was a 'perfect redemption, propitiation, and satisfaction, for all the sins of the whole world', it condemns masses as 'blasphemous fables, and dangerous deceits'.

Articles 32 to 36 deal with matters of *Church discipline*. Bishops, priests and deacons are permitted to marry 'at their own discretion, as they shall judge the same to serve better to godliness' (31). Dealing with the traditions of the Church, Article 34 establishes the principle that traditions and ceremonies need not always be alike, but states equally clearly the need for individual conformity. Wilful individualism is frowned upon as an offence against the common order of the Church, proper authority and as possibly wounding 'the consciences of the weak brethren'. The last three articles deal with the position of the sovereign and civil power in relation to the Church.

Subscription to the Thirty-nine Articles has never been required of any but the clergy and, until the nineteenth century, members of the universities of Oxford and Cambridge. From 1865 English clergy were required only to affirm that the doctrine of the Church of England as set out in the *Book of Common Prayer* and the Articles was agreeable to the Word of God, and to undertake not to teach anything which contradicted them. Since 1975, to the disappointment of some, the clergy have simply been required to acknowledge the Thirty-nine Articles as one of the historic formularies of the

Church of England 'which bear witness to the faith revealed in Scripture and set forth in the Catholic creeds' (Canon C 15).

Parker and Jewel

In the first five years of her reign Elizabeth completed the foundations of the English Church, helped by her chief minister William Cecil and her first Archbishop of Canterbury Matthew Parker (1504–75). Parker was learned and modest, a historian who had not fled to Europe during Mary's reign. He had kept out of bitter doctrinal controversy. Much of the ethos and shape of the Church of England is the result of Parker's energy, tact and moderation. He was intimately involved in the preparation of the Thirty-nine Articles.

Parker was fortunate in having an able Devonian as his main colleague. John Jewel (1522–71) was born in Berrynarbor near Ilfracombe, Devon, and educated at Barnstaple and Merton and Corpus Christi Colleges, Oxford. He had absorbed reformed doctrines early in his career. On Mary's accession he had gone to Germany, but on his return Elizabeth made him Bishop of Salisbury.

Jewel provided a magnificent defence of the national church in his *Apologia Ecclesiae Anglicanae* (1562). The early use of the word *Anglicanae* is interesting. Jewel was a man of genuine scholarship and wide knowledge of the early Church. He had great respect for Catholic forms of theology and churchmanship and maintained his independence of view. He opposed John Knox and extreme Calvinists, but remained hostile to *Roman* Catholicism. He based his theology only on assertions which he thought could be justified by reference to the Scriptures and the doctrine of the primitive Church, as expressed by the authoritative councils and the teaching of the Church fathers of the first six centuries.

Jewel's *Apologia Ecclesiae Anglicanae* was the best defence of Anglicanism which had yet been published and remains one of the finest. Jewel built the library of Salisbury Cathedral; and among a number of poor boys he maintained and prepared for university was another Devonian, Richard Hooker, whose work was also destined to be influential (see pages 54–66).

The Church in the country

Early in Elizabeth's reign England was still a mainly rural country. For many people Christian belief and practice were an integral part of their lives in the hamlets, villages or small towns of the land. Within this society the Church occupied a central part and played a central role. The local church was usually accepted as an essential part of society and most people appear to have believed its teaching. Most English men and women seem to have believed in God; there were a few who admitted to being atheists, but they were oddities.

In Elizabeth's reign the state expected everyone to attend church. Whether they were committed Christians or not, prayers, homilies and biblical passages were familiar to many people. The Anglican Church was the nation at prayer and the prayer-book religion of the parish church became the fabric of their lives. Every child was deemed to be born into it, baptised and catechised. It was a criminal offence to stay away from church on a Sunday (the legislation has never been repealed).

Protestantism, however, was a religion of the word – Scriptures, books and sermons – and it was perhaps more easily embraced by merchants, tradespeople and artisans in towns, than by country folk. Illiteracy was widespread.

This may be partly the reason why the Reformation took hold slowly in England. Many people clung to their traditional ceremonies, to their processions and holy water, and also to the mass, long after the legislation of Elizabeth's first Parliament made such things illegal. For many adults in Elizabeth's early years the Reformation was a stripping away of familiar and sometimes well-loved observances, an interference with a world of symbols which they understood.

By the 1570s, however, a generation was growing up which had known nothing other than Protestantism, which believed the Pope to be Antichrist and the mass a theatrical performance. This new generation did not look back to the Catholic past as their own, but as another world.

The Pope excommunicates Elizabeth and her subjects

On 25 February 1570 Pope Pius V issued the bull *Regnans in Excelsis* which pronounced the Queen excommunicated and deposed. It stated that there was 'no salvation outside the one Holy Catholic and Apostolic Church'. It said that 'resting then upon the authority of him who has willed to place us (albeit unequal to such a burden) in this supreme throne of justice, we declare the aforesaid Elizabeth a heretic and an abettor of heretics, and that those that cleave to her (have) incurred the sentence of anathema, and to be cut off from the unity of Christ's body.'

Few English men and women probably heard that the Pope had pronounced them heretics. What they heard instead was that a doughty Devonian, Francis Drake, was cheekily attacking Spanish harbours in the Americas, and in 1580 returned in triumph from sailing around the world. In 1583 Sir Humphrey Gilbert claimed Newfoundland for England and the following year Sir Walter Raleigh tried to establish a colony near Roanoake Island in North Carolina. In 1588 Philip II launched his 'Invincible Armada' against England, but Drake and Admiral Howard sent them packing. William Shakespeare (born in Stratford-upon-Avon in 1564) began to direct and act in his own plays in the 1590s. They were heady days in which to be alive.

RICHARD HOOKER

Heavitree, when I grew up there, had been for many years a suburb of Devon's county town. But when Richard Hooker (1554–1600) was born, Heavitree was separated from Exeter by fields and meadows. Though his parents had neither wealth nor influence, Hooker proved to be an exceptionally bright child with an ability to apply himself to study, and John Jewel managed to get him a place at Corpus Christi College, Oxford, where he became a Fellow in 1577 and deputy Professor of Hebrew a couple of years later.

In March 1585 Walter Travers, the author of a book about

Presbyterian churchmanship, wrote a note setting out *Sundry unsound Points of Doctrine at divers times delivered by Mr Hooker in his public sermons*. They included various quotes from Hooker's sermons which, Travers argued, proved that Hooker was favourably disposed to Roman Catholicism and believed that you could be a Roman Catholic and a Christian. Hooker produced an initial reply and then, in 1586, began work on what became his magisterial book, *Of the Laws of Ecclesiastical Polity*, eventually published between 1594 and 1597.[7]

Hooker's Laws

Hooker's famous *Laws* were an extended answer to the Puritan case against the Church of England. The eight volumes are lengthy, detailed and judicious, but not dull. There are passages where he uses gentle humour, but he never writes with malice even when taking apart his opponents' arguments. Sometimes his arguments on points of detail are difficult to grasp, but overall – despite his love of very long sentences – his English prose is masterly. His writings played their part in checking extreme Puritanism in England.

Hooker opened his *Laws* with a warning that there is a limit to the extent that we as humans can understand the ways of God. 'Our safest eloquence concerning him is our silence, when we confess . . . that his glory is inexplicable, his greatness above our capacity and reach.'

Hooker spoke of the different kinds of law – Eternal Law, Nature's Law, Celestial and Heavenly Law, the Law of Reason, Divine Law and Human Law – and defined them. He argued powerfully that right reason suggests that obeying eternal laws is best. The reflective person will recognise that obeying good laws is good for us. 'If reason err we fall into evil.' He explains why the Kingdom of God must be the first thing in our lives.

Reason and Scripture

Whatever we believe about Christ's salvation, says Hooker, although Scripture is the ground of our belief, 'yet the authority of man is, if we mark it, the key which opens the door of entrance into the knowledge of the Scripture. The Scripture could not teach us the things that are of God unless we did credit men who have taught us that the words of Scripture do signify things.'

Hooker stresses that he is not arguing that men can, with their unaided reason, arrive at divine truth. But the word of God is a 'two-edged sword' only in the hands of reasonable men. Reason was the weapon which killed Goliath: but only when David used it.

He argued that no branch of science in the world led people into knowledge without first making a number of presuppositions about things which were already known. Science normally assumed that a number of first principles were either taken as self-evident or taken for granted due to previous work. In the same way, he argued, 'Scripture teaches all supernatural revealed truth without the knowledge whereof salvation cannot be attained.' We believe this because we accept that 'Scriptures are the oracles of God himself.' We cannot, however, say that this is self-evident. 'There must be therefore some former knowledge presupposed which herein assures the hearts of all believers.'

Reason and experience

So how do we learn that the Scriptures are the oracles of God? Some say we can only learn this by tradition: 'we believe because both we from our predecessors and they from theirs have so received'. But is this enough? What about experience? Hooker insisted that experience was important. By experience we notice that the whole Church of God has the opinion that Scripture is authoritative. We judge, by experience, that a man is impudent if he is not prepared to submit to widely accepted sources of authority. Then the more we apply ourselves to reading the Scriptures and hearing its mysteries, the more we find that its note of authority corresponds to what others have told us about it.

If we exclude the use of natural reasoning about the sense of Holy Scripture concerning the articles of our faith, then 'that the Scripture concerns the articles of our faith who can assure us?'

The same passages of Scripture which by right exposition *build up* Christian faith, being misconstrued *breed error*. We need reason to show us the difference between true and false exposition. Jesus understood both the need for and importance of rational argument. He disputed with people hoping to do good and to establish truth. That Christ was the son of David was truth, yet, says Hooker, 'against this truth our Lord in the Gospel objecteth, "If Christ be the son of David, how doth David call him Lord?" [Matt. 22:43–5]. There is as yet no way known how to dispute, or to determine of things disputed, without the use of natural reason.'

Worship

Hooker answered the Puritan objection that the Church of England was hopelessly 'corrupted with Popish orders and ceremonies'. Reformed churches on the continent of Europe had banished these practices and people told him that England ought to have followed their example.

He said that the purpose of the outward form of all religion is that the Church may be edified. People are edified, he said, either when their understanding is in some way increased, or when their hearts are moved appropriately, or 'when their minds are in any sort stirred unto that reverence, devotion, attention, and due regard which in these cases seems requisite'. To achieve these purposes in worship it has always been thought that not only speech but also means which appeal to the eye, 'the liveliest and most apprehensive sense of all', make a strong impression. From this starting point 'have risen not only a number of prayers, readings, questionings, exhortings, but even of visible signs also; which being used in performance of holy actions are undoubtedly most effectual'.

Words in worship are not enough; 'sensible actions' are better and more memorable than mere speech. 'The things which so long experience of all ages hath confirmed and made profitable, let not us presume to condemn as follies and toys, because we sometimes know not the cause and reason of them.'

Puritans told him that the Church of England had departed from the ancient simplicity of Christ and his apostles. They told him that the English Church had embraced too much 'outward stateliness';

that they did things better in New Testament times. In the days of the early Church, faith was soundest and godliness abounded. The best thing to do now was to cut later inventions and reduce things to the ancient state of things.

He could not agree with this. Nobody was quite sure how things were done in the apostles' times, since the Scriptures only gave sketchy details and the Puritans rejected other records. 'So that in tying the Church to the orders of the apostles' times, they tie it to a marvellous uncertain rule.'

Hooker pointed out that rites and ceremonies in which the Church of England followed the Church of Rome were also often followed by the Church of Geneva. 'We follow the Church of Rome in more things; yet they in some things of the same nature about which our present controversy is: so that the difference is not in the kind, but in the number of rites only, wherein they and we do follow the Church of Rome.'

He answered the Puritan criticism that the Church of England had retained from Rome much that was simply superstition. In deciding what outward forms were appropriate in the Church, Hooker suggested the test of 'intrinsic reasonableness'. Church customs or rites should demonstrate 'their conveniency and fitness in regard of the use for which they should serve . . . Duties of religion performed by whole societies of men ought to have in them according to our power a sensible excellency correspondent to the majesty of him whom we worship.' Church customs should be appropriate to the greatness of God, the dignity of religion and correspond with 'celestial impressions in the minds of men'.

The public reading of Scripture

The Puritans accused the Church of England of making the public reading of Scripture more important than preaching, but Hooker refused to be defensive about this. The Word of God saves, he said, because it makes 'wise to salvation'. Those who live by the Word must know it. The Scriptures are the best way to make God's treasures known to the world.

But as with everything of value, this requires hard work. We do not bring the knowledge of God with us into the world. 'And the less our own opportunity or ability is that way, the more we need the help of other men's judgments to be our direction. Nor does any man ever believe into whom the doctrine of belief is not instilled by instruction some way received at the first by others.'

Preaching

Sermons are not the only preaching which saves souls. You can preach by writing as well as speaking, as for example the apostles did. But certainly,

> we should greatly wrong if we did not esteem preaching as the blessed ordinance of God, sermons as keys to the Kingdom of Heaven, as wings to the soul, as spurs to the good affections of man, unto the sound and healthy as food, as physic unto diseased minds. So how highly soever it may please them (the Puritans) with words of truth to extol sermons they shall not herein offend us.

What offended Hooker, however, was the Puritan accusation that the Church of England's emphasis on the simple reading of the Word of God was mistaken. They underestimated the power of God's Spirit. The public reading of Scripture is 'for the endless good of men's souls, even the virtue which it has to convert, to edify, to save souls'. The Puritans played this down in their high opinion of sermons. The Church has always believed Scripture to be 'the law of the living God'.

He believed that the public reading of Scripture was the ordinary method 'whereby it pleases God of his gracious goodness to instil that celestial verity which being but so received is nevertheless effectual to save souls'. He drew attention to the horror of good kings and leaders in the Old Testament when they realised that reading God's law had been neglected. By simple reading of the Word of God true repentance may come about.

But there is, of course, a very important role for preaching. Salvation belongs to none but such 'as call upon the name of our

Lord Jesus Christ'. Neither individuals nor nations can be converted until they believe. 'What they are to believe, impossible it is they should know till they hear it. Their hearing requires our preaching unto them . . . That which must save believers is the knowledge of the cross of Christ, the only subject of all our preaching. And in their eyes what does this seem as yet but folly? It pleases God by "the foolishness of preaching" to save.'

The thing which makes sermons attractive and effective is 'the wit of man'. The problem, however, is that sermons 'oftentimes accordingly taste too much of that over corrupt fountain from which they come'. When preachers use devices to attract their listeners' attention, like saying new or startling things, then damage can result. We should beware of this. The same danger does not arise with the public reading of the Scriptures.

Prayer

For Hooker, prayer was the first thing in which a righteous life began and the last in which it ended. Two things help public prayer: first, the holiness of the place where it is offered and second, the authority, zeal and holiness of the minister who leads it. The people of God join themselves in prayer with the one who stands and speaks in the presence of God for them. The minister needs to 'praise God with all his might'.

Virtue and godliness of life are required of the minister of God. He is to teach and to instruct the people. But if he sets a bad example they will be led away from godliness. Even if the minister gives them good instruction, they will not benefit if his life is inconsistent with the doctrine he teaches.

Liturgy

In Hooker's view, a third thing also helps public prayer: a solemn liturgy. He addresses those who do not like the idea of a set form of Common Prayer. He gives precedents in Scripture for a set form of prayer and quotes Numbers 6:22–6 where God speaks to Moses and says, 'Speak to Aaron and his sons, saying, Thus you shall bless the Israelites: You shall say to them, "The Lord bless you and keep you; the Lord make his face to shine upon you, and be gracious to you; the Lord lift up his countenance upon you, and give you peace."'

Jesus, says Hooker, has left us the Lord's Prayer as a part of the Church's liturgy and a pattern by which to frame all other prayers with economy of words. He quotes a number of set forms of poetic and repetitive prayer in Scripture. He speaks of Jewish liturgies and argues that as the Jews had their songs of Moses and David, so the Church of Christ had always used these and had sung Mary's song (the Magnificat had been sung at least since the time of St Benedict), the song of Zacharias and the song of Simeon. Hooker also refers to a group of Puritans who previously had just extempore prayers but who now had a liturgy.

Sacraments

Sacraments, says Hooker, are 'signs and tokens of some general promised grace, which always really descends from God unto the soul that duly receives them'.

The Church is to us that very mother of our new birth 'in whose bowels we are all bred, at whose breasts we receive nourishment'. Therefore those who are born of God 'have the seed of their regeneration by the ministry of the Church which uses to that end and purpose not only the Word, but the Sacraments, both having generative force and virtue . . .'

Sacraments are the powerful instruments of God to eternal life. As our natural life consists in the union of the body with the soul, so our supernatural life consists in the union of the soul with God. God is in Christ; Christ is in us; and the sacraments serve to make us partakers of Christ. This is why sacraments are needed.

The Eucharist

Those who by baptism have 'laid the foundation and embarked on a new life' have in the Eucharist their nourishment and food prescribed for *continuance of life* in them. Those who will live the life of God must eat the flesh and drink the blood of the Son of Man, because this is a part of that diet without which we cannot live. 'The strength of our life begun in Christ is Christ, that his flesh is meat and his blood drink, not by imagination but truly, even so truly that through faith we perceive in the body and blood sacramentally presented the very taste of eternal life.'

Hooker's doctrine of the Eucharist is close to that which later became known as 'receptionism': he said that the real presence of Christ's body and blood is not to be sought for in the sacrament, but in the worthy receiver of the sacrament. The real presence is 'not corporal but mystical and effectual'.

Priesthood

Although he was often an uncritical defender of Anglicanism, Hooker made no secret of his preference for the term *presbyter* rather than *priest*. 'I would', he said, 'not willingly offend their ears to whom the name of priesthood is odious without a cause.'

Seeing that sacrifice is now no part of the Church ministry, he admits that the word *presbyter* does seem more in line with the drift of the whole gospel of Jesus Christ. He went on to deny the need for the ordination of priests by bishops and this has made him popular with some Evangelicals.

Bishops

The Puritans maintained that there ought not to be in the Church bishops who enjoyed the sort of authority and honour which the Church of England gave them. In answer, Hooker maintained that for over fifteen hundred years the Church of Christ had never been planted in any kingdom throughout the world except with the government of bishops.

In England, even before the Saxons, the chief pastors of the souls of Christians were bishops. In the history of the Church bishops are mentioned from the earliest times. The first bishops in the Church of Christ were his apostles. The apostles were sent by Christ to publish his gospel throughout the world, and were named bishops in that the care of government was also committed to them. The apostles therefore were the first who had such authority, and all others who have had it after them are their lawful successors.

Justification

In writing about justification, Hooker's abilities as a judicious writer were fully tested. He was rather like a man walking along a tightrope above a circus ring where snarling lions with the labels 'Protestant' and 'Catholic' pinned to their manes waited eagerly for him to miss his footing.

In a detailed section of his Laws, he sets out four respects in which the Church of England agreed with the Church of Rome on justification. Then he turned to the disagreements.

> We disagree about the nature of the very essence of the medicine whereby Christ cures our disease; about the manner of applying it; about the number and the power of the means which God requires in us for the effectual applying thereof to our soul's comfort. When they are required to show what the righteousness is whereby a Christian man is justified, they answer that it is a divine spiritual quality; which quality received into the soul does first make it to be one of them who are born of God: and secondly, endues it with power to bring forth such works as they do who are born of him.

The Church of Rome believed that

> unto such as have attained the first justification, that is to say, the first receipt of grace, it is applied further by good works to the increase of former grace, which is the second justification. If they work more and more, grace does more and more increase and they are more and more justified. To such as have diminished it by venial sins, it is applied by holy water, Ave Marias, crossings, papal salutations, and such like, which serve as reparations of

grace decayed. To such as have lost it through mortal sin, it is applied through the sacrament (as they term it) of penance; which sacrament has force to confer grace anew.

This was the 'maze the Church of Rome does cause her followers to tread' when they asked her the way of justification.

When Roman Catholics spoke of justification, they made the essence of it 'a divine quality inherent' – a righteousness which is in us. In teaching justification by inherent grace, the Church of Rome perverted the truth of Christ. From the teaching of Christ's apostles, said Hooker, 'we have received otherwise than she teaches'. He did not deny that the righteousness of sanctification was inherent; that 'unless we work, we do not have it'. But the Church of England distinguished the righteousness of sanctification from the righteousness of justification.

Hooker made detailed comparisons of the Epistles of Paul, John and James. 'What way is there', he asked, 'for sinners to escape the judgment of God, but only by appealing to the seat of his saving mercy?'

Against the Puritans, Hooker argued that the Church of Rome did grant that Christ alone has performed sufficiently for the salvation of the whole world. But when it came to *applying* 'this inestimable treasure, that it may be effectual for their salvation . . . they teach, indeed, so many things pernicious to Christian faith, in setting down the means whereof they speak, that the very foundation of faith which they hold, is thereby plainly overthrown, and the force of the blood of Jesus Christ extinguished'.

However, he was prepared to be far more generous than the Puritans in his assessment of the eternal state of Catholics who had had the misfortune to live before the Reformation. He believed that 'thousands of our fathers in former times, living and dying within her walls, have found mercy at the hands of God'. Many Roman Catholics in previous times in their writings 'held the foundation, to wit, salvation by Christ alone, and therefore might be saved. For God has always had a Church among them which kept firmly his saving truth.'

For Hooker (as with Newman 250 years later), 'the faith of true believers cannot be divorced from hope and love'. Faith is certainly made perfect by good works, 'and yet no works of ours good without faith'. It may sound a paradox, but we 'are justified by faith alone, and yet hold truly that without good works we are not justified'. He quoted the 'sense they of Wittenberg [Lutherans] have in their Confession: "We teach that good works commanded of God are necessarily to be done, and that by the free kindness of God they merit their certain rewards".'

Having argued, in an eloquent and Evangelical-sounding passage, that once you have justifying faith you always have it, Hooker asked what the word 'alone' means in the doctrine of justification. His answer was that we say our salvation is 'by Christ alone' in the sense that 'however, or whatsoever, we add unto Christ in the matter of salvation, we overthrow Christ'. But he argued that when we say that our salvation is by Christ alone there are a series of things which actually we do not mean to exclude. We do not mean to exclude our own faith. We do not mean to exclude the works which are essential evidence of our sanctification. We do not mean to exclude either hope or love which are 'always joined as inseparable mates with faith in the man that is justified'. We do not mean to suggest that works are not necessary duties 'required at the hands of every justified man'.

What we do mean, says Hooker, when we state that we are justified by faith alone, is that 'faith is the only hand which puts on Christ unto justification'. Christ is the only garment which, when we have put it on, 'covers the shame of our defiled natures, hides the imperfection of our works' and 'preserves us blameless in the sight of God'.

Christ, says Hooker, 'without any other associate, finished all the parts of our redemption, and purchased salvation himself alone'. But so that this blessing of redemption is conveyed to us, many things are required, such as being known and chosen of God before the foundation of the world; being called, justified, sanctified; and after we have left the world, being received into glory. In all these things, Christ has something which he works alone.

What is the mistake made by the Church of Rome? It is not 'that she requires works at their hands that will be saved, but that she attributes to works a power of satisfying God for sin; and a virtue to merit both grace here, and in heaven glory'. And then to the annoyance of the Puritans, Hooker added: 'That this overthrows the foundation of faith I grant willingly; that it is a direct denial thereof, I utterly deny.'

Hooker's memory kept alive

One of my favourite places to enjoy a summer's afternoon is the cathedral close in Exeter. In the cool shadow of the 850-year-old cathedral towers, I marvel at the wisdom of the citizens of Exeter in commissioning Alfred Drury to carve his fine statue of Richard Hooker. There he sits in an armchair with his Bible, a pigeon perched disrespectfully on his head. How many carefree tourists are aware of the wisdom and scholarship of one of the most attractive theologians the English Church has ever produced?

JAMES I

On 24 March 1603 Elizabeth died and was succeeded by James VI of Scotland as James I of England (until 1625). In governing the English Church, James was wise, shrewd and calculating, putting his theological knowledge to use. He wanted uniformity and obedience. He knew that both Puritans and Catholics could thwart these aims and adopted a policy of trying to detach moderates from radicals.

The Puritans had high hopes that they would fare better under James than Elizabeth, and that the reforms they favoured for the Church of England would be promoted by a king who had been brought up in the Presbyterian Church of Scotland.

However, both James I and later Charles I, showed a greater degree of tolerance towards Rome and English Catholics than was usual for many of their Protestant subjects.

The Hampton Court Conference

In January 1604 the Hampton Court Conference discussed the issues raised by the Puritans in the Millenary Petition. In this, a thousand ministers (hence the title) pleaded with the King to relieve them of their 'common burden of human rites and ceremonies'. The practices they objected to included making the sign of the cross in Baptism, Confirmation, the surplice, the ring in marriage, the length of services, failure to observe the Lord's Day, bowing in the name of Jesus in church, and the reading of the Apocrypha.

The Authorised Version

Although the Puritans were disappointed in the response to their requests, the most famous outcome of the conference followed an intervention from Dr John Rainolds (1549–1607), the President of Corpus Christi College, Oxford. Rainolds, a Puritan, suggested that there should be a new translation of the Bible which would be the sole one used in the churches of England. After Richard Bancroft (1544–1616), the Bishop of London, reluctantly agreed, James I ordered that the work should be begun. A strong body of revisers was formed, including the professors of Hebrew and Greek at Oxford and Cambridge and other leading scholars, over sixty in all, who sat in six groups, two at Oxford, two at Cambridge and two in Westminster, each with a special portion of the Bible assigned to it initially.

Tyndale's influence plus various later translations fixed the tone of the new Bible. The work took two years and nine months to prepare for the press and was published in 1611. It began with a famously flowery message from the translators to 'the most high and mighty Prince James, by the Grace of God, King of Great Britain, France and Ireland', reminding him that 'great and manifold were the blessings, most dread Sovereign, which Almighty God, the Father of all mercies, bestowed upon us the people of England, when first he sent Your Majesty's Royal Person to rule and reign over us'. The preface went on to explain that the translators had the original Greek and Hebrew texts before them as they went about their work.

On the title page were the words 'Appointed to be read in Churches', but it was never otherwise officially 'authorised'. It won widespread favour by its intrinsic merits rather than by official backing. It retained its popularity until the proliferation of translations in the second half of the twentieth century. For over three hundred years, most English-speaking families who read books, and some who did not, owned a copy of the Authorised or 'King James' version. Phrases from it became and remain part of the fabric of the English language.

James I's Canons

The Convocations of Canterbury in 1604 and York in 1606 passed the principal body of canonical legislation since the Reformation. Richard Bancroft, now Archbishop, had done much of the work on them while he had been Bishop of London. They were a collection of 141 canons which dealt with subjects like the conduct of services, the administration of the sacraments, the duties and behaviour of clerics, the furniture and care of churches, churchwardens and marriage regulations. They amounted to a comprehensive catalogue of conditions for conforming to the established Church and several of them were directed against Puritans.

The result was that between 100 and 300 Puritan clergy resigned. The failure (in the main) of the Hampton Court Conference and the severely conformist demands of the new canons stimulated dissent. From 1603 to 1625, however, the Church of England was kept broad enough to contain all but the most extreme radicals, and non-conformity remained a relatively insignificant force.

Church life under James I

The sixty-six bishops who sat on the episcopal bench in the early years of James's reign were among the first generation to grow up in a settled Protestant Church. They possessed a higher overall level of academic qualification and experience of administration than their Elizabethan counterparts.

At the heart of seventeenth-century Anglicanism was the *Book of*

Common Prayer which was now establishing itself as part of the English way of life for most people. The Prayer Book encapsulated the Church of England's focus on Scripture in the set cycle of Bible readings, psalms, canticles, 'comfortable words' and other scriptural texts which punctuated its services. The repeated use of the Creeds linked Anglicanism to the first centuries of Christianity.

England's churches still retained powerful visual images from the medieval world, such as wall panels inscribed with the Apostles' Creed, the Ten Commandments and the Lord's Prayer. All English men, women and children were expected to learn these words in the catechism. The early seventeenth century saw a surge in the output of catechisms, tracts, manuals and devotional aids.

By this time, too, there was a widespread interest in expository preaching and, especially in the areas of the country most influenced by Puritanism, this was seen as the key part of the minister's activity. Yet this existed alongside the older idea of the clergyman as part of the community, providing the rites of passage (at birth, confirmation, marriage, death) and faithfully ensuring regular prayer and Sunday worship.

Guy Fawkes and his plot

By 1603 most Roman Catholics realised that there was no longer any prospect of the restoration of their faith in England, and that the most they could hope for was some measure of toleration.

Guy Fawkes (1570–1606) had been born in York of Protestant parents and baptised in the Church of St Michael-le-Belfry, many years later to become famous under the leadership of the Rev. David Watson. Fawkes became a Catholic at an early age and served in the Spanish army in the Netherlands. Inspired with fanatical zeal for the Catholic religion, he plotted with several other Catholics to blow up James I, his ministers and the members of both houses of Parliament.

On 5 November 1605 he was caught red-handed with the gunpowder in the cellar of the Palace of Westminster. For his pains he was tortured, tried and hanged for treason the following year, together with his fellow plotters.

The whole affair was widely publicised and it planted firmly in the minds of English people the conviction that Catholicism was to be identified with treason, and that Jesuits were arch-conspirators. Guy Fawkes's failed plot is still celebrated throughout England every 5 November.

Arminianism

Jacobus Arminius (1560–1609) was a Dutch theologian who became Professor of Theology at Leiden in 1603. Arminius rejected the Calvinistic doctrine of predestination and maintained that God bestows forgiveness and eternal life on all who repent of their sins and believe in Jesus. God wills that all people should attain salvation, and only in the sense that he has from eternity foreseen the belief or unbelief of individuals has he destined the fate of each. As is often the case in Church history, he was actually less 'Arminian' than his followers who continued the ensuing dispute with Calvinism for many years.

In England the Laudians were to be Arminian in tendency, as were the Wesleys. Arminius's refutation of Calvinism was so systematic that he gave his name to the anti-Calvinist movement generally.

'What do the Arminians hold?' someone asked in the 1630s.

'All the best bishoprics and deaneries in England,' was the reply.

Lancelot Andrewes

Although not an Evangelical, Lancelot Andrewes (1555–1626) is one of the benchmark Anglicans with whom it is useful to compare others. From 1605 until the end of James I's reign he preached regularly at the royal court. One of the translators of the Authorised Version of the Bible, Andrewes was intensely devout, apparently spending about five hours every day in prayer and devotion to God, refusing to be disturbed before noon. He wove Scripture into his prayers.

Andrewes thought of the Church of England as an integral part of Catholic Christendom. He believed that Anglicanism must show itself in prayer, worship and Christian living to be a worthy member of the Holy Catholic Church.

A man of great scholarship, he mastered fifteen languages. Although Andrewes displayed many weaknesses, such as his frequent absences from his dioceses, there seems also to have been an aura of genuine and attractive godliness about him. His sermons arose out of his devotional life and he had the ability to move the hearts of his listeners. His love of ordered beauty transformed the services of Westminster Abbey while he was Dean there. Later he became Bishop (successively) of Chichester, Ely and Winchester.

The most striking thing about Andrewes' theology which distinguished him from the Evangelicals was the importance he attached to the incarnation. He distrusted individualism in the sense that he denounced the practice of interpreting Scripture in the light of individual conscience. Scripture, he said, can only be interpreted in the Church. He did, however, want to encourage a personal relationship between his hearers and Christ. He attached considerable importance also to the Holy Spirit. He frequently referred to the fathers of the early Church, but did not regard them as infallible.

His doctrine of the episcopacy and the Eucharist ranks him as 'the first great preacher of the English Catholic Church'. A friend of Richard Hooker in his youth and of George Herbert in his old age, Andrewes was one of the figures who demonstrated that Anglicanism had its own body of theology and a historical continuity with the Church through the ages.

Andrewes held a high doctrine of the Eucharist and constantly used sacrificial language when speaking of it. He wanted the Church of England to express its worship in an ordered ceremonial, and in his own chapel he used the mixed chalice, incense and candles.

James I was enthralled by Andrewes' preaching. 'No one has spoken so well since the days of the apostles,' said the King after one of his sermons. Another Andrewes sermon delighted the King so much that he slept with the text of it under his pillow.

When Charles I received his daughter Princess Elizabeth at Whitehall on the eve of his execution, he commended Lancelot Andrewes' sermons to her.

The emergence of the High-Churchmen

In 1611 William Laud (1573–1645) was elected President of St John's College, Oxford. Immediately his Catholic, anti-Puritan views annoyed many people. In 1616, he was appointed Dean of Gloucester and was able to translate his ecclesiastical convictions into action and to demonstrate publicly his determination to introduce ecclesiastical, liturgical and disciplinary reforms.

Under James I, the High-Churchmen could be recognised by a general cluster of attitudes and actions which they had in common. They accepted the main tenets of Arminianism; they stressed the sacraments as sources of grace; they were wary of placing too much importance on preaching; they had reservations about the personal interpretation of Scripture by the laity; they emphasised the central importance in the life of the Church of divinely instituted bishops and the clergy as constituting God's appointed order; and they stressed royal authority and the duty of all subjects to obey monarchs without question.

High-Churchmen accepted that there were errors and abuses within Roman Catholicism, but (like Hooker) they denied that the Pope was Antichrist and that it was impossible for Catholics to attain salvation. They disliked some (but not all) aspects of the asceticism of Calvinism, and wanted to return to what Laud called 'the beauty of holiness' by means of well-ordered churches and proper use of the liturgy.

CHARLES I

On 27 March 1625 James I died at his palace of Theobalds and was succeeded by Charles I (until 1649). Charles married a French princess, Henrietta Maria. The protracted negotiations which gave England a Catholic Queen ensured a considerable measure of toleration for Roman Catholics in spite the laws against them.

In his religion Charles had grown up an unswerving Arminian Anglican. In his political beliefs he inherited from his father the belief in Divine Right, saying in 1628, 'I must avow that I owe the account of my actions to God alone.'

By the end of James I's reign, the Arminians had made remarkable progress in a relatively short time. Although Protestantism was by far and away the dominant religious tradition in England during the reign of Charles I, however, Catholicism was by no means extinct.

Nicholas Ferrar and Little Gidding

In 1625 Nicholas Ferrar (1592–1637) bought the manor house of Little Gidding, an estate eleven miles north-west of Huntingdon. A Fellow of a Cambridge College, and a one-time extensive traveller, for a while Ferrar served as an MP. His brother, brother-in-law and their families joined him at Little Gidding in order to establish a kind of community life in accordance with the Church of England – a place where they would seek retirement from the world and complete dedication to God. The Puritans said it was an 'Arminian monastery'.

In 1626 William Laud ordained Ferrar deacon and under his direction the household of some thirty people began a life of prayer and work. In 1633 Charles I visited Little Gidding and was impressed. He borrowed a book which he kept much longer than he had intended. When he returned it, he apologised for writing in the margins.

The Puritan hostility to Little Gidding was unfair given Ferrar's love of the Scriptures. T. S. Eliot included a poem entitled 'Little Gidding' in his *Four Quartets* in 1944. In 1977 a new (ecumenical) community was founded at Little Gidding with a membership of about thirty-five people who recite a simple daily office, receive guests, publish books in the field of Christian spirituality, and keep a small farm.

William Laud in the ascendancy

In 1625 and 1626 William Laud was appointed to preach at the opening of Parliament; in October he was promised the Archbishopric of Canterbury for the future. Laud possessed a clear vision of the kind of Church he wanted to see. Some would criticise him as a reactionary who sought to restore the Church of England to its medieval power and status, subject only to the authority of King instead of Pope. In 1628 he became Bishop of London.

For Laud preaching was subordinate to prayer and the sacraments in public worship. Both Laud and Charles I preferred liturgy to preaching. The King was not hostile to all preaching, but hated Evangelical Puritanism as a movement which resisted all forms of authority and hierarchy. In 1629 Charles issued instructions which constituted a severe programme for binding preaching to the liturgy and discipline of the Church.

GEORGE HERBERT

In 1619 George Herbert (1593–1633), who had listened to Lancelot Andrewes preach early in his life, became Public Orator of the University of Cambridge. In December 1625 he visited London where he met John Donne, who had become Dean of St Paul's four years earlier. Donne had succeeded Andrewes as the most admired preacher in the country.

Herbert decided to turn his back on the life at court to become a country parson living the life of his calling in an atmosphere of peaceful seclusion. Izaak Walton recalled that when Herbert told one of his court friends of his decision to seek ordination, his friend tried to persuade him to change his mind.

'The life of a clergyman', said his friend to Herbert, 'is too mean an employment and too much below your birth, excellent abilities and the endowment of your mind.'

'I will work to make the sacred name of the priest honourable', Herbert replied, 'by consecrating all my learning and all my poor abilities, to advance the glory of God that gave them – knowing that I can never do too much for him, that has done so much for me as to make me a Christian. And I will work to be like my Saviour, by making humility lovely in the eyes of all men, and by following the merciful and meek example of my dear Jesus.'

In 1626 he became incumbent of Layton Ecclesia, about two miles from the new Little Gidding community. Herbert set about the restoration of Leighton Bromswold Church (completed after his death). He believed that only the best could be used in the service of God and the layout of the church demonstrates the way in which he drew from both Puritan and high-church understandings of worship. Herbert wanted prayer and preaching to be of equal importance.

Herbert moves to Bemerton

On 6 April 1630 George Herbert was instituted as rector of the parish of Fugglestone-cum-Bemerton, near Salisbury. His friends waited outside, as was the custom. They listened as he rang the bell of St Andrew's Church to indicate that he had taken possession of his living. After the sound of the bell stopped ringing out across the Wiltshire countryside, Herbert failed to appear at the church door. So one of his friends looked through a window and saw him lying prostrate on the ground in front of the altar. Herbert later told his friend that he had spent the time setting rules for himself and the future conduct of his life, and had made a vow to keep them.

One of the attractive features of Herbert is that you cannot readily associate him with any party in the Church. It is better to say that he belonged to the Anglican tradition of 'thoughtful holiness' which combined a love of tradition with intellectual enquiry in which prayer and study are held close together. Perhaps the description 'sturdy Protestant of the middle way' fits him quite well. He has left us a record of his beliefs and spirituality in his extended poem *The Temple* and his book *The Country Parson*.

Herbert's writing, especially his poetry, is popular today. He touched upon the essential features of parish ministry which remain unchanged over the passage of time. And in his day, Herbert's parishioners and friends saw in this tall, gracious man something of Christ.

Herbert is principally concerned in his writings with the Christian faith as a way of life for all, believing that true Christianity is a response, in worship and in personal conduct, to God's love as made known in Christ. He communicates the eternal beauty of holiness.

As Anthony Russell has pointed out, at one level *The Country Parson* can be read as a simple guide to how the clergyman should perform his duties, but it is also a description of a saintly life lived among ordinary people in the countryside.[8]

Herbert's aim was to establish a living Christian community in his parish centred upon constant teaching and daily worship in the village church. For him, the worshipping community started with his own household. But he soon attracted others either to attend the services with him or at least to mark with some simple act of devotion the canonical hours of 10 a.m. and 4 p.m., as they heard the bell toll.

Izaak Walton recorded that 'some of the meaner sort of his parish did so love and reverence Mr Herbert, that they would let their plough rest when Mr Herbert's Saints Bell rang to prayers, that they might also offer their devotions to God with him; and would then return back to their plough'. Herbert emphasised order, beauty and music. The daily offices became part of the life of the community, as Herbert aimed to make the whole parish aware of the presence of God.

Herbert on preaching

The prayers of the Church formed the centre of Herbert's life, but he also saw preaching as a vital task. While vast congregations flocked to hear John Donne preach at St Paul's, Herbert preached in a tiny Wiltshire church which would scarcely hold a hundred people.

In *The Parson Preaching* he lays down the principles which guided his preaching. He wanted his words to move his hearers to goodness by means of a simple sincerity. Herbert rejected the use of witticisms and splendid oratory in favour of a simple desire to communicate that sense of a yearning for God and a knowledge of his salvation. 'The character of [the preacher's] sermons is holiness,' he wrote. 'He is not witty or learned or eloquent but holy.'

'Sometimes,' Herbert wrote of the preacher's task, 'he tells them stories and sayings of others . . . for them also men heed and remember better than exhortations which though earnest, yet often die with the sermon, especially with country people; which are thick and heavy and hard to raise to a point of zeal and fervency and need a mountain of fire to kindle them; but stories and sayings they will remember . . .'

Herbert believed that you can only open the secret of the Scriptures to those who genuinely wish, with God's help, to follow a holy life. The preacher, he said, must have a deep sense of conviction. Every word must be 'heart deep'.

The country parson's library is a holy life. Herbert knew that the preacher's inner being is exposed in a sermon, and if he does not communicate a desire to love and serve God, then no amount of words will make good the lack. He combined a sense of God's mercy and glory with a realisation of human enslavement to sin; and at the centre of his sermons is a picture of a loving God calling his erring children back to himself.

George Herbert recommended the practice of inviting parishioners into the parson's home for a meal. 'There is much preaching in this friendliness.' In the course of a year he tried to invite everyone in his parish to dinner. His all-too-short life was a mixture of piety and common sense. 'The parson is full of all knowledge,' he wrote. 'He condescends even to the knowledge of tillage and pasturage and makes great use of them in teaching, because people by what they understand are best led to what they understand not.'

On 1 March 1633 George Herbert died of tuberculosis, just before his fortieth birthday.

Herbert's *The Country Parson* lies at the heart of the Anglican tradition of pastoral ministry. Its author sought, by prayer and by love, to draw people to God and to show them through his life something of God's nature and love. His main point was that the priest must imitate Christ in his life as well as in his preaching and the celebration of the sacraments. Herbert's memory is kept alive every time Christians from across the Church spectrum sing the hymns 'King of glory, King of Peace', 'Let all the world in every corner sing' and 'Teach me my God and King', or are enchanted by his beautiful poetry.

Towards an Anglican Evangelical party

Although it is generally said that it was not until the eighteenth century that Anglican Evangelicals began to think of themselves as a party, we can already identify fascinating developments in the first half of the seventeenth century. By the early 1630s Puritans who remained within the Church of England had succeeded in establishing a largely informal and unstructured network of preachers which worked to a large extent independently of, though not in direct conflict with, the Church authorities. They were linked together by ties of friendship as well as by conviction and interest.

These early Anglican Evangelicals tended to look mainly to the University of Cambridge for inspiration and intellectual leadership. Already they enjoyed the support of many peers and gentry, merchants and lawyers, especially in East Anglia, the Midlands, London and the Home Counties.

London Evangelical preachers and their supporters were becoming a well-organised body which was well supplied with funds. We can now use the words Puritanism or Evangelicalism to speak of a continuation of the English Reformed tradition in seventeeth-century England.

The Puritans in the years before the outbreak of Civil War were zealous reformers who wanted to rid the Church of popish ceremonies. Most of them showed no desire to destroy the framework of the established Church or to get rid of bishops. It was not until the Arminians began to have a real impact on the liturgy and practice of the Church of England that Puritans found themselves in serious conflict with the authorities.

Growing hostility to Laud

Although in the 1630s William Laud dominated Church affairs in England, most English men and women had by now embraced the values associated with Protestantism. They were woven into the fabric of society and the English were proud of their Protestant traditions.

In the year that Herbert died (1633), William Laud was appointed

Archbishop of Canterbury. This gave him new platforms for influence and action, as had his election as Chancellor of Oxford University in 1630.

During his time as Archbishop, Laud launched into his campaign to remove the 'Protestant' Communion table from the nave and rail it off in the chancel as (in the eyes of his opponents) a 'popish' altar, requiring communicants to receive Communion at the rail. This created widespread opposition. At the same time, both Laud and Charles I denounced sabbatarianism and commended Sunday recreations such as dancing, maypoles, ales and archery. The Puritans found this obnoxious.

RICHARD BAXTER

Richard Baxter (1615–91) was born in Rowton, Shropshire, and was educated at Donnington Free School, Wroxeter, and privately. He studied divinity at home, especially the writings of the medieval Schoolmen.

Baxter was a big man both physically and in his personality. During his life, he did an immense amount of good, but also made some big mistakes. He had a remarkable capacity for instant analysis, could beat most people in debate, but did not always use these gifts in the best way. Theologically, he devised a middle way between the Reformed, Arminian and Roman doctrines of grace, adopted a controversial position on justification by faith, and interpreted the Kingdom of God in terms of contemporary political ideas.

In 1638 the Bishop of Worcester ordained him deacon and he became assistant minister at Bridgnorth. He found his sympathies moving from conventional Church of England Puritanism in the direction of Nonconformity. He was troubled by what he regarded as indiscriminate giving of the Lord's Supper, and while at Bridgnorth he never administered the Holy Communion. He refused to baptise any child with the sign of the cross and did not wear a surplice.

Church on fire in Kidderminster

Baxter stayed in the Church of England, however, and in 1641 became curate in Kidderminster where, from 1647 to 1661, he served as Vicar. His achievement there was remarkable: England had not seen a ministry like it before. The town consisted of about eight hundred homes and two thousand people, many of whom were hand-loom workers. They were 'an ignorant, rude and revelling people'[9] when Baxter arrived, but this was to change dramatically.

His church in Kidderminster held up to a thousand people and it was usually full in Baxter's time. He built five galleries to hold the crowds. 'On the Lord's days,' he recorded, 'you might hear an hundred families singing psalms and repeating sermons as you passed through the streets . . . when I came thither first there was about one family in a street that worshipped God and called on his name, and when I came away there were some streets where there was not past one family in the side of a street that did not do so; and did not by professing serious godliness, give us hope of their sincerity.'[10]

By instinct Baxter was a schoolteacher and he believed that teaching the people was the minister's main task. He preached once each Sunday and Thursday, for an hour each time, and taught basic Christianity, or as he put it: 'the great fundamental principles of Christianity contained in [the] baptismal covenant'.

In addition to his teaching programme from the pulpit, Baxter held a weekly pastor's forum for discussion and prayer, distributed Bibles and Christian books and taught individuals through personal counselling and catechising. He urged that Christians should regularly come to their pastor with their problems and let him check their spiritual health, and that ministers should regularly catechise their congregations.

He tried to ignore differences between Presbyterians, Episco-palians and Independents in the town and managed to secure co-operation among the local ministers in common pastoral work. Although a spokesman for Presbyterians, he was never a fully fledged Presbyterian himself. He was an advocate for Nonconformists but remained a moderate Episcopalian (believing in a place for bishops). He spoke of 'all true Christians throughout the world' as 'united with Jesus Christ as the head'.

Church on fire with reforming zeal

OLIVER CROMWELL

In the years 1637 to 1640 a rapid series of events occurred which hastened the drift towards Civil War.

In 1640 Oliver Cromwell (1599–1658) was elected Member of Parliament for Cambridge and sat in both the Short and Long Parliaments. Cambridge-educated, he had previously been MP for Huntingdon. Cromwell regarded religion as the most important thing in his life. His Christian faith was rooted in his Calvinism, although it was wider, more tolerant and more tender than many of his contemporaries. He seems genuinely to have longed for the creation of a godly nation.

In 1641 the English Parliament began to dismantle the regime of Charles I. There were systematic attacks on the Church of England. Between 1641 and 1646 Laudian innovations in the Church were overturned, and those in holy orders banned from holding secular offices.

Civil War

On 22 August 1642 Charles raised his standard at Nottingham and the Civil War began (lasting until 1645). The majority of England's citizens were surprised to find themselves at war. Even in the King's camp at Nottingham there was a strong body of feeling which favoured negotiation rather than fighting. With such an initial lack of enthusiasm for war, and generally inexperienced generals and rank-and-file soldiers in each of the opposing armies, early battles were inconclusive.

The war began a period during which there was much devastation of church buildings and property. Many English churches today bear marks of axe or bullet, or record that Cromwell's cavalry was stabled there. Cromwell's troops thought themselves to be fighting against the Church and made the churches and their ornaments objects of destruction. They vandalised works of art, peppered hammer-beam roofs with shot, mutilated and decapitated statues, smashed stained glass and cut vestments to pieces.

Cromwell's New Model Army was largely recruited from Baptists. Baptists had been active in England since establishing their first church in London in 1612; and Baptists in Cromwell's army often preferred the prayer meeting to the ale house.

The Westminster Assembly and Confession

On 1 July 1643 the Westminster Assembly began to meet. It went on to meet over 1,100 times between 1643 and 1649 and continued meeting until 1653 under the Commonwealth. The Assembly prepared the Directory of Public Worship (1645) which superseded the Prayer Book for the next sixteen years. The Assembly also produced the two Westminster Catechisms and the famous Westminster Confession.

The Westminster Confession established itself as the definitive statement of Presbyterian doctrine in the English-speaking world and embodied Puritan theology in its classical form. It expounded all the leading articles of the Christian faith from the creation to the last judgment. It taught the Calvinistic doctrine of election, though it also recognised freedom of the human will. It talked about two covenants, one of works made with Adam and one of grace made in Christ with believers.

By 1644 all Church of England bishops were either imprisoned, exiled or had retired. In the same year the balance of the war tilted in favour of the Parliamentary forces.

The execution of Laud

Archbishop Laud had been imprisoned in the Tower of London since 1641, but his trial did not begin until 1644. This is generally held to have been conducted with little regard for the demands of justice. Laud denied accusations of 'popery' and declared his adherence to the Protestant Church of England, but they executed him nonetheless on Tower Hill on 10 January 1645. He seems to have been unable to understand the popular leaning towards Puritanism and the hatred he had aroused by his measures against all who did not share his views on ritual. In matters of pure doctrine, however, he had in fact been rather broad-minded and conciliatory.

The end of the war

The New Model Army and the genius of Cromwell played their part in what proved to be decisive battles at Naseby and Langport in the summer of 1645, and in the spring of the following year the King gave up the military struggle.

Cromwell was afraid of indiscipline and anarchy. He sought a church system which would provide order and stability, and a measure of uniformity, but at the same time he seems genuinely to have wanted to allow some tolerance and flexibility.

Parliament approved the abolition of the Prayer Book and its replacement by the Presbyterian Directory of Worship. The Ordinance establishing Presbyterianism in England, which was finally approved in 1646, gave Parliament the supreme voice in Church affairs.

Charles I was imprisoned and among the few books he read during his captivity was a collection of George Herbert's poems. In 1649 they tried him for treason and executed him. Cromwell established the 'Commonwealth'. The King's execution outraged many people and alienated some who had been, or might have continued to be, supporters of Cromwell.

JEREMY TAYLOR

Jeremy Taylor (1613–67), though by no means an Evangelical, stands in interesting relationship to them. The best of his devotional writing has been read with profit by Evangelicals, yet some of his views have been severely criticised by them.

A native of Cambridge, he was educated at Gonville and Caius College where he later became a Fellow. After ordination, he went to London to preach in place of a friend and attracted the attention of Archbishop Laud. In 1635 he was appointed chaplain to Charles I. Some suspected him of Roman tendencies, but he cleared himself of this charge.

In 1642 Taylor became a chaplain in the Royalist army. He was imprisoned for a short time and then retired in 1645 to Wales where he lived as chaplain to Lord Carbery at Golden Grove, near Llandeilo (Dyfed). Here Taylor wrote many of his best books, including his devotional classics *The Rule and Exercise of Holy Living* (1650) and *The Rule and Exercise of Holy Dying* (1651). These books (often since published in a single volume) are written in beautiful prose which combines lucidity with vigour and powerful imagery. The same qualities made Taylor a popular preacher who possessed insight, imagination and practicality directed by a pastoral heart.

Many people regard Taylor's books as fine expressions of Anglican spirituality which insist on moderation and a well-ordered holiness of life. However, Taylor's theology is controversial. Some said, even in his day, that Taylor's ideas were Pelagian (holding that people can take steps towards salvation by their own efforts apart from God's grace).

In this century some Evangelicals have attacked Taylor.[11] They have argued that there was a classical Anglican position on justification which was held, among others, by Richard Hooker, James Ussher, John Donne and Lancelot Andrewes. These men defined the position of Anglicanism and distinguished it from that of Rome, on the one hand, and from the Reformed position on the other. But Evangelical critics of Taylor argue that a new school of thought arose during the English Civil War which was 'moralistic' and out of line with orthodox Anglicanism. This new school of thought was represented, among other people, by the contrasting figures of Jeremy Taylor and Richard Baxter.

The nature of true faith

Since confusion about the *nature of faith* often lies at the heart of disagreements between Evangelicals and Christians with a more Catholic understanding of justification, it is worth noting how Taylor understood faith.

In his *Holy Living*, he devotes two pages to a definition of faith.[12] He argues that to have faith is to 'believe everything which God has revealed to us' and 'when once we are convinced that God has spoken it, to make no further inquiry, but humbly to submit'. We should always remember, he says, that there are some things we shall never understand 'nor search out their depth'.

Faith, says Taylor, is 'the parent of charity; and whatsoever faith entertains must be apt to produce love to God'. To have faith is to 'give ourselves wholly up to Christ, in heart and desire, to become disciples of his doctrine with choice (besides conviction), being in the presence of God but as idiots, that is, without any principle of our own to hinder the truth of God; but sucking in greedily all that God has taught us, believing it infinitely, and loving to believe it'.

Taylor insisted that faith involved believing the *conditions* of God's promises 'or that part of the revelation which concerns our duty'. Many, he said, 'are apt to believe the article of remission of sins, but they believe it without the condition of repentance, or the fruits of holy life'. The great object of faith, for Taylor, was 'the covenant of the gospel' and 'that supposes our duty to answer his grace, that God will be our God, so long as we are his people'.

Taylor said that thinking of faith as simply trusting that our sins are forgiven is 'not faith but flattery'. He argued that faith was 'to profess publicly the doctrine of Jesus Christ, openly owning whatsoever he has revealed and commanded, not being ashamed of the word of God, or of any practices enjoined by it . . .'

Finally, faith was 'to pray without doubting, without weariness, without faintness'. All of these 'acts of faith' were present in the servants of Jesus in varying degrees: 'some have it but as a grain of mustard-seed; some grow up to a plant; some have the fulness of faith: but the least faith that is must be a persuasion so strong as to make us undertake the doing of all *that duty which Christ built upon the foundation of believing*'.

So much for the Acts and Offices of faith. What about the *Signs of True Faith*? Taylor's list of such signs includes *earnest and vehement prayer*: 'it is impossible that we should heartily believe the things of God and the glories of the gospel, and not importunately desire them'. Then there is 'desiring God to be all in all to us, as we are, in our understanding and affections, wholly his'. The person of faith should be 'a stranger upon earth' who has all his or her 'thoughts and principle desires fixed upon the matters of faith, the things of heaven'.

Taylor approved of James's sign of faith when the apostle wrote in his New Testament letter that faith without works was dead (Jas 2:20). 'No man can possibly despise, or refuse to desire, such excellent glories as are revealed to them that are servants of Christ; and yet we do nothing that is commanded us as a condition to obtain them.' All Christians are quick to believe the truth that through Christ their sins are forgiven; but they equally quickly forget that Jesus himself attached a condition to that forgiveness. 'For if you forgive men when they sin against you, your heavenly Father will also forgive you. But if you do not forgive men their sins, your Father will not forgive your sins' (Matt. 6:14–15).

True faith, says Taylor, 'is confident, and will venture all the world upon the strength of its persuasion. Will you lay your life on it, your estate, your reputation, that the doctrine of Jesus Christ is true in every article? Then you have true faith. But he that fears men more than God, believes men more than he believes God.'

It was when Taylor listed the last of his signs of faith, that he most obviously ran counter to popular Evangelical preaching and teaching. 'Faith,' he wrote, 'if it be true, living, and justifying, cannot be separated from a good life; it works miracles, makes a drunkard become sober, a lascivious person become chaste, a covetous man liberal; it "overcomes the world", it "works righteousness", it makes us diligently to do, and cheerfully to suffer, whatsoever God hath placed in our way to heaven.'[13]

Some Evangelicals would argue that the way to combat potential abuse of the doctrine of justification by faith is not to try to broaden justification to include the moral change but to say that the Lord never justifies without regenerating. John Stott, for example, maintains that justification is 'the work of the Father through the Son' while regeneration is 'the work of the Father through the Spirit'. But the two always go together. Stott told me that he agrees with Taylor that faith cannot be separated from a good life, but that he prefers Handley Moule's formula: '"Christ for us" our only righteousness before God, "Christ in us" our only hope in an ungodly world. "Christ for us" is justification, "Christ in us" is sanctification.'

I discuss these issues again in the concluding part of this book.

In 1658 Taylor moved to Lisburn in Northern Ireland as a lecturer. At the Restoration in 1660 they made him Bishop of Down and Connor and Vice-Chancellor of Dublin University.

The Reformed Pastor

Meanwhile Richard Baxter had also been engaged in writing a work which was to prove both enduring and controversial. In 1656 he completed his book called *The Reformed Pastor*. Baxter believed that 'all churches either rise or fall as the ministry doth rise or fall (not in riches or worldly grandeur) but in knowledge, zeal and ability for their work'.[14]

The book has maintained its appeal until today when new editions are still being published. Bishop Hensley Henson, no great admirer of Anglican Evangelicals, wrote of *The Reformed Pastor* that it 'is the best manual of the clergyman's duty in the language, because it leaves on the reader's mind an ineffaceable impression of the sublimity and awfulness of the spiritual ministry'.[15]

The book demonstrates the great care Baxter took in pastoral organisation and his deep concern for Christian unity. Jim Packer believes that Christian ministers today should read the book for three reasons: first, because of the book's energy, written from the heart as well as the head; second, because of its reality, being transparently honest and straightforward; and third, because of its rationality. Baxter is utterly thorough in working out means to his end.[16]

Baxter insisted in his book that preaching, though vital, on its own often failed to bring things home to ordinary people. Therefore 'personal work' was necessary. 'I know that preaching the Gospel publicly is the most excellent means, because we speak to so many at once. But it is usually far more effectual to preach it privately to a particular sinner...'[17]

Baxter's call to holiness

Baxter is very blunt by modern standards. He begins his book with a chapter on the 'oversight of ourselves' and refers to 'many a preacher now in hell, who hath a hundred times called upon his hearers to use the utmost care and diligence to avoid it . . . God never saved any man for being a preacher, nor because he was an able preacher; but because he was a justified, sanctified man, and consequently faithful in his Master's work . . . It is a fearful thing to be an unsanctified professor, but much more to be an unsanctified preacher.'

Over and over again he calls ministers of the gospel to holiness. He loathed hypocrisy and double-standards:

> It is a palpable error of some ministers, who make such a dispro-portion between their preaching and their living; who study hard to preach exactly, and study little or not at all to live exactly. All the week long is little enough to study how to speak two hours; and yet one hour seems too much to study how to live all the week. They are loath to misplace a word in their sermons, or to be guilty of any notable infirmity (and I blame them not for the matter is holy and weighty), but they make nothing of misplacing affections, words, and actions in the course of their lives. Oh how curiously I have seen some men preach; and how carelessly I have seen them live their lives! . . . Let me then entreat you, brethren, to do well, as well as say well. Be 'zealous of good works'. Spare not for any cost, if it may promote your Master's work.[18]

Baxter on justification by faith

Baxter spent his life sparing no effort to preach the gospel to crowds and to individuals. Addressing pastors, he spoke of 'that saving grace of God which you offer to others' and 'the effectual working of that gospel which you preach', proclaiming 'to the world the necessity of a Saviour'.[19] At the same time, he was a vigorous opponent of antinomianism (the error that so stresses the free grace and mercy of God that it plays down and neglects our call to be holy). And all his life he was involved in heated controversies on justification following the publication of his first book *Aphorisms of Justification* (1649).

Baxter was, like Taylor, a chaplain to the forces in the Civil War, though on the Parliamentary rather than the Royalist side (despite the fact that he opposed republicanism). Although the two men were on opposite sides in the war and came from different ends of the church spectrum, some Evangelicals in this century have claimed that Baxter, like Taylor, was unsound in his view of justification.

What offends them, and indeed some of Baxter's contemporaries, is Baxter's view of faith as 'obeying trust'. This has always been a sensitive area for Evangelicals, although you will rarely hear them criticise the theology of the chorus of the hymn 'When we walk with the Lord':

> Trust and obey, for there's no other way
> To be happy in Jesus,
> But to trust and obey.

On the contrary, they sing it lustily. Now in his *Aphorisms* Baxter argued that no one was justified unless they produced 'Evangelical' works which rendered them worthy of justification. Some Evangelicals have put Baxter in the same 'holy living' category of Anglicans who believe that 'faith includes obedience and charity . . . and that antinomianism is to be shunned by an emphasis on holy living'.[20]

One of the twentieth century's best-known Evangelical theologians has offered his own perspective on Baxter's theology. Jim Packer, an admirer of Baxter, wrote a doctoral thesis at the University of Oxford entitled: *The Redemption and Restoration of Man in the Thought of Richard Baxter*.

Packer argued that Baxter's entire theological system was governed by a coherent leading principle; and, as he put it, he found in Baxter 'nothing but the dazzling precision of a man who knows exactly what he thinks and how to say it'. Packer summarised Baxter's doctrine of redemption in the statement that 'Christ satisfied the lawgiver, procured the new law, which requires faith and confers justification on those who obediently recognise it'.[21]

More recently Packer has argued that 'in an age in which self-ignorance, secular-mindedness, moral slackness and downright sin are as common among Christians as they are today, it is doubtless from the stern side of Puritanism – the side that forces on us realism about our sinfulness and our sins – that we have most to learn'.[22]

The Church of England during the Interregnum

In 1654 Cromwell himself, now 'Lord Protector', quarrelled with Parliament and the following year the 'rule of the major-generals' began. But despite the abolition of episcopacy and the banning of the *Book of Common Prayer*, the Church of England survived the Interregnum. Throughout these years, loyal Church of England clergy were stigmatised as 'Prayer Book' men.

The extent of the disruption should not be exaggerated, however: two-thirds of English parishes had no change of minister under the Commonwealth. Frequently the attempt to oust a minister led to resistance from parishioners. Despite the severity of the attack on the Church of England as an established Church, the parochial structure and parish ministry survived the storms of the Civil War and the Interregnum. There was no mass desertion from the established Church. Although there was no obligation to attend the parish church, many of the clergy managed to preserve worship in their churches according to the *Book of Common Prayer*, or by reading the book privately in aristocratic and gentry households up and down the land. Anglican services were held discreetly in many places, especially baptisms, weddings and funerals. Even Cromwell's daughter was married in Oxfordshire according to the Prayer Book service.

In 1657 Cromwell refused to accept a suggestion that he should become king. In 1658 he dissolved Parliament. Later in the year he died and was succeeded by his son Richard as Lord Protector. Unlike his father, Richard was a weak and mild man whom his enemies named 'Tumble-down Dick'. The army, still the main power in the land, turned him out. The forty-two members of the earlier 'Rump' Parliament were recalled and persuaded Richard to resign.

Amid all this chaos there was a strong revival in England of Royalist feeling. Finally a Devon man came to the rescue when General George Monk organised new elections. On 4 April 1660 the Declaration of Breda promised an amnesty to Charles I's son Charles, and on 22 April 1660 the Convention Parliament recalled him from exile to become King (he reigned until 1685).

CHARLES II

Charles II said he wanted to contribute to the binding up of those wounds which had for so many years kept bleeding as a result of the general confusion throughout the kingdom. The new king offered a general pardon to all who would declare their loyalty and obedience to the new regime.

An astute man, Charles II proved in some respects to be a successful king. During his twenty-five-year reign he re-established the monarchy on a popular footing and a sound financial basis. He was a tolerant ruler and skilful enough not to antagonise Parliament. But self-indulgence was the dominant trait in his character throughout his life. He had many mistresses and was reckoned to have fourteen illegitimate children. He ostentatiously practised as an Anglican, but showed little sign of genuine religious devotion. His many defects of character, however, were unknown to most English people, who were simply overjoyed to have a king once more.

The Church of England established again

Although Charles's first Parliament was split on religious lines between the Anglicans, Presbyterians and Independents, the Church of England returned to its position as the established Church. The Prayer Book was revised and its use enforced by the Act of Uniformity in 1662. Most of the mainly minor revisions leaned towards meeting Puritan objections. The book continued to be used in English churches without successful challenge for well over three hundred years, becoming part and parcel of the life, ethos and language of the nation.

Savoy Conference

Richard Baxter took part in the Savoy Conference which met from April to July in 1661 at the Savoy in the Strand to review the *Book of Common Prayer*. The Presbyterians hoped in vain to gain concessions which would enable them to remain members of the established Church. But the Bishop of London, Gilbert Sheldon, ignored Baxter's alternative service book (*Reformed Liturgy*) and his appeal that ministers not ordained by Anglican bishops should not be required to seek reordination. Baxter set out the 'Exceptions' to the *Book of Common Prayer* – a long list of Puritan objections to the existing (1604) Prayer Book with a view to its revision. A few of these 'Exceptions' were taken into account in the revised Prayer Book of 1662, but for the most part they were disallowed.

The 1662 Act of Uniformity confronted Presbyterian clergy with the choice between total submission to the rule of bishops or the loss of their livings. Over two thousand clergymen decided to leave. The loss to the Church of England of so many good men was great. They often left with a sense of sadness rather than anger and bitterness, feeling that they were doing God's will.

The majority of English parish clergy accepted the changes introduced in 1660–2 as they had those of the previous decades. And just as many Puritans could not stomach the 1662 Act of Uniformity, so many Anglican clergy who had been ejected in the 1640s returned in considerable numbers to livings under the patronage of Anglican gentry patrons.

Anglican services after 1660

The services of the Church of England after 1660 were characterised by a higher ceremonial than that to which most English people had become accustomed. Candlesticks were put back on the altar, organs returned to the churches, the church year with its different seasons was celebrated, crosses and religious artefacts were used again, and gestures expressive of reverence were seen once more. But trends in the Restoration churches were not all in one direction. Some Puritan influence did remain.

With the growth of dissent the Church of England became more established and accepted as the national Church but also, for the first time, regarded as only one among many expressions of Christian belief and practice. The modern age was dawning in which no one tradition could assert its right to be the only representative of the Christian faith in the country. Dissent was now recognised as a permanent factor in British life.

Between 1662 and the Declaration of Indulgence of 1687, which allowed full liberty of worship, Richard Baxter endured persecution, suffering at the hands of the notorious Judge Jeffreys on the questionable charge of having 'libelled the Church' in his *Paraphrase of the New Testament* of 1685.

Many London churches destroyed

In 1665 the Great Plague killed the astonishing number of 68,596 people in London out of a total population of about 460,000 – nearly 15 per cent of the capital's citizens; and the following year the Great Fire of London destroyed 180 hectares of the city. The fire was devastating for the Church of England, which lost 89 of London's parish churches.

The Duke of York goes over to Rome

In the same year that Samuel Pepys made his last Diary entry, 1669, the King's brother, James, Duke of York, grew convinced there was no salvation outside the Catholic Church. He openly professed his Roman Catholicism the following year and in 1672 was admitted into the Catholic Church. His second wife was also a Catholic. For the remainder of his brother's reign, James epitomised the danger of popery to all anti-Catholics.

In 1673 the Test Act excluded Catholics and Nonconformists from holding public office. The Act insisted that the holder of any civil or military office must take the Oath of Allegiance and Supremacy, must receive Communion according to the rites of the Church of England, and must make a declaration against the Catholic doctrine of the mass. The Duke of York resigned his office as Lord Admiral rather than take the 'test' stipulated by the Act. Up and down the country Roman Catholics toasted the Duke. Charles II himself kept people guessing about his own religious opinions.

In 1675 they laid the foundation stone of a building to replace the old St Paul's Cathedral destroyed in the Great Fire nine years earlier. Thirty-five years on, in 1710, Sir Christopher Wren's masterpiece would be complete.

In 1678 the Disabling Act barred Roman Catholics from Parliament; and a member of an Independent congregation in Bedford, John Bunyan, published the first part of *The Pilgrim's Progress* written in prison while he suffered from the same repressive measures which hurt Baxter.

Charles II grew seriously ill in 1685 and his brother talked to him about religion. When the King was sure there was no hope, he consented to receive a Catholic priest. Anglican clergy were ushered out of the bedchamber and a toothless, shabby old man, John Huddleston, carrying a stole and an oil bottle, hurried through a side door from the antechamber in which he had long been kept waiting. The priest was a Benedictine who, many years before when a priest-missioner in Staffordshire, had helped to shelter the King as he fled after the battle of Worcester. He had been protected from persecution and awarded a life pension. Huddleston now received the King into the Catholic Church. The following morning Charles died.

JAMES II

Charles was succeeded by his brother James II (until 1688). Charles had no legitimate children, but by various mistresses he had fourteen illegitimate sons and daughters. The most well-known of his sons was James, Duke of Monmouth, who set out to contest the throne.

The Duke of Monmouth returned to England from Holland, landing at Lyme Regis in the summer. He proceeded to Taunton where devoted followers crowned him King. He attempted a surprise attack by night at the battle of Sedgemoor, which failed miserably and he fled from the battlefield, leaving his followers to be butchered. He was eventually captured in a ditch in the New Forest and, despite pitiful pleas to James for mercy, was executed on Tower Hill. The sequence of the Rebellion was the brutal punishment of the rebels by Lord Chief Justice Jeffreys in 'the Bloody Assize'. Nearly three hundred of the Duke's followers were executed and a further eight hundred were sold as slaves to Barbados.

James II's attack on the position of the Church of England was one of the main factors bringing about his eventual downfall. However, he began his reign by making it clear that he did not want to establish Catholicism as the sole religion of the country or eradicate Protestantism by force. He sensibly resisted many of the outlandish proposals of his Catholic advisers. He told them that he simply wanted to establish the rights of English Catholics to worship unmolested and to take a full part in the political life of the country. But it was widely felt that Catholicism and toleration were incompatible. Protestants believed that you could never bring together liberty and infallibility.

The King's household and the offices of state remained firmly in the hands of Tory Protestants, and the Anglican Chapel Royal remained the spiritual centre of the Government. At the coronation service in Westminster Abbey the Catholic convert King and his devoutly Catholic second wife, Mary of Modena, together with some forty Catholic peers and peeresses, submitted to the unamended Anglican service.

William secretly invited to save England from its Catholic King

Seven leading noblemen invited the Dutch Protestant Prince William of Orange to come and deliver the country from its unpopular ruler.

William had a good claim to the throne in his own right, as the son of Charles I's daughter Mary, and he had married James II's daughter Mary, whose mother was the Protestant Anne Hyde.

As soon as William landed in England in 1688, to little opposition, revolts broke out all over the country, and James found he could not rely on his army. He fled, but was captured on board ship and brought back to London. There he was felt to be an embarrassment, so he was allowed to escape again. This time he reached France. James's attempt to raise an army in Ireland was frustrated when William later defeated him at the Battle of the Boyne (1690). James escaped again. The victory is still celebrated annually by the Protestants in Ulster (the Orange Men), causing much distress to the Catholic population.

WILLIAM AND MARY

The Revolution of 1688 was accomplished with little or no blood-shed, and has gained the name of the 'Glorious Revolution'. The 1689 'Convention Parliament' declared James to have abdicated and offered the throne to William III (to 1702) and Mary II (to 1694). The Toleration Act passed in the same year gave Nonconformists freedom of worship. This marked the end of the Church of England's claim to be the national Church, the single, all-inclusive Church of the English people. Only Roman Catholics and those who denied the doctrine of the Trinity were specifically excluded from the benefits of the Act. The Glorious Revolution thus conferred on orthodox Dissenters freedom to worship in their own way.

The Nonjurors

Members of the Church of England who after 1688 refused to take the Oaths of Allegiance to William and Mary were known as Nonjurors. Their grounds were that by taking the new oaths they would break their previous oaths to James II and his successors. The

Nonjurors numbered nine bishops and some four hundred priests who were deprived of their livings, as well as a number of prominent laymen. The Nonjurors' guiding principles were the sanctity of the oath and the distinctive Anglican doctrine of the Divine Right of Kings. They thought of the Church as a spiritual society with its own laws and stressed the importance of external forms of worship. These ideas link them with the Caroline Divines of the early seventeenth century and the Tractarians of the nineteenth century (see pages 72–4, 239–46).

Death of Richard Baxter

Baxter was in complete sympathy with those responsible for the overthrow of James II and readily complied with the Toleration Act. He died on 8 December 1691 at the age of seventy-six. He left over two hundred writings including the hymns 'Ye holy angels bright' and 'He wants not friends that hath thy love', which breathe a spirit of genuine love for God and his fellow men and women, as well as reflecting his love for moderation.

PART TWO

Church on fire
in revival

England, 1700–1800

O thou who camest from above
The pure celestial fire to impart,
Kindle a flame of sacred love
On the mean altar of mine heart!
(Charles Wesley)

EIGHTEENTH-CENTURY ENGLAND

Since William had no children, Princess Anne's (Queen Mary's sister) only surviving child had died when young, and the son of James II was a Roman Catholic, Parliament passed the Act of Settlement in 1701 to guarantee a Protestant succession. By the Act, the Crown was settled on the Electress Sophia of Hanover and the hereditary rights of the descendants of Charles I were set aside. Sophia was the daughter of Elizabeth of Bohemia, the daughter of James I. The Act also extended the Bill of Rights by ordaining that all future sovereigns should 'join in Communion with the Church of England as by law established'.

The Act was passed just in time, because the following year William died and was duly succeeded by his sister-in-law Anne (who ruled until 1714). By giving up her right to the first year's emoluments of a priest taking up fresh office in the Church, Queen Anne established a fund to help the poorer clergy of the Church of England which became known as Queen Anne's Bounty. For more than two hundred years the fund helped needy parishes.

The year 1707 saw the Union of England and Scotland, by which the Scots kept their own Presbyterian Kirk, law courts and legal system. They called the resulting kingdom Great Britain.

When Queen Anne died in 1714 she was succeeded by the Elector of Hanover as George I (to 1727). Hanoverian kings were to rule Britain for 123 years. In 1715 Robert Walpole became First Lord of the Treasury and the first British politician to be known as 'Prime Minister'. Some years later he moved into 10 Downing Street as his official residence. Walpole had been destined for the Church, but when his two elder brothers had died, he had been left the family estate and sufficient wealth to follow a political career in the Whig party (forerunners of the Liberals). Over what sort of England did he preside?

Drunkenness

In some respects there was a good deal of prosperity. Wages were good for many, taxes light and trade expanding, but the proverbial drunkenness of these times affected all classes in society. Walpole himself drank heavily, as did his Tory political opponent the First Viscount Bolingbroke, together with many other leading statesmen. Many of England's country squires were 'six-bottle men', drinking six bottles of port in one sitting. Most business was transacted in taverns.

'Drunk for a penny, dead drunk for tuppence,' ran the refrain, 'and clean straw for nothing!'

Immorality

Neither King George II, the Prime Minister, nor the Prince of Wales made any secret of their adultery; and to supplement their wages, it was not unusual for labourers to sell their wives by auction at the cattle market. Baptismal registers show how widespread immorality was in England's villages.

Cruelty

With 253 capital offences on the Statute Book, a particularly popular form of entertainment was an execution. If you picked a pocket, stole a sheep, cut a hopbind or damaged a bridge the law said that you should expect the death penalty. Charles Wesley preached in one prison to fifty-two criminals who were waiting to be hanged and among them was a child of ten. In London on Mondays crowds turned out for the Tyburn hangings, where the well-off paid for seats on the grandstand and thousands of others watched the contortions of the poor victims of this barbaric form of punishment as they slowly choked to death.

Cruelty was a feature of other pastimes also. They baited bulls on every village green and even in cathedral closes. Some clergy kept fighting cocks and recorded their victories in parish registers.

Crime

The threat of brutal punishment did not deter the bands of young men who terrorised London streets, slitting faces and rolling respectable ladies in barrels. In Hampstead, Hackney and Islington highwaymen ambushed coaches, while on the south coast of England many of the landed gentry were in league with smugglers.

The mob idolised men like Jack Sheppard (1702–24) of Stepney who committed the first of many robberies in 1720, and in the year of his death was caught five times and escaped four times. When, at the age of twenty-two, he was hanged at Tyburn, 200,000 people turned up to watch. Dick Turpin (1705–39) was, successively or simultaneously, butcher's apprentice, cattle-lifter, smuggler, house-breaker, highwayman and horse-thief.

In 1750 novelist Henry Fielding, then acting as a magistrate at Bow Street Court in London, established the Bow Street runners, precursors of the police. But there were never more than eight or ten of them and after Fielding's death they grew corrupt themselves. The runners plus a few elderly night watchmen were quite unable to deal with crime on the streets of the capital and Horace Walpole recorded in 1752 that the private citizen was 'forced to travel, even at noon, as if he were going to battle'.

THE CHURCH IN THE EIGHTEENTH CENTURY

According to one view, the eighteenth century was a 'glacial epoch in our church history'. Puritan enthusiasm had been driven out at the Restoration and some high-church zeal left with the Nonjurors. And so, on this view, 'only the cautious and the colourless remained, Laodiceans whose church was neither hot nor cold'.[1]

Certainly the Church was weakened by the loss of the Puritans and Nonjurors; no doubt there was an acute shortage of suitably qualified candidates for the ministry. Many vicarages and rectories had fallen into disrepair and some clergy were forced to do other tasks to supplement their meagre stipends.

However, the picture was not one of unrelieved gloom. Arthur Warne, having studied churches in eighteenth-century Devon, argues that at the grassroots the Church was 'intimately involved in the life of the people, providing a great deal of their justice, acting the unenviable role of moral policeman, settling their disputes over legacies, protecting their rights, educating their children, and even pioneering much that has become known as social security'.[2] And the two great religious movements of the eighteenth century, Methodism and the Evangelical revival within Anglicanism, were nurtured in the bosom of the Church, even if she often proved an unsympathetic mother.

One view of the country clergyman of the early eighteenth century is given in Henry Fielding's novel *The Adventures of Joseph Andrews* (1742) as 'a parson on Sundays, but all the other days may be properly called a farmer'. He occupied a small piece of land of his own, besides which he rented considerably more. His wife milked the cows, managed his dairy, and followed the markets with butter and eggs. The hogs fell chiefly to his care. Lord Macaulay wrote that the clergy were 'regarded, on the whole, as a plebeian class . . . his boys followed the plough and his girls went out to service'.[3]

The Curate of Lastingham in the early eighteenth century had thirteen children to support on a stipend of £20. His wife kept a public house and he was able to convince the Archdeacon that this arrangement, taken with his fiddle playing, caused the parishioners to be 'imperceptibly led along the paths of piety and morality'.

Benjamin Newton, Rector of Wrath, combined his priestly duties with the interests and occupations of a moderately well-to-do country gentleman. He hunted with all the neighbouring packs, shot at the manor where he had sporting rights, fished, kept greyhounds, and attended the race meetings at Richmond and Catterick as well as the local balls. He farmed on a considerable scale his own glebe and rented land, bred horses, sat on the county bench, visited and entertained his friends in a constant round of hospitality. Taking all these activities together, it is unlikely that George Herbert would have entirely approved.

The English Reformation had established lay supremacy in many areas of church life. In the eighteenth century almost all patronage was in lay hands and the resident squire frequently appointed the clergyman. Often, as the lay rector, the squire had the responsibility of repairing the chancel and exercised his right to occupy a pew in the chancel during services.

Preaching

Eighteenth-century sermons often had little meaning for congregations. The Rev. John Coleridge of Ottery St Mary, Devon, father of the author of *The Ancient Mariner*, used to introduce lengthy Hebrew quotations into his sermons, regarding Hebrew as the 'immediate language of the Holy Ghost'.[4] Hogarth's cartoon of the sleeping congregation recorded an experience with which many could identify. Sermons were often too learned or too dull to hold the attention of the ordinary parishioner. It was no wonder that those who could escape the eye of the squire or parson often preferred to sit under the homelier and livelier discourses of Methodist preachers with their more energetic and colloquial preaching.

Archbishop Tillotson's example

Anglican preaching at this time was often dominated by the example of John Tillotson (1630–94) who had become Archbishop of Canterbury in 1691. Regarded by some as the best preacher of his age, Tillotson had established a school of preaching markedly different from that of Lancelot Andrewes. His preaching was especially concerned with morality, and appealed to reason and common sense (or 'natural wisdom') rather than to divine revelation. In this sense, he differed markedly from the Evangelicals.

Many eighteenth-century clergymen did not compose their own sermons, but read those written by others; or, later in the century, patronised the ingenious Dr Trusler who, in the 1770s, established a business in abridging the sermons of eminent divines and printing them in copperplate, so that if the pulpit was overlooked by the gallery the onlookers would think that the clergyman was reading his own composition.

Church music and worship

The musicians and singers usually occupied the west gallery of the church. During the service the congregation stood and turned west during the musical parts of the service (hence the expression 'to turn and face the music'). The musicians had a reputation for doing their own thing and were quite likely to respond to any interference by the clergyman with a noisy demonstration of their disapproval, often during the service itself.

Although much that went on in eighteenth-century Anglican church services would almost certainly have disturbed George Herbert, it was in one sense the offering of the whole community in an act of worship which included the village choir and band, with fiddle, bass, viol and serpent, the charity children in blue uniforms under the eye of the parish beadle, bell-ringers in the tower, and the parish clerk. However, parsons rarely celebrated Holy Communion more than three or four times a year and often neglected the systematic catechising and pastoral work of which Herbert and Baxter had written in the previous century.

Non-residence

During much of the eighteenth century before the Industrial Revolution began to create a drift of population to the towns, five out of every six English people lived in villages. Here in the country, the Church suffered from the curse of pluralities and non-residence – until, in 1838, the Pluralities Act finally made it illegal for any Anglican clergyman simultaneously to hold more than one living without special dispensation from the Archbishop of Canterbury.

All too often parishes were looked upon as sources of income rather than spheres of service, and thousands of villagers never saw their rector, except perhaps when he visited them to settle a dispute about the tithe. A skilful and ungodly man would accept as many livings as he could and never think of ministering to his flock in any one of them. Many bishops did little to interfere for they were often the worst offenders. A few years after becoming Bishop of Llandaff in 1782, Richard Watson (1737–1816) became rector simultaneously of two parishes in Shropshire, two in Leicestershire, two in the Isle of Wight, three in Huntingdonshire and seven in Wales while he lived the life of a prosperous farmer on his estate on Windermere.

In areas where the clergy were largely non-resident, such spiritual work as was done was performed by 'gallopers', curates who were known principally for their ability to race from one parish to another, to serve as many churches as they could on a Sunday for a fee of half a guinea per service. The procession of curates leaving the city of Oxford over Magdalene Bridge on a Saturday afternoon to lead worship in the surrounding parishes was a familiar sight in the mid-eighteenth century. Sunday services were at no fixed time and the sextons kept watch on the church towers for sight of the parson on his horse. When he spotted him in the distance he rang the bells to summon the congregation.

Dilapidated churches

Many churches were allowed to fall into a very poor state of repair. When the Bishop of Carlisle visited his diocese, these were some of the entries he made in his journal: 'The church is in a very ill state'; 'church and chancel are both in ruins'; 'the inside of the church was full of water'; 'the church looked more like a pig-sty than the house of God'. And this is how he recorded his visit to one church: 'The roof is miserably shattered and broken. Not one pane of glass in any of the windows. No flooring. No seats. No reading-desk . . .' In many dioceses surplices were not used, not through any Puritan scruples, but from simple slovenliness.

OXFORD IN THE 1720S

Our story of English Evangelicalism began in the University of Oxford where the Master of Balliol College, John Wycliffe, developed his reforming ideas. From the early sixteenth century and through the seventeenth century, Evangelicalism tended to look to Cambridge for its inspiration and leadership. The eighteenth-century Evangelical revival, however, was to a large degree born in the hearts of Oxford men before it spread across England.

What sort of university are we talking about? For Oxford undergraduates in the early eighteenth century there were no examinations, no athletics and hardly any lectures. John Wesley, in a University sermon he preached in 1744, said that 'pride and peevishness, sloth and indolence, gluttony, sensuality, and a proverbial uselessness' were the seven predominant features of common-room life.[5] The younger men organised innumerable clubs like the Poetical, the Amorous and the Drinking Clubs. Not all of these were frivolous though: the members of one club, as a contemporary of George Whitefield discovered, used to spend their time reading Greek and drinking water.[6]

THE WESLEYS AND WHITEFIELD

Although correctly thought of as the founder of what was to become an international Christian denomination, John Wesley (1703–91) was determined to remain loyal to the Church of England and urged his followers to do the same, even though much later in life he began to ordain men himself. He always regarded Methodism as a movement within the Church of England and it remained so during his lifetime. Since he devoted most of his long adult life to preaching the gospel, and because of his key role in the Evangelical revival of the eighteenth century, Wesley deserves our attention as we tell the story of Anglican Evangelicalism. Precisely what happened, and when he became a Christian, is something which perplexed some of his contemporaries and about which his own views appear to have modified over the years.

The son of Samuel Wesley, the impracticable little high-church rector of Epworth, Lincolnshire, John Wesley was a fraction over five foot in height, less than nine stone in weight, exact, fastidious and logical. For two years he had been acting as his father's curate – the only experience he ever had in England of work as a parish priest. But in 1729, in one of Oxford's bouts of academic reform, he was recalled to Lincoln College to resume his duties as a Greek lecturer.

The 'Holy Club'

'In November, 1729,' Wesley wrote, 'four young gentlemen of Oxford, Mr John Wesley, Fellow of Lincoln, Mr Charles Wesley, Student of Christ Church, Mr Morgan, Commoner of Christ Church, and Mr Kirkham of Merton College, began to spend some evenings in a week reading chiefly the Greek New Testament.'[7] Charles Wesley (1707–88), five years younger than his brother John, was the real founder of what became known as the 'Holy Club'. The young, frank and jovial Kirkham had known the Wesleys at their Epworth home; Morgan was a warm-hearted, enthusiastic Irishman. At first the club devoted several evenings a week to the study of classical authors, but gradually their interest in religious authors began to dominate.

William Law's (1686–1761) *A Serious Call to a Devout and Holy Life* had been published that year (1729) and the book was widely discussed and read in Oxford. 'The short matter is this,' Law had written in his first chapter, 'either reason and religion prescribe rules and ends to all the ordinary actions of life, or they do not; if they do, then it is as necessary to govern all our actions by those rules, as it is necessary to worship God.' Nowhere did Law find more eager disciples than the young men who met in John Wesley's rooms at Lincoln College. Night after night, they asked themselves the question, 'By what rules should a Christian regulate his life?' They tried to devise fixed and definite duties for every moment of the day.

As rumours of what they were doing spread around the colleges, the activities of the new group became something of a joke. Lively minds outdid each other in coining nicknames for the club, including 'Bible Bigots', 'Godly Club', 'Bible Moths', 'Sacramentarians' and 'Holy Club'. One Christ Church man unearthed a word which had originally been used of a school of French Calvinists in the seventeenth century. 'Here is a new sect of Methodists,' he announced.

'The Methodists'

Many years later, speaking of himself and his friends in the third person, John Wesley recalled:

> The name clave to them immediately, and from that time both these four and all that had any religious connection with them were distinguished by the name of Methodists. In the three or four years following others joined the club, till in the year 1735 there were fourteen of them who constantly met together. Three of these were tutors in the various colleges, the rest Bachelors of Arts or undergraduates. They were orderly to a fault, and observed for conscience sake every rule of the church and every statute of the university. They were orthodox in every point of Christian doctrine, firmly believing, not only in the creeds, but whatever they judged to be the doctrine of the Church of England.

For nine months they continued to meet every evening in John's comfortable rooms on the first floor on the south side of the first quadrangle (where you can see his bust today), the famous Lincoln vine twining round the windows outside. 'The chief business was to review what each had done that day, and to consult what steps were to be taken next.'[8] One step they decided to take was to make prison visits.

Missionaries to Oxford

Oxford Castle prison was overcrowded and dirty with men and women, debtors and violent criminals, crammed together by day; and at night the women were driven into a dungeon to sleep on filthy straw left by friends of previous prisoners. The unpaid jailer lived by the sale of beer and therefore encouraged drunkenness. Smallpox and prison fever frequently broke out, but there was no infirmary or chaplain and the chapel was never used.

In the summer of 1830 Morgan of Christ Church, one of the original members of the Holy Club, heard of a man in Oxford Castle who had been condemned to death for murdering his wife. After visiting the man, Morgan graphically described to the members of the club what he had seen at the prison, and persuaded the two Wesleys to go and see for themselves. The result of this visit was that the club sought permission from the Bishop of Oxford to begin missionary work among the Castle prisoners. The Bishop encouraged them to go ahead and the club members began to make daily visits, talking to the prisoners and then inviting them to the disused chapel where they read aloud Herbert's *The Country Parson's Advice to his Parishioners*, and the litany, and held services with a sermon on Sunday afternoons. In time, they extended their work to Bocardo, the debtors' prison, and to the workhouse.

Members of the Holy Club also started a school in the Oxford slums, paying a school teacher and providing clothes for the children. They visited the school themselves, examining the children's work, listening to them read and hearing their prayers and catechism.

Reading the early Church fathers

One member of the club had studied the lives and works of the early Church fathers (just as the Tractarians were to do a century later), and encouraged Wesley to read the fathers more thoroughly than he had done before. And so Wesley and the other members of the club immersed themselves in Tertullian (*c*. 160 to *c*. 220) of Carthage (near modern Tunis) and read of the stern enthusiasm, austere discipline and intensely practical religion of the North African Church. They began to model their lives on Carthaginian lines: to the practice of weekly Communion which they had already begun they added the observance of the canonical hours of prayer and the set fasts on Wednesday and Friday. They treated the Saturday Sabbath as a festival in itself and kept Sunday as a still greater festival in honour of the resurrection.

To the end of his life Wesley was a student of the fathers and translated them for the benefit of his preachers. Many aspects of Methodism which were considered innovations – class meetings, love feasts, quarterly membership tickets, daybreak services, the watch nights, separate seats for men and women – were actually revivals of customs from the early Church.

A new recruit to the Holy Club

In 1732 a shy eighteen-year-old arrived in Oxford from Gloucestershire to be a humble student at Pembroke College, across St Aldate's Street from lordly Christ Church. He had been born in the Bell Inn, Gloucester, where, during his teens, in his own words, he 'put on my blue apron and my candle-snuffers, washed mops, cleaned rooms, and . . . became a professed and common barman'.[9] He soon heard about the Methodists and admired them for a while from a distance. Then one day he sent a note to Charles Wesley informing him that an old woman in one of the Oxford workhouses had committed suicide. On receiving his message, Charles Wesley invited the Pembroke man to breakfast, and within a few days he was enrolled as a full member of the club.

The new recruit was retiring, self-deprecating and shabbily dressed with dark-blue eyes and an unusually handsome face: his name was George Whitefield (1714–70) and despite his personal diffidence he was soon to develop a talent for dramatic preaching.

Less than a year later the Holy Club dissolved. Whitefield spent a year of informal ministry in and around Gloucester and Bristol and experienced his 'new birth' three years before the Wesleys. On Trinity Sunday 1736, he was ordained deacon in Gloucester and preached his first sermon in the Crypt Church there. Later he followed the Wesleys and Benjamin Ingham to Georgia. The other members of the club went to country parishes.

Although the club disbanded, the young men took with them their commitment to personal austerity – with Whitefield kneeling for hours in the snow and John Wesley maltreating his body till he gave himself a haemorrhage of the lungs. Relentlessly, they carefully timed their duties and undertook a rigid system of self-examination. Many years later Wesley reflected that they may have had the faith of servants, but it was unlike the faith of sons.[10] By this I think he meant that a servant often obeys his master from a motive of fear, whereas a son obeys his father because he loves him (see John 15:14–15).

The Wesleys set off for Georgia

In 1732 George II granted a royal charter for the establishment of a colony 'in that part of Carolina which lies from the northern part of the Savannah river, all along the sea-coast to the southward'. The name of the new colony was chosen in honour of the monarch who had granted the land. The idea had originated with General James Edward Oglethorpe (1696–1785), soldier and Member of Parliament, who had been educated at Corpus Christi College, Oxford, before entering the army.

Oglethorpe had taken an interest in trying to help debtors and in prison reform. As chairman of a House of Commons committee he put his mind to the problem of how to help released debtors. His thought was that the new colony would be a refuge for them and also that they would help protect the southern frontier of Carolina against attack from the Indians. So each male planter was to be regarded as a planter *and* a soldier. Oglethorpe believed that the new colony would help in 'the rapid conversion of nations, relief from religious persecution, and the increase in wealth and trade of Great Britain'.[11]

The religious element was important in the foundation of Georgia. Liberty of conscience was to be allowed to all, 'except papists', in the worship of God. To the west of the colony were the French, to the south the Spanish, who were 'all papists'. Oglethorpe and his colleagues were afraid that 'persons opposed to the Protestant religion' would be introduced into the new colony.

The native Indians appear to have abandoned their initial opposition to the scheme and were seen by Oglethorpe as wanting to be instructed in the religion of the white man. Writing of one of the Indian tribes in 1733, Oglethorpe recorded: 'Their chief comes constantly to church, is desirous to be instructed in the Christian religion, and has given me his nephew, a boy who is his next-of-kin, to educate.'

'We do not', said Chief Tomo-chi-chi (according to Oglethorpe's account), 'know good from evil, but desire to be instructed and guided by you that we may do well with, and be regarded amongst, the children of the Trustees [who had established the colony].'

When Tomo-chi-chi visited England he made a great impression so that the whole Georgia scheme attracted many sympathisers, including John Wesley's father Samuel, who said, 'If I were ten years younger, I would join the colonists myself.'

When his father died John Wesley went to London to present to Queen Caroline a volume Wesley senior had written on the Book of Job. It was on this visit that he met some of the Georgia trustees who were looking for a man to preach the gospel to the settlers and to the Indians. An Oxford colleague introduced Wesley to Oglethorpe. 'Here is a man eminently qualified for the work,' he said.

At first Wesley hesitated, thinking of his newly widowed mother, Susannah. 'I am the staff of her age, her support and comfort,' he said. However, he consulted his older brother Samuel (who seems to have been a kind of second father to the whole family) and William Law, author of the book *A Serious Call* which had so influenced him and Charles. Encouraged by the advice of the two men, he travelled home to Epworth to talk the matter over with his mother.

'Had I twenty sons', Susannah told him, 'I should rejoice that they were all so employed, though I should never see them more.' That settled it. John's imagination was fired by the prospect of a work for God among the Indians in Georgia.

'I hope', John Wesley told a lady friend, 'to learn the true gospel of Christ by preaching it to the heathen. They have no comments to construe away the text; no vain philosophy to corrupt it; no luxurious, sensual, covetous, ambitious expounders to soften its unpleasing truths. They are as little children, humble, willing to learn, and eager to do the will of God, and consequently they shall know of every doctrine I preach, whether it be of God. By these, therefore I hope to learn the purity of that faith which was once delivered to the saints, the genuine sense and full extent of those laws which none can understand who mind earthly things.'

'Why, Mr Wesley,' the lady replied with faultless logic, 'if they are all this already, what more can Christianity do for them?'

Undeterred, John Wesley had no doubt that he should go to Georgia as a *missioner* (his word) among the Indians. The Society for the Propagation of the Gospel (SPG) proposed to send him out with a stipend of £50 a year. With his characteristic disregard for money, Wesley was inclined to refuse the stipend and live on the proceeds of his Lincoln College Fellowship. But his brother Samuel (who himself donated a set of Communion plate to the church in Savannah) persuaded him against this. 'It would be unfair on your successor not to take the stipend and if you don't need it for yourself you can spend it in doing good.'

Charles Wesley decided to go with his brother, as secretary to Governor Oglethorpe. Two other young men joined them, Benjamin Ingham of Queen's College, one of the Oxford Methodists, and Charles Delamotte, son of a London merchant. John Wesley said that their whole object in going was 'to save our souls; to live wholly to the glory of God'.

On board ship, they rose early and continued the disciplined regime they had practised as members of the Holy Club in Oxford. From four in the morning until five they each spent the time in private prayer. From five until seven they read the Bible together, comparing what they read with the writings of the fathers. They ate breakfast at seven and said public prayers at eight. From nine to twelve John usually learned German (for reasons we shall discover) and Charles Delamotte studied Greek or navigation. Charles Wesley, who had been recently ordained, wrote sermons while Benjamin Ingham gave lessons to the children aboard. At twelve they met to give an account to one another of what they had been up to since their previous meeting and what they planned to do before their next.

They dined at one and then spent their time until four in the afternoon reading or talking to the other passengers. At four they led public evening prayers, explaining the set Bible readings, catechising and instructing the children. They spent the hour between five and six in private prayer. From six to seven, John and the two Charleses read in their cabins to two or three passengers (there were about eighty English on board) while Benjamin Ingham read between decks to as many as cared to listen. At first they took supper at seven, but early in the voyage gave this up, 'finding nature did not require so frequent supplies as they had been accustomed to'. At eight they met to give one another an account of what they had done and to whom they had talked, discussing the best way of making progress with particular individuals, 'what advice, direction, exhortation, or reproof was necessary for them'. Sometimes they read a little more, before concluding with prayer and going to beds of mats and blankets between nine and ten.

Not surprisingly, John recorded in his journal that 'neither the roaring of the sea nor the motion of the ship could take away the refreshing sleep which God gave us'.

The Moravians

The twenty-six Moravians whom Wesley met on this voyage to Georgia were an important influence in his life and more generally on the eighteenth-century Evangelical revival. A few years later another Moravian, Peter Böhler, was to counsel Wesley on his return to England. Moravians were the spiritual descendants of John Huss (c. 1369–1415), the son of a Bohemian peasant who, while studying theology in Prague, had come under the influence of Wycliffe's writings and had sought to introduce reforms in the Church which resulted in his being burnt at the stake. His followers had chosen their own bishops and had sought to live strictly as they interpreted the New Testament.

Driven from their homeland (now part of the Czech Republic), the Moravians had scattered throughout Europe. In 1722 some of them had settled in Germany on the estate of Count von Zinzendorf, who allowed them to build the town of Herrnhut, near Dresden. The town became a haven for Protestant refugees from many parts of Europe and the Moravians were an important influence on the growth of European Protestantism.

Following a renewed bout of persecution in Herrnhut, Zinzendorf had sent the group the Wesleys met on board ship to Georgia as missionaries. John Wesley was deeply impressed with their unaffected holiness, their readiness to do menial work which the English passengers had refused to do, and above all their courage in facing death when a storm arose.

The Moravians seemed to the Wesley brothers and their two colleagues to be a reproduction in the eighteenth century of the early Christians of the first three centuries. Benjamin Ingham wrote:

They are more like the primitive Christians than any other church now in the world; for they retain both the faith, practice and discipline delivered by the Apostles. They have regularly ordained bishops, priests, and deacons. Baptisms, confirmation, and the Eucharist are duly administered. Discipline is strictly exercised without respect of persons. They all submit to their pastors being guided by them in everything. They live together in perfect love and peace, having, for the present, all things in common. They are more ready to serve their neighbours than themselves. In their business, they are diligent and industrious; in all their dealings strictly just and conscientious. In everything, they behave themselves with great meekness, sweetness, and humility.

The Moravian way of life will have appealed to John Wesley's love both of practical holiness and of church doctrine and discipline. So that he could talk to the Moravian party he set himself the task of learning German on the voyage.

The Wesleys in Georgia

After a stormy voyage the men from Oxford arrived in Georgia on 5 February 1736. A few days after landing John Wesley met Chief Tomo-chi-chi.

'You are most welcome,' the chief told Wesley. 'I am glad to see you here. I have a desire to hear the Great Word for I am ignorant. When I was in England, I desired that some might speak the Great Word to me. Our nation was then willing to hear. Since that time we have been in trouble. The French on one hand, the Spaniards on the other, and the traders that are amongst us, have caused great confusion, and have set our people against hearing the Great Word. Their tongues are useless; some say one thing, and some another. But I am glad that you are come. I will assemble the great men of our nation, and I hope, by degrees, to compose our differences; for without their consent I cannot hear the Great Word.

'However, in the mean time,' the chief concluded, 'I shall be glad to see you at my town; and I would have you teach our children. But we would not have them made Christians as the Spaniards make Christians, for they baptise without instruction; but we would hear and be well instructed, and then be baptised when we understand.'

John Wesley's reply was brief: 'God only can teach you wisdom, and if you be sincere, perhaps he will do it by us.'

Unexpectedly, however, Wesley found himself preoccupied with work for which he had never bargained. Instead of spending his time as a missionary to the unconverted, he was forced by the withdrawal of another clergyman to become parish priest to the settlers. The new town of Savannah was to be his special sphere of service, although the SPG made him more or less responsible for the spiritual guidance of the whole colony of Georgia. Charles had travelled out as Governor Oglethorpe's secretary, but now worked as a clergyman at Frederika.

Characteristically, in Savannah John Wesley carried out with vigour the church system he loved, and also introduced some practices which foreshadowed later Methodism. He immediately established the double daily service and weekly Communion. On Sundays he 'divided the public prayers according to the original appointments of the church'; he refused to baptise the child of an influential parishioner except by immersion; he formed a society which met on the evenings of Sunday, Wednesday and Friday for devotional purposes; he spent three hours a day on house-to-house visitation; he preached against the love of fine dress, encouraging his congregation to dress in plain, clean linen or woollens; he learnt Spanish so that he could talk to his Jewish parishioners and also conducted services in French and Italian; he put a stop to the children of better-off parents jeering at boys and girls who came to school without shoes and socks by himself attending the school with bare feet.

'We cannot tell what religion you are of'

When he heard that Charles was finding things difficult in Frederika, John changed places with him for a while. After a month a member of his congregation in Frederika said to him: 'I like nothing you do; all your sermons are satires on particular persons. Besides, we are Protestants; but as for you, we cannot tell what religion you are of. We never heard of such a religion before; we know not what to make of it. And then your private behaviour. All the quarrels that have been since your arrival here have been because of you; and there is neither a man nor woman in the town minds [takes notice of] a word you say.'

John and Sophia

Soon after his arrival in Georgia, John Wesley had been introduced to Miss Sophia Christina Hopkey, niece of the chief magistrate, as an anxious enquirer. She often consulted him about her spiritual state; he gave her French lessons; she dressed in simple white clothes in deference to his hatred of finery; she was a regular member of his congregation in Savannah during the week and on Sundays; and she nursed him through an illness. They grew very close.

John asked the Moravians whether he should marry Sophia. When the Moravians decided that he should not, John simply replied: 'The will of the Lord be done.'

Sophia soon consoled herself by marrying a Mr Williamson and it is a pity that was not the end of the matter. However, when Wesley continued to show a spiritual and pastoral concern for Sophia, Mr Williamson understandably objected. Williamson drew up a list of grievances against Wesley, including the allegation that when John was dissatisfied with Sophia's spiritual condition he had prevented her from taking Communion. Williamson sought to have his grievances examined in a civil court, but Wesley said that most of the complaints were 'matters of an ecclesiastical nature' and refused to acknowledge the authority of a civil court to examine them.

When Mr and Mrs Williamson planned a visit to England, Wesley's friends urged him to return too in case the Williamsons should misrepresent him at home. Charles and Benjamin Ingham had by this time returned in any case. The matter was finally settled when the Savannah magistrates appointed another clergyman to take Wesley's place. And so, with a heavy heart, he left Georgia never to return.

Was Georgia a failure?

Although it is often said that John Wesley's time in Georgia was a failure, this is an over-simplification. A fortnight after his arrival, he had told Charles, 'I have hitherto no opposition at all; all is smooth, and fair, and promising. Many seem to be awakened; all are full of respect and commendation.'

A little later he told Oglethorpe, 'Savannah never was so dear to me as now. I found so little either of the force or power of godliness at Frederika, that I am sincerely glad I am removed from it.' He wrote home to a friend at Lincoln College that there was great need for others to come over to Georgia and work with him in 'this harvest'.

A letter he wrote to a Mrs Chapman while he was in Georgia throws light on his personality, spiritual state and self-understanding at this time and helps us judge how successful he regarded the visit.

You seem to apprehend that I believe religion to be inconsistent with cheerfulness, and with a social friendly temper. So far from it, that I am convinced that religion has nothing sour, austere, unsociable, unfriendly in it; but, on the contrary, implies the most winning sweetness, the most amiable softness and gentleness. Are you for having as much cheerfulness as you can? So am I. Do you endeavour to keep alive your taste for all the truly innocent pleasures of life? So do I. Do you refuse no pleasure but what is a hindrance to some greater good, or has a tendency to some evil? It is my very rule . . .

He recorded in his journal:

All in Georgia have heard the word of God. Some have believed, and begun to run well. A few steps have been taken towards publishing the glad tidings both to the African and American heathens. Many children have learned 'how they ought to serve God' and be useful to their neighbour. And those whom it most concerns have an opportunity of knowing the state of their infant colony, and laying a firmer foundation of peace and happiness to many generations.[12]

George Whitefield said, 'What the good Mr John Wesley has done in America is inexpressible. His name is very precious among the people, and he has laid a foundation that I hope neither men nor devils will be able to shake. I hope that I follow him as he has followed Christ.'

'Who shall convert me?'

After the Sophia Williamson debacle, John Wesley and Charles Delamotte made their way to Charleston and boarded a ship on 22 December 1737. On board ship and soon after his return, he recorded his thoughts and feelings in language he later modified or retracted: 'I went to America to convert the Indians; but oh! who shall convert me? I have a fair summer religion. I can talk well, but let death look me in the face, and my spirit is troubled. Alienated as I am from the life of God, I am a child of wrath, an heir of hell.'

Many years later he added a note to this assertion that although he went to convert the Indians he was not himself converted: 'I am not sure of this'; and to the words, 'I am a child of wrath' he wrote later: 'I believe not'. His more mature explanation was to draw a distinction between the faith of the servant (which is characterised by fear and duty) and that of the son (which is characterised by love and freedom).

Later, too, he revised his view of Moravian teaching, coming to adopt the view that they attached exaggerated importance to feelings.

J. H. Overton has commented: 'If John Wesley was not a true Christian in Georgia, God help millions of those who profess and call themselves Christians!'[13]

Wesley and Delamotte arrived back in England on 1 February 1738.

Too easy for Englishmen

'I want that faith,' John Wesley noted at this time, 'which none can have without knowing it.' It was in this frame of mind that, within a week of landing at Deal, on 7 February 1738, he was introduced to yet another Moravian, Peter Böhler, who had just arrived in England on his way to work as a missionary in Carolina. At twenty-five, Böhler was ten years younger than Wesley, but the older man seems readily to have accepted the younger man's spiritual maturity.

Faith, to Wesley, was still very much an intellectual process involving 'a firm assent to all the propositions contained in the Old and New Testaments'. To Böhler it was a much simpler matter involving trust in Christ; and he told Count von Zinzendorf in a letter home: 'Our way of believing is so easy to Englishmen, that they cannot reconcile themselves to it: if it were a little more artful, they would much sooner find their way into it.'

'My brother, my brother,' Böhler told Wesley during their second meeting in Oxford, 'that philosophy of yours must be purged away.'

Böhler set about the purging process. 'March 4th. I found my brother [Charles],' Wesley recorded in his journal, 'at Oxford and with him Peter Böhler; by whom (in the hand of the great God) I was on Sunday the 5th clearly convinced of unbelief; of the want of that faith whereby alone we are saved.'

'How can I preach to others when I haven't faith myself?' Wesley asked Böhler. 'Should I leave off preaching?'

'By no means,' Böhler replied.

'But what can I preach?'

'Preach faith till you have it,' said Böhler, 'and then *because* you have it, you *will* preach faith.'

So the following day, Monday 6 March, Wesley began preaching 'the new doctrine', but, he recorded, 'my soul started back from the work'.

Böhler spoke to Wesley about the idea of saving faith being given in a moment. At first Wesley rebelled against this notion as would have many early eighteenth-century Anglicans: indeed, he had refused to visit a man who had been condemned to the gallows, because he thought there was not enough time for him to become a Christian. But then he consulted his New Testament and rather reluctantly decided that Böhler had the Bible on his side.

'But surely', he objected, 'times have changed today.'

Böhler met this objection by producing actual, recent examples of what he claimed were instantaneous conversions.

'Lord, help thou my unbelief!' Wesley cried out.

Böhler left for America in May, but he had sown seed in Wesley's mind.

What happened in Aldersgate Street

On Wednesday 24 May 1738, at about five in the morning, Wesley opened his Greek New Testament to these words: 'Thus he has given us through these things, his precious and very great promises, so that . . . you may become participants in the divine nature' (2 Pet. 1:4). Just before he left his house, he read again: 'You are not far from the Kingdom of God.'

That afternoon he was invited to go to the new St Paul's Cathedral (still less than thirty years old). He listened carefully to the words as the choir sang the anthem:

Out of the deep have I called unto thee, O Lord. Lord, hear my voice. O let thine ears consider well the voice of my complaint. If thou, O Lord, wilt be able to mark what is done amiss, O Lord, who may abide it? But there is mercy with thee; therefore thou shalt be feared . . . O Israel, trust in the Lord: For with the Lord there is mercy, and with him is plenteous redemption. And he shall redeem Israel from all his sins (Ps. 130:1 4, 7 8 BCP).

In the evening, as he recorded in his journal, he went 'very unwillingly' to a society in Aldersgate Street. This was almost certainly a society which met in Nettleton Court. George Whitefield had ministered there the previous year and Peter Böhler had formed the members into small groups who met together for Christian fellowship, Bible reading and prayer.

That evening at Aldersgate Street an Anglican, William Holland, read from Luther's Preface to the Epistle of the Romans. 'About a quarter before nine,' Wesley's famous journal entry reads, 'while he was describing the change which God works in the heart through faith in Christ, I felt my heart strangely warmed. I felt I did trust in Christ, Christ alone for salvation, and an assurance was given me that he had taken away my sins, even *mine*, and saved me from the law of sin and death.'[14]

Wesley spoke to all who were there that evening, telling them, as he put it, 'what I now first felt in my heart'. But before very long, Wesley thought, 'This cannot be faith; for where is your joy?' After he returned home, he noted, 'I was much buffeted with temptations; but cried out, and they fled away.' In his journal he recorded what he learnt during this period in these words (the italics are Wesley's): 'Then was I taught that *peace and victory over sin are essential to faith in the Captain of our salvation; but that as to the transports of joy* that usually attend the beginning of it, especially to those who have mourned deeply, *God sometimes giveth, sometimes withholdeth them, according to the counsels of his own will.'*[15]

After Aldersgate Street

On the Sunday following the Aldersgate experience Wesley was present at a meeting of a religious society in James Hutton's house in Little Wild Street, London. During the reading of a sermon by Bishop Blackall, Wesley stood up and amazed the society.

'I have never been a Christian till within the last five days,' he said. 'I am perfectly certain of this. The only way for you to become Christians is to trust in Christ.'

'Have a care, Mr Wesley,' James Hutton cautioned, 'how you despise the benefits received by the two sacraments.'

James Hutton, like Wesley's friend William Law, was a nonjuring clergyman of the second generation and, like all Nonjurors, a high churchman (though he later joined the Moravians). His wife was even more vehement.

'If you have not been a Christian ever since I knew you,' said Mrs Hutton irritably, 'you have been a great hypocrite, for you made us all believe that you were one.' It was a very understandable reaction.

'When we renounce everything but faith,' John Wesley replied, 'and get into Christ, then, and not till then, have we any reason to believe that we are Christians.'

In her alarm, Mrs Hutton wrote and told John's brother Samuel about the incident. Samuel (who always referred to his younger brother as Jack) replied, 'What Jack meant by his not being a Christian till last month, I understand not. Had he never been in covenant with God? Then, as Mr Hutton observed, baptism was nothing. Had he totally apostatised from it? I dare say not; and yet he must either be unbaptised or an apostate to make his words true.' The two brothers also had a very blunt but amicable correspondence between themselves on the subject, though over the years the differences between them widened.

It was not until over six months after the Aldersgate experience that Wesley felt settled. During this restless period he spoke of being 'troubled and in heaviness'; of 'grieving the Spirit of God'; of 'want of joy'; of his not being able to 'find in himself the love of God or of Christ'; of deadness and wanderings in public prayer; and 'even in the Holy Communion having frequently no more than a cold attention'.

When did Wesley become a Christian?

During the next two years Wesley reflected on his life up to and after Aldersgate Street and the significance of what had happened. He came to see it like this: he decided that until he was about ten years old he had not 'sinned away that "washing of the Holy Ghost"' which was given him in baptism. He had always been taught that he could only be saved 'by universal obedience, by keeping all the commandments of God'. He had always followed these instructions as carefully as he could. But during those early years of his life, 'all that was said to me of inward obedience or holiness I neither understood nor remembered. So that I was indeed as ignorant of the true meaning of law as I was of the gospel of Christ.'

While he was at Charterhouse School, from 1714 to 1720, where the restraints of home were removed, he neglected outward duties and was 'almost continually guilty of outward sins, which I knew to be such, though they were not scandalous in the eye of the world.

However, I still read the Scriptures, and said my prayers, morning and evening.'

As an undergraduate at the University of Oxford (1720–4), he still said public and private prayers, read the Bible and other religious books, especially commentaries on the New Testament. But he still had no notion of *inward holiness*. He carried on 'habitually and (for the most part) very contentedly in some or other known sin'.

At the age of twenty-two he read Thomas à Kempis's *The Imitation of Christ*. This book (which he continued to keep by him all his life) taught him that true religion was 'seated in the heart' and that God's law extended to all our thoughts as well as words and actions. But when he first read à Kempis, he was angry with the author for being *too strict*. However, he began to take Communion every week and to aim and pray for inward holiness. He thought of himself as a good Christian.

After he was elected a Fellow of Lincoln College, Oxford (May 1725), he first grew methodical. He tried hard to keep himself from *actual sins* and advised other people to be more religious. It was then that he first read William Law's *Christian Perfection* and *A Serious Call to a Devout and Holy Life*. Parts of both books annoyed him, but they convinced him even more of the 'exceeding height and breadth and depth of the law of God'. The effect of this was to make him cry out to God for help. He tried very hard to *keep the whole law* inward and outward '*to the utmost of my power*'.

In the year 1730, as we have seen, he began visiting prisons and helping Oxford's poor and sick, got rid of all his possessions except bare necessities, observed fast days, and generally practised self-denial.

Then, as he records, 'a contemplative man convinced me still more than I was convinced before that outward works are nothing . . . and in several conversations instructed me how to pursue inward holiness, or a union of the soul with God.' Wesley never revealed who the 'contemplative man' was, but his journal does record that in July 1732 he paid his first visit to William Law, who set him reading the *Theologia Germanica* – an anonymous medieval book by a German priest which recommends poverty of spirit and renunciation of self as the way of union in and with God. Luther was impressed by it as were the Pietists.

But none of this passion for holiness in his own strength gave him any real joy until the time he left England for Georgia. On board the ship the Moravians began to show him 'a more excellent way' though he still did not fully understand this. In America he still preached and practised a life which consisted of 'trusting in that righteousness whereby no flesh can be justified'.

So he looked back on all the time he was in Georgia as 'beating the air' (presumably a reference to 1 Corinthians 9:26 where the picture is of a boxer who has no clear strategy in his fight). He was still trying to establish his own righteousness, still properly 'under the law' fighting the battle Paul records in Romans 7. It was a struggle between nature and grace (a state he later thought most who were called Christians were content to live and die in). He lacked the 'witness of the Spirit' (Rom. 8:16) which brings assurance of salvation.

It was against this background that Wesley had his Aldersgate Street experience. The question arises as to whether Wesley was suddenly converted. The answer, I think, is that if you had asked Wesley what he had learnt from Böhler in 1738 he would have summarised it like this: true faith cannot be separated from power over sin and a constant peace arising from a sense of forgiveness; saving faith is given in a moment; and instantaneously a person may turn from sin and misery to righteousness and joy in the Holy Spirit. Later in his life Wesley abandoned this insistence on the suddenness of the change, and his own experience did not in any case entirely bear the notion out.

Wesley, justification and holiness

A superficial understanding of Wesley would say that until May 1738 he tried desperately hard to make himself a Christian by striving to keep the commandments and follow God's external law; and that, from Aldersgate on, when he discovered that we are justified by faith alone, he abandoned the struggle for holiness and simply 'trusted in Christ', urging others to do the same.

This, however, would be seriously to misunderstand Wesley. He was quite clear that his mission was to 'spread scriptural holiness throughout the land'. Justification by faith was certainly a funda-mental strand in Wesley's teaching, but the doctrine never led him into the trap of antinomianism (the error that so stresses the free grace and mercy of God that it plays down our call to be holy). Indeed this was one of the factors in his break with the Moravians in 1740. If he was at all inclined to antinomianism, when the Moravian influence was still fresh, he soon corrected himself. 'I fell,' he writes, 'among some Lutheran and Calvinist authors, *whose confused and undigested accounts magnified faith to such an amazing size, that it quite hid all the rest of the commandments.*' This would never do for Wesley.

Nor did the doctrine of justification by faith lead Wesley to make light of the need for repentance. 'Repentance absolutely must go before faith,' he wrote. 'Justifying faith cannot exist without previous repentance. "Whoever desires to find favour with God should cease to do evil, and learn to do well." '

John Wesley was a preacher of righteousness and was sometimes opposed for laying too much stress on good works. Faith, for Wesley (as it was for Augustine), was a moral and spiritual act of the will – and in this his ideas more resembled those of Jeremy Taylor and Richard Baxter (see pages 84 to 90) than the Lutherans and Calvinists. 'What', Wesley asks, 'is faith? Not an opinion nor any number of opinions, be they ever so true. A string of opinions is no more Christian faith than a string of beads is Christian holiness.'[16]

Wesley and Christian perfection

Although it proved controversial during his lifetime and has re-mained so ever since, Wesley regarded the promise of Christian perfection as the very essence of the whole Methodist movement. The present-day 'Faith and Worship' course for training Methodist local preachers, while stressing the importance of this teaching, tends to soften its implications and demands. The course says: 'Translated into today's terms we might say that the path of Christian perfection is making more and more room for love.' But is that a fair representation of what Wesley taught?

In his famous sermon on Christian perfection, Wesley took as his text Philippians 3:12: 'Not as though I had already attained, either were already perfect: but I follow after, if that I may apprehend that for which also I am apprehended of Christ Jesus' (AV).

Wesley begins his sermon by saying that perhaps no expression in Scripture has given more offence than 'perfection'. 'The very sound of it is an abomination to [some].' Whoever '"preaches perfection" (as the phrase is), that is asserts that it is attainable in this life, runs great hazard of being accounted by them worse than a heathen man or a publican.'

Some, he says, have given up the expression because of the offence it gives. But is the phrase not found in Scripture? If so, by what authority can any messenger of God lay it aside, even though all men should be offended? He quotes Paul in his farewell to the Ephesian elders (Acts 20:27): 'For I have not hesitated to proclaim to you the whole counsel of God.'

We may not, he says, leave these expressions aside since they are the words of God, and not of man; but we must explain the meaning of them. Quoting his text, Wesley then sets out the senses in which Christians are not perfect and the senses in which they are. First, *the senses in which Christians are not perfect*: they are not perfect in knowledge; nor free from error; nor free from infirmities (but he does not take the word infirmity to include 'known sins'). He means bodily infirmities and inward imperfections not of a moral nature – for example, 'slowness of understanding, dullness, confusedness, apprehension, incoherency of thought, limited imagination, poor memory'; and they are not wholly free from temptation.

He says that Christian perfection is another term for holiness. 'Everyone that is perfect is holy, and everyone that is holy is, in the Scripture sense, perfect.' But there is no 'absolute perfection' on earth: no perfection which does not allow room for continual increase. 'So how much soever any man hath attained, or in how high a degree soever he is perfect, he hath still need to "grow in grace", and daily to advance in the knowledge and love of God his Saviour.'

Then, he speaks of the *senses in which Christians are perfect*. First, he points out that there are several stages in the Christian life. In 1 John, the apostle writes to 'dear children'; to 'young men'; and to 'fathers' (he quotes the verses in each case). He says it is to these (the 'fathers') he speaks chiefly in the remaining part of his sermon. But even 'infants in Christ' (1 Cor. 3:1) are in such a sense perfect, or 'born of God' (1 John 3:9). 'Those who have been born of God do not sin, because God's seed abides in them; they cannot sin, because they have been born of God.'

We should not make up our minds about these things, he says, on the basis of 'abstract reasonings' or the experience of this or that particular person. We have to decide these things on the basis of what the Bible says. 'Now the Word of God plainly declares that even those who are justified, who are born again in the lowest sense, do not "continue to sin"; that they cannot "live in it any longer"' (Rom. 6:1–2). He gives many references from Paul which speak of the old man being crucified with him; the body of sin being destroyed; 'they do not serve sin'; 'being dead with Christ they are freed from sin'; 'dead to sin alive to God'; 'sin no longer has dominion over them'; 'being freed from sin and servants of righteousness', and so on.

Wesley says: 'The very least which can be implied in these words is that the person spoken of therein, namely all real Christians or believers in Christ, are made free from outward sin.' He quotes Peter's Epistle to the same effect and says that all these expressions from Paul and Peter must at least denote ceasing from the outward act of sin, from any outward transgression of the Law.

But the most important verses, he says, are 1 John 3:8f. and 1 John 5:18: 'We know that those who are born of God do not sin . . .' People explain these verses in various ways, says Wesley. They say: it means that he sins not wilfully; or he does not commit sin *habitually*; or *not as other men do*; or *not as he did before*. By whom is this said? Not by John. 'If you would prove that the Apostle's words, "anyone born of God does not continue to sin" (1 John 5:18) are not to be understood according to their plain, natural, obvious meaning, it is from the New Testament you are to bring your proofs; "else you will fight as one that beateth the air".'

He examines all the relevant New Testament passages in detail and concludes: 'A Christian is so far perfect as not to commit sin.' 'This the glorious privilege of every Christian, even if he is just a babe in Christ.' But it is only of those who are 'strong in the Lord' (Eph. 6:10) and 'have overcome the evil one' (1 John 2:13), or rather of those who 'have known him who is from the beginning' (1 John 2:14), that it can be said they are in such a sense perfect 'as to be freed from evil thoughts and evil tempers'. 'I have been crucified with Christ and I no longer live, but Christ lives in me' (Gal. 2:20). These words 'manifestly describe a deliverance from inward as well as from outward sin. This is expressed both negatively, "I no longer live" – my evil nature, the body of sin, is destroyed – and positively, "Christ lives in me" – and therefore all that is holy, and just, and good . . . what communion has light with darkness?'

He, therefore, who lives in true believers (Christ) has 'purified their hearts by faith' (Acts 15:9) insomuch that 'Christ in you the hope of glory' 'purifies himself just as he is pure' (1 John 3:3). He is purified from pride, for Christ was lowly of heart; pure from self-will or desire, for Christ desired only to do the will of the Father, and to finish his work; pure from anger, in the common sense of the word, for Christ was meek and gentle, patient and longsuffering. Thus Jesus 'saves his people from their sins' (Matt. 1:21) and not only from outward sins, but also from the sins of their hearts.

Wesley's case for Christian perfection (as he carefully defined it) cannot easily be dismissed by those who take Scripture seriously.

The significance of the Wesley story

Wesley's story gives us an insight into how one child of the eighteenth-century Church of England found a type of Christianity which touched his heart, bringing him to speak of a living faith in Christ. His massive influence on the Evangelical revival within Anglicanism in Britain and America cannot be underestimated.

Wesley never left the Church of England. The early Methodists were simply Christians, usually Anglican, who wanted to meet regularly in small societies to encourage one another to live out a genuine Christianity. They had no intention of becoming a new denomination. Indeed, Wesley thought that when the Methodists left the Church of England, then God would leave them.

It is true that Wesley organised the first Methodist Conference at a former Foundry in Moorfields, London, as early as 1741. This was not a Conference to run a new denomination but, as he found

Anglican churches closing to him, a gathering to organise the growing band of lay preachers whom he encouraged to preach the Christian gospel up and down England. These annual events were only provided with a legal constitution much later in 1784.

In 1741 Wesley began his ministry of travelling and preaching that would take him throughout Britain, covering an estimated 250,000 miles, mainly on horseback. He was not always well received, frequently facing mobs, stoning and hostile Anglican clergy. Eventually, however, he became a respected national figure. His chief centres were London, Bristol and Newcastle-upon-Tyne. Altogether he preached over 40,000 sermons as well as writing thousands of letters.

From small beginnings in the 1760s the Methodist system gradually developed also in America. The needs of this new field induced Wesley to ordain Thomas Coke as Superintendent or Bishop and, controversially as we shall see, to instruct Coke to ordain Francis Asbury as his colleague.

Wesley rose every morning at 4.00 a.m., ate sparingly and preached four or five times a day. He was a prolific writer, writing his sermons as he rode and publishing many books and pamphlets in support of his concerns. He had a remarkable devotion to George Herbert and included forty-seven poems from *The Temple* in his various collections of hymns and sacred poems. Personal magnetism and an enormous capacity for self-discipline and organisation helped him control the growing Methodist movement.

He mixed easily in a variety of company and impressed that devout Anglican and wit, Samuel Johnson, with his conversation. He was an effective spiritual counsellor to women. However, his marriage in 1751 to Mary Vazeille, a woman who had nursed him after a fall on London Bridge, was most unhappy.

Politically a Tory, he was a pioneer of popular education, founded Christian schools and foundling hospitals, opened dispensaries for the sick and poor, and wrote the *Primitive Physick: or An Easy and Natural Method of Curing Most Diseases* for those with no access to medical help. He experimented with electrolysis and wrote a pamphlet on electricity. Remarkably, he used a machine which produced an electric shock to help people suffering from depression.

Wesley campaigned for prison reform, helping to pay prisoners' debts and hiring teachers for the children of debtors. He started lending societies, advancing small amounts of working capital to those wanting to start their own businesses. When England was under threat from Napoleon he offered to raise a private regiment since he felt that the country was not well enough defended.

Whitefield and Wesley

In 1738 Whitefield had followed the Wesleys to Georgia and was appointed minister at Savannah. His preaching was very popular. He returned to England in 1739 and was ordained priest in Christ Church Cathedral, Oxford. Whitefield began to preach in the fields of Kingswood Hill near Bristol. He was threatened with excommunication by the Chancellor of the diocese, but disregarded this and went from success to success in his new irregular ministry. He even managed to involve, at that stage reluctant, John Wesley.

In August 1739 Whitefield left England once more for America with a collection of £2,530 for his orphanage in Georgia. He arrived in Savannah in January 1740. In the course of the next thirty years, he made five more evangelistic missions to America and, despite his untimely death at the age of fifty-five, left – as we shall see – a permanent mark on American Christianity as a part of the first 'Great Awakening'. During his time in England, his supporters built him a chapel in Bristol as well as the Moorfields 'Tabernacle' in London. He reached immense audiences, but founded no distinct sect, and his followers ultimately helped to form the Calvinistic Methodists. The Countess of Huntingdon appointed him her chaplain, and built and endowed many chapels for him.

Whitefield's career was more spectacular than Wesley's in some respects, but he left no organisation to carry on his work and his message was less original. But, as a popular spokesman for Calvinism, he had no equal.

In his doctrine, predestination tended to be more presupposed than argued out, but Whitefield asserted it so vigorously that Wesley, the Arminian, came to regard it not only as a denial of free will but as an encouragement to the relaxation of Christian discipline. In 1740 Wesley preached and published a fierce attack upon the doctrine of predestination and all its spokesmen in a sermon called 'Free Grace'. This caused an irreparable breach between what became 'two sorts of Methodists'. Wesley and Whitefield both sought reconciliation but not compromise – and Whitefield never lost his personal admiration for Wesley and for his mission. The two men exchanged letters, but not very frequently, and they preached occasionally in each other's pulpits. But they never again enjoyed a cordial friendship or hearty co-operation. Nevertheless, they did justice to each other's motives and virtues.

In September 1770 Whitefield died in Newburyport, Massachusetts (near Boston). The previous month, Wesley and his Conference had issued a public warning to all Methodists who had 'leaned too much toward Calvinism'. Although this hugely offended Whitefield's closest friends and sponsors – the Countess of Huntingdon and her 'Connection' (see page 149) – they dutifully complied with Whitefield's previously expressed desire that Wesley be invited to preach his funeral sermon.

On Sunday 18 November 1770, John Wesley duly preached the funeral sermon at the Chapel in Tottenham Court Road, London. He recorded: 'It was an awful season. All were still as night; most appeared to be deeply affected; and an impression was made on many which one would hope will not speedily be effaced.' The conclusion of the sermon is a moving tribute to the man whose talents at least for dramatic oratory were greater than Wesley's. Whitefield was certainly the most striking orator of the Evangelical revival and his influence, particularly on the tone of American Evangelical Christianity, has been profound.

WILLIAM GRIMSHAW

Haworth, the bleak village on the edge of the West Yorkshire Moors, where in later years the three Brontë sisters lived and died, is also the place where Anglican Evangelicalism established itself in the north of England.

William Grimshaw (1708–63) was born into a family of small

farmers in the little village of Brindle, six miles south of Preston in Lancashire. He was educated at Blackburn Grammar School and Heskin Free School; and in 1726, at the age of eighteen, he entered Christ's College, Cambridge, as a student.

During the four or five years Grimshaw spent in Cambridge taking his Arts degree he lived a carefree life, learning to drink and swear like most of his fellow students, and decided on ordination as a way of getting a good living. Ordained deacon in 1731, he became a priest the following year in Todmorden, West Yorkshire, where he spent eleven years. In 1734 he married a widow and a few happy years began, during which a son and daughter were born.

As a young clergyman he visited his parishioners only 'in order to drink and be merry with them'. He read prayers and a sermon once every Sunday, and enjoyed hunting, fishing and playing cards. On one occasion, a reflective parishioner named Mary Scholefield asked him a serious question.

'What may I do for the good of my own soul?'

'Put away these gloomy thoughts,' Grimshaw replied. 'Go into merry company; divert yourself; and all will be well at last.'

The answer failed to satisfy either Mary or, if he were honest, Grimshaw himself.

In about 1734 he began to take life more seriously, started to give the young people in Todmorden solid Christian teaching using the catechism, and preached the need to live a devout life. He energetically condemned sin and urged his flock to flee from the wrath to come. But his sermons were rather cheerless affairs with no message of hope to balance the calls to good behaviour. He began to visit his parishioners more conscientiously.

In October 1739 a blow struck the Grimshaw home. William's wife fell ill and died, after only five years of marriage. Grimshaw was overwhelmed with grief and continued to visit his wife's grave for the rest of his life. He slipped into a period of depression, one element of which was lurid sexual temptation. He later told a close circle of Christian friends that he had at this time 'lusted after every woman he saw' and fantasised about the Virgin Mary.

Grimshaw becomes an Evangelical

His conversion to Evangelicalism occurred during the course of a spiritual struggle arising from his inability to answer his parishioners' spiritual questions, his sexual difficulties, and reading Owen's writings on justification. John Owen (1616–83) was an Oxford educated Puritan who had been appointed Vice-Chancellor of that university by Cromwell in 1652. He disagreed with Richard Baxter and the Arminians on justification, but his writings were tolerant and fair, displaying spiritual insight.

Grimshaw's change of heart seems to have had little, if any, connection with the stirrings of Evangelical revival in London and the south of England associated with the Wesley brothers and Whitefield. His contacts with these men occurred later.

Grimshaw's friend Joseph Williams described how, 'At the house of one of his friends he lays his hand on a book and opens it with his face towards the pewter-shelf; and instantly an uncommon heat flashes in his face. He is surprised, and turning about cannot imagine how the pewter could reflect fire at such a distance. He turns to the title-page and finds it to be Dr Owen on Justification, and immediately his face is saluted with such another flash.' Reading Owen, Grimshaw decided that he should look to Christ alone for salvation. Reflecting on Paul's New Testament letters strengthened him in this belief. The outcome was a 'great joy . . . a Bridal Bliss in Christ', which brought with it physical fitness and energy. After a while the old depression returned, but less seriously.

'I was now willing', he later told Henry Venn, 'to renounce myself, every degree of fancied merit and ability, and to embrace Christ as my all in all. O what light and comfort did I enjoy in my own soul, and what a taste of the pardoning love of God!'

He sought out Mary Scholefield to correct his earlier advice. 'O Mary,' he told her, 'what a blind leader of the blind was I, when I came to take off your burden by exhorting you to live in pleasure, and to follow the vain amusements of the world!'

In 1741 Grimshaw married again. By the time he arrived in Haworth in May 1742 he was firmly in the Evangelical camp.

In those days, before the growth of Bradford and Halifax, Haworth was one of the loneliest spots in England, cut off from the rest of the world by miles of rugged moorland. It stands on the line of hills which runs down from the Lake District in the north to the Peak District of Derbyshire and divides West Yorkshire from Lancashire. Haworth is about four miles from the town of Keighley and eight from Bradford; in those days it consisted of little houses built of brown stone, was almost bare of trees and approached by a steep rise either from Hebden Bridge or Keighley.

Grimshaw found a hard task waiting for him. Many of the people in and around Haworth were small, independent workmen who farmed a few acres of land, and combed and wove at home for the new worsted industry. They divided their time between the sheep on the open moorland and their work in little low rooms where they heated their combs over red-hot charcoals. Craftsmen who were proud of their skill, they were not immediately inclined to pay much attention to deep matters of the mind or soul; and suspicious of strangers, they eyed warily a Lancashire man who had been educated at the University of Cambridge.

To make matters worse, Haworth, in the huge parish of Bradford, had been without a clergyman for three years following a scandal which ended in Grimshaw's predecessor being suspended from the ministry. The village had become almost entirely godless. Weddings featured entertainment in the form of races in which near-naked runners were a scandal to respectable visitors. Funerals had degenerated into alcoholic orgies, with bodies being laid in graves without the performance of religious rites.

'When I arrived in Haworth', Grimshaw told his friend John Newton years later, 'I could ride for a full half-day east, west, north, south, and not meet a single godly soul, nor even hear tell of one.'

The work in Haworth begins

The people of Haworth found in their new vicar a man as blunt and strong-willed as they were, with an enormous capacity for hard work and an evident sincerity.

'Football matches on the Sabbath must stop,' he announced. 'I expect to see you all in church.'

Grimshaw refused to practise or to tolerate anything which was merely formal or conventional. But even in the first twelve months of his time there, he began to see the first signs of what looked like a work of God. He later looked back on his first year at Haworth and wrote: 'In that year, our dear Lord was pleased to visit my parish. A few souls were affected under the Word, brought to see their lost estate by nature, and to experience peace through faith in the blood of Jesus. My church began to be crowded, in so much that many were obliged to stand out of doors.' In the early days, the Haworth church saw scenes like those described by Wesley in his journal, with members of the congregation overcome with a vivid sense of their own guilt and the wrath of God: they would cry out in anguish or weep with remorse.

Haworth appeared to be experiencing a work of the Spirit of God in which converts were soon to be counted not in ones or twos, but in scores if not hundreds. Scenes like this were unusual in the Church of England; rarely since Richard Baxter's years at Kidderminster had Anglicanism been troubled by the excessive popularity of a preacher.

Grimshaw's dress was plain, even shabby at times. Often he only had one coat and one pair of shoes. He ate plain food and hated any form of waste. Picture the scene in one of his services. He is short but well built, robustly healthy and with sharp eyes. Before the prayers he casts a searching eye over every man, woman and child in church. If he sees anyone lounging forward rather than kneeling, he rebukes the offender by name. If he sees a stray dog in the church, he chases it out himself.

When he reads the Scriptures, he avoids the accent he has heard at the University of Cambridge and translates every sentence into the broadest Yorkshire and intersperses homely comments of his own. After the Third Collect, he may engage in extempore prayer, addressing the Almighty with a fervour which suggests to his congregation that he has been walking closely with God. Then he ensures that the psalm before the sermon is a long one, for at this point he has important business to perform.

He takes his stout riding stick from the vestry wall and marches out of the church. He looks around to see if any lazy parishioners are idling their time in the churchyard, the street, or one of the four alehouses within a stone's throw of the church. If he finds any, he rounds them up and drives them into church.

A friend of John Newton's, passing one of the alehouses on a Sunday, saw several people jumping out of the windows and leaping over a low wall just beyond, and thought the building must be on fire.

'What's the cause of this commotion?' he asked.

'Parson Grimshaw's coming!' they shouted.

John Newton himself, who sometimes visited Haworth, noted that the villagers were more afraid of Grimshaw than the Justice of the Peace, but added that 'his reproof was so authoritative and yet so mild and friendly, that the stoutest sinner could not stand before him'.

At last, when the patrons of the Black Bull are rounded up and have taken their seats in church, Grimshaw mounts the steps of a brand-new pulpit of the old-fashioned, three-decker style.

He announces his text. 'For I determined not to know anything among you, save Jesus Christ and Him crucified' (1 Cor. 2:2). He delivers his sermon, hot and strong, full of uncompromising dogma, yet complete with vivid imagery and the sort of dry humour which Yorkshire people appreciate.

'Does the flesh tempt you?' he asks his congregation. 'Flee and pray. Does the world tempt you? Resist and pray... Think not to dance with the devil all day, and sup with Christ at night: or to go from Delilah's lap to Abraham's Bosom.'

He preaches in what he calls 'market language' which is sometimes so racy and unconventional that it offends his closest friends. But John Newton (his mind infinitely broadened by his years on a slave ship) defended him: 'Frequently a sentence, which a delicate hearer might deem vulgar, conveyed an important truth to the ear and fixed it on the memory for years. I give my judgment on this point something in his own way – that is the best cat which catches the most mice.'

Grimshaw himself summarised the aim of his preaching as 'debasing man and exalting my dear Lord'. He had no patience with those who, as he put it, 'to gain the admiration of the ignorant and the praise of men, affect in their preaching high-flying words, pompous language, rhetorical strains and philosophical terms'. Instead he sought to be 'a soul searching, a soul winning, and a soul enriching minister, one who maketh the hard things easy, and dark things plain'.

Sometimes Grimshaw would preach for two hours, but managed to hold the attention of his congregation with his flair for the common things of life and use of homely illustrations.

When he preached about temptation he knew what he was talking about – especially as, after his second wife died in 1746, the sexual difficulties returned. The touch of a woman's hand fanned 'the smouldering fires of passion' into flame, or sometimes the spark would be a visit to a bedridden woman parishioner. But he was now better equipped to deal with his difficulties and there is no record of him behaving improperly. He seems to have fought temptation partly by asceticism and almost incessant activity, but chiefly by way of regular written covenants with God. He also considered marrying for a third time and, curiously, decided to be guided by the toss of a coin.

'Heads I marry, tails I don't.' He tossed and the coin came up tails.

'For God's sake don't flatter them!'

Many of the leaders of the eighteenth-century Evangelical revival preached from Grimshaw's pulpit: George Whitefield, the two Wesleys, Henry Venn and William Romaine. Once, when George Whitefield visited the church, he began his sermon in a smooth, conciliatory way, making some remarks about how privileged the members of the congregation were to have Grimshaw as their minister.

'For God's sake don't speak so,' cried Grimshaw, springing to his feet at the reading desk. 'I pray you do not flatter them. The greater part of them are going to hell with their eyes open!'

Grimshaw would not tolerate excuses for staying away from church. 'Our clothes are poor and foul,' some told him. So he introduced a special lecture for them on Sunday evenings followed by prayers in his own house (which still stands).

'It's too far for us to walk across the moor to church,' others complained. So Grimshaw began to hold barn services in remote hamlets.

A man of prayer and spirituality

The first members of the Evangelical party always stressed the importance of getting up early in the mornings. They saw it as a crucial element in the disciplined Christian life. If you understood the value of time you did not lie in bed after the sun was up. Grimshaw rose earlier than that, having already meditated in bed. 'As soon as you awake in the morning', he wrote, 'employ an hour in five things: bless God for the mercies of the night past; praise him for a new day, and for the blessing of it; examine well your own hearts; meditate upon some spiritual subject; and plan out the business of the day.'

He sang a hymn or prayed as he dressed, spent a further half an hour in private worship in his study, and then led family worship. Prayer punctuated the rest of his day. When he had no preaching duties he would spend up to six further hours praying, in addition to time spent reading. He ended his day with yet more family and private prayer.

'At going to bed', he wrote, 'revise the thoughts, words and actions of the day. What is amiss, beg pardon of; what is well, bless God alone for. Conclude with prayer. Undress and lie down with prayer. And never fall asleep with an unforgiven sin upon your conscience.'

He spent many of those hours alone with his God in self-examination, undertaking an unending search for sin, but he gave at least as much time to meditation on the Bible. The soul, he thought, needs food as well as medicine. Grimshaw has been compared with the great spiritual masters in that he sought the reality of a relationship with God, but also understood dryness.

At Haworth Grimshaw introduced a daily service at five in the morning (six in winter) and this became a feature of many eighteenth-century Evangelical parishes. And, much as George Herbert had done over a century earlier, Grimshaw gradually taught his people to match each day's work with prayer in church. To hear him pray was a never-to-be-forgotten experience. Friends described him as 'a man with his feet on earth and his soul in heaven . . . He would take hold of the very horns of the altar, which he would not let go till God had given him the blessing.'

Then he had what he called his monthly visitations: in twelve different parts of his parish he borrowed a farmhouse kitchen and used to summon seven or eight of the families there to meet him. He expected everyone to turn up – parents, servants and children. During the visitation he would question them individually on their knowledge of the Christian faith; teach them where they needed instruction; rebuke them for anything in their conduct of which he disapproved; and warn them of temptations they would be likely to face. Then he would dismiss them with a blessing which they could see came from his heart.

Sometimes when he met parishioners while he was out and about, he would challenge them about their spiritual life.

'Do you make a habit of prayer?' he would ask.

'Yes, parson,' might come the reply.

'Well, kneel down and let me hear you!' he would say.

'Mad Grimshaw'

After Grimshaw had persuaded the young men to abandon their Sunday football, some of them took to meeting on the moors for card-playing and other games. Grimshaw had adopted what the poet Robert Southey described as the 'dismal puritanical notion that it is sinful to walk in the fields for recreation on the Sabbath day'. Other sources suggest that the activities Grimshaw objected to were less innocent than simple recreation. However, he decided not only to condemn them from the pulpit, but to adopt a course of action typical of many which earned him the nickname 'Mad Grimshaw'.

He disguised himself one evening – some said he borrowed an old woman's skirt and shawl – so that no one would recognise him. Then he set off for the spot some distance from the village where the young people used to assemble. As soon as he was near enough to discover who they were, he threw off his disguise.

'Don't any of you move!' he shouted.

He wrote down all their names and instructed them to report to his parsonage at a certain date and time. They turned up as punctually as if they had been served with an arrest warrant. He instructed them to form a circle.

'Kneel down,' he told them.

After they and he were all kneeling, he prayed for them at great length. Then, getting up, he delivered a moving but not unfriendly lecture. It is said that he never had to repeat the performance.

On one Sunday a man on his way to fetch a midwife needed his horse shod in the village. The blacksmith refused to do the job until the two of them went together to the parsonage. Grimshaw granted permission for the work to be done, agreeing that this was a genuine emergency.

In addition to all his other work, he also took over the teaching in the local school when necessary, and constantly supervised its work. After some years under Grimshaw's leadership his congregation grew too large to be contained in the village church. By 1757 giving by his congregation proved ample enough for Grimshaw to complete an enlargement of the church. But it was still too small.

'What has God wrought in the midst of these rough mountains!'

'I took horse for Haworth,' John Wesley recorded in his journal on 22 May 1757. 'A December storm met us on the mountain, but this did not hinder such a congregation as the church could contain. I suppose we had near a thousand communicants, and scarce a trifler among them. In the afternoon, the church not containing more than a third of the people, I was constrained to be in the churchyard.'

Two years later Wesley visited Grimshaw's church again. 'The church would not contain the congregation; so after prayers I stood on a scaffold close to the church, and the congregation in the churchyard. The communicants alone filled the church. In the afternoon the congregation was nearly doubled, and yet most of those were not curious hearers, but men fearing God.'

Again, two years after that, Wesley found that, 'the church would not near contain the people. However, Mr Grimshaw had provided for this by fixing a scaffold on the outside of one of the windows, through which I went after prayers, and the people likewise went out into the churchyard. The afternoon congregation was larger still. What has God wrought in the midst of these rough mountains!'

On one of his visits George Whitefield noticed that thirty-five bottles of wine were needed at Haworth for one administration of Holy Communion.

Grimshaw and the Church of England

Notwithstanding his Evangelicalism, Grimshaw was a robust church-man. He took great care of the fabric as well as the worship of his church, having a new font consecrated in 1742 and a new pulpit installed.

The Archbishop of York's visitation returns for June 1743 show that Grimshaw catechised (i.e. gave formal Christian instruction in question and answer form) from Easter to Whitsun each year. Grimshaw told John Wesley that it was his custom to expound the Church of England's Articles and Homilies each year, and he urged people to use all the means of grace the Church made available. He believed that neglect of the Articles was the main cause of dissent; and he disagreed with an old clergyman he knew, who, when asked by his curate if he might read from the Homilies, replied: 'No. For if you should do so, the whole congregation would turn Methodist!'

'I am determined to live and die a member and minister of the Church of England,' he told Charles Wesley in 1755. 'For although I can by no means endure the doctrine and deportment of the clergy in general, yet I have no reason to quarrel with our Church. Her Articles, Homilies, Catechism, and Liturgy, for the main, are orthodox and good.' He never wavered from this belief and wrote again to Charles Wesley in 1760. 'I see nothing so materially amiss in the Liturgy or the Church constitution as to disturb my conscience or justify separation. No; where shall I go to mend myself? I believe the Church of England to be the soundest, purest, most apostolical Christian Church in the world; therefore I can in good conscience, as I am determined, God willing, to do, live and die in her.'

Unlike some strong churchmen, however, he also wrote: 'I love all denominations ... so far ... as I find them endued with the Holy Spirit.'

Grimshaw's theology

In December 1762 Grimshaw sent the scholarly London Evangelical William Romaine a statement of his theology: he was, he said, a Calvinist on his knees and an Arminian on his feet, and he tried to strike a balance between the two. He held that the doctrine that God had elected some to be eternally saved was of special value for the already assured, but he could not believe it was a useful doctrine for the unconverted.

'My business', he said, 'is to invite all to come to Christ for salvation, and to assure all that will come of a hearty welcome.'

John Newton thought that on the whole Grimshaw was a Calvinist, but reckoned that 'many Calvinists would scarcely have acknowledged his claim to that name if he had made it'.

The key to his theology is that he had a heart which was full of Christ and the Scriptures. He was convinced of the vileness of sin, the value of souls, the need for repentance, the call to holiness, and the life of the world to come. 'When I die', he said, 'I shall then have my greatest grief and my greatest joy; my greatest grief that I have done so little for Jesus, and my greatest joy that Jesus has done so much for me.'

Carrying fire across parish boundaries

As Grimshaw's preaching fame spread beyond Haworth, scores of people came to hear him from surrounding villages and beyond. Strangers from neighbouring Yorkshire towns would ride over on a Sunday morning, and as many as a hundred would dine at the village inns before the afternoon service. Then they asked him to preach at cottage meetings in their own towns, promising him a hearty welcome. They told him alarming stories of neglected parishes, of absentee or alcoholic clergy, and of children growing up ignorant of the basics of religion.

Grimshaw decided that the state of eighteenth-century England needed exceptional action and so, unlike most of his Anglican contemporaries, he decided to travel from place to place – conducting an 'itinerant ministry'.

At its best the English parochial system was designed to bring the gospel to every home – but surely it should not be allowed to hinder the spread of the good news. And so Grimshaw mounted his horse, leaving Haworth behind him, and rode across parish boundaries, preaching in barns and in the open moorland air, wherever they would listen in Yorkshire, Lancashire, Cheshire and north Derbyshire. He rarely preached less than twenty times a week and once managed thirty-one times.

'A few such as him,' Wesley said of Grimshaw, 'would make a nation tremble. He carries fire wherever he goes!' At another time, Wesley shrewdly observed: 'It is not easy to ascribe such unwearied diligence, chiefly among the poor, to any motive but the real one.'

'You do too much,' friends told Grimshaw. 'You should spare yourself.'

'Let me labour now,' he always replied, 'I shall have enough rest by and by. I cannot do enough for Christ who has done so much for me.'

Idleness seems to have troubled Grimshaw's conscience. 'Today I have trifled,' he once wrote in his diary. 'I have loitered it away doing little, or I fear but little to God's glory . . . Be ashamed, O my soul, before ye Lord, for so embezzling thy golden moments!'

He did, however, allow himself breaks in his hectic schedule for meditation. 'A day of net-mending,' he wrote in his diary in 1756. 'No preaching – reading, meditation and prayer have been my chief exercise and employment.' He thought of meditation as 'the soul's chewing'.

Grimshaw and the Methodists

Grimshaw greatly admired John Wesley and welcomed the travelling Methodist preachers to his parsonage. Sometimes he filled the house with them, giving up his own bed and, unknown to his visitors, sleeping in the hayloft. He would rise early and clean their boots himself.

They preached in his kitchen and he always announced in church when this was to be. And in case, after his death, he should be succeeded by a less godly minister and his flock scatter, he built a chapel and house for the travelling Methodists at his own expense. After one sermon by one of the itinerant preachers, he embraced the man. 'The Lord bless thee, Ben. This was worth a hundred of my sermons!' He fell down in front of another and told him: 'I am not worthy to stand in your presence.'

The Archbishop's verdict

Twice neighbouring clergy sent complaints to the Archbishop of York about Grimshaw's extra-parochial preaching.

'How many communicants had you when you first came to Haworth?' Archbishop John Gilbert asked him, after he had received the first complaint.

'Twelve, my lord,' replied Grimshaw.

'How many have you now?'

'In the winter, from three to four hundred,' Grimshaw told him, 'and in the summer, near twelve hundred.' (Later, the numbers taking winter Communion rose to five hundred.)

'We cannot find fault with Mr Grimshaw', his Grace replied to the first complaint, 'when he is instrumental in bringing so many to the Lord's Table.'

On the second occasion Archbishop Gilbert visited the Haworth church for a confirmation service. He told Grimshaw that he had heard some critical reports of his activities and asked him to preach in two hours' time on a text which he named. Grimshaw thought he was about to be turned out of his parish. When he climbed into the pulpit he engaged in such an ardent prayer that it is said the Archbishop was moved to tears. He then preached a powerful sermon on the required text.

At the end of the service, Gilbert took hold of Grimshaw's hand. 'Would to God,' he said in the presence of all the assembled clerics, 'that all the clergy in my diocese were like this good man.'

Grimshaw and Henry Venn

From 1754 to 1759 Henry Venn was Curate of the village of Clapham near London, later to become famous in the history of Anglican Evangelicalism, and in 1757 he worked with George Whitefield on a preaching tour in the western counties of England. In 1759 he moved to Huddersfield, south of Haworth. Venn embarked on a work which was in many ways similar to Grimshaw's, spending a good deal of time on horseback, searching out obscure parishioners in lonely farms and cottages. Like Grimshaw, he began to draw large congregations so that often his church could not hold the people and he had to preach in the open air.

'He was one of the most eminent examples', Sir James Stephens wrote of Henry Venn, 'of one of the most uncommon of human excellencies, the possession of perfect and uninterrupted mental health.' Over the years many people visited his study to take his advice about farms or quarrels or marriages.

Years later Charles Simeon wrote to one of Venn's grandsons: 'I wish you had known your grandfather; the only end for which he lived was to make all men see the glory of God in the face of Jesus Christ.'

Henry Venn and William Grimshaw became close friends, and Venn was later to tell his own son: 'There is nothing that I know of worthy a thought compared with possessing so much grace that everyone who comes near you is enlivened and edified in his own soul. Thus it was with my very dear friend Mr Grimshaw.' At another time Venn wrote: 'Indeed, Mr Grimshaw was one of God's servants, and of so loving a disposition, I scarce saw anyone go beyond him, and very few of the dearest of God's sons and daughters are so affectionate.'

Venn's son, John, became the first chairman of the Church Missionary Society and his grandson, another Henry, ran the CMS for more than thirty years in the middle of the nineteenth century.

The Huntingdon connection

Selina, Countess of Huntingdon (1707–91), devoted her life and fortune to the spread of Evangelical teaching. The daughter of Earl Ferrers, in 1728 she married the Earl of Huntingdon, who died in 1746 leaving her to live the life of a wealthy widow for nearly half a century. She was earnest, strong minded and imperious. As churches were closed to Evangelical clergy, she opened her house to them and made them welcome. As a countess, she could have as many private chaplains as she pleased; if she decided to build a chapel in her grounds, no one could stop her. William Romaine became her senior chaplain.

'Good Lady Huntingdon', wrote George Whitefield, 'goes on acting the part of a mother in Israel. Her house is indeed a Bethel. We have the Sacrament every morning, heavenly conversation all day, and preach at night. For a day or two she has had five clergymen under her roof.'

She aimed to evangelise the aristocracy, and her 'spiritual routs', as the wits called them, became a well-known phenomenon in the fashionable world. Few hostesses in London could assemble a better-connected company of guests: the Prince of Wales and the Duke of Cumberland, Lord North and the Earl of Chatham, Horace Walpole and Baron Melcombe, Lord Chesterfield and Lord Bolingbroke, the Duchess of Marlborough and Lady Suffolk – all would meet in her drawing room and listen to her preachers. The most important of her converts was the Earl of Dartmouth, who was President of the Board of Trade, later Colonial Secretary, President of the Royal Society and patron of James Watt's inventions. After his conversion in 1756 he made it his business to secure livings for Evangelical clergy and it was he who sent Henry Venn to Huddersfield and John Newton to Olney.

In August 1762 Lady Huntingdon was in Yorkshire with George Whitefield and William Romaine as her chaplains, and visited Haworth. Three months later, Grimshaw wrote to the Countess:

I hope ere long to see my dear brother Whitefield in his own pulpit again. When will Your Ladyship revive us with another visit? What blessings did the Lord shower upon us the last time you were here! And how did our hearts burn within us to proclaim his love and grace to perishing sinners! Come and animate us afresh; aid us by your counsels and your prayers; communicate a spark of your glowing zeal, and stir us up to renewed activity in the cause of God!

But Grimshaw did not live to see the Countess again.

'My time is come'

Only once during the twenty-one years that he worked at Haworth did Grimshaw stop work due to illness, even though it was said of him that he 'used his body with less compassion than a merciful man would his beast'.

But early in 1763 typhus broke out in Haworth. Grimshaw knew that it was highly infectious, but carried on visiting the sick and dying. In the spring, at the age of fifty-five, he caught the disease himself and knew it would be fatal.

One of his first visitors as he lay dying was the Rev. Benjamin Ingham. Ingham, a Yorkshireman, had been one of the members of Wesley's Holy Club at Oxford and had travelled to Georgia with the two Wesleys. Now he rode over twice from the other side of Leeds, to visit Grimshaw and tell Lady Huntingdon how he was doing.

'My last enemy is come!' Grimshaw told Ingham on his first visit. 'The signs of death are upon me. But I am not afraid – No! No! Blessed be God, my hope is sure, and I am in his hands.'

On his second visit Ingham found Grimshaw much worse and knelt beside him in prayer. 'I harbour no desire of life,' Grimshaw told Ingham. 'My time is come, and I am wholly resigned to God.'

Then he raised his hands towards heaven, and said: 'Tell her ladyship that I thank her from the bottom of my heart for all her kindnesses to me during the years I have known her. With my dying breath, I implore every blessing, temporal and spiritual, to rest upon her!'

Later he placed his hand over his heart and said: 'I am quite exhausted, but I shall soon be at home for ever with the Lord, a poor miserable sinner redeemed by His blood.'

As Benjamin Ingham left, Henry Venn arrived and asked Grimshaw how he felt. 'As happy as I can be on earth,' he told Venn, 'and as sure of glory as if I was in it. Never have I had such a visit from God since I knew him.'

As the end drew near, he ran a high fever and one of his attendants asked him how he was. 'I have nothing to do', he replied, 'but to step out of my bed into heaven.'

He gave detailed directions for his burial, including the instruction that he should be placed in 'a plain poor man's coffin', inscribed: 'For me to live is Christ, and to die is gain' (Phil. 1:21). He had had the same text engraved on the sounding board of his new pulpit twenty years earlier.

On 7 April 1763 he murmured, 'Here goes an unprofitable servant!' and died.

According to Wesley's account, 'His body was interred with what is more ennobling than all the pomp of a royal funeral, for he was followed to the grave by a great multitude, with affectionate sighs and many tears; who cannot still hear his much-loved name without weeping for the guide of their souls, to whom each of them was dear as children to their father.'

Henry Venn preached the funeral oration both at Luddenden where he was buried (alongside his two wives), and at Haworth. 'He did his utmost for God,' Venn told the huge crowd which assembled for the funeral. 'Seldom had the sun ever run half his daily course before this minister had once or oftener declared the testimony of the Lord, which enlightens the eyes of the mind and rejoices the hearts of the poor. All intent on this work, every day had its destined labours of love, morning and evening, to fill up. Labours so great, that it is almost incredible to tell how many hours of the twenty-four were constantly employed in instructing those who dwelt in his parish or neighbouring places. Never was any sordid child of this world more engrossed by the love of money and more laborious in heaping it up, than William Grimshaw was in teaching and preaching the Kingdom of God!'

Grimshaw's children

Grimshaw's daughter had attended Wesley's school at Kingswood, Bristol, but died at the age of twelve. Wesley said that she 'departed in the Lord'.

His son, who had also received a Christian education, became an alcoholic. On one occasion, when he was riding home on a horse which his father had ridden on his preaching tours, he said to the animal: 'Once thou carried a saint, but now thou carriest a devil.'

Grimshaw junior survived his father by three years and died childless. But he repented of his ways before he died, and some of his last words were, 'What will my father say, when he sees that I am got to heaven!'

FLETCHER OF MADELEY

John William Fletcher (1729–85) was the saint of Evangelicalism. 'In four-score years', wrote John Wesley, 'I have known many exemplary men, holy in heart and life, but one to equal him I have not known, one so inwardly and outwardly devoted to God.'

Gentleness, humility, long nights of prayer, self-denial, a love of children, a love of birds, courage, a practice of the presence of God – these characterised Fletcher's life. 'No country or age', wrote the poet Robert Southey, 'has ever produced a man of more fervent piety or more perfect charity.'

All contemporary writers seem to have been equally impressed. Even the unbelieving French author Voltaire, when challenged to name a character as beautiful as that of our Lord, pointed to his fellow countryman Fletcher of Madeley.

For Fletcher was not an Englishman. His real name was Jean Guillaume de la Flechère, but as his English friends could never spell this correctly he consented to be known as John William Fletcher. Born in Switzerland, he was educated in Geneva for the ministry of the Swiss Church. But finding the doctrine of election as taught by Swiss Calvinists offensive, he moved to England as a private tutor. He taught for a while in the home of Thomas Hill of Tern Hill, Shropshire.

'I shall wonder if our tutor doesn't turn Methodist by and by,' Mrs Hill joked.

'Methodist, madam,' asked Fletcher, 'pray what is that?'

'Why,' replied Mrs Hill, 'the Methodists are a people that do nothing but pray.'

'Then,' said Fletcher, 'by the help of God I will find them out.'

At a Methodist preaching house in London, Fletcher found a type of Christianity very different from stern Genevan Calvinism: it seemed joyous, generous and exuberant with love for God and man.

In March 1757 Fletcher was ordained deacon by the Bishop of Hereford, and made a priest on the following Sunday. In 1760 he obtained the living of Madeley, a large Shropshire village in the Severn valley.

Fletcher's parishioners were a mixed bunch: a few well-to-do farmers mainly interested in their cattle, hunting and ale; agricultural labourers; colliers from two coal pits; and the forgemen of Coalbrookdale, the cradle of England's Industrial Revolution where the famous Darby family had begun to smelt iron with coal. It was a strange contrast: three thousand mainly rough, rowdy, often drunken parishioners under the care of a scholar with delicate health, a sensitive handsome face and foreign ways and accent. But Fletcher worked in Madeley for twenty-five years from 1760 to 1785. George III inquired through the Lord Chancellor what promotion would be acceptable to Mr Fletcher.

'Tell his majesty', Fletcher replied, 'that I want nothing but more grace.'

Wesley tried to persuade him to give up his parish and become a travelling preacher. Although he occasionally joined Wesley on short preaching tours, however, he was determined to stay in his parish.

His first task was to make his parishioners realise that the church was as important a place as the bull-ring. He visited every home and urged his people to come to church. Some of them answered that they could not wake early enough to get there on time. So taking a bell in his hand, he set out every Sunday morning at 5 a.m. and went round the most distant parts of the parish, inviting the villagers to the house of God.

In the early months he was discouraged by the small congregations who came. But gradually the numbers grew so that in time the little church could not hold all the people. He took out one of the windows near the pulpit, so that some could stand in the churchyard to listen to the sermon. Many walked long distances, bringing their dinners with them. Well into the twentieth century you could see deep indentations in the pillars of the vicarage gates where they used to sharpen their knives.

Fletcher catechised the children every Sunday afternoon. He started six Sunday Schools in various parts of the parish. In the summer he held classes in the woods, teaching the children to pray and sing hymns which he wrote for them. Every night of the week he held a service in some part of the parish – in church, in a cottage or in the open air. He gathered people into small groups and rose at five in the morning to instruct them in the Christian faith.

Young people were in the habit of meeting in the evenings into the early hours for 'dancing, revelling, drunkenness and obscenity'. Fletcher managed to stop this after a long struggle. He used to burst in on these gatherings in 'holy indignation'. He would take the names of all who were present and send them to their homes with stern rebukes. Whenever these miscreants saw Fletcher coming they used to take to their heels, but their vicar would run after them. It is said that 'many a man's life was changed by the conversation that followed'.

He worked hard at personal conversations and always tried to draw lessons from the everyday things of life. If a woman was poking a fire, he spoke of the way the fire of love in the soul is apt to burn low.

Another was sweeping a room. 'Are you taking equal care', he asked, 'to drive uncleanness out of every corner of your heart?'

He met a farmer with a gun. 'Sin', he said, 'is missing the mark.'

He met a woman carrying a basket to market. 'Let me tell you of the one who died to bear a heavier burden for you.'

Of course the wags in the parish mimicked this habit of Fletcher's unmercifully. But he carried on and those to whom he spoke seldom forgot what he told them.

All sorts of rumours did the rounds. 'Did you know he's a Jesuit in disguise?' some said. His foreign accent made it almost believable. A neighbouring squire sent a message that he intended to cane Fletcher publicly in the street; some farmers refused to pay their tithes. The colliers decided they would hold a great bull-baiting event in which Fletcher would take the place of the bull. One group set out to capture him while another stayed to get the dogs ready. But a funeral kept him from going to the place they had expected to find him and he escaped his fate.

He took up his pen to intervene in the debate between Calvinism and Arminianism. He had seen Calvinism at its most severe in Geneva and wrote his six *Checks to Antinomianism* (1771–5). He believed strongly in Wesley's doctrine of Christian perfection. He also wrote against the Unitarian doctrines of the Presbyterian minister and scientist Joseph Priestley (1773–1804).

'I know not which to admire most,' John Wesley said of his writings, 'the purity of the language, the strength of the argument, or the mildness and sweetness of spirit that breathes throughout the whole.'

Fletcher died of a fever caught while visiting a sick parishioner. His last words were typical of the man: 'O my poor! What will become of my poor?'

JOHN NEWTON

John Newton (1725–1807), the son of the stern captain of a small trading ship, spent his childhood in the docks and streets of strange towns in many parts of the world. His mother was a devout Dissenter who laid the foundations of his later conversion; however, she died when John was only six, and at the age of eighteen he decided he was an atheist. He joined a ship bound for West Africa, 'in order', he said, 'that I might now be as abandoned as I pleased without any control'.

At Sierra Leone Newton entered the service of a white slave-trader. He worked for a year on the coast of Sierra Leone being treated badly by the slave-trader's black mistress, who enjoyed making a white man miserable.

Newton's father asked another ship's captain to look for his son. The search was successful and Newton was set free. His rescuer was disgusted by the blasphemous stories Newton told aboard the ship. Newton then served a term as mate on a slave ship, and later as captain of his own vessel.

John Newton was a complex character. Along with his love of adventure and tendency to fall into bad company, he loved books. On African sands he had taught himself Euclidean geometry, and on the slave ship he studied Latin. When he read Thomas à Kempis's *The Imitation of Christ* the book shook his atheism. He remembered some of the Christian words and attitudes instilled into his young mind by his mother. A storm at sea made him reflective and a gradual change in his outlook began. He dated his conversion to Christ as 10 March 1748, when he was twenty-three years old.

As a young man Newton had fallen in love with a thirteen-year-old girl and in 1750 he returned to England to claim Mary Catlett ('Polly') as his wife. Living the steady life of a married man, he made friends with some of the leaders of the eighteenth-century Evangelical revival: Wesley, Whitefield, Berridge, Grimshaw, Venn and Romaine. He considered becoming a Dissenter, but Lord Dartmouth persuaded him to enter the Church of England.

The Bishop of Lincoln ordained him in 1764 and he was offered the curacy of Olney in Buckinghamshire. In the eighteenth century, Olney was a squalid little town, 'inhabited', wrote William Cowper, 'chiefly by the half-starved and ragged of the earth'. There was a long street of tumbledown cottages with holes in their thatched roofs. The people had traditionally lived by lacemaking, but the trade was doomed.

Newton threw himself into the work at Olney with energy. He obtained funds from Lord Dartmouth to relieve the physical conditions of his new parishioners and then addressed himself to the needs of their souls. A page of his diary gives us details of his weekly timetable:

SUNDAY	*6 a.m.*	Prayer Meeting
	Morning. Afternoon. Evening	Full service with sermon
	8 p.m.	Meeting for prayer and hymn-singing in the Vicarage

MONDAY	*Evening*	Men's Bible Class
TUESDAY	*5 a.m.*	Prayer Meeting (good average attendance)
	Evening	Prayer Meeting (the largest meeting of the week)
WEDNESDAY		Classes for young people and enquirers
THURSDAY	*Afternoon*	Children's meeting 'to reason with them, and explain the Scriptures in their own little way'
	Evening	Service in church with sermon – attended by many people from the villages around
FRIDAY	*Evening*	Meeting for members of the Society

John Newton had no one to assist him at Olney and had to take every meeting himself. In addition, he was a conscientious parish visitor, held many cottage meetings in remote corners of his parish, and constantly arranged additional meetings.

Preaching was not Newton's strongest point. Certainly his personality and earnestness commanded attention, but the effect was spoiled by his poor delivery and awkward gestures. His greatest gift was as a counsellor. He understood sin from personal experience, and a constant stream of people made their way to Olney to be guided by Newton. If they were struggling with temptation, they found in him a man who could sympathise.

Others wrote to him from every part of England and could be sure they would get a reply which combined understanding and sturdy common sense with spiritual insight. 'It is the Lord's will', he said, 'that I should do most by my letters.'

Newton and William Cowper

In 1767 some new parishioners came to live at Olney. The red house in the marketplace was taken by a Mrs Unwin, a clergyman's widow with a son and daughter, and a shy, sensitive friend who had come to be a part of the family.

The shy young man was William Cowper (1731–1800), the son of an Anglican clergyman. Cowper's life had been traumatic since the death of his mother when he was six. This had been a shattering blow to him and his early school days were miserable. He grew convinced that he was under a curse. He was a little happier at Westminster School, though lacking in self-confidence. Leaving school, he entered training for a career in law but began to suffer from severe depression.

Cowper fell in love with a woman named Theodora, but his father forbade them to marry. After his father died in 1756, he became morbidly introspective. When faced with an examination for a legal position, he panicked and made an unsuccessful attempt to hang himself. They put him in Dr Cotton's House for Madmen in St Albans.

Dr Cotton was an Evangelical and patiently set about helping Cowper as best he could, in the process drawing him towards a faith in Christ. When Cowper was somewhat better, Dr Cotton sent him to live with the Unwins and it was with them that he eventually arrived at Olney. Unable to cope with the idea of paid employment, he turned from the law to poetry. He wrote:

> I was a stricken deer that left the herd
> Long since; with many an arrow deep infixed
> My panting side was charged, when I withdrew
> To seek a tranquil death in distant shades.
> There was I found by One who had himself
> Been hurt by the archers. In his side he bore
> And in his hands and feet, the cruel scars.
> With gentle force, soliciting the darts
> He drew them forth, and healed, and bade me live.[17]

William Cowper and John Newton became close friends. Cowper

grew well enough, between his recurring bouts of depression, to help in the work of the parish. The friendship between the two men has enriched the Church with some well-loved hymns.

The Olney hymns

One of Newton's devices for keeping up his flock's attendance at the main parish prayer meeting was to provide a new hymn every Tuesday evening which he often took as a text for his talk. Sometimes Newton wrote them; sometimes Cowper. Between them, the two men wrote over three hundred hymns, many of which are still among the most popular in the English language. Among those Newton gave us is the autobiographical hymn which is probably more popular at the end of the twentieth century than it has ever been in its history:

> Amazing grace, how sweet the sound
> That saved a wretch like me!
> I once was lost, but now am found,
> Was blind but now I see.

Others from Newton's pen include: 'How sweet the name of Jesus sounds', 'Glorious things of thee are spoken', 'One there is above all others', and 'Begone unbelief, My Saviour is near'.

Cowper's hymns include: 'Oh for a closer walk with God', 'Hark my soul it is the Lord', 'There is a fountain filled with blood', 'God moves in a mysterious way' and 'Jesus, where'er thy people meet'. Evangelicals are sometimes accused of triumphalism or of being blessed with an excess of certainties. Cowper escapes the criticism and his honesty is refreshing when he asks,

> Where is the blessedness I knew
> When first I saw the Lord?

or when he confesses,

> Lord, it is my chief complaint
> That my love is weak and faint;

> Yet I love Thee and adore;
> O for grace to love Thee more!

One of Cowper's achievements was to write the poem *The Task*. This work carried the Evangelical message to places others could never reach. People who might have scorned Grimshaw's preaching read *The Task*. Cultured people acknowledged that Evangelicalism had something to say to thoughtful people.

The subject of *The Task* was remarkable: 'You can write about anything,' his friend Lady Austin had told Cowper. 'Write about this sofa!' Cowper accepted the challenge.

'I sing the sofa,' *The Task* begins, but in a thousand charming lines Cowper discusses theology, gardening, politics, literature and contemporary life – returning to the sofa in the closing lines. Four thoughts stand out: the beauty and sanctity of family life at home; a call to the simple life; an interest in what was happening in the world; and a call to a right relationship with God.

Newton moves to London

While Cowper was composing *The Task*, a part of Olney was destroyed by fire. John Newton decided that the Guy Fawkes celebrations on 5 November posed a threat to the thatched roofs of the cottages and tried to put a stop to the annual event. Unruly elements of the town strongly resented Newton's proposal and attempted to destroy the vicarage. Newton had to back down, and his influence in the town was damaged.

When, in 1780, he was offered the rectorship of St Mary Woolnoth, an important parish at the heart of the City of London, he decided to accept. Despite the limitations of his preaching, crowds came to hear him at St Mary's and he continued his counselling.

Newton used his position in London to good effect. He was prominent in the campaign against the slave trade, his earlier experiences enabling him to supply the factual detail which the reformers needed. He was a director of the Sierra Leone Company which settled freed slaves. He served on the committee of the Church

Missionary Society, and helped found the London Missionary Society as well as the British and Foreign Bible Society.

Death of Wesley

In 1784 the young Charles Simeon – soon to become one of the most famous Anglican Evangelicals – visited a now aged John Wesley. The two men discussed the Calvinist–Arminian dispute and concluded that they agreed on the most important issues of theology.

Wesley preached his last open air sermon at Winchelsea on 6 October 1790, and his last sermon at Leatherhead on 2 February 1791. On 24 February of that year he wrote his last letter, to William Wilberforce, encouraging him in his campaign against the slave trade. The next day he returned to London and died at his home on 2 March 1791, aged eighty-seven. Thus ended the life of one of the great Christians of all time.

At the time of the death of this consummate organiser there were 294 Methodist preachers and 71,668 members of Methodist societies in Britain; 19 missionaries and 5,500 members on mission stations; and 198 preachers and 43,265 members in America. Wesley remained a member of the Church of England until the end and, as a result of his influence, the established Church, despite often closing its doors to him, had experienced something of a revival itself.

Death of Newton

Newton lived into his eighties and continued preaching almost until the end came. William Jay of Bath visited him in the closing weeks of his life. The old man was now frail, but Jay never forgot his parting words.

'My memory is nearly gone,' Newton told him, 'but I remember two things – that I am a great sinner, and that Christ is a great Saviour.'

He neatly encapsulated Evangelicalism. After he died a few weeks later, they erected an epitaph in St Mary's:

JOHN NEWTON

Clerk,
Once an Infidel and Libertine,
A servant of slaves in Africa
was
by the mercy of our Lord and Saviour
Jesus Christ
Preserved, Restored and Pardoned
And appointed to preach the Faith he
had so long laboured to destroy

Michael Hinton, in *The Anglican Parochial Clergy*, concludes that Newton was 'one of the most attractive of Anglican parish priests' who 'sat lightly to party lines'. Although Newton described himself as a Calvinist, he hated theological disputes. 'He lacked both a systematic theology and an ordered mind; but his sermons and writings were full of shrewd observation and practical wisdom.'[18]

THOMAS SCOTT

After a brief interregnum, Newton was succeeded at Olney by Thomas Scott (1747–1821). On leaving school Scott had worked for nine years on a farm, but all the time, he had a passionate love of books and at last succeeded in his ambition of going into the Church. He was ordained in 1772, despite secretly holding Unitarian beliefs.

Not long after his ordination he travelled to Olney to hear Newton preach, but was unimpressed. 'I thought his doctrine abstruse, imaginative, and irrational.' The only result of his visit to Olney was that he began to treat his village congregation in neighbouring Stoke Goldington to a series of controversial sermons against Methodism. But two months later Newton impressed Scott in a more effective way.

'Two of my parishioners,' wrote Scott, 'a man and his wife, lay at the point of death. I heard of the circumstance, but, not being sent for, I took no notice of it, till one evening – the woman being now dead and the man dying – I heard that my neighbour Mr Newton had been several times to visit them. Immediately my conscience reproached me with being shamefully negligent in sitting at home within a few doors of dying persons and never going to visit them. It occurred to me that whatever contempt I might have for Mr Newton's doctrines, I must acknowledge his practice to be more consistent with the ministerial character than my own.'[19]

His next step, curiously, was to open a correspondence with Newton with the aim of converting him to Unitarianism. Scott's own account of the correspondence demonstrates the strength of Newton's character and ability. 'I filled my letters', Scott wrote, 'with definitions, inquiries, arguments, objections, and consequences, requiring explicit answers.' The older and wiser man gently parried every stroke as it fell, never yielding an inch of his ground, but never thrusting back, taking care never to wound his young opponent. The controversy drove Scott to study his Bible more carefully. Day after day he walked up and down the beautiful park at Weston, his Greek New Testament in his hand, until in the end he decided that the truth was on Newton's side.

In 1781 Scott arrived in Olney as Curate after Newton had moved to the city of London. The appointment was unpopular at first. Some of the people knew and violently disliked Scott. For his part, Scott did not have a high regard for them.

'They are almost all Calvinists,' he wrote, 'even the most debauched of them.' Scott was fearless, honest, outspoken and tactless. 'Mr Scott', Cowper wrote to Newton, 'would be admired were he not so apt to be angry with his congregation. Warmth of temper indulged to a degree that may be called scolding, defeats the end of preaching. But he is a good man and may perhaps outgrow it.'

'I am very unpopular in the town,' Scott noted, 'and preach in general to small congregations. I am generally looked upon as unsound and legal.'

When it was suggested that he should move to London to be morning preacher at the Lock Chapel, he did so with a sense of relief.

Scott's commentary on the Bible

In London Thomas Scott wrote the commentary on the Bible which made his name famous. Bellamy, an enterprising but hard-up publisher, noticing the revived interest in the Bible, hit on the idea of issuing a Bible commentary in weekly parts, and offered Scott a guinea a week if he would begin at once. The offer was tempting. Scott had often longed to work through the Bible, seeking to understand the message of every verse, and in those days a guinea a week was not to be despised by a married man whose whole income was barely £120 a year. He accepted the challenge.

The work had to be done at a killing pace. Each weekly part had to be written in a week. 'Sick or well,' recalled Scott, 'in spirits or out, the tale of bricks must be delivered ... I am convinced that I did not deliberate, consult, and pray, as I should have done. I was too hasty in determining.'

'I have known him', wrote Scott's son, 'with great difficulty and suffering prepare as much copy as he thought would complete the current number, and then, when he had retired to bed, and taken an emetic, called up again to furnish more.'

This explains some of the book's unusual features: it has no quotations from the early Church fathers and no discussion of the views of other commentators. To make matters worse, Scott developed asthma and a fever; his wife died; his congregation was divided by theological differences; and extreme Calvinists in his flock were trying to drive him from them.

Scott's publisher turned out to be a scoundrel. Before the sixteenth weekly part appeared, Bellamy announced that he had no more money and that, if the work was to continue, the author himself would have to find the funds.

After Scott had succeeded in borrowing what he needed, Bellamy went bankrupt and Scott found himself saddled with a debt of £500. 'It was needful that the whole progress of the work', he wrote, 'should be stamped with mortification, perplexity and disappointment, if the Lord meant me to do any good to others by it, and to preserve me from receiving hurt to my own soul. Four years five months and a day were employed in the work with unknown sorrow and vexation.'

Yet in its way, Scott's commentary was a great work. He aimed to 'speak plainly and intelligibly to persons of ordinary capacity'. He refused to indulge in fanciful interpretations, such as finding Paul's system of theology hidden in the tassels of the Tabernacle. His theory was that 'every passage of Scripture has its literal and distinct meaning, which it is the first duty of a commentator to explain, and speaking generally the *spiritual meaning* is no other than this *real* meaning with its fair legitimate application to ourselves'. In other words he tried to discover the meaning of each passage of Scripture for himself and then share this with his readers.

During his lifetime 37,000 complete sets of his commentary were sold, bringing to the publishers almost £200,000. Although Scott never became a rich man, his book was profoundly influential. In many Evangelical homes, the head of the house read it aloud at family prayers; and Scott stamped his sane and sober methods on the minds of thoughtful Evangelicals. Cardinal Newman said of Scott that he 'made a deeper impression on my mind than any other, and to whom, humanly speaking, I owe my soul' (see page 240).

Scott left London in 1803 for the rectory of Aston Sandford, Buckinghamshire, where he died in 1821.

CHARLES SIMEON

Charles Simeon (1759–1836) came from a wealthy family and was educated at Eton and King's College, Cambridge. When he arrived at King's from Eton, he was known as a wild undergraduate, famous for his love of horses and extravagant dress. At King's he discovered that the rules of the college compelled him to receive Communion a certain number of times a year. He decided to take this requirement seriously and bought a copy of a book on the Lord's Supper which introduced him to the doctrine of the atonement for the first time. Under the influence of Henry and John Venn, Simeon was converted to Christ and devoted the rest of his life to trying to make the rest of Cambridge grasp the truth of the Christian gospel.

Simeon became a Fellow of King's in 1782, was ordained and

appointed the following year Curate of Trinity Church by the Market Place. The bishop had foisted on the parishioners a young, inexperienced man, instead of the curate they had hoped to get. Simeon's ministry began amid bitter opposition when the seat-holders deserted the church in a body, and locked the doors of the pews so that no one else should use them. When Simeon placed benches in the aisles, the churchwardens threw them out into the churchyard.

Rowdy bands of undergraduates used to try to break up Simeon's services. One contemporary wrote, 'Those who worshipped at Trinity were supposed to have left common sense, discretion, sobriety, attachment to the Established Church, love of the liturgy, and whatever else is true and of good report, in the vestibule.' Certainly, in the early years of his ministry he was ostracised by respectable Cambridge people, and he was detested by many dons. His readiness to co-operate with Dissenters made him an object of suspicion. Michael Hinton notes that he 'was exposed to the obloquy which anyone who takes the Christian faith seriously attracts from those whose commitment is demonstrated by comparison to be shallow'.[20]

Thomas Dykes, who in 1786 went up to Magdalene College, recorded that Simeon was 'one of the most unlikely persons to become extensively useful that he had known . . . much zeal but not according to knowledge . . . apparent affectation of manner . . . egotism and self-importance which seemed likely to neutralise any good effect of his ministry . . .' His early preaching was said to be crude and undigested, containing many striking remarks but full of incorrect statements and allusions which offended good taste.

Simeon persevered with his work, however, rarely deliberately doing anything to provoke opposition, but never flinching from preaching what he believed to be the truth. First he earned toleration, and then recognition as the most inspiring teacher in Cambridge. After some years, Trinity came to be crowded with undergraduates every Sunday. His Friday Conversation Circle for the discussion of religious questions, his Bible classes and doctrine classes always filled his room at King's with eager disciples. Many of the Evangelical preachers of the next generation were trained at his sermon classes. Simeon published his sermon outlines in the twenty-one volume *Horae Homileticae*. When he eventually gained the respect of the University of Cambridge, he held the college posts of Dean of Arts, Dean of Divinity and Vice-Provost.

Simeon got up every morning, even in winter, at four o'clock, and after lighting his fire, devoted the first four hours of the day to private prayer and the study of the Scriptures.

Some said that Simeon was pompous and imperious; others that he was aware of his own failings and worked hard to correct them. Certainly a graciousness of character shines through his many surviving letters. He himself wrote of 'the three things a minister has to learn, (1) Humility, (2) Humility, (3) Humility'.

Simeon is remembered as a clear thinker who possessed spiritual insight. He was extremely hardworking: one of the most active early members of the British and Foreign Bible Society, of the Church Missionary Society, and of the London Society for Promoting Christianity among the Jews. Unlike other Evangelicals, however, he did not espouse the cause of the abolition of the slave trade; nor indeed that of any other social reform.

Simeon is well known as the founder of the Simeon Trust. 'The greatest reform that the Church needs', he wrote to the Bishop of Oxford, 'is an improvement in the method of appointing to the cure of souls.' When he inherited some money following a brother's death, he decided to buy the patronage of a certain number of livings. As the years passed, other Evangelicals gave money for the same purpose, or handed over to him livings that were in their gift. In this way the Simeon Trust arose and by the end of the nineteenth century it had the right of appointing to more than a hundred parishes, including some of the most important in the country. The Trust Deed which Simeon drew up is characteristic of him. All his trustees, and those who succeeded him, were to be careful to elect 'no one who is not a truly pious and devoted man, a man of God in deed and truth, who, in his piety, combines a solid judgment and a perfectly independent mind'. On no account must they 'be influenced by any solicitation of the great and the powerful, or by any partiality towards a particular individual, or by compassion towards anyone on account of the largeness of his family or the smallness of his income'. They must 'examine carefully, and judge before God, how far any person possesses the qualifications suited to the particular parish, and by that consideration alone they must be determined in their appointment of him'.[21]

Simeon's ministry in Cambridge continued for over fifty years and he came to achieve a unique position in the Church of England. Lord Macaulay was at Cambridge in Simeon's later years and wrote in a letter to his sister, 'If you knew what his authority and influence were and how they extended from Cambridge to the remote corners of England, you would allow that his [Simeon's] real sway in the church was far greater than that of any Primate.'[22] Even in the twentieth century, a Cambridge undergraduate who was an earnest Christian was known as a 'Sim'.

Simeon's influence on John Stott

John Stott told me that he had been introduced to the Simeon story when he was himself an undergraduate at Cambridge. He read the biographies of Simeon by Carus (1842) and Moule (1892) and Simeon has always been one of his heroes. Two aspects of Simeon's life impressed Stott: first, his expository biblical preaching; and second, his emphasis on the truth not being at one extreme or at the opposite extreme or in a confused admixture. The truth, said Simeon, is at both extremes even if you cannot reconcile these extremes. This thought has been helpful to Stott in the controversy between divine sovereignty and human responsibility.

PART THREE

Church on fire
in the New World

North America, 1730–1900

We went through fire and water,
but you brought us to a place of abundance.
(Psalm 66:12)

EARLY CHRISTIANITY IN THE COLONIES

In 1606 James I granted a charter to the Virginia Company, a group of English merchants who, the following year, founded a successful colony in Jamestown – the first permanent English settlement in America. In May 1607 the settlers joined the Rev. Robert Hunt in a service of Holy Communion.

Religious observances such as this were common during the critical moments of the colony's early history. When a new governor arrived in 1610, as the colony teetered on the brink of collapse, one of the first things he did was to organise a worship service in order to issue a call for sacrifice and industry. Virginia's earliest legal code made attendance at Sunday services compulsory and contained harsh reprisals against violations of the Sabbath, adultery, extravagant dress, and other moral lapses.

In the Virginia Company's charter, the King had included instructions for propagating the 'Christian religion to such people as yet live in darkness and miserable ignorance of true knowledge and worship of God'. In 1611 the Rev. Alexander Whitaker went to Virginia to serve as chaplain to the Governor and minister to the settlers. Whitaker helped to steer the colony's religion towards low-church Anglicanism.

From the beginning, the Church of England was established by law as the official church of Virginia. When the Civil War broke out in England in the 1640s, Virginia sided with the King and the bishops against Parliament and the Puritans. Such Puritanism as the first colonists in Virginia practised existed firmly within the framework of the established Church. In this they contrasted with the thirty-five or so 'Pilgrim Fathers' who settled in Plymouth, Massachusetts, in 1620: these were Puritans who had less patience with the Church of England.

By the middle of the eighteenth century the coastal region between the Appalachians and the sea was colonised by British,

Dutch, Swedish and German settlers. Many early colonists were Puritans, but there were also middle-of-the-road Anglicans, Lutherans, Roman Catholics, Baptists, Presbyterians, Congregationalists, Quakers and Jews.

DEVEREUX JARRATT

Devereux Jarratt (1733–1801) was a parish priest of the Church of England in Virginia (known after independence as the Episcopal Church) from 1763 until his death. During his lifetime the religious scene in Virginia changed from one dominated by the established Church of England into a landscape where Methodists, Presbyterians, Baptists and other Evangelical denominations threatened to wipe the now disestablished Episcopal Church from the territory altogether.

Jarratt was born on 6 January 1733 in New Kent County, Virginia, about twenty-five miles south-east of Richmond, the present state capital. The area was a mixture of agricultural and swamp lands. Although his parents were not particularly religious, they were members of the Church of England, and taught him to repeat a whole chapter of the Bible before he learnt the letters of the alphabet. By the time he was thirteen, both his parents had died and he was looked after by an elder brother.

The parish church, about three miles from where he lived in New Kent County, was well attended, but Jarratt only went occasionally. The clergyman was known as a poor preacher with weak eyesight, who preached from a text written out verbatim and 'kept his eyes continually fixed on the paper, and so near, that what he said seemed rather addressed to the cushion than to the congregation. Except at a time when he might have a quarrel with anybody – then he would straighten up, and speak lustily, that all might distinctly hear.'[1]

When he was nineteen Jarratt left New Kent County to take up the post of schoolmaster in Albemarle County, about a hundred miles to the north-west, on the edge of the Appalachian Mountains. He set off carrying all his luggage on his back and taking a pair of coarse breeches, a couple of shirts, a pair of shoes and socks, an old felt hat and a bearskin coat.

Whitefield's early influence in Virginia

After two or three days, Jarratt arrived at the home of his new employer, Jacob Moon. Albemarle was virtually a frontier county and there was no church in the area. Someone did, however, show him a book of George Whitefield's sermons.

Whitefield preached the need to be 'born again' – you had to 'feel your sins', repent, believe in Jesus Christ, and experience a new birth to be saved. He attacked formalism, spiritual deadness, and salvation by works – all characteristics which many associated with the Church of England. By the early 1840s Anglican ministers in Philadelphia, Charleston, New York and Boston had refused Whitefield access to their pulpits, closed their churches to his meetings, and had written bitter attacks criticising him and his message. Probably no single American group rejected him more angrily than his fellow Anglican clergy.

The Church of England clergy in the colonies criticised Whitefield for implying that 'in the work of regeneration, we are wholly and absolutely passive'. According to his Anglican critics, Whitefield preached that no act of moral or religious duty, no sacrament, and no obedience to religious ritual could encourage or instil salvation. They argued that this was not the doctrine of the Church of England. For them, conversion was not something which happened suddenly: it came about gradually as a man or woman co-operated with the Holy Spirit who led them through a process which involved reason, faith, good works and habits of piety.

For most Anglican ministers, Whitefield's 'new birth' meant enthusiasm and enthusiasm led to social disruption and sectarianism. In spite of Whitefield's impeccable Church of England credentials, most Anglican colonial leaders found his brand of religious revivalism alien to their tradition.

The term 'Great Awakening' came to be used by historians to describe a wave of religious revivals that peaked in many of the colonies in the years 1740–62. These revivals marked the beginning of popular Evangelicalism in the American churches.

On his preaching tours George Whitefield eclipsed local ministers in captivating the crowds who flocked to hear the Englishman preach in stirring terms about the new birth. Devereux Jarratt's employer told him that Whitefield was 'New Light'. By this he meant the new revivalist party of which the Northampton Congregationalist preacher Jonathan Edwards (1703–58) emerged as the main champion.

Life with the Cannons

Jarratt moved to the home of a wealthy man named John Cannon, who owned a large estate with many slaves. Mrs Cannon was New Light – rigid and severe, having no truck with levity of any kind. The slightest hint of ungodliness would be met with a stern rebuke.

When he arrived at the Cannons on a Sunday afternoon, Mrs Cannon told him that she read sermons aloud every evening and invited him to come and listen. Jarratt accepted and pretended to listen very carefully to what she read. He described the sermons as 'experimental and Evangelical'. Gradually the sermons began to have their effect and he resolved to abandon sin and try to save his soul. 'But my resolution', he wrote, 'was made in my own strength, for I had not yet learned how weak and frail we are by nature, and that all our sufficiency is of God.'

Jarratt was the first person Mrs Cannon had come across actually to be affected by what she thought of as 'vital religion'. She persuaded him to stay on with them; and so he came to spend a year at the Cannons' house, listening to sermons in the evenings and teaching at a nearby school by day, taking the two little girls of the family with him on horseback.

At the end of a year with the Cannons, Jarratt returned to working for Jacob Moon and began teaching at a school with twelve or thirteen pupils at twenty shillings a scholar. When he began to talk to the Moons about religion, they made light of what he said.

'That's all New Light cant,' they told him. 'You've caught it from Mrs Cannon! *We're* Church people and can listen to nothing except that which comes through that channel.'

'Unless we repent,' Jarratt told them, 'we shall perish. Except a man be born again, he cannot see the Kingdom of God.'

'We must all be born again,' the Moons replied, 'but that is to be after we are dead.'

Jarratt accepted a new, better paid position with the Cannons to teach their son. He found that Mrs Cannon was just as religious as before. At the same time, a Presbyterian minister arrived in the county of Cumberland to the south of Albemarle and began to visit a venue near the Cannons to preach once a month. The man was not a good preacher, but Jarratt never missed his sermons and had some long conversations with him. The Presbyterian also introduced him to the works of a number of English Christian writers, including Richard Baxter and Philip Doddridge (1702–51) as well as to the hymns of Isaac Watts (1674–1748). Jarratt now attended church regularly, tried to live morally, and was considered a Christian by all who knew him.

Heaven arrives on earth

Jarratt's Evangelical conversion occurred at some point in the 1750s while, as a young man in his mid-twenties, he was living with the Cannons. The episode was similar to John Wesley's in the sense that observers of both men considered them good Christians before the crisis came; and the actual experience seems to have been characterised by a transition from doubt to joyful assurance. There is no evidence that Jarratt had at this time read the details of Wesley's Aldersgate experience which had occurred fifteen or so years earlier. He described his own experience like this:

I was blessed with faith to believe, not one promise only, but all the promises of the gospel with joy unspeakable and full of glory. I saw a fullness of Christ to save to the uttermost, that, had I ten thousand souls as wretched and guilty as mine was, I could venture all on his blood and righteousness without one doubt or fear . . . Not that I suppose I never had true religion before this – I believe I had true religion, or I could not have gone through so many trials – but such a bright manifestation of the redeemer's all-sufficiency and willingness to save, and such a divine confidence to rely on, I never had till that moment – it was a delightful little heaven on earth – so sweet, so ravishing, so delightful, I uttered not a word, but silently rejoiced in God my Saviour.[2]

Friends now tried to persuade Jarratt to enter the ministry. But he knew that Presbyterians required their ministers-in-training to learn Latin and Greek. So a few men, including John Cannon, clubbed together to subsidise his education.

Until about this time, Jarratt had lived and moved entirely among Presbyterians. He had acquired a prejudice against the Church of England on account of what he had heard and experienced of the clergy's cold and uninspiring style of preaching. And he did not care for the idea of set public prayer. But as he began to read more widely, his ideas grew less certain.

English Evangelical books reach Virginia

Hervey became Jarratt's favourite author. James Hervey, of Lincoln College, Oxford, had been a member of the Wesleys' Holy Club. Dismissed from a curacy in Bideford, Devon, because of his views, in 1752 he became Rector of the first Evangelical parish in the Midlands – the village of Weston Favell, near Northampton. His first book went through twenty editions and copies quickly found their way across the Atlantic and captured Jarratt's imagination.

He learned that Wesley and Whitefield were members of the Church of England. And so he came to feel that a man could be as useful for God in the Church of England as in any other denomination – perhaps more so.

He had never examined the *Book of Common Prayer* in detail, but had previously read a few short extracts which he had been told were objectionable. Now, however, on further reflection, and on reading the whole book, he decided that on the whole it contained an excellent system of doctrine and public worship.

He began to think of the Church of England as 'no way inferior to the Presbyterian'. If he prepared for ordination in the Church of

England, however, he would incur the expense and danger of a perilous voyage to England at a time when the country was at war with France. Which way should he go?

Jarratt becomes C of E

In the spring of 1762, at the age of twenty-nine, Jarratt began to prepare for ordination in the Church of England. He obtained a title to a parish, and visited both the Governor of Virginia and the Bishop of London's Commissary in the colony. These two granted him the papers he needed to take to the Bishop of London.

One of his brothers had died, leaving him about three hundred acres of land. He sold this to help finance the necessary visit to England.

Trials at sea

In October 1762 Jarratt boarded the *Everton*, bound for England. As a temporary peace with France was not signed until the following year, the *Everton* headed out into the Atlantic well armed with fourteen carriage guns, swivelling guns, muskets and weapons for close-quarter fighting.

They enjoyed a smooth and uneventful voyage across the Atlantic, eventually sighting land off the north coast of Ireland and then sailing south-east through the North Channel between Mull of Kintyre and Fair Head. Close to Llandudno on the north coast of Wales, with the weather deteriorating, they took a pilot aboard who agreed with the crew that it would be impossible to reach the port of Liverpool in the storm and that they would head south-west and try to reach shelter in Beaumaris harbour. Beaumaris lies on the south-east coast of the Isle of Anglesey, looking across the Menai Strait to the mountains of North Wales.

As they edged their way towards Beaumaris in the storm it seemed as if the *Everton* was going to be driven on to the rocks. The captain pushed the helmsman from his post and took to steering the ship himself.

At about nine or ten in the morning, the pilot ran the ship aground on Lavan Sands opposite Beaumaris.

'There's nothing we can do', the captain announced, 'until the tide rises in six hours or so. I shall lower the yawl and we'll row to Beaumaris to regale ourselves on fresh provisions.'

Aboard the little boat, the captain, Jarratt, a few passengers and crew members slipped across the narrow Menai Strait into Beaumaris harbour. It was Devereux Jarratt's first proper sight of Britain. He looked up at the curiously truncated towers of Beaumaris Castle, begun at the end of the thirteenth century by Edward I, but never finished.

The town of Beaumaris seemed to him to be totally delightful and, he recalled, 'the inhabitants looked so fresh and ruddy, that I thought no people in the world could live better than the Welsh'. He looked back across the water to the mainland of Wales where the tops of the mountains were hidden in cloud, and the visible parts blanketed in snow. It was the most majestic view he had ever seen.

In Beaumaris, they bought fresh food, including meat and butter, which they ate in the town. Jarratt said the food was better than anything he had tasted all his life.

Aboard the *Everton* again, the tide rose but the ship remained firmly stuck on the sand, badly battered by the waves. They were carrying a cargo of over five hundred hogshead of best Virginian tobacco and even when the tide reached its highest point the *Everton* refused to budge.

On the Friday morning they tied long ropes to the bow of the *Everton* and secured the other ends to the stern of the yawl and the long boat. The captain selected strong oarsmen from the crew to man the two smaller boats. As the tide reached its highest point, at an order from the captain, the men began to row with all their strength. Within about five minutes the ship slipped slowly forward into the deeper water of the Menai Strait.

Now, as they edged their way out into Conwy Bay bound for Liverpool, they discovered to their dismay that the pilot had been drinking. When the captain suggested to the pilot that he was in no fit state to steer a ship, a furious row broke out and the pilot shouted, 'If your ship sinks to hell, I won't lift a hand or say a word to prevent it!'

Captain and crew were strangers to the coast of North Wales and knew only that the coastline looked rocky. The captain began first to shake all over and then to cry. The rest of the crew tried to steer the *Everton* as best they could.

Then the rudder broke, the ship turned right round and began to drift helplessly in the wind. Eventually the crew managed to repair the rudder. But they now had no one, pilot or captain, to direct them and no knowledge of a safe route to Liverpool.

The diplomat

Jarratt left the passenger cabin to look for the pilot. He found him sitting alone.

'I beg you to come and take charge of the ship,' Jarratt said.

'I will not!' the pilot replied firmly. 'I have been maltreated by the captain and cannot submit to his insults.'

'Perhaps in the heat of the moment', said Jarratt, 'the captain may have spoken improperly. But you should not on that account allow your resentment to go as far as putting this ship, its cargo, and perhaps the lives of its passengers and crew, in danger. Surely neither the passengers nor the rest of the crew have offended you? I must add that your own welfare and your family's may depend on how you conduct yourself in the next few hours.'

After a while, Jarratt succeeded in calming the pilot.

'Alright,' he said at last. 'I will take charge of the ship and bring her safely into port.'

The pilot was as good as his word, and despite running into a strong headwind, he navigated the *Everton* to within eight miles of Liverpool where they dropped anchor. From here, the captain and passengers boarded the small boat and went ashore.

Jarratt in England

On the Sunday morning they hired horses and rode into Liverpool as the sound of church bells was ringing out across the River Mersey. Entering the first church they came to, Jarratt was intrigued to experience his first Church of England service in the mother country. 'It was an elegant building,' he recalled, 'large and roomy, and crowded with hearers. The minister that preached made a noble appearance being full dressed in all his canonicals. But his sermon was as empty as his dress was full. It was merely historical; and nearly of the same cast were all the sermons I heard in that town.'

Jarratt travelled by stagecoach to London where he visited the Bishop of London and presented his papers to him. Bishop Richard Osbaldeston referred him to his chaplain for examination for ordination.

Jarratt was ordained deacon in the King's Chapel at Christmas 1762 after four weeks in London. Several men were ordained on the same day, all English except Jarratt, and all educated either at Oxford or Cambridge. On the afternoon of the ordinations, Bishop Osbaldeston received the new deacons and Jarratt always recalled his remarks with pride.

'I have never been so well pleased', the bishop said, 'with any ordination before. Your performances at your examinations were all well done.'

Then, looking at Jarratt, the bishop concluded, 'I am especially pleased with yours from Virginia.'

Just a week after being ordained deacon by the Bishop of London, Jarratt was ordained priest by the Bishop of Chester, Edmund Keene.

By early January 1763, Jarratt was ready to return to Virginia. But, as the River Thames was frozen solid, no ships would be likely to sail for several weeks. During this enforced stay in London, Jarratt preached in a number of churches. His manner, and the content of his sermons, suggested to his congregations that Jarratt was a Methodist. Evidently his experience of the Great Awakening had affected his style.

While in London Jarratt heard both Wesley and Whitefield preach, plus one of Whitefield's lay preachers, but was not carried away with enthusiasm. 'I got little edification from either of the three,' he commented, 'though the two first spoke well, and to the purpose.'

Before the ice thawed, at the end of February, Jarratt contracted smallpox. The fever lasted for five or six weeks, but by April Jarratt was fully fit again. Eventually he took a stagecoach to Liverpool and booked a passage home. They sailed on the last day of April and eventually dropped anchor in Yorktown, Virginia, on the first Sunday in July 1763. Jarratt had been away for nine months. Now he faced the task of finding a parish.

A parish in Dinwiddie County

His search took him to the parish of Bath in Dinwiddie County, Virginia, south of Petersburg, thirty miles or so from where he was born and brought up. He arrived in late August with a short note from a friend recommending him. He was invited to stay with a member of the church's vestry (the equivalent to an English Parochial Church Council). The parish had three churches, at Butterwood, Hatcher's Run and Saponey.

Jarratt got on well with his host and it was arranged that he should preach at the church in Butterwood on his first Sunday. Word quickly spread and there was a full church.

The following Thursday had been designated by the Virginian authorities as a day to celebrate the Peace of Paris which ended the Seven Years' War between England and France. Large congregations turned out to hear Jarratt preach and he appears to have acquitted himself well. The vestry met on the Monday evening following his third service.

The verdict was unanimous and the chairman instructed the clerk to record that the Rev. Devereux Jarratt was received as minister of Bath parish on 29 August 1763. Jarratt was now thirty-one.

He begins his ministry in Bath parish

Devereux Jarratt was a little less than middle height but with what contemporaries described as a 'manly appearance'. He was corpulent but active, blessed with an unusually retentive memory, good judgment and a strikingly powerful voice. He was in his element at a reading desk or in a pulpit.

A long letter he wrote over thirty years later to his friend the Rev. John Coleman is very revealing in what it tells us about Jarratt's attitude to his new parishioners, his theology at this time, and the reasons for the tensions that developed.

He told Coleman that for about nine months before his arrival Bath parish had had no settled pastor, but the churches had been supplied by neighbouring clergy. He goes on to give his assessment of the shortcomings of his predecessors: 'I found the principles of the Gospel – the nature and condition of man – the plan of salvation through Christ – and the nature and necessity of spiritual regeneration, as little known and thought of, as if the people had never attended a church or heard a sermon in their lives. Yet, as it appeared, they thought themselves a wise and understanding people, and as religious, as was necessary, or their Maker required them to be.'[3]

Jarratt was unshakeable in his conviction that the doctrines, as he understood them, of the eighteenth-century religious revival were correct, and that the attitudes and presuppositions of conventional churchgoers of the time were wrong. He goes on to tell us: 'Such being the state of things, every well informed mind will readily conceive, in a measure, the difficulties I had to encounter. I had to encounter gross ignorance of divine things, combined with conceited wisdom and moral rectitude.'[4]

Jarratt felt that his congregation in Bath parish could not bear to hear 'the self-abasing doctrines of free grace' which, he says, he tried to preach in 'a close, plain, searching, pungent, animated manner'. He thought they found it 'too mortifying for human pride to bear'; and however much they had approved of him at first, they now wished they had never seen him.[5]

When Jarratt told his flock to observe this or abstain from that, he would be asked: 'Why didn't other ministers tell us that? Were they not as learned as you?'

At the start of his work in Bath parish, Jarratt saw himself as isolated – a man standing alone. 'I was opposed,' he wrote, 'and reproached by the clergy – called an enthusiast, fanatic, visionary, dissenter, Presbyterian, madman, and what not.'

He would not be put off. He was utterly convinced of the importance of what he was preaching. No opposition would daunt his spirit. He refused to preach cosy sermons or flatter his congregations.

Despite his doubts about the doctrines of predestination and election, he appears to have preached a gospel which had strong elements of Calvinism in it which he combined with a Wesleyan strand of perfectionism. Describing his approach to preaching, he said that he 'judged it necessary to adopt that method of preaching which might have the most direct tendency to make sinners feel their situation and be sensible of their guilt and helplessness. Nothing short of this will properly turn the attention of the human race to the invitations of the Gospel, and render a Saviour precious to their souls.'[6]

So he preached the doctrine of original sin. In Jarratt's view, the words *virtue* or *moral virtue* were simply cant terms used by 'velvet-mouthed preachers'. In fact he refused ever to use the word 'virtue' in his preaching. Instead of advising his listeners, in the cool, dispassionate manner of contemporary Anglican preachers, to 'walk in the primrose paths of decided, sublime and elevated virtue', he aimed to expose in vivid and alarming colours the guilt of sin, 'the entire depravity of human nature – the awful danger mankind are in by nature and practice'.

Jarratt's method of preaching was to convince his congregations of their sin; tell them that they could do nothing to save themselves; press them to 'fly to Jesus and rest on him for complete salvation'; and exhort those who believed to be careful to maintain good works, and go on to perfection. In the words of the apostle Paul, his aim was that they should cleanse themselves 'from all filthiness of the flesh and spirit, perfecting holiness in the fear of God' (2 Cor. 7:1 AV).

Jarratt's energy cannot be faulted. He refused to confine himself to working in the three churches in his parish and simply preaching in their pulpits. He began to visit people in their homes regularly and arrange meetings in private houses for prayer, singing, preaching and conversation. He thought the meetings in homes did more good than services in the churches. He allowed his people to ask him questions and air their doubts in these home meetings. He also used to put questions to them to gain their concentration and impress on them how much they needed to learn. It was a little like a catechism class except that he did not tell them the answers until the end of the exercise.[7]

News of Jarratt's style of preaching and energetic work outside his churches spread to neighbouring parishes and counties. People now travelled considerable distances to hear him preach and his churches began to be crowded. The number of conversions grew.

Jarratt arranged for the building of two large extensions to the Butterwood church. Recalling these days many years later, he wrote, 'It gives me pleasure now to review those happy times, and the many precious and reviving seasons, when the Spirit was poured out from on high, and such a number of souls was gathered into the field of the Great Shepherd.'

Then, in response to requests, Jarratt began to travel beyond the boundaries of his parish into an area of five or six hundred miles, east, west, north and south.

Most of the clergy were still opposed to him and unwilling to allow him to preach in their churches. So, like Wesley and White-field, he began to preach in the open air. Crowds at these meetings grew large too. To the south, Jarratt now travelled into North Carolina to preach over a wide area, as well as many counties in Virginia.

Jarratt began to preach the importance of Holy Communion. By the early 1770s, between nine hundred and a thousand people were celebrating the Lord's Supper in his three churches, including those who attended regularly from neighbouring parishes. These large numbers attended despite Jarratt's practice of 'fencing the table': by this he meant 'laying down as clearly as I could the marks and characters of such as were invited, and such as were not, and pointing out the danger of unworthy receiving'.

The celebration of Holy Communion in Bath parish gave Devereux Jarratt genuine pleasure:

To see so many hundreds convened from different quarters joining devoutly in the divine service; to see them singing the praises of their God and common Saviour, lustily, and with one heart and voice – to see them listening to the word preached, with attention still as night – eagerly drinking in the balmy blessings of the gospel, dispensed by the instrumentality of one whom they esteemed their pastor, their teacher, their guide, their father, and their friend – sweetly communing with me and one another, and myself with all. O, it was a little heaven upon earth – prelibation of celestial joys.[8]

But sadly for Jarratt these days of heaven on earth were not to last.

The Baptists come to Virginia . . .

Roger Williams (1603–83) had established the first Baptist church in America soon after settling in Providence, Rhode Island, in 1639. Throughout the seventeenth century the Baptists had remained weak. In 1707, however, five churches in New Jersey, Delaware and Pennsylvania had united to form the Philadelphia Baptist Association. By 1760 the association extended from Connecticut to Virginia. By 1769 the Baptists had begun to make converts in Amelia, a county immediately to the north-west of Dinwiddie.

Naturally, the Baptists preached the importance of adult baptism by immersion and this caused tension and disputes with members of the Church of England, shaking the faith of some. Gradually the Baptists began to take on recruits, including from among church people. As they made inroads into Dinwiddie county, Jarratt reported that very few from his parish joined the Baptists. But the development was divisive and it lowered his morale and that of his congregations.

Jarratt's reaction to the arrival of the Baptists is interesting. Over twenty years later he recalled:

As far as I can judge, I have, at least for thirty years, possessed a truly catholic spirit. I was bigoted to no party whatever . . . My wish was that souls might be saved, and was willing the Lord should choose his own instruments for that purpose. But it was grievous to me to behold the unity of brethren destroyed, and especially by such notions as I was and am fully persuaded were nothing but notions, and answered no other end but a bad one – I mean the destruction of love and peace which Christianity is designed to promote.

I endeavoured to act prudently and inoffensively and by lenient methods. I prevented this notion of going into the water, and its evil train of consequences, from breaking into my parish. But I could not prevent its spreading to other counties where I used sometimes to preach. In these counties many were disunited and the peace of neighbourhoods destroyed. I did what I could to prevent this evil, but it was too much for any one man to do.[9]

... and then the Methodists

Less than thirty years after John Wesley's Aldersgate experience, the first Methodist congregations in America began to meet in New York and Virginia in the 1760s. The first Methodist preacher Jarratt came across in Virginia was Robert Williams, and he took to him as 'a plain, simple-hearted, pious man'. In about 1772 Williams visited Jarratt in his home in Bath and stayed with him for almost a week, preaching several sermons in the parish. On the whole, Jarratt liked his preaching, 'especially the affectionate animated manner in which his discourses were delivered'.

'Methodists are true members of the Church of England,' Williams told Jarratt. 'Their intention is to build up and not to divide the Church. Methodist preachers do not assume the office of priests. They administer neither the ordinance of baptism nor the Lord's Supper, but look to parish ministers in all places to do this. Their task is to call sinners to repentance; to encourage converts to join together to build one another up and to work for spiritual improvement.'

'He who leaves the Church,' Williams added, 'leaves the Methodists.'

All this impressed Jarratt and he grew to like Williams. He warmly welcomed Methodist preachers to his home and parish. When people expressed fears to Jarratt that the growth of Methodism would divide the Church of England, he would reply that he believed the Methodists were sincere in their attachment to the Church.

Methodist societies began to be established all across Virginia, and preachers were appointed to take charge of them. Later in his life, Jarratt looked back and wondered whether he had been mistaken in encouraging the Methodists in the way he did.

Independence, and Anglicanism in crisis

To the north, in April 1775, the first shots of the American War of Independence were fired at Lexington, Massachusetts. In August, King George III proclaimed that the Americans were rebels.

Just a few hundred miles to the north-east of Virginia, on 4 July 1776, the Continental Congress met in Independence Hall, Philadelphia. It adopted the famous Declaration of Independence which proclaimed the thirteen original colonies of America 'free and independent states'. Thomas Jefferson had prepared the first draft, which explained in short sentences and simple but eloquent words the American complaints against George III. The document described the kind of republic the Congress wanted to establish in America. It rested on the belief that 'all men are created equal' and that governments exist to guarantee 'life, liberty and the pursuit of happiness'.

The colonies celebrated with bonfires, drums beating, fifes playing, guns firing, bells ringing and cannon booming. Congress made General George Washington Commander-in-Chief of the American army.

The Declaration of Independence put the Anglican churches in America in crisis. The Church of England had been the established Church in most colonies and was associated with loyalty to colonial governors and the English crown. In Virginia, all Anglican ministers were deprived of their livings, and many churches were put to secular uses. Baptismal fonts were turned into cattle troughs.

In the midst of the upheaval (in 1780) Jarratt wrote of his continued love for the Church of England:

I dearly love the Church. I love her on many accounts – particularly for the following: I love her because her mode of worship is so beautiful and decent, so well calculated to inspire devotion, and so complete in all parts of public worship. I love her because of the soundness of her doctrines, creeds and articles, etc. I love her because all her officers, and the modes of ordaining them are, if I mistake not, truly primitive and apostolic. Bishops, priests and deacons were, in my opinion, distinct orders in the church, in her earliest and purest ages. These three particulars, a regular clergy, sound doctrine, and a decent comprehensive worship contain the essentials, I think, of a Christian church. And as these three are in the possession of the old Church, I have been, and still am, inclined to give her the preference.[10]

The end of the war came suddenly in 1781 in Virginia itself, when the British General Cornwallis surrendered to an army of French and American troops commanded by Washington at Yorktown. In 1783 Britain signed the Treaty of Paris which gave the colonies their independence.

The Methodists go their own way

John Wesley had drawn up a list of twelve reasons why American Methodists should not leave the Church of England. One of his reasons was that to leave would be 'throwing balls of wild-fire among them that are now quiet in the land'. Leaving would bring about 'inconceivable strife and contention between those who left and those who remained in the church'. Wesley claimed to believe that God had sent all Methodist preachers to what he called 'the lost sheep of the Church of England'. Would it not, he asked, be 'a flat contradiction of this design to separate from the Church?'

However, in 1784, at a meeting in Baltimore on 24 December, the 'Christmas Conference' recognised Thomas Coke and Francis Asbury as the first independent leaders of Methodism in America. The conference made a commitment to John Wesley's ideal of spreading scriptural holiness.

This decision by the Methodist leadership in America to abandon Wesley's original intention of using the societies to revive Anglicanism and instead to form an independent Methodist Church shattered Jarratt. He turned bitter.

The Methodists are a designing people, void of the generous and catholic spirit of the Gospel – and so entirely under the influence of Pope John [Wesley] – and countenance so many illiterate creatures void of prudence and discretion that I have no expectation of any good and lasting effects from their misguided zeal. Their professed adherence to the Church is amazingly preposterous and disingenuous and nothing but policy either in England or here.[11]

Sadly, he was vilified by many of his former friends in the Methodist movement.

Formation of the Protestant Episcopal Church

Before the American Revolution, there were no bishops in the colonies (partly because the British government was reluctant to give the colonies the kind of autonomy that this would have implied, and partly because many of the colonists were violently opposed to their presence). After the Revolution, the establishment of an American episcopate was essential. A group of Connecticut clergy attempted to secure the consecration of Samuel Seabury (1729–96) as bishop for their diocese and the first American bishop. After failing to gain consecration in England, Seabury was consecrated in 1784 by Scottish 'Nonjuring' bishops.

In 1786 the Consecration of Bishops Abroad Act made possible the consecration in England of bishops for dioceses in other parts of the world. In 1787 William White and Samuel Provoost, having been elected to the bishoprics of Pennsylvania and New York respectively, sailed to England and were consecrated bishops.

William White

William White (1748–1836) was born in Philadelphia, went to England in 1770 to be ordained deacon and priest, returned in 1772 and became first an assistant and then the Rector of the Church of Christ and Saint Peter in Philadelphia. He served as Chaplain of the Continental Congress from 1777 to 1789, and then as Chaplain of the Senate.

In the years following independence, White played the dominant role in guiding and inspiring the scattered Anglican parishes of the thirteen colonies to unite in a national Church. He is often called the Father of the Episcopal Church. He was largely responsible for the Constitution of the Protestant Episcopal Church in the USA ([P]ECUSA). Under his direction, the system of Church government was established more or less as it exists today. National business is conducted by the General Convention, which meets every three years and consists for voting purposes of three Houses: Bishops, Clerical Deputies and Lay Deputies. A majority of each is required to pass a measure.

Samuel Seabury had been an outspoken loyalist during the Revolution and struggled to make the American Church as Anglican as possible. High-church Connecticut Episcopalians, led by Seabury – who favoured a strong episcopacy, clerical control of the Church, and a theology emphasising sacramentalism and apostolic succession – contrasted with lower-church Episcopalians in the middle and southern states.

The first General Convention met in Philadelphia in 1785 and took preliminary steps towards the establishment of a duly recognised denomination. With the episcopal succession secured, the Episcopal Church in the United States formed itself into an autonomous body in full communion with the Archbishop of Canterbury. The General Convention in 1789 produced its own revision of the *Book of Common Prayer*. In the same year George Washington became the first President of the United States of America.

Soon after peace between Britain and America was concluded the Virginian state assembly incorporated the Protestant Episcopal Church by law. The Church called a convention at Richmond to devise rules for its government. Jarratt attended – but as an Evangelical who had also welcomed the Methodists to his area he was received coolly.

In 1790 James Madison, president of the College of William and Mary and cousin of a later President of the United States, was elected first Bishop of the Episcopal Church of Virginia. Madison shared certain beliefs of the Evangelicals and in 1792 he invited Jarratt to deliver the keynote sermon to the annual conference of the diocese at Williamsburg. Jarratt accepted the invitation and advised the conference delegates to 'take heed to yourselves'. He drew a contrast between ministers 'grave in their deportment, strict and holy in their lives, warm and animated in their preaching, and diligent and laborious in their vocations' with clergy who were 'cold and languid, slothful and vicious'.

Following the 1792 convention Jarratt became even more isolated when he broke with his initially sympathetic bishop. As part of an effort to fill vacant parishes, Bishop Madison travelled to Petersburg for an ordination service. Jarratt had previously examined the candidates as to their suitability for holy orders and voted against two young men, only to find himself outvoted. Unwilling to watch Madison ordain the two men – even if he could not avoid hearing his voice – Jarratt sat in a corner pew throughout the service with a handkerchief covering his face. He never attended another convention of his Church.

Jarratt and the Virginian church in decline

Burdened from 1794 by a painful, malignant tumour on the side of his face, the ageing Jarratt gradually withdrew from evangelism and society, though still preaching on Sundays. His personal decline mirrored the decline of the Episcopal Church in Virginia.

He attributed the decline in attendance at Episcopal churches partly to 'the machinations of the Methodists' and partly to a general increase in godlessness: 'The morals of mankind have become so corrupt, and their rage for sensual and unlimited gratification so great, that they would gladly seize on any pretext for casting off the restraints of the Bible.'

Jarratt died from cancer on 29 January 1801, aged sixty-nine, bearing great pain courageously. He had served faithfully for almost forty years in the parish ministry in Virginia. A good and loyal friend to people with whom he agreed, he seems to have been a loving husband (though he rarely mentioned his wife in his journals), a conscientious pastor, and an indefatigable preacher, taking the gospel to almost thirty counties in Virginia and North Carolina.

Bath Parish still exists and according to its 'parish profile' now consists of two churches and a shrine: 'Calvary in Dinwiddie, Good Shepherd near McKenney, and Sapony Shrine'. It seems that 'Sapony Shrine' is the former Sapony Church, but services are only held there now on the fifth Sunday of the month. The other two churches seem unlikely to be the ones known in Jarratt's day. There is, however, a statue of Jarratt in one of the parish towns.

JOSEPH PILMORE

Joseph Pilmore (1734–1825), in many ways the successor to Devereux Jarratt, illustrates the strong links between the eighteenth-century Evangelical revival in England and the strength of Evangelicalism in the nineteenth-century American Episcopal Church. Pilmore was a one-time lay preacher among the English Methodists. His parents had been members of the Church of England and he had been commissioned by Wesley as an itinerant lay preacher.

After some years spent preaching in America, he returned to England during the War of Independence. At the end of the war, he went back to America and applied to Bishop Seabury for Holy Orders.

'Mr Pilmore, I have heard a good account of you,' Seabury replied, 'and will ordain you with pleasure.'

Ordained deacon on 27 November 1785, and priested three days later, he became Rector of Christ Church, New York City. Ten years later he returned to Philadelphia, where he had worked in the 1770s, as Rector of St Paul's Church. He soon had a church of seven hundred communicants.

'His soul would be all on fire'

Describing his preaching, a member of Joseph Pilmore's congregation referred to his Evangelical fervour and simplicity. 'He never wandered far away from the cross. He spoke of the character and work of Christ and the grace of the Holy Spirit.' He was interested in practical Christian living. He preached from short notes, beginning with little animation and then gradually warmed to his theme. 'You would see his eyes begin to kindle and the muscles of his face move and expand, until at length his soul would be all on fire, and he would be rushing onward extemporaneously almost with the fury of a cataract.'[12]

James Milnor, later Rector of St George's Church, New York City, remembered hearing Pilmore preach at St Paul's Church, Philadelphia. Milnor was happy with the evangelical style of Pilmore's preaching, because, as he wrote:

he allies with it, and makes it auxiliary to the inculcation of morals; and he sets forth the atonement of the Saviour, in the general way in which it is viewed by most Christians, without proposing the perplexing intricate and dark theology which the stricter Calvinists deduce from it. He enters on no critical disquisitions upon nice and disputable doctrinal points, but endeavours to fix the faith and the affections of his hearers upon the blessed redeemer, as the alone means of salvation.[13]

Pilmore died on 24 July 1825, aged ninety-one.

JOHN HENRY HOBART

The Great Awakening and the departure of Methodists from the Church had made American Episcopalians less tolerant of enthusiasm than ever and anxious to emphasise the freedom of the will and the value of human reason. So alongside Evangelicalism, which was strong in the American Episcopal Church in the middle years of the nineteenth century, came a high-church revival. The movement bore similarities to, and was to some extent influenced by, the Oxford Movement in England. Much of the revival revolved around the life and thought of John Henry Hobart (1775–1830) and his associates. It is one of the remarkable coincidences of history that the leader of the English Oxford Movement (Newman, b. 1801) should have had the same Christian names as the leader of the equivalent movement in America.

Hobart had been born in Philadelphia to an old Puritan family which had been Episcopalian for two generations. William White had ordained him to the diaconate in 1798 when he was a young man of only twenty-two. White gave him a list of books to help him in his study of theology. Through this list Hobart gained a window into the wide spectrum of Anglican thought, which included a rejection of Calvinism. Apart from the Evangelicals, most leading American Anglicans criticised Calvinism for its tendency towards fanaticism and for what they saw as its undermining of morality. But Hobart also recorded that White 'earnestly recommends me to study the Bible to form my opinions'. The only figure from the English Reformation which White included in the reading list was Richard Hooker.

In 1801 John Henry Hobart was ordained to the priesthood. He had inherited from his mother a fervent religion which gave to his preaching style an intensity that was unusual in American Episcopal preaching. Bad eyesight meant that he could not easily read his sermons and many found his freer style of preaching electrifying.

In his writings Hobart blended an appeal for emotional piety and a strong defence of elevated church doctrine. He stressed two principles: 'That we are saved from guilt and from dominion of sin, by the divine merits and grace of a crucified Redeemer', and that this merit and grace are only with certainty applied to the soul 'in the devout and humble participation of the ordinances of the church, administered by a priesthood who derive their authority by regular transmission from Christ'.[14]

Hobart was consecrated Bishop of the diocese of New York in 1811. For the nineteen years that he was bishop, Hobart directed and instructed the religious life of the New York church as well as a vast diocese which reached up to the Canadian border. He became a vigorous champion of the high-church vision of Episcopalianism, writing numerous tracts and books.

Differing views on salvation and holiness

In the nineteenth century, high-church writers addressed themselves to the question of the state of non-Episcopalians in the eyes of God. They raised the importance of the visible Church and claimed that through it alone God promised the covenant of salvation. Some of them argued that although non-Episcopalians could have no claim on these promised or covenanted mercies, they might still benefit from the general, or 'uncovenanted', mercies of God. This concept of 'uncovenanted mercies' was offensive to many and easily misunderstood. Evangelicals took small solace in the uncovenanted mercies offered to them and the phrase became a focus for Evangelical resentment of the ecclesiology of the high-church movement.

Hobart argued that he did share the basic *sola gratia* (only by grace) theology of the Reformers, agreeing that salvation could only be a gift from God. Even the greatest human endeavours, he wrote, 'can neither merit pardon for the past, nor procure favour for the future'. All grace had to be given by God through Christ, and it was God who freely pardoned and gave the sinner a righteous status. Yet Hobart was wary of what he saw as the 'faith alone' excesses of the Great Awakening and the apparent separating of faith from the effort he thought people ought to put into living a good life.

For Hobart, like Jeremy Taylor two hundred years earlier, justification was a persuasion of the truth of the promises of God. He made justifying faith more intellectual than the Evangelicals; it was no longer an emotion, but a truth to be accepted. The Hobartians, in line with the moralistic emphasis of seventeenth- and eighteenth-century Anglicanism, and also of the Oxford Movement, tied justification closely to the fruit it produced. The individual by an act of will, in co-operation with grace, concerned himself with good works, since true faith ought to lead to a spirit of humble reliance upon God. Playing down the passive aspect of justifying faith, and emphasising the link between love and action, 'faith formed by love', they did not talk in the same way about conversion.

For Hobart the new birth came via the sacrament of Baptism. 'In a certain sense', he wrote, 'every baptised person undergoes a change of spiritual condition – is born again.'

American Bible Societies

By 1816 more than one hundred Bible Societies had been organised in the United States. They met for a convention and established the

American Bible Society (ABS). Hobart tried to distance the New York Episcopal Church from it. Bishop William White, the first Presiding Bishop, had openly supported the interdenominational Philadelphia Bible Society and served as its first president. In praising it, White noted with approval that the Bibles 'shall be separated from all notes and commentaries whatsoever, and, except the contents of the chapters, shall contain nothing but the sacred text. It is therefore manifestly a design in which all denominations of Christians, without exception, may unite.'[15]

Hobart, however, strongly urged New York Episcopalians to support the Episcopalian Bible and Common Prayer Book Society rather than the ABS. Bible Society controversy entailed eight years of sporadic pamphlet warfare. Hobart disliked the idea of separating the Word of God from the Church of God. Some important Episcopalians disagreed with Hobart on this issue and continued to support the ABS. Others supported him.

The Episcopal Church during the years of the Hobart episcopate grew steadily in size and influence. There was also a growing number of Evangelicals in New York, including Milnor and McIlvaine (see pages 201 and 202–208).

ALEXANDER VIETS GRISWOLD

Alexander Griswold (1766–1843) was the first Evangelical Bishop of the American Episcopal Church. Confirmed by Bishop Seabury and ordained in 1795, he was, in 1810, elected Bishop of the Eastern Diocese – encompassing New Hampshire, Vermont, Massachusetts, Maine and Rhode Island.

When Griswold arrived in the diocese, there were fifteen clergymen in the five States; Vermont did not have a single church building, Massachusetts had thirteen, New Hampshire five, Rhode Island four, and Maine two.

In his first eighteen years he ordained 148 deacons and 111 priests, confirmed nearly ten thousand people and travelled twenty thousand miles – mostly by stagecoach. New England had never taken kindly to bishops, but Griswold was so earnest, faithful and humble that he gradually overcame the prejudice against the Church and his visitations became of special interest to the whole community.

His modesty impressed people. 'He's the best representative of an apostle that I have ever seen,' an elderly Congregationalist said of Griswold, 'particularly because he doesn't know it.'

He was a man of few words. Once, at dinner in his own house, Dr Stephen Higginson Tyng turned to him and said, 'Bishop, why don't you talk more?'

'I talked a great deal when I was young,' Griswold replied, 'and said a great many foolish things, but I have never been sorry for anything I have not said.'

Looking back on the early years of his ministry he wrote:

Adopting the practice of my brethren whom I thought wiser than myself, my preaching had been far too much on sectarian distinctions, and types of controversy, especially against High Calvinism and schismatics; and quite too frequently in defence of the distinctive principles of the Protestant Episcopal Church to the great neglect of the essential doctrines of Christ, and the necessary duties of Christians. This manner of preaching among our clergy very much strengthened the belief among other denominations that *churchmen*, as we were called, were but formalists and bigots; regarding the church more than religion, and the Prayer Book more than the Bible; departing from their own Articles and Homilies, and destitute of true piety and renovation of heart.[16]

In 1836 Griswold became fifth Presiding Bishop of the Episcopal Church. On 15 February 1843, he went to visit another Evangelical, Manton Eastburn, who had recently been elected assistant Bishop of Massachusetts. On Eastburn's doorstep, Griswold suddenly collapsed and died.

Thomas March Clark said: 'If ever there was a good man, a true man, an honest disciple of Jesus Christ, Bishop Griswold was that man.'

CHURCH ON FIRE AGAIN IN VIRGINIA

Evangelicalism, which had been quiet since the golden years of Devereux Jarratt's middle life, quietly began to revive in Virginia during the first quarter of the nineteenth century. A few godly men and women made their homes houses of prayer. The result was that Virginia became the nursery of Evangelical Christianity within the Episcopal Church during much of the nineteenth century.

RICHARD CHANNING MOORE

The second Bishop of Virginia, Richard Channing Moore (1762–1841), was an Evangelical of whom it was said that he preached the gospel of the grace of God.

At the close of one Sunday afternoon service in New York, prior to his becoming a bishop, a member of the congregation rose and said, 'Dr Moore, the people are not disposed to go home; please give us another sermon.'

Dr Moore obliged, but still they asked for more. Dr Moore preached a third sermon and then concluded: 'My beloved people, you must now disperse – for although I delight to proclaim the glad tidings of salvation, my strength is exhausted, and I can say no more.'

As a result of that service sixty communicants were added to the parish. Vast congregations attended his services in New York and Bishop Hobart challenged him about his departures from strict use of the liturgy.

'They are neither inconsistent with the principle,' Moore replied to Hobart, 'nor prohibited by the canons of the church. And, although some condemn them as irregular and Methodistical, I cannot, as a minister of Christ, give them up. For I know that God's blessing is on them. They are the nurseries of my communion.'

'I am determined', said Moore, 'to preach the glorious doctrines of grace, instead of mere morality.'

Anglicans in Virginia elected him their Bishop in 1814 and for twenty-seven years 'with burning eloquence he went through the waste places of Virginia like a flame of fire'. Under his leadership, old parishes were revived, churches long closed were reopened, and new parishes were established. Although personally devoted to the liturgy, and requiring its full use in the set services of the Church, he encouraged informal gatherings for fellowship and prayer.

VIRGINIA THEOLOGICAL SEMINARY (VTS)

In 1822 the Virginia diocesan convention adopted a constitution for the 'Theological School of the Diocese of Virginia', later to be located at Alexandria. Two years later the college had twenty-one students.

In 1859, when Bishop John Johns spoke at a service of dedication of Aspinwall Hall, he said, 'Care has been taken that in this school the doctrines of the Protestant Reformation, which are the doctrines of the Scriptures, and of which justification by faith is the key-note, should be taught with distinctness and decision . . .

'We may further say that one thing which has distinguished the teaching of the Seminary has been its firm and unshaken faith in the system of doctrine once delivered to the saints, and as held in the Articles of our Church. We have held fast the atoning work of our Lord as a satisfaction to the divine justice as well as a revelation of the divine love; justification only by the righteousness of Christ; regeneration only by the power of the Holy Spirit; the sacraments as signs and seals of spiritual grace.'

Dr Reuel Keith, who came from Andover, Massachusetts, VTS's first dean and Professor of Systematic Divinity, brought New England Calvinism to the college. He held 'low' sacramental views.

'He knows no more of the Church than my horse,' Bishop Ravenscroft, a Hobartian High-Churchman, said of Dr Keith.

After Keith had delivered a strongly Calvinist lecture at VTS, a bold student posed a question. 'When, Doctor, are we to have the other side?'

'There is no other side,' Keith replied.

Mixed attitudes to Calvinism in the mid-Atlantic states at this time is illustrated by a story which is told of the Rev. Dr Fowles of Philadelphia. Fowles secured as a supply for one Sunday a clergyman of pronounced Calvinist views, and left for him the order of service and the notices. Underneath he pencilled the words: 'We still give poor sinners a chance at the Epiphany.'

THE EPISCOPAL CHURCH AND OTHER DENOMINATIONS

Throughout the first half of the nineteenth century the backbone of Episcopal Church membership was primarily the upper middle-class professional and business community. They were attracted to the restrained emotionalism and decorum of Episcopal worship. The town churches in particular aimed to combine good church architecture, fine music (paid choirs were introduced as early as 1818), and dignified worship.

The members of the Methodist Church by contrast were drawn largely from the middle and working classes. Evangelical Episcopalianism seems to have been a way for élite early Americans to be Evangelicals without the taint of 'enthusiasm' that would have come from associating with Methodists and Baptists.

PHILANDER CHASE

Philander Chase (1775–1852) attended Dartmouth College in Hanover, New Hampshire, discovered the *Book of Common Prayer* and became an avid Episcopalian. Chase was Bishop of Ohio (1818–31) and first Bishop of Illinois (1835–52).

On a visit to England in the early 1830s Philander Chase noted in his journal that he dined with the 'venerable Mr Simeon who spoke of his expected departure for a better world with pleasure' (Simeon died in 1836).

Chase hated the doctrines of the Church of Rome. In a Pastoral Letter he condemned what he called 'the blasphemous doctrine of transubstantiation, and the abominable idolatries of the mass', the doctrine of purgatory, invocation of saints and the supremacy of the Pope.

By 1824 the Episcopal Church had two Evangelical Seminaries – Virginia and Kenyon College in the diocese of Ohio. Kenyon College began in Philander Chase's home with one teacher, the bishop, and one student. Chase's memory was enshrined in a college song which began:

> The first of Kenyon's goodly race
> Was that great man, Philander Chase,
> He climbed the hill and said a prayer,
> And founded Kenyon College there.

JAMES MILNOR

The leader of the New York Evangelicals was the Rev. Dr James Milnor (1773–1845), who was brought up a Quaker, but disowned by that body when he married an Episcopalian. He learned his theology from Joseph Pilmore and was ordained in 1814. The text of his first sermon was 'I am not ashamed of the gospel of Christ'.

Milnor became Rector of St George's Church, New York City in 1816. Bishop Hobart instituted him. Disliking the weeknight prayer meetings which were held in the parish, Hobart called on the Rector.

'You must disband the weeknight prayer meeting,' he told Milnor.

'Very well,' Milnor replied, 'but you must go with me and break it up.' The prayer meetings continued.

In 1845 Stephen Higginson Tyng succeeded Milnor as Rector of St George's Church, and ministered there for thirty-four years. He vehemently opposed both high-church Tractarianism and broad-church Liberalism.

GOLDEN AGE FOR EVANGELICAL EPISCOPALIANS

At the 1832 General Convention, four bishops were consecrated together – John Henry Hopkins for Vermont, George Washington Doane for New Jersey, Benjamin Bosworth Smith for Kentucky, and Charles P. McIlvaine for Ohio. Smith and McIlvaine were Evangelicals; Hopkins and Doane were High Churchmen.

The golden age for the Evangelical Episcopalians was the 1830s to the 1850s. They had strong bishops like Griswold, Moore, Chase, Smith, McIlvaine, William Meade, John Johns, Stephen Elliott, and a little later Alfred Lee, Manton Eastburn, Henry Washington Lee, J. P. K. Henshaw of Rhode Island and Thomas March Clark.

Bishop Clark, who entered the Episcopal ministry in 1836, recorded that at that time 'the growth of the Church was very much in the Evangelical direction, and it looked as if this party might soon attain a decided ascendancy'. In the ten-year period which followed, the number of clergy doubled, and the Evangelicals were strengthened by the coming into the Church of ministers from other Christian bodies.

At the height of their influence in the 1840s and 1850s, however, Evangelicals still made up slightly less than half of the House of Bishops and approximately one-third of the clergy.

CHARLES MCILVAINE

Charles P. McIlvaine (1799–1873) served the Episcopal Church for fifty-three years. He was one of the most remarkable and complex characters that American Anglican Evangelicalism has produced: 'a powerful and dynamic preacher, a capable theologian, a forceful and authoritarian bishop, an obdurate controversialist, a sentimental husband and father'.[17]

If a feature of Evangelicalism is its activism, McIlvaine was a classic example. Inclined to be always on the go, he also struggled with a lifelong battle against nervousness, anxiety and depression, which forced him to rest periodically from his duties by travelling to Europe.

McIlvaine published over seventy works during his lifetime. He inspired great loyalty and devotion among those who admired and agreed with him and was a formidable opponent to those with whom he disagreed. He counted among his friends many of the great Evangelical leaders of the day, as well as top political and military figures.

The secret of McIlvaine's early success, said Clowes Chorley, was that he preached the unsearchable riches of Christ. 'Just as I am', the hymn written by an Evangelical member of the Church of England Charlotte Elliott, which was to become so popular in Moody and later Billy Graham crusades, was also McIlvaine's favourite.

McIlvaine believed that the spread of righteousness depended on faithful Evangelical ministers carrying out God's work in the Episcopal Church.

When one of Washington's largest parishes Christ Church in Georgetown lost its rector, McIlvaine arrived to replenish the ranks and served there from 1820 to 1824. During his five years at Christ Church, McIlvaine was a popular preacher, well liked for his ardour and piety. The early 1820s were heady days for Evangelical Episcopalians in the nation's capital. They believed that deadened by formalism, the Episcopal Church lacked zeal and prayed that they could revive the Church.

West Point revival

In 1824 the Government appointed McIlvaine Chaplain and Professor of Ethics at West Point Military Academy. Under his leadership something of a revival broke out. Although McIlvaine tried to limit publicity, word of the revival leaked out, and McIlvaine became a nationally known preacher and revivalist. But he worried about fanaticism at West Point. McIlvaine eventually lost his position at West Point as a result of the revival. In a response to excesses there, he developed a guarded form of revivalism – one heavily dependent on trained leadership.

McIlvaine in New York

In 1827 McIlvaine accepted a call from St Ann's Church in Brooklyn, New York City, and stayed there until 1832. St Ann's was a parish in the middle of the Episcopal Church's most high-church diocese. McIlvaine and his friend James Milnor were the only Evangelical Episcopal ministers in New York City.

During his five years at St Ann's McIlvaine joined in many of the great Christian causes which were dear to the hearts of American Evangelicals of many denominations. New York was a strategic centre for the American Bible Society, the American Tract Society, seamen's societies, temperance societies, and many moral-reform groups.

In his third year at St Ann's, McIlvaine was taken ill and his doctor sent him to Europe to rest. He spent most of his time in England with his friend James Milnor. He attended the Islington Conference, held at the home of Daniel Wilson, met Hannah More and attended the meetings of the British Anti-slavery Society where he met William Wilberforce. He spent a week in Cambridge, where he dined with Charles Simeon. For nearly eight months he travelled with Milnor and together they visited many of England's leading Evangelicals.

Bishop of Ohio

In 1832 McIlvaine was consecrated the second Bishop of Ohio. The post would be coupled with the post of President of Kenyon College, the seminary which had been founded by Philander Chase. It was an interesting move for the cultivated, Princeton-educated man to leave the cosmopolitan New York for the Wild West. But in his forty years as Bishop of Ohio, his diocese grew from 17 clergy to 106, with 116 parishes, 9,745 communicants, and a missionary budget of over $200,000.

In September 1834 McIlvaine delivered his first address to the diocese of Ohio. Entitled 'The Preaching of Christ Crucified', he set out in it his view of the Christian ministry.

'You are well aware', he began, 'that the great work for which your sacred office was established, is the preaching of the gospel. The primary job of the clergy isn't reading the liturgy or celebrating sacraments. Ministers are called to preach the atoning work of Christ. I urge my clergy to examine the Evangelical character of their preaching. Does it bear witness to Christ? Since the centre of the Gospel is Christ himself, every sermon must point to some aspect of Christ's life, ministry, or kingdom. Sin, justification, sanctification, and the final glory of believers are appropriate topics for Evangelical sermons. The purpose of such preaching is to overturn the kingdom of Satan in the hearts of men. Such gospel preaching distinguished the ministry of the early apostles, and if the Ohio clergy preach in the same way, God will increase the church.'[18]

Throughout his sermon McIlvaine never once referred to the Episcopal Church or its distinctive practices and doctrine. Diana Butler has pointed out that in this first address to his diocese, he preached a sermon that could have been preached in any Evangelical church.

McIlvaine changes his tune

A few years later, however, the Bishop's tone changed. Living in the West had taught him a few things. He discovered that there were about thirty divisions of Baptists in the West and this bolstered his convictions about the strength of Episcopalianism. Even in his early months in Ohio, McIlvaine had become concerned about the 'appetite for excitement and novelty in the mode of awakening and converting sinners' that he had seen among some Christians in the state.

In 1836 McIlvaine delivered his second message to the diocese of Ohio. 'If we would promote the spirit of vital godliness in the world', he said, 'we must promote it in connection with, and by means of, that only body – the Church – which the Lord has built in the earthly house of its tabernacle in this wilderness. You may as well expect your minds to be in health while your bodies are diseased, as that the spirit of religion will flourish, while the body of religion, the visible church is disordered.'[19]

In McIlvaine's view, Episcopalians gave Ohio a Church with

'distinctive sobriety, dignity and purity' in the face of the 'appalling exhibition of the religious temper of the times'.

In his first message to the clergy, and indeed, in his own West Point revival, the Bishop had preached the gospel. Now it seemed, at least to some Ohioans, that the bishop was preaching the Episcopal Church. In a cry which Anglican Evangelicals have uttered in many parts of the world, they wondered whether their Evangelical Bishop had changed his views since taking office.

The Oxford Movement comes to America

When, during the 1830s, the publications of the Oxford Tractarians began to arrive in America, the battle between the Evangelicals and the High-Churchmen intensified. McIlvaine came down firmly on the Evangelical side.

McIlvaine believed that Tractarianism was 'an abandonment of all that we have been taught by our Church to believe to be true, the narrow, the only way that leadeth unto life'. To him, the Oxford Movement complicated Christ's good news to men and women in need of a Saviour. In his book *Oxford Divinity Compared*, McIlvaine attacked the Tractarians' doctrine of justification and other aspects of their theology, including the elevation of tradition over Scripture, the doctrine of baptismal regeneration, and Isaac Williams's doctrine of 'reserve'.

He criticised the Tractarians on the grounds that they rejected the theology of the Reformation, although of course the Tractarians made no secret of this. In Tract 80 Isaac Williams argued that the deepest Christian truth should only be communicated to people as by moral growth they were able to receive it. According to Williams the Evangelical system unduly exalted preaching at the expense of an emphasis on obedience as the best means of promoting Christianity in the world. Evangelicalism tended to exclude everything that might alarm its followers: obedience to Church authority, practices of mortification, and the performance of duty. It set out religion in ways which were attractive to the world, rather than by purifying and humbling the heart.

Instead of the process of painful self-discipline and the ancient

Church's system of penance, said Williams, Evangelical Christianity offered an instant route to the privileges of being a Christian. Evangelicalism took all that was agreeable and attractive in Christianity, and rejected what was stern and self-denying. Religious truth can only be received in a certain state of heart, said Williams, and he singled out the atonement as an example of such truth, suggesting that the tone of Evangelical presentation of the doctrine magnified grace and minimised the need for obedience. Teaching on the atonement should therefore be 'reserved' until a person had progressed to a life of good works and would, at that time, be unlikely to separate grace from works.[20]

Against this, McIlvaine (and most Evangelicals) argued that the very heart of Christian theology was 'the preaching of Christ crucified'. To him, all other doctrines were based on the atonement. Christ's saving work on the cross was to be preached openly and without reserve; to do less would be to disobey God and contradict the clear teaching of Scripture. 'St Paul', he said, 'waited not till men were well initiated into Christian mysteries, before he unveiled the grand subject of atonement and justification through the blood of Christ.' The atonement, when embraced and believed by contrite sinners, was the only sure ground for 'unreserved obedience'.

Actually, Isaac Williams had himself said that he did not lower the doctrine of atonement, but heightened and exalted it. 'All I say is that it should be looked upon and spoken of with reverential holiness . . . The whole business of the church is to impart true saving knowledge.' Alarmed by antinomianism, the Tractarians stressed the role of obedient good works in shaping Christian character. But, said Williams, 'it is only through the blood of Christ that we are able to think or do what is good. It is through the blood alone that our deeds are accepted.' The Tractarians wanted to present the cross in a way which did not encourage an attitude which cheapened grace.

As so often in Christian history, the differences between the two sides were less than the ensuing battles and polarised positions suggested. However, most Evangelicals were convinced that if the Tractarians gained a powerful position in the Episcopal Church, the Evangelical message would be weakened.

After McIlvaine

In 1871 Bishop George David Cummins (1822–76) visited McIlvaine's home in Cincinnati. The two men discussed the forthcoming General Convention.

'We are looking to you, my dear bishop,' Cummins said to McIlvaine, 'to lead us, like another Moses, out of our present state of bondage to freedom and liberty.'

'Ah!' said McIlvaine, 'I am too old for any such contest and too feeble. The younger bishops, such as you, must fight the battle which is inevitable.'

In 1872, troubled by controversies in the Church and suffering from nervous exhaustion, McIlvaine went to England to visit old friends and escape some of the ecclesiastical pressure. At the age of seventy-four his health and strength were worn. After several months in England, feeling rather better, he decided to tour Italy with some friends.

In February 1873 McIlvaine suddenly became quite ill, and on 13 March he died quietly in his sleep. They sent his body back to England, where he was honoured by the Archbishop of Canterbury with a funeral service in Westminster Abbey.

MANTON EASTBURN

For twenty-six years Manton Eastburn (1801–72) was Rector of Trinity Church, Boston. In some respects a strong churchman, for a time some thought he inclined to the high-church party. His theology was Evangelical, however, and, to their indignation, he always addressed the fashionable and cultured congregation of Trinity Church as 'vile earth and miserable sinners, worms and children of wrath'.

Bishop T. M. Clark said of Eastburn's preaching that 'he rarely gave offence by the introduction of novel thoughts, or over-taxed the mental powers by abstruse arguments'. His sermons were always precisely thirty minutes long, and they followed a uniform pattern.

He always alluded to 'man's fallen state by nature', justification by faith, worldliness and temptation.

Manton Eastburn was inclined to be wordy in his language. He spoke of the broad road as 'that vast arena frequented by far the largest numerical majority'; he described 'man' as 'a denizen of the earth'; Europe as 'a foreign strand'. As a boy in Boston, Phillips Brooks heard Eastburn preach on the parable of Dives and Lazarus. After quoting the rich man's plea that Lazarus might be able to dip his finger in water to cool his burning tongue, Eastburn solemnly remarked: 'To that wholly inadmissible request the patriarch returned a negative reply.'

Although a classical scholar, he boasted that he had not changed his views since he was seven years old. Henry Codman Potter, who was his assistant in Trinity Church, said of him:

He had made up the parcel of his opinions – had neatly tied them up with the red tape of a cherished tradition, and had deposited the package on the top shelf of his mental storehouse, not to be taken down or disturbed under any conceivable conditions. He was a scholar; and he had a sincere love of letters which made him one of the best students of the classics whom I ever knew. Indeed, it was my commonest experience, whenever I entered his library to find him with a volume of some Greek or Latin poet in his hand. But living, as he did, through an era which witnessed some of the most tremendous readjustments of Christian faith and dogma, he never, so far as I could learn, consented to read a line of the authors who discussed them, or to talk about them or their work with anyone who had.[21]

In 1842 Manton Eastburn was elected Assistant Bishop of Massachusetts. Anyone who differed from him was 'the victim of detestable prejudice'. Novelties in the Church disturbed his peace. He used to say that 'the Ritualists and the Broad-Churchmen, like the canker worm and the palmer worm, were destroying his diocese'. He hated Ritualism. He refused to allow flowers in the chancel at his visitations. He dismissed out of hand any suggestion of change in the Prayer Book.

Eastburn and ornaments . . .

When the clergy at the Church of the Advent, Boston, placed a cross and candles on the altar there, Eastburn announced that he would not visit the parish for Confirmation until the offensive ornaments were removed. The rector and vestry refused to remove them. But after the passage of a canon requiring a bishop to visit a parish at least once in three years, Eastburn at last consented to visit the church – though he found the ritual extremely distasteful.

Prior to the visit, but after Bishop Eastburn had arranged a date, the senior warden called on him.

'Bishop,' the warden asked, 'could we postpone the confirmation for a few weeks, because by that time a larger class can be prepared?'

'No,' replied Bishop Eastburn, 'the fewer confirmed after instruction at the Church of the Advent the better!'

When he eventually made the visit, he waited patiently until the time came for his address to the candidates. His address has been wittily paraphrased by Thomas Clark.

'I have now,' said the Bishop to the Confirmation candidates, 'in compliance with the usages of our Communion, laid my hands upon you, and you have been confirmed. To what extent you comprehend the real nature of this act of dedication, and what instruction you have received respecting it, I do not know. I think it possible that you have been taught that this table is an altar, but it is not, inasmuch as no sacrifice has ever been offered there, or ever can be. You may have been told by these gentlemen in the rear (the clergy) that they are priests in the Church of God.

'In any real sense you are as much priests as they are, for we are taught in the New Testament that all the faithful alike are priests in the kingdom of Christ. I made them what they are with a breath, and I can unmake them with a breath! They may have told you that it is your duty to confess your sins to them. You have as much right to insist that they should confess their sins to you! There is but one Being to whom we can go with our transgressions with any hope of being absolved.'[22]

... and flowers

On a visit to Grace Church, Newton, while Peter Henry Steenstra was Rector, the Bishop, when vested and about to enter the chancel, noticed two vases of flowers on the altar.

'Mr Steenstra,' he said, 'although I know that you make no idolatrous use of these flowers, I cannot, on principle, take part in a service with them on the Holy Table.'

'Since the congregation are already in the church,' Steenstra replied, 'it would look odd if I went in now and removed the flowers. Perhaps we may both go in to begin the service and immediately kneel at opposite ends of the altar. While the congregation have their eyes closed in prayer, we could reach up and each take a vase from the top of the altar and put it underneath.'

Bishop Eastburn agreed, and this they did!

Eastburn's friends warned him that if he persisted in expressing certain convictions, he would be ostracised.

'I shall not mind,' he replied, 'as long as God is with me.'

Preaching a Memorial Sermon in 1872, Phillips Brooks referred to Eastburn's relationship to the Evangelical Movement. 'His whole life was full of it,' Brooks said. 'He had preached its gospel in New York with wonderful success and power. He bore his testimony to it to the last in Boston. A faith that was very beautiful in its childlike reliance upon God; a sturdy courage which would have welcomed the martyrdom of more violent days; a complete, unquestioning, unchanging loyalty to the ideas which he had once accepted; a deep personal piety, which, knowing the happiness of divine communion, desired that blessedness for other souls; a wide sympathy for all of every name who were working for the ends which he loved and desired; these, with his kindly heart and constancy in friendship, made the power of the long ministry of Bishop Eastburn.'

PHILLIPS BROOKS

Phillips Brooks (1835–93) is widely known today as the author of the carol 'O little town of Bethlehem', which he wrote in 1868. He studied at Harvard, received his formal theological training at VTS, and was ordained in 1859. From 1862 to 1869 he was Rector of Holy Trinity Church, Philadelphia.

At Philadelphia, and perhaps earlier, he became attracted to a more Liberal outlook than the Evangelicalism he had been taught at VTS. In A. V. G. Allen's *Life of Brooks*, the points on which Brooks differed from Evangelicalism are listed as follows:

- Its view of Baptism as a covenant
- Its literal theory of inspiration and its conception of Scripture as a whole
- Its separation of things secular and sacred
- Its failure to recognise truth in other religions and in non-Christian people
- Its indifference to intellectual culture
- Its tendency to limit the Church to the elect
- Its view of salvation as an escape from endless punishment
- Its insistence upon the necessity of acknowledging a theory of the atonement as central to salvation
- Its insufficient conception of the incarnation and of the person of Christ
- Its tendency to regard religion too much as a matter of the emotions, rather than of character and will[23]

In 1869 Brooks became Rector of Trinity Church, Boston. Although many historians recognise Brooks as a leader of the Broad Church movement, Clowes Chorley maintained that Brooks 'never drifted from the heart of Evangelical religion', arguing that the keynote of his preaching remained Christ. Some American Evangelicals, however, would regard this assessment as wide of the mark. They point out that Brooks played down the centrality of Christ's atonement and rejected a Calvinist view of the 'total depravity' of man.

It is true that Brooks retained a profound, if patronising, respect for the early Evangelical leaders. Preaching in 1872, he said: 'The Evangelical movement had its zealous men here and there throughout the land. The peculiarities of the movement were an earnest insistence on doctrine, and upon personal spiritual experience, of neither of which had the previous generation made very much. Man's fallen state, his utter hopelessness, the vicarious atonement, the supernatural conversion, the work of the Holy Spirit – these were the truths which men of those days, who were what we called "Evangelical" men, urged with the force of vehement belief upon their hearers. There were crude, hard, and untrue statements of them very often, but they went deep; they laid hold upon the souls and consciences of men. They created most profound experiences. They made great ministers and noble Christians. It was indeed the work of God.'[24]

Brooks and the EES

The Evangelical Education Society (EES) was designed to give grants of money to theological students preparing for the ministry. In 1870 the Society's Board decided that before any grant was made the student had to answer a series of questions expressing his belief in Evangelical tenets. This policy so aroused Phillips Brooks's indignation that he resigned his membership of the Board, writing to the secretary objecting to the principle and saying:

> It is not so very long since we were students ourselves. I am sure that if these questions had been laid as tests upon the Alexandria Seminary when you and I were there they would have excluded all the men who have been most useful in the ministry since. I cannot doubt it, and yet I cannot at this moment think of one man of our time who has turned out a high churchman.

Gillis Harp, Associate Professor of History at Acadia University, who has studied Brooks in depth, has observed that the other members of the Board would have understood only too well that Phillips Brooks's defection would have serious consequences for the

Evangelical movement within the Episcopal Church. When Phillips Brooks embraced a brand of the broad-church Liberalism of his day, American Evangelicalism lost one of its more influential and original thinkers.

In 1887 Brooks wrote to Dr Henman Dyer, saying, 'I am more and more sure that the dogmatic theology in which I was brought up was wrong.' In 1891 he became Bishop of Massachusetts, the post he held until his death.

THE EPISCOPAL THEOLOGICAL SCHOOL

Bishop Griswold had pressed for the establishment of a theological college in New England, but it was not until 1867 that The Episcopal Theological School (ETS) was eventually established in Cambridge, Massachusetts.

ETS's Francis Wharton

The most colourful figure to have been involved in the early years of ETS was Francis Wharton. Some say he was the real founder of the school. Wharton had studied the workings of institutions at Gambier, Philadelphia and Virginia and had noted their limitations.

Francis Wharton was born in Philadelphia in 1820. When he married an Episcopalian he became one himself. Graduating from Yale in 1839, Wharton thought seriously of preparing for the ministry, but being dissuaded by his father, studied law in his father's office instead. At the age of twenty-six he published a treatise on criminal law which passed through nine editions during his life and ran to five thick volumes. New editions of these volumes were still being published in the 1930s.

In 1862, at the age of forty-two, Wharton was ordained, and the next year called to the rectorship of St Paul's, Brookline, which he held till 1871, although from 1867 he combined it with service to ETS. In 1867 the Trustees appointed him Dean of ETS, an office which he only held for eleven weeks, resigning in favour of John Seely Stone, although he continued to teach courses at the school on Evidences of Christianity, Apologetics, Liturgy, Polity, Canon Law, Homiletics, and Pastoral Care.

'He could lecture in an interesting way on almost any subject,' said Bishop Lawrence, 'throwing in pleasant anecdotes, dryly humorous quotations, kindly advice, and hunks of wisdom, drawn from experience.' An infection of the throat which gave his voice a high falsetto quality, amusing his students, finally made it impossible for him to speak at all.

In 1885 he was appointed Chief of the Legal Division of the Department of State in the first of President Cleveland's administrations. At the request of Congress, he wrote major multivolume works on international law and diplomacy. He was reading the proof-sheets of one of these when he died in 1889. The eleventh edition of the *Encyclopaedia Britannica* calls him 'the foremost American authority on International Law'.

John Bassett Moore, who knew Wharton in his last years in Washington, said that 'he possessed in the highest degree vivacity of intellect'; 'the activity of his mind was incessant'; he had 'quickness and breadth of comprehension', an exceptional memory, an almost unlimited capacity for work, and a sparkling sense of humour. There were humorous passages even in his treatises on criminal law.

Not the least of Wharton's contributions to ETS was his ecumenical spirit, rare in those days of partisanship. He often pointed to 'the tolerant and Catholic platform which the Anglican Communion adopted at the Reformation'.

Wharton maintained that parties in the Church were not only a sign of her vitality but also of her perpetuity and unity. They were called into being by the need for emphasis on neglected phases of truth. If they ignored the truths which other parties stood for, they might become less than Christian, but on the whole they had shown a tendency to learn from each other and enrich the common heritage. He expressed the hope that Evangelicals would 'not become less evangelical', but 'more and more sacramental, more and more impressed with an appreciation both of the ethical and of the institutional sides of the faith, more and more loyal to the

Catholic creeds, and more and more fearless in appealing to reason'.[25]

EVANGELICAL EPISCOPALIAN CHRISTIANITY

Although nineteenth-century Evangelical Episcopalians allowed more scope for extempore prayer than other Church people, they also loved the *Book of Common Prayer*. In the sermon at the opening of the General Convention of 1838, Bishop Meade described it as 'the most perfect of all liturgies' and begged that it might 'be maintained in its purity and integrity'. Bishop Richard Channing Moore spoke of the liturgy as 'combining with the soundest sense the purest and most sublimated devotion; a liturgy which has commanded the respect and admiration of some of the greatest and most enlightened men who have lived since the Reformation'.

Dress

The rule for the wearing of surplices varied. In early colonial times in Virginia the surplice was always worn, but later it fell into disuse. Cassocks were unknown. Bishop Moore himself always took his seat in the chancel in ordinary dress, except when about to perform some official act.

Bishop White often attended the evening service at St Paul's, Philadelphia, and Dr Tyng described how he 'was seen walking up our middle aisle, with his cane in his hand, and his green spectacles on his eyes. He came up to the chancel, and laid his hat and cane down upon the cushion, and seated himself quietly in a chair.'

Sundays

Sundays were high days in Evangelical parishes. In 1845 at St Andrew's, Philadelphia, there was Sunday school at 9 a.m.; morning prayer and sermon at 10.30 a.m.; Sunday school again at 2 p.m.; afternoon service at 3 or 4 p.m.; and from time to time a special evening service.

A history of St Ann's, Brooklyn, describes a Sunday at that parish:

> The children and youth assemble at nine. At ten, the Pastor enters to inspect the schools, and to smile on the dear lambs of the flock. At half past ten the morning service begins: Confession, Prayer, Praise, Chanting, Litany, Commandments, Psalms, Hymn, Preaching. At two the children are questioned on the lesson of the day. At three they join the congregation, and re-enter the church for a second service and sermon. After this the parish library is opened for the use of the congregation, and the children assemble at the libraries of their respective schools, select their books from a thousand at their disposal, and retire with the smiles and often the caresses of the female teachers. At a quarter past seven there is a third service and a plain and practical discourse, in the chapel, brilliantly illuminated with gas. Sunday was without doubt the Sabbath, and was kept in 1845.[26]

Prayer meetings

The weeknight prayer meetings became an established Evangelical institution. They were usually held on Saturday nights. Most of the time was, as Bishop Clark wrote,

> occupied by the singing of hymns and prayers offered by a few elderly men of high repute for piety, who rarely, if ever, violated the laws of propriety and good taste, although there might be some degree of sameness in their petition. Occasionally a younger person, more inflamed by zeal, would take occasion to lay the supposed short-comings of the rector in word and doctrine before the Lord, and implore that he might be directed from above to improve his ways, but this was a very rare occurrence.

Weeknight prayer meetings became a badge of the Evangelical party. They used to say in Philadelphia that St Peter's was 'high' and

St Paul's was 'low', because the former had a celebration of the Holy Communion early on Sunday mornings, and the latter had a prayer meeting. Bishop Clark said, 'No one could expect to be called to an Evangelical church if he bowed in the creed, and no low church rector was regarded as faithful to his trust unless he cultivated the informal prayer meeting.'[27]

Episcopal *form* and the *spirit* of true Christianity

Anglican Evangelicals in nineteenth-century America believed that the forms of Episcopalianism were only as good as long as they promoted the *spirit* of true Christianity. Episcopal forms had to be enlivened by an inward and spiritual experience of new birth.

'The power of godliness', said Charles McIlvaine, 'is the *substance*, or *reality* of godliness, as distinguished from all its forms . . . [It is] that inward and spiritual grace which is the life and being of all genuine piety before God. Its only abiding place is in the heart.' Such grace comes, he argued, only through 'a new and inward birth' in which God would give power for personal transformation into a 'new creature'. McIlvaine complained that some Episcopalians acted as if '*the more form, the more godliness*'. He rejected this.

Episcopal forms should be 'highly valued for their proper uses, affectionately cherished, faithfully observed, [and] jealously guarded'. But they should not be 'lifted into a false importance, and made to hinder instead of helping truth'. Formalism, the elevation of forms above inward reality, would always result in the 'denial of the power of godliness'.

McIlvaine urged Evangelical Episcopalians to resist what he saw as the short-comings of American revivalism and forge an orderly, decorous, church-oriented Evangelicalism that would provide stability and promote the gospel in a rapidly changing world.

He agreed with the High-Churchmen that extreme Evangelicalism injured Christian faith. The Church must act to guard true doctrine, fight innovation, and stand as a bulwark against schism and sectarianism.

Evangelical Episcopalians certainly did not completely reject the use of Episcopal forms. They only rejected high-church formalism.

They tried to inject the forms of the Episcopal Church with the spirit of true Christianity. They wanted to see the liturgy invigorated by individuals filled with a personal experience of God's saving grace.

Revivals

Evangelical Episcopalians conducted revival meetings, but they aimed to achieve a more restrained and generally less emotional form than was current in American revivalist Christianity generally. They prided themselves on the decorum of their revivals, adopting such means as prayer meetings and preaching, but avoiding measures which they believed created unhealthy excesses and fanaticism.

During his years at St Ann's, New York, McIlvaine faced the question of how to incorporate revival-style Christianity into the weekly life of his parish. How could the forms and rites of the Episcopal Church be used to promote what he believed to be true religion? He reflected on what distinguished true revivals from mere 'extravagances'. Revivals, he came to believe, must produce both conversions and holy living. Many so-called revivals were little more than excitement. In genuine revival, converts would demonstrate the fruit of the Holy Spirit.

McIlvaine told a congregation in Ohio: 'Never does a Church need a liturgy, a form of prayer for public worship, more than in a revival of religion. It serves as a help to all that is of the Holy Ghost, as a check against that disposition to extravagance and novelty by which so many revivals have been deformed.'[28]

Preaching

Evangelical Episcopalians believed that ministers should not just perform certain rites and liturgies: they should proclaim new life in Christ. They believed in the supreme value of the ministry of the Word. Many of them were regarded as great preachers.

For them, preaching the gospel meant something definite and radical. It meant the strong call of God to a careless and godless people, awakening in their hearers a sense of their accountability to God, their need of personal salvation through accepting Christ's redemption and the obligation to lead a godly and consistent life in view of the judgment to come.

They said of the Evangelical Episcopalian Gregory Townsend Bedell that 'in the pulpit he was unrivalled'. Not only did residents in Philadelphia crowd to hear him preach, but travellers would pause in the city on their travels in order to attend St Andrews.

THE REFORMED EPISCOPAL CHURCH

In December 1873 a group of eight clergymen and nineteen laymen organised the Reformed Episcopal Church as a protest against what they described as the Romanising tendencies of the Protestant Episcopal Church and as a guardian of the Protestant and Evangelical doctrines of the Anglican tradition.

The founding bishop of the new Church was George David Cummins, who had visited McIlvaine shortly before his death.

The Reformed Episcopalians argued that they were guardians of the faith as it had been delivered to their Evangelical forebears. By the 1870s the Evangelical party of the Episcopal Church was moving towards what would later be called fundamentalism. Stemming from the 1850s and their loss of confidence in the Church, Episcopalian Evangelical identity had become more Evangelical than Episcopal. They were alarmed about scepticism, rationalism, Liberalism, biblical criticism and Roman Catholicism.

Evangelicals who believed that the Episcopal Church had been incompletely reformed left to join the Reformed Episcopal Church in 1873 or soon after; those who still believed that the Anglican Reformation was true to the spirit of Evangelical religion stayed.

THE END OF OLD-STYLE EVANGELICALISM

In the years following 1873 Evangelicals within the Episcopal Church faced problems which effectively destroyed old-style Evangelicalism within the Church for about eighty years. The new generation of leaders, initially Evangelicals, slowly abandoned old party loyalty in favour of the Broad Church whose new emphasis on critical theology and social ministry seemed to them better fitted to address the problems of post-Civil-War America.

At Evangelical Episcopal seminaries in Virginia and Cambridge (ETS) younger faculty members embraced Liberalism, Darwinism and biblical criticism. By the end of the century, all the Evangelical educational institutions had become Liberal. By 1900, there were very few people left in the Protestant Episcopal Church to carry on the Evangelical Episcopal vision.

St George's Church, New York

St George's Church in New York is a sort of microcosm of Evangelical Episcopalianism generally. The elder Stephen Tyng had been Rector of St George's for more than thirty-five years and under him the church had been a centre for the most committed forms of old-fashioned Evangelicalism.

After securing an evangelical succession for his pulpit, Tyng retired in 1878. However, his Evangelical heir, Walter Williams, by all accounts a weak leader and ineffective preacher, resigned after only five years. His successor was the Rev. William Rainsford, who is remembered in Episcopal history as a Liberal and 'social gospel' leader.

Rainsford became inspired by Phillips Brooks and discovered the works of Frederick Robertson, an Anglican preacher who had abandoned Evangelicalism for Broad Church Liberalism. While serving in a parish in Toronto he had distanced himself from Evangelical views. He doubted the substitutionary theory of the atonement, the verbal inspiration of Scripture and the doctrine of eternal punishment. On pragmatic matters, however – such as the tone of

221

the messages he preached, drawing large numbers of people to church, leading exciting Bible classes, and balancing the church budget – Rainsford continued to please his Evangelical congregation in New York. Although he was slowly abandoning Evangelical doctrine, Rainsford still embodied Evangelical style.

Rainsford reorganised St George's Sunday school, abolished pew rents, encouraged congregational singing and launched an urban ministry programme into the surrounding community. But he did not obviously make a clear break with his Evangelical past.

As late as November 1885, Rainsford held a massive revival meeting at St George's which included Evangelical stars such as Bishop Bedell and Ira D. Sankey. Nevertheless, by the mid-1890s Evangelical leaders noticed a change at St George's which was complete by the turn of the century. In 1903 eleven Philadelphia clergymen (who called themselves 'members of both the great historic schools of the Church' – high church and Evangelical) accused him of heresy. In 1905 he declared: 'I am confident that unless our creeds are treated as symbols of divine truth, beautiful and necessary if you will – but still as symbols and not as complete and final expression of divine truth – these creeds that we have been brought up to love and reverence, will seem to our fellow-men as bandages we insist on binding on their eyes – not as lamps we would if we might place in their hands.'[29]

If you think that labels are useful, you could say that the former Evangelicals who remained in the Episcopal Church had become Liberals.

PART FOUR

Church on fire in nineteenth-century England

Fire goes before him and consumes his foes on every side.
(Psalm 97:3)

THE CLAPHAM SECT

By the year 1800 Anglican Evangelicalism had become a power in England. Most Evangelical churches were crowded on Sundays; thousands attended weeknight meetings for prayer and Bible study. Would the movement now produce fruit that would last?

One answer came from Clapham, still, at the turn of the century, a village of a couple of thousand people separated from London by pleasant meadows. Around Clapham Common – a wilderness of gorse bushes, gravel pits and ponds – some merchants and MPs, who wanted to live in the country and yet be within easy reach of the city, had built a number of substantial homes.

John Venn was rector there from 1792 to 1813. The son of Henry Venn, Evangelical vicar of Huddersfield, Venn organised his parish on vigorously Evangelical lines, including a Sunday evening service (still a novelty at that time) and a system of district visiting.

When a lady who was staying at Fulham Palace wanted to visit Venn, the Bishop of London would only lend her his carriage on condition that she would get down at a neighbouring public house. 'On no account must the episcopal horses be seen at the door of an Evangelical vicarage,' the Bishop told her.

A remarkable group of laymen was now living in Clapham, devoted to the Church of England, fervent in prayer, diligent in studying the Bible, able and successful in the world of business and politics. There was Henry Thornton, MP, banker, financier and son of John Thornton, said to be the second-wealthiest merchant in Europe. Next door to Thornton lived William Wilberforce, another MP, whom Pitt and Burke declared to be the greatest orator of the day. Nearby were the homes of Charles Grant, Chairman of the East India Company; James Stephen, the famous lawyer; Zachary Macaulay, former Governor of Sierra Leone; and Lord Teignmouth, a former Governor-General of India.

Sydney Smith, writing in the *Edinburgh Review*, nicknamed the group 'The Clapham Sect'. Rich and prosperous, they lived in large houses, dressed well, fed well, rode well-groomed horses. William Thackeray, the novelist, sneered at them. 'In Egypt itself', he wrote in *The Newcomes*, 'there were not more savoury fleshpots than at Clapham.'

Nevertheless, despite their wealth, these men ordered their lives with monastic self-discipline. They were hospitable because they believed this to be a Christian duty. Like all the best Evangelicals at that time, they rose early in the mornings and spent time in the presence of God. They mapped out every hour of the day beforehand, with so many hours for prayer, for study, for business, for rest. They did not regard their wealth as their own, but gave to the Lord's work generously and methodically.

Wilberforce and the slave trade

Peaceful African villages suddenly raided at night; men, women and children dragged in chains to the coast; the long, slow voyage across the Atlantic; the filth and stench of the poisonous hold where the slaves were packed in layers; and then the work on sugar plantations urged on by the overseer's whip. More than two hundred English vessels were engaged in the slave trade at the end of the eighteenth century, and yet good people, including Evangelicals, saw no harm in it.

Whitefield bought slaves for his orphanage in Georgia and Newton continued in the business for some years after his conversion. But now the Evangelicals of Clapham, led by William Wilberforce (1759–1833), made up their minds that the trade must stop. Wilberforce, the son of a wealthy merchant, had been educated at St John's College, Cambridge. After being elected MP for Hull in 1780 he became a close friend of William Pitt the Younger. As a result of reading the New Testament while travelling in Europe during 1784 and 1785, he was converted to Evangelicalism and made up his mind to live a more disciplined Christian life.

John Newton, once he had seen the light about slavery, opposed Wilberforce's wish to take Holy Orders and persuaded him to serve the cause of Christianity in Parliament. This is something

Wilberforce was well fitted to do, possessing a combination of self-discipline, a capacity for hard work and great skills as an orator. In his Practical View of the *Prevailing Religious System of Professing Christians* (1797) Wilberforce argued that religion depended on vital revealed truths and was not merely a matter of ethics and applied benevolence.

In 1788 Wilberforce, supported by Thomas Clarkson and the Quakers, began a nineteen-year struggle for the abolition of the slave trade. Wilberforce and the Clapham Sect had to face formidable opposition. An immense amount of English capital was invested in the trade. The ship-owners, the merchants, the planters and the financiers were united in their determination to keep both the trade and practice of slavery going.

King George III was quite sure the pious men of Clapham were dangerous revolutionaries. Admiral Nelson had no time for Wilberforce. 'I was bred in the good old school,' he wrote from the Victory, 'and taught to appreciate the value of our West Indian possessions, and neither in the field nor the Senate shall their rights be infringed, while I have any arm to fight in their defence, or a tongue to launch my voice against the damnable doctrine of Wilberforce and his hypocritical allies.'[1]

Wilberforce introduced his Bill eleven times, only for it to be debated and defeated. He had to collect witnesses from all over the world; he had to examine the witnesses for the other side and expose their false or misleading assertions. He had to educate public opinion by an endless succession of meetings. He wrote hundreds of pamphlets, attended almost daily committees of one kind or another, and organised petitions and deputations. He also interviewed and briefed Cabinet ministers.

At one stage of the fight, Wilberforce's friends agreed to sacrifice one night's sleep a week in order to help him sift through the mass of evidence that was pouring in. At last they won the victory, when in 1807 the Bill was carried by 283 votes to 16. The historian and philosopher William Lecky called the abolition of slavery one of 'the three or four perfectly virtuous acts recorded in the history of nations'. The men who bore the brunt of the fight, who supplied the leaders, the organisation, the fire and the funds, were British Anglican Evangelicals.

After 1807 Wilberforce supported the movement for the complete abolition of slavery (as distinct from the trade in slaves) and this was brought about by the Emancipation Act of 1833 which became law shortly before his death – abolishing slavery in the British Empire.

CHURCH MISSIONARY SOCIETY

Methodist missionary work had begun to flourish in the middle of the eighteenth century. In 1792 the Baptist Missionary Society had sent Carey to India; in 1795 the non-denominational London Missionary Society sent its first band of workers to the South Sea Islands; Scots Presbyterians founded two societies in 1796. The Church of England, on the other hand, was doing little.

The Society for the Propagation of the Gospel was nearly a hundred years old, but its sphere was limited by its Charter and its work at this time was confined to the white colonists. The Society for Promoting Christian Knowledge (SPCK) was subsidising a small Lutheran mission in India, but this lay outside its normal sphere of work. The Church of England had no organisation for making a real impact in countries where the gospel was never preached.

Since its foundation in 1783, almost all London Evangelical clergy belonged to the Eclectic Society which met fortnightly to discuss matters of mutual concern. (In November 1997 it was announced that the Society is to merge with the Senior Evangelical Anglican Clergy (SEAC) and to get a new lease of life as 'New Eclectics'.) In 1799 Henry Venn of Clapham opened a discussion of the original society under the title, 'What methods can we use more effectively to promote the knowledge of the gospel among the heathen?'

Originally, the idea had been for the Eclectic Society to send out a few missionaries itself. But at Charles Simeon's suggestion, and under his guidance, the Society resolved to form a special society for the purpose. Not far from where John Wesley's heart had been 'strangely warmed' sixty years earlier, they held a public meeting in the Castle and Falcon Hotel in Aldersgate Street. There, twenty-five people founded the Society for Missions to Africa and the East, later to become famous as the Church Missionary Society (more recently the Church Mission Society). Henry Venn was Chairman, Henry Thornton Treasurer, and Thomas Scott the Bible commentator, the Secretary.

Little happened immediately. Foreign missionary work was still virtually unheard of: there was no literature on the subject, no stories to tell of missionary adventures, the scheme seemed rather vague, and nobody came forward. The committee did not do much except make plans for some Bible translations. After two years, when Scott left London to become Vicar of Aston Sandford, Josiah Pratt took over as Secretary and served in the post for the next twenty-two years.

Josiah Pratt's instinct was to think big. He set about the task of collecting facts about the most distant countries and quickly grasped the problems to be faced. He worked with wisdom and untiring energy and, in 1815, was joined as Secretary by a familiar name in Anglican Evangelical history.

Edward Bickersteth's son of the same name was a famous Evangelical Bishop of Exeter and his grandson became Bishop of South Tokyo. His nephew was Bishop of Ripon and his great-great-grandson preceded the present Archbishop of Canterbury as Bishop of Bath and Wells (until 1987). Eugene Stock, who wrote a massive and detailed multi-volume history of the CMS, said of the first Edward Bickersteth's period as secretary:

He represented the highest spiritual side of the Society's principles and methods. His Evangelical fervour was irresistible; and wherever he went, from county to county and from town to town, he stirred his hearers to their hearts' depths, and set them praying and working with redoubled earnestness. His beautiful loving influence healed many divisions, and bound both workers at home and missionaries abroad in holy fellowship. If ever a CMS secretary was filled with the Spirit, that secretary was Edward Bickersteth.[2]

Pratt and Bickersteth were the two men who laid the foundations on which all the later work of the CMS was built.

A large part of the east coast of India was now in British hands. Charles Simeon was determined to begin an Anglican missionary work in India through East India Company chaplains. He successfully persuaded many young Cambridge Evangelicals to apply for chaplaincies as they became vacant.

One of the most famous Anglican missionaries to India was Henry Martyn (1781–1812), a brilliant Cornishman, Senior Wrangler, Prizewinner and Fellow of St John's, Cambridge, who sailed for India in 1805 as an East India Company chaplain. Besides missionary work among Indians, Martyn translated the New Testament into Hindustani and set to work on an Arabic version, living in Shiraz to improve his style. He also translated the *Book of Common Prayer* into Hindustani. Then his health broke down and he started on the journey home across burning plains, only to die alone in Tibet, a stranger in a foreign land. Armenian clergy gave him a Christian burial.

The CMS undertook major pioneering work in West, and later East, Africa, many parts of India, Pakistan and Bangladesh, Sri Lanka, China, Japan, and the Middle East. The CMS of Australia, New Zealand and Ireland are sister societies.

DANIEL WILSON

The son of a wealthy silk merchant, whom he was expected to succeed in business, Daniel Wilson was ordained in 1801. In 1807 he became Vice-Principal of St Edmund Hall, Oxford, and in 1812 he succeeded Richard Cecil at St John's Chapel, Bedford Row. St John's was one of the 'Proprietary Chapels' which the bishops had allowed to be built as the simplest way of coping with the increase of the population. St John's has been demolished, but in the nineteenth century it was a stronghold of Evangelicalism, its congregation including William Wilberforce and other members of the Clapham Sect. At St John's, Daniel Wilson became the leading Evangelical clergyman in London.

In 1824 Wilson was appointed Vicar of Islington. He began a Sunday evening service, abolished pew rents and made all the seats free. He mapped the whole parish into districts and enrolled house-to-house visitors; he opened fifteen Sunday schools.

Daniel Wilson well illustrates why 'activism' is often regarded as one of the key features of Evangelicalism. Incredibly, at his first Confirmation service as Vicar of Islington, Wilson presented to the Bishop 780 candidates! He introduced an early morning Holy Communion, the use of the Litany on Wednesday and Friday and a service on every Saint's Day. He built three new churches to seat more than five thousand people. When he became Bishop of Calcutta in 1832, at the age of fifty-four, he left behind him a strong and efficient parish.

Wilson's energy was phenomenal. As a young man he translated or retranslated all of Cicero's letters in order to acquire a good Latin style. He kept a journal and corresponded for years in Latin with familiar friends for the same reason. At the age of seventy-eight he entered Burma, lived in houses made of mats and founded churches. He wearied others, but rarely himself.

Some said he was ambitious and loved power. But if so, this was surely a means to a noble end. His object was to do all he could so that souls would be saved; and to this he devoted all his time, talents, influence and property. 'We may err in administering the diocese,' he used to say in Calcutta, 'but we cannot err in preaching the gospel. I have made ten thousand mistakes, but I have preached five thousand sermons.'

Wilson was a man of prayer. He referred every event to God. If you met him on business, he began the conversation with prayer and prayed after a decision had been made. If you called on him when he was ill, he would say, 'My dear friend, please pray with me.'

Towards the end of his life, he would spend half days in prayer. He prayed in St Paul's Cathedral in Calcutta (built under his direction), in his private rooms, at the altar, with sick people, with friends in confidence, when the sun was setting and when it was time for bed. Towards the end of his life, when he was unable to kneel down, he prayed with folded hands and eyes lifted up to heaven.

Rising from prayer one evening, after reading Ephesians 4, he said to a lady, 'Oh! my dear child, if we could live much more in the spirit of Ephesians 4, we should be much happier. I am quite overwhelmed when I think of what the true tendency of the gospel is, and of what we ought to be.'

'See what a poor creature I am,' he said on entering his breakfast room one morning, 'and pity me. I fell asleep last night at my prayers.'

He read the whole Bible through every year. 'Tell me how much time you give to the Bible,' he used to say, 'and I will tell you what you are as a Christian. The more we read the Bible, the more we may. It is certain that we shall never exhaust it.' In private he always read an edition with notes by Thomas Scott.

He had immense missionary zeal and wanted every clergyman in India to be a missionary. He worked hard at Bengali, Hindustani and Sanskrit to improve his own effectiveness in the task.

The theme of Wilson's preaching and teaching was always Jesus Christ. When he quarrelled with any scheme of doctrine, it was always because it took from Christ the honour due to his name. The name of Jesus was in every sermon Daniel Wilson preached and every prayer he prayed.

THE BIBLE SOCIETY

Mary Jones, a little girl from Tynoddol, Wales, used to walk four miles every Saturday to read the nearest Bible, until, by hoarding up the halfpence that she earned, she managed to save enough to buy a copy of her own. In bare feet she walked thirty miles over the mountains to find Thomas Charles of Bala, a Methodist leader and the only man in Wales likely to have Bibles to distribute. On her arrival, he told her that he had sold the last Bible many months earlier and that there was no prospect of any more being printed.

Thomas Charles was, however, in correspondence about the possibility of establishing a Bible Society. On his next visit to London, he raised the matter with the Committee of the recently founded Religious Tract Society.

'Surely a Society might be formed for the purpose,' said one of the Committee members in a memorable remark, 'and if for Wales, why not for the Kingdom? And if for the Kingdom, why not for the world?'

The men of the Clapham Sect quickly announced their support for the scheme, and the British and Foreign Bible Society was founded. Lord Teignmouth was its President, William Wilberforce its Vice-President, Henry Thornton its Treasurer and Josiah Pratt of the CMS one of its Secretaries. The group held its first meeting at the London Tavern in Blackfriars on 7 March 1804.

These men were Anglican Evangelicals, but they believed that the provision of Bibles for the world was a cause in which churchmen and nonconformists could work cordially together. They adopted an interdenominational basis: one secretary must always be a member of the Church of England and the other a nonconformist minister. Of the committee of thirty-six, fifteen must be Anglicans, fifteen nonconformists, and six foreign residents in England.

The Society's first prospectus said that its 'exclusive object' was 'to diffuse the knowledge of the Holy Scriptures by circulating them in the different languages throughout Great Britain and Ireland; and also, according to the extent of its funds, by promoting the printing of them in foreign languages and the distribution of them in foreign countries'.

Naturally, the first country they dealt with was Wales. They prepared a Welsh version of 25,000 Bibles and New Testaments, the leather-bound edition costing 3s 3d, and the cloth-bound New Testament twopence. An eyewitness described the arrival of the Bibles in Wales:

When the arrival of the cart was announced, which carried the first load, the peasants went out in crowds to meet it, welcomed it as the Israelites did the Ark of old, drew it into the town, and eagerly bore off every copy, as rapidly as could be dispersed. The young people could be seen consuming the whole night reading it. Labourers carried it with them to the field, that they might enjoy it during the intervals of their labour, and to lose no opportunity of becoming acquainted with its truths.

The General Committee of the Bible Society then turned its attention to the Canadian Indians, and printed the Gospel of John in Mohawk. Next they produced a cheap edition of the English Bible; then a Gaelic Bible for the Highlands. Then came the New Testament in Spanish, Portuguese, Italian, Dutch, Danish, Eskimo, Irish, Manx and modern Greek.

Twice, in its early years, the Society was almost wrecked by controversy. In 1825 a bitter dispute arose over whether the Society should circulate Bibles with the Apocrypha included. At last, in spite of protests from Simeon and many other Evangelicals, the anti-Apocrypha party won and the General Committee decided to circulate only the Old and New Testaments.

Five years later another violent controversy erupted, this time over Unitarianism (or Socinianism). In 1830 the Guernsey Auxiliary of the Society passed a resolution 'pledging themselves to discountenance all union with Socinians', and 'earnestly recommending the parent society totally to withdraw from those who deny the Divinity of our Lord'.

The Society's General Committee in London declined to impose any restrictive test or to refuse the help of anyone who recognised the value of the Bible and wished to help circulate it. Agitation began which ended in terrible uproar at the annual meeting. For six hours a storm raged in Exeter Hall. Speaker after speaker was howled down and the Chairman could not make himself heard. Eventually, when it came to the vote, those who wanted the test were decisively defeated. Many English supporters withdrew from the society and formed the Trinitarian Bible Society. However, the General Committee maintained the confidence of the majority of supporters.

The founding of a Bible Society in London was quickly imitated elsewhere. In less than twenty years from 1804, Europe, the British Empire and America were dotted with Bible Societies and auxiliaries, many of them – including the American Society – helped financially from London.

From the 1830s the Society worked through agents, salaried workers sent out from London to organise Bible Society work over a large area. They set up depots and employed *colporteurs* – a name which originated in France where pedlars went from door to door, or person to person, to distribute the Scriptures. This system was extended to nearly every country in the world. Colporteurs still work in this way in some countries today.

THE EARL OF SHAFTESBURY

'I am essentially an Evangelical of the Evangelicals,' said the seventh Earl of Shaftesbury (1801–85) in his old age. 'I have worked with them constantly, and I am satisfied that most of the great philanthropic movements of the century have sprung from them.'

Shaftesbury (known as Lord Ashley before the death of his father) was educated at Harrow and Christ Church, Oxford, where he obtained a first-class honours degree in Classics. In 1826 he began his Parliamentary career as a member of the Conservative Party. By birth an aristocrat, he spent his life fighting for causes that neither his party nor his class always tackled with such enthusiasm. He must be awarded the title of the most eminent social reformer of the nineteenth century.

While at Harrow he had been horrified by the sight of a pauper's funeral, and had from that moment dedicated his life to the cause of the poor and friendless. 'I have a great mind to found a policy upon the Bible,' he wrote, 'in public life observing the strictest justice, and not only cold justice, but active benevolence.'[3]

'What am I fit for?' he wrote at another time. 'I want nothing but usefulness to God and my country.'

Basing Government policy on Christian principles

Shaftesbury entered Parliament at a time when many children were caught in the grip of the new industrial system. Lancashire factory owners bought children by the barge-load from London workhouses and held them for years, nominally as apprentices but really as slaves. Even children as young as five were made to stand on stools and feed great machines for fourteen hours a day. Underground, in the mines, six-year-olds sat all day in darkness opening and shutting doors as the trucks ran by. The treatment of the mentally ill was equally appalling: the main thought was by whip and chain to protect the community from danger.

Shaftesbury always insisted that the best policy for the British Government was to declare emphatically that its conduct was based on Christian principles, that everything should be done in a Christian character to a Christian end.

Towards the end of his life, he said:

> I made it an invariable rule to see everything with my own eyes, to take nothing on trust or hearsay. In factories, I examined the mills, the machinery, the homes, and saw the workers and their work in all its details. In collieries I went down the pits. In London I went into lodging-houses and thieves' haunts, and every filthy place. It gave me a power I could not otherwise have had. I could speak of things from actual experience, and I used often to hear things from the poor sufferers themselves which were invaluable to me. I got to know their habits of thought and action, and their actual wants. I sat and had tea and talk with them hundreds of times.[4]

Charles Dickens, who was always a warm admirer of Shaftesbury, became his close ally in his reforming work.

On entering Parliament, Shaftesbury made it his first task (successfully) to persuade Parliament to appoint fifteen 'Lunacy Commissioners' of whom he became one. In time all the asylums in the country were indeed reformed.

His task was much more difficult in the case of employment conditions for adults and children in factories and mines. The mill and mine owners were present in large numbers in the House of Commons. Shaftesbury had to fight the wealth and political power of England.

'British industry will be ruined', they told him, 'if your measures are introduced.' Over and over again his reforming measures were defeated. His opponents tried every method of obstruction, including holding lengthy Commissions of Inquiry and bringing forward half-measures. But he persevered, enduring seventeen years of abuse.

Eventually he succeeded. His Factory Act of 1833 stipulated that no under-nines were to work in factories and introduced a nine-hour day for nine- to thirteen-year-olds. His Act of 1844 limited women to working a twelve-hour day and eight- to thirteen-year-olds to six and a half hours. His Ten Hours Bill of 1847 introduced a ten-hour day for children aged thirteen to eighteen and for women. These conditions are alarming by modern standards, but they represented a huge achievement by Shaftesbury in the mid-nineteenth century.

There was more to be done. Children were forced up narrow chimneys by pricking the soles of their feet or threatening them with lighted straw. Shaftesbury protected young chimney sweeps by introducing the Climbing Boys Act.

On 3 August 1872, when he was seventy-one, Shaftesbury laid the first stone of the new buildings on the Shaftesbury Park estate in London. Following the destruction of houses by the building of railways and other public works, a company had been formed to erect homes for working people which were comfortable and sanitary and which, over a period of years, they could afford to buy. The estate, in Battersea near Clapham Junction Station, was opened in July 1874. There were 1,200 houses, schools, an ornamental garden, a lecture hall and shops – but no pub or pawnshop. At the opening of the estate, Shaftesbury, Disraeli and Lord Granville made speeches. Disraeli, the Prime Minister, spoke in glowing terms of Shaftesbury's efforts to improve the lot of the working classes.

Shaftesbury and the 'Palmerston bishops'

From one point of view, Evangelicals were now in a stronger position than ever before. But as far as the appointment of bishops was concerned, when Lord Palmerston became Prime Minister in 1855, even though he was Shaftesbury's father-in-law, there seemed little cause for rejoicing.

'I fear,' wrote Lord Shaftesbury, 'Palmerston's ecclesiastical appointments will be detestable. He does not know, in theology, Moses from Sydney Smith.'

Palmerston, however, recognised the limits of his own knowledge and wisely turned to his son-in-law for advice. He consulted Shaftesbury constantly for nine years so that the Earl became known as 'the Bishop-maker'. The results were a drastic change in the methods of selection. Until this time, with a few exceptions, appointments to the Episcopal Bench had been regarded as one of the Government's most important sources of patronage, and bishoprics had been distributed among members of the governing families, largely with the hope of winning votes in the House of Lords. Shaftesbury was the first to break down this system, and to recommend the appointment of men on religious rather than political grounds.

Shaftesbury's nominations were not all Evangelicals: Ellicott (for Gloucester) and Jacobson (for Chester) were High-Churchmen, though of the old school rather than Tractarian. Tait (for London) and Philpott (for Worcester) were Broad-Churchmen. Longley, Thomson and Harold Browne were non-party men. The only group Shaftesbury never recommended were Tractarians. Certainly, seven Evangelicals did become bishops on Shaftesbury's recommendation, but perhaps this was fair given their under-representation in the past.

The Church Pastoral Aid Society

The Industrial Revolution was changing Britain from a nation of villagers to a nation of town-dwellers, but the bulk of the clergy still worked in the villages. So a small group of Evangelical laymen from Islington inserted a paragraph in the *Record* for 12 March 1835, drawing attention to the need for a Church Home Missionary Society. They called a meeting in the committee room of the Church Missionary Society and on 19 February 1836 formed the Church Pastoral Aid Society (CPAS) 'for the purpose of benefiting the population of our own country by increasing the number of working clergymen in the Church of England, and encouraging the appointment of pious and discreet laymen to the clergy in duties not ministerial'.

They invited the Earl of Shaftesbury to be their first President. William Ewart Gladstone, then the MP for Newark and son of the leading Evangelical layman in Liverpool, was a member of the CPAS Committee. In the first year the CPAS made grants for nearly sixty additional curates and thirteen lay assistants.

At the end of the twentieth century, CPAS is seen as the major home mission agency of the Church of England. It supports a team of evangelists, provides parish consultancy, produces resources for worship, is the major player in parish-based youth work through organisations like Pathfinders and CYFA, encourages young people to consider ordination, and administers the patronage of over five hundred parish churches.[5]

John Bird Sumner

One man who gave great support to the CPAS in its early years was John Bird Sumner. Following service as Bishop of Chester from 1828, Sumner became Archbishop of Canterbury in 1848, the first Evangelical to hold this office since they began to think of themselves as a party within the Church of England. But even as Archbishop, Sumner lived the quiet, frugal life of a country clergyman, rising at dawn, lighting his fire, and dealing with most of his letters before breakfast. He refused to wear an episcopal wig or drive in a state coach. He preferred to walk to the House of Lords with his umbrella under his arm. 'I cannot imagine', he said, 'that any greater reproach could be cast on the Church than to suppose that it allowed its dignity to interfere with its usefulness.'

THE OXFORD MOVEMENT: EVANGELICALISM UNDER ATTACK

The leaders of the Oxford Movement (1833–45) stressed the identity of the Church as a divine society, with an apostolic ministry continued through the historic line of bishops, and sacramental worship as the means of grace. They saw themselves as working for the renewal of the Church in the face of growing secularism and Liberalism.

Some historians have seen the movement as a period of renewal in the Church of England to which the Evangelical movement gave the spirit and the Catholic movement the form. It is true that although the followers of the two parties in the Church were often locked in fierce controversies, they actually had much in common, as some of them even acknowledged at the time – a shared concern for a religion of the heart.

John Keble preached a sermon in St Mary's Church, Oxford (where Cranmer had recanted on his recantation), on 14 July 1833, which is usually regarded as marking the beginning of the movement. In his sermon (the Assize Sermon) he defended the rights of the Church of England against Government interference. With the Church under threat from various quarters, no one, Keble argued, could devote himself too much to the cause of the apostolic Church or to personal devotion and prayer. Many people came to see, in the writing and life of Keble and its preoccupation with purity and sanctity, a poetic mind and a pastoral ministry that had strong similarities to George Herbert.

John Henry Newman

Newman was Vicar of St Mary's from 1828 until he resigned the post in 1843, two years before becoming a Roman Catholic. Newman had grown up amongst Anglican Evangelicals and wrote about them warmly in his famous *Apologia*. Thomas Scott and Daniel Wilson were two Evangelical writers who greatly influenced him.[6]

Under Newman's lead St Mary's became a focal point of the Oxford Movement, and during the fifteen years of Newman's ministry there the church's pulpit exerted a greater influence than at any other time in its momentous history. Dons and undergraduates flocked to hear Newman preach and many of the students copied his mannerisms and imitated every inflection of his voice.

Although Newman had abandoned his Calvinism by the time he became Vicar of St Mary's, he still spoke of Evangelical themes. He talked of the cross as the heart of religion; he said that 'the sacred doctrine of Christ's atoning sacrifice is the vital principle on which the Christian lives, and without which Christianity is not'. But he was already moving towards the Oxford Movement's doctrine of 'reserve', referring to the atonement as 'the deepest Christian truth' which 'should only be communicated to men and women as by moral growth they are able to receive it'.

The Tractarians and justification

In Adam de Brome's chapel on the north side of St Mary's, Newman delivered his Lectures on Justification which, though he was still an Anglican, marked the abandonment of the Evangelicalism of his younger years. Newman and the other leaders of the Oxford Movement – Keble, Ward, Pusey and Williams – set out their views in a series of lengthy tracts: hence they came to be known as the Tractarians.

They came to the view that Evangelicals were obsessed with the slogan 'justification by faith', which had come to prominence in the stormy years of the Reformation and represented one strand only of biblical truth. This alleged obsession had distorted Evangelical thinking and dominated their presuppositions.

Claiming to make the Bible the ultimate authority in their faith, Evangelicals actually used selected passages – especially parts of Paul's epistles – to support their version of Christianity. The men of the Oxford Movement found Evangelicals guilty of paying too little attention to passages such as the Sermon on the Mount, with its high standard of Christian righteousness and absence of obvious references to the atonement. Evangelicals consciously or subconsciously thought of these passages as mere moralising – not the gospel.

William Ward

The outspoken Fellow of Balliol, William Ward (1812–82), pushed Tractarian principles to their furthest extreme. He argued vigorously that the Lutheran principle of justification by faith destroyed the whole idea of self-conquest. It involved a total passivity so that the average standard of saintliness and the normal level of Christian attainment was miserably low. Evangelicalism denied the first principles of morality, and too often had become a religion of feeling rather than duties. Popular Evangelical Christianity aimed at salvation rather than morality. Accepting Calvin's teaching of 'total depravity', Evangelicals forgot that, as Newman put it, human nature 'has the promise upon it of great things'.

According to Ward, Luther had found Christians in bondage to their works; he released them by his doctrine of faith, and left them in bondage to their feelings. Evangelicalism placed too little emphasis on obedience. Whereas Scripture always introduced the warning clause 'if you keep the commandments', Evangelicals tended to say 'if you don't think of them too much'. Evangelical teaching which led people to think that good works were of minor importance, and spoke slightingly of them – that is works of love, of humiliation, and prayer, taught a false and dangerous doctrine. This teaching flattered human laziness, but opposed Scripture, opposed classic Church teaching, and opposed the first principle of our moral nature.[7]

Newman, and the leaders of the Oxford Movement, stressed the role of the conscience as 'the voice of God within'. They spoke of the importance of a sense of duty: 'thou shalt' whispering within us. They stressed that obedience must come first, then knowledge – that obedience was the air in which religious faith lived. It was, as Jesus said, the pure in heart who see God.

The Church, Ward argued, should insist on the value of moral effort and recognise that religion should develop from and not contradict the natural religion of which Paul speaks in the second chapter of Romans. An important function of the Church was to 'train up saints'; ascetic discipline was needed to raise the moral tone. Although good works cannot be done except through the grace of God, there must be careful moral discipline as the foundation on which to build Christian faith.

Sin was the great enemy to be feared, not self-righteousness; obedience to the will of God was the great thing needed. Love was the discriminating mark and moulding principle under which mere belief (which demons exercise) was converted into faith and made justifying. Faith was not justifying unless informed and animated by love.

Justification and the atonement

Justification, said Newman, comes through the sacraments; is received by faith; consists in God's inward presence; and lives in obedience. Justification is a real and actual communication to our souls of the atonement through the work of the Spirit: the dwelling in us of God the Father and the Lord incarnate through the Holy Spirit. To be justified is to receive God's very presence within us, and be made a temple of the Holy Spirit. 'Christ in us' – that, Newman said, is our justification.

On this debate, John Stott suggested to me that what Newman ought to have said was that 'God never justifies without regenerating; and that justification and regeneration always go together. When you put it like that it's no longer necessary to try and subsume under the heading of justification the change that does take place in the justified. But this change isn't part of their justification, it's part of their regeneration.'

Stott agrees with the leaders of the Oxford Movement where they draw attention to the dangerous effects that the Protestant doctrine of justification can have on behaviour – that it could lead to passivity or antinomianism. He refers to Romans 6: 'That's what Paul was combating when he wrote "What then are we to say? Should we continue to sin in order that grace may abound? By no means!" (Rom. 6:1). The fact that Paul put it like that shows that there were some people who were arguing in that way – and they have been ever since!'

He also agrees with Newman's emphasis in his lectures when he speaks of the cross in two ways: first as a place where Christ has done something for us, but second as a picture of what should happen in the life of the believer – being crucified with Christ and taking up the cross.

Newman saw justification as the setting up of the cross within us. For him, it was wholly the work of God; it came from God to us; it was a power exerted on our souls by him, but Christ's cross did not justify by being looked at but by being applied. Christ atoned by the offering of himself on the cross; and he justified by the mission of his Spirit.

The faith which justifies

Newman's emphasis on the nature of the faith which justifies echoes that of Jeremy Taylor (see pages 84–7). Newman argued that preachers should take care to encourage congregations to make sure their faith was justifying, that it was not dead, formal, self-righteous, or merely moral instead of glorifying him 'whose image fully set out, destroys deadness, formality and self-righteousness'. Newman said we should think of faith as a habit of the soul; and a habit is something permanent which affects the character.

Religious doctrines and articles of faith can only be received in a certain state of heart; and this state of heart can only be formed by the repetition of certain actions. The obedience of Christians was the light of the world; example was a more powerful persuasion than preaching. God would reveal himself to the pure in heart, to the humble, and to those who, in his strength, kept his commandments.

Pusey on Evangelicalism

Unlike Newman, Edward Bouverie Pusey (1800–82) was not brought up among Evangelicals. But though critical, his attitude to Evangelicals was warmer than some of his Tractarian colleagues. His assessment of Evangelicals was almost certainly more accurate than that of the other men of the Oxford Movement (the leaders were all men). Educated at Eton and Christ Church, he was elected a Fellow of Oriel College in 1823. In 1828 he was ordained deacon and priest and appointed Regius Professor of Hebrew and Canon of Christ Church, offices he held for the rest of his life. Also unlike Newman, he remained a loyal member of the Church of England to the end of his days.

In his fifties, Pusey said this of Evangelicals:

When I was a child, I never knew an Evangelical. But over the last twenty-five years I have met many. And ever since I knew them I have loved those who are called Evangelicals. I love them because they love our Lord. I love them for their zeal for souls. I have often thought them narrow; yet I have been drawn to individuals among them more than to others who hold truths in common with myself, which Evangelicals don't hold, at least explicitly.

I believe Evangelicals to be 'of the truth'. I have ever believed and believe that their faith is, on some points of doctrine, much truer than their words ... I have always sought Evangelicals out, both out of love for them, and because I believe that nothing, with God's help, so dispels prejudice as personal discussion, heart to heart, with those against whom that prejudice is held. I sought to point out to them our common basis of faith ...

From time to time, as in some of our struggles at Oxford, Evangelicals and I have acted together. I have united with them whenever they would join me in defence of our common faith ...

I tell friends who are dissenters that one thing alone of which the Church of England is jealous: that nothing should be seen to overshadow, or interfere with, or supplement the meritoriousness of the one sacrifice of our dear Lord upon the cross. This is what she everywhere guards: 'The offering of Christ once made is that perfect redemption, propitiation, and satisfaction, for all the sins of the world, original and actual, and there is none other satisfaction for sin but this alone ...'

God blesses through the sacraments; and God blesses through truth. If a Wesleyan minister preaches his simple gospel that 'we are all sinners', that 'Christ died to save sinners', that 'he bids all sinners to come to Him' and says 'whoever comes to me I will never drive away', this is of course fundamental gospel truth, and, when God blesses through it those who know no more, he blesses them through faithful reception of his truth ...

Protestant bodies have their revivals; the Church of England has multiplied the celebration of its sacraments. After more than three centuries, the English Church alone has a more vigorous life than ever. What's the reason? We haven't rejected Catholicism.[8]

The Tractarians on holiness

Like Newman and Ward, Pusey believed that Evangelicals fell short in both their teaching and practice of holiness:

> Evangelicals often seem to me to carry their ideas of corrupt human nature too much into the new man. They think that because we are by nature infected with evil, and have ourselves gone yet further astray, therefore we are incapable of rising to any great heights of holiness (though this is always God's free gift, and not of ourselves). Evangelicals almost seem to look upon it as derogatory to Christ's atonement, if we are thought of as anything other than weak, miserable, sinning creatures, who are to go on sinning and polluted unto our lives' end. They forget that since it's not ourselves but God who makes us holy, all boasting and self-righteousness is excluded by the very conditions.
>
> The result is a miserably low standard of human attainment among Evangelicals. Or, to put it another way, a lack of faith as to what God can and has and does work in us for our redemption, or of Christ's being at the right hand of God to make intercession for us. They don't think of that almost more stupendous mystery, man united with God, our human nature (which has not been vouchsafed to angels) united with our God, and all the high inconceivable privileges ensuing from that.[9]

There was force in these Oxford Movement arguments in that they highlighted weaknesses in Evangelical doctrine and emphasis. However, in their assessment of Evangelicalism, the Tractarians underestimated the seriousness with which Evangelicals treated sin and failed to take sufficient account of the effect on the quality of their lives of either the high Evangelical view of Scripture or their doctrine of sanctification. Pusey was the most astute in recognising this and therefore wisely had tried hard to establish good relationshps with Evangelicals. I say more about this in the concluding section of this book (pages 453–4).

THE PEARSALL SMITHS AND HOLINESS

Across the Atlantic in 1867 many Americans were reading a weekly magazine called *Revival*. The November edition included an article by a Quaker, Mrs Pearsall Smith, entitled 'The Way to be Holy'. Her husband wrote similar articles and the couple's ideas were to become a talking point on both sides of the ocean.

The keynote of the Pearsall Smiths' message was that the normal Christian life was intended to be one of sustained victory over sin; that true salvation is not only from the guilt of past sins, but also from the power of those sins in the future; that this salvation is the gift of God, not the work of self, and is to be appropriated by faith, just like the gift of justification. The emphasis was very different from Oxford Movement teaching.

In 1874 the Pearsall Smiths arrived in England. Although Pearsall Smith had no theological training, he received many invitations to address meetings. What Pearsall Smith said often betrayed his ignorance of theology and included both distortion and error. However, four Anglican Evangelicals – Hopkins of Holy Trinity, Richmond, Moore of Brunswick Chapel, Thornton of St Nicholas's, Nottingham, and Hankin of Christ Church, Ware – decided that the kernel of what Pearsall Smith was saying was soundly scriptural and a message needed by the Church.

They organised a Convention in July 1874 at Broadlands, near Romsey, to discuss 'the Scriptural possibilities of faith in the life of the Christian (a) as to maintained communion with God, (b) as to victory over all known sin'. Further conferences followed, one of which was attended by Canon Harford-Battersby, Vicar of St John's, Keswick.

Many Evangelical leaders regarded the new movement with suspicion. Two Evangelical publications, the *Record* and the *Christian Observer* were entirely hostile, as was Bishop Ryle (whose criticisms are set out on pages 254–7). In the twentieth century Jim Packer criticised this approach to holiness. Eventually, the strain of criticism and controversy began to tell on Pearsall Smith, who had in any case come to England to convalesce from an illness, and his public addresses became rambling and wild. Some English friends insisted that he return to America. Contrary to what many believed, however, the movement was not dead.

THE KESWICK CONVENTION

In July 1875 Canon Harford-Battersby, who was attracted to the Pearsall Smiths' ideas, held the first Keswick Convention. A cultured Balliol man, Harford-Battersby had worked his way from the Oxford Movement position to the Evangelical one. He wanted to give Christians in the north of England an opportunity to hear the new ideas.

He hired a tent and sent out invitations. The Convention has been held almost every July from then until now. By no means every speaker over the years has taken the excessively passive 'let go and let God' line on holiness which Ryle and others severely criticised at the time and Jim Packer has rounded on in recent years. Many have simply taken seriously the Convention's call to a life of practical holiness. Others have been drawn by the 'All One in Christ Jesus' motto, realising sometimes for the first time that there are sincere Christians in denominations other than the one in which they grew up. Yet others have been attracted to the message that the Christian life need not be a succession of miserable failures, that victory over sin is possible. All have enjoyed the beautiful Lake District scenery in summer.

The Convention has given a great impetus to foreign missionary work, as young people have taken to heart the words of the second verse of Francis Ridley Havergal's hymn of consecration:

> Take my hands and let them move
> At the impulse of thy love;
> Take my feet, and let them be
> Swift and beautiful for thee.

BISHOP RYLE

John Charles Ryle (1816–1900) stated the Evangelical position with clarity on many disputed issues, establishing a line which in some areas remains unchanged today. He went some way to answering Tractarian attacks on Evangelicalism and distanced himself from the passivity of the Keswick teaching of his day.

J. C. Ryle stood literally head and shoulders above his contemporaries. Grave, dignified, of magnificent presence, he was an athlete who had captained teams at both Eton and Oxford. He was able academically, became a good administrator and a vigorous, clear-thinking preacher and writer. On the surface at least, his Christian faith appears rarely to have been troubled by doubt. By 1897 more than twelve million English copies of his tracts had been sold and in addition many had been translated into a dozen foreign languages.

'My first serious thoughts about religion', declared Canon Knox-Little, 'have been derived from reading one of Ryle's tracts.' The English author John Ruskin (1819–1900) said: 'The pleasantest and most useful reading I know on nearly all religious questions whatever are Ryle's tracts.' Bishop Chavasse described Ryle as 'a man of granite with the heart of a little child'. Charles Haddon Spurgeon called him the best man in the Church of England. In 1880 he became the first bishop of Liverpool.

'You know my opinions,' he told the Bishopric Committee in his new diocese. 'I am a committed man. I come among you a Protestant and Evangelical: but I come with a desire to hold out the right hand to all loyal churchmen, holding at the same time my own opinions determinedly.' He told one of his diocesan conferences: 'I have no love for men who have no distinct opinions, theological jelly-fish without bones, brains, teeth or claws.'

However, he always tried to be scrupulously fair to 'each of the three historic parties in the church' – meaning, presumably, Evangelical, Catholic and 'Broad Church'. 'In a fallen world like ours,' he said, 'and in a free country it is vain to expect all men to see all things alike: but so long as a brother walks loyally within the limits of the Articles and Prayer Book, let us respect him and treat him courteously, even when we do not agree with him. I entreat every clergyman in my diocese, for Christ's sake, to abhor all needless divisions, and to follow after peace as well as truth.'[10]

Despite fierce controversies with 'Ritualists' in his diocese, he was successful in his work as a bishop. When he arrived in Liverpool, there was no diocesan machinery at all; when he resigned in 1900 he left behind one of the best organised dioceses in England.[11]

Ryle on Evangelical Christianity

'The clouds are gathering round the Church of England; her very existence is in peril.' Similar words have been spoken at various times for three hundred years at least. The exact quote is taken from a paper written by Bishop Ryle in 1896. He had in mind conflicting opinions which he believed threatened to split the Church, especially the divisions over Ritualism which characterised the Church of England in the second half of the nineteenth century. He was not sure whether his beloved Church would survive the struggle.

In the belief that clarity of thought aids debate, he attempted to define Evangelical Christianity. He set out five leading features of Evangelicalism.

First, the *absolute supremacy it assigns to Holy Scripture.*

Second, *the depth and prominence it assigns to the doctrine of human sinfulness and corruption.* And so, said Ryle, 'we dread fostering man's favourite notion that a little church-going and sacrament-receiving, a little patching and mending, and whitewashing, and gilding, and polishing, and varnishing, and painting the outside – is all that his case requires . . . Man is radically diseased and needs a radical cure.'

Third, *the paramount importance it gives to the work and office of our Lord Jesus Christ,* and to the nature of the salvation which he has wrought for men and women. 'We hold that an experimental knowledge of Christ crucified and interceding, is the very essence of Christianity . . . We say that life eternal is to know Christ, believe in Christ, abide in Christ, have daily heart communion with Christ, by simple personal faith – and that everything in religion is useful so far as it helps forward that life of faith and no further.'

Fourth, Ryle emphasised the high place which Evangelicalism assigned to *the inward work of the Holy Spirit in the hearts of men and women.*

Fifth, he stressed the importance which Evangelicalism attached to *the outward and visible work of the Holy Spirit in people's lives.*

Ryle's nine points setting out what Evangelicalism *is not* are revealing as much for the list of what he felt it necessary to deny as well as for the substance of his denials.

First, he said Evangelicalism *does not despise learning, research, or the wisdom of days gone by.* Looking over a list of those who had been eminent for theological scholarship, Ryle claimed that some of the most distinguished were Evangelicals: Ridley, Jewel, Ussher, Lightfoot, Davenant, Hall, Whittaker, Willett, Reynolds, Leighton, Owen, Baxter, Manton. Evangelicals do read and can think, he said, but they refuse to place any uninspired writings on a level with revelation.

Second, Evangelicalism *does not undervalue the Church* or think lightly of its privileges. 'In sincere and loyal attachment to the Church of England we give place to none. We value its form of government, its Confession of faith, its mode of worship as much as any within its pale.' However, Ryle insisted that Evangelicals refused to exalt the Church above Christ, or to teach people that membership of the Church was identical to membership of Christ. They refused to assign to the Church an authority for which they found no warrant either in Scripture or in the Articles.

Third, Evangelicalism *does not undervalue Christian ministry.* 'We regard it as an honourable office instituted by Christ himself, and of general necessity for carrying on the work of the Gospel.' But Evangelicals refused to admit that clergy were in any sense sacrificing priests, mediators between God and humanity, lords of people's consciences, or private confessors. 'We find that sacerdotalism, or priestcraft has frequently been the curse of Christianity, and the ruin of true religion. And we say boldly that the exaltation of the ministerial office to an unscriptural place and extravagant dignity in the Church of England in the present day, is likely to alienate the affections of the laity, to ruin the church, and to be the source of every kind of error and superstition.'

Fourth, Evangelicalism *does not undervalue the sacraments of Baptism and the Lord's Supper*. Ryle maintained that Evangelicals honoured them as holy ordinances appointed by Christ himself, and 'as blessed means of grace, which in all who use them rightly, worthily, and with faith, "have a wholesome effect or operation"'. But Evangelicals refused to admit that the sacraments conveyed grace *ex opere operato*, and that in every case where they were administered good must necessarily be done. They could not accept that the sacraments were above preaching or prayer.

Fifth, Evangelicalism *does not undervalue the English Prayer Book*. Evangelicals honoured the Prayer Book as a matchless form of public worship and admirably adapted to the needs of human nature. But Evangelicals did not presume to say that there can be no acceptable worship of God without the Prayer Book. It did not possess the same authority as the Bible.

Sixth, Evangelicalism *did not undervalue Episcopacy*. 'We give our bishops as much honour and respect as any section of the Church of England and in reality a great deal more.' Episcopal government, rightly administered was the best form of Church government in an evil world. But Evangelicals could not believe that bishops were infallible, or that Presbyterian orders were not valid orders or that non-episcopal Christians were to be handed over to the uncovenanted mercies of God (as many High-Churchmen taught). Evangelicals believed, like others, that from the beginning there had been bishops, priests and deacons, but they could not accept the slogan 'No bishop, no church'.

Seventh, Evangelicalism *did not object to handsome churches*, good ecclesiastical architecture, a well-ordered ceremonial, and a well-conducted service, but they hated slovenliness and disorder in God's service. They maintained that simplicity should be the foremost characteristic of Christian worship. Human nature is so easily led astray, and so thoroughly inclined to idolatry, that ornament in Christian worship should be used sparingly. The inward and spiritual character of the congregation is more important than architecture and adornments.

Eighth, Evangelicalism *did not undervalue unity*. Evangelicals loved harmony and peace; but there could be no real unity without oneness in the faith. They protested against the idea of unity based on a common episcopacy and not a common belief in Christ's gospel. 'We abhor the very idea of reunion with Rome unless Rome first purges herself from her many false doctrines and superstitions.'

Finally, Evangelicalism *did not undervalue Christian holiness and self-denial*. Evangelicals wanted as much as anyone to promote habitual spirituality of heart and life in Christians. 'We give place to none', said Ryle, 'in exalting humility, charity, meekness, gentleness, temperance, purity, self-denial, good works, and separation from the world. With all our defects, we are second to no section of Christ's church in attaching the utmost importance to private prayer, private Bible-reading and private communion with God.'

Bishop Ryle offered three suggestions about the present duties of Evangelicals. Some will say that they are as relevant at the close of the twentieth century as they were at the close of the nineteenth.

First, he suggested that Evangelicals *should be very careful about their own personal religion.* They should ensure that it was thoroughly and entirely Evangelical. 'The times we live in are desperately unfavourable to a sharply-cut, decided, distinct, doctrinal Christianity. A fog of vague Liberalism over-spreads the ecclesiastical horizon. A settled determination to think everybody is right, and nobody is wrong, everything is true, and nothing is false, meets us at every turn. The world is possessed with a devil of false charity about religion.' Instead, Ryle advocated standing fast in the old paths, 'the good way of our Protestant Reformers'.

Second, he recommended that Evangelicals *took care not to compromise their principles by compromising with the world.*

This plausible pretext of making our services more attractive, and cutting the ground from under the feet of Ritualists, too often induces Evangelical ministers to do things which they had far better let alone. New church decorations, new church music, and a semi-histrionic mode of going through church worship, are things which I suggest we must watch most narrowly and keep at arm's length. They are points on which we must take heed that we do not let in the Pope and the devil . . .

Worshippers who are not content with the Bible, the cross of Christ, simple prayers and simple praise, are worshippers of little value. It is useless to please them because their spiritual taste is diseased.

Finally, Ryle *warned against allowing Evangelicalism to be thrust out of the Church of England without a struggle.* Evangelicalism was worth a struggle. 'In the day when Evangelical religion is cast out of the Church of England, the usefulness of the church will be ended and gone. Nothing gives the Church of England more power and influence as genuine, well-worked, well-administered Evangelical religion.'[12]

Ryle on holiness

What Bishop Ryle said about holiness, and his stress on the subject, is important in two respects. First, as a rebuke of Keswick Convention teaching which told people that, because faith was the key to holiness, you need not *strive* to be holy; and second, in his answer to the allegation of the leaders of the Oxford Movement that Evangelicals were poor achievers in the realm of holiness.

Ryle issued his rebuke to Keswick teaching in the form of gentle questions. Was it wise, he wondered, to speak of faith as being the one and only thing required, as many seemed to be doing in handling the doctrine of sanctification? Was it wise to proclaim, in as bald and unqualified a way as many did, that the holiness of converted people was by faith only and not at all by personal exertion? Ryle did not think such teaching reflected the balance of God's Word.

Against the background of Keswick teaching, Ryle pointed out that Scripture taught that in following holiness the true Christian needed personal exertion and work as well as faith. 'The very same apostle who says in one place, "The life I live in the body, I live by faith in the Son of God", says in another place, "I fight", "I run", "I beat my body", and in other places, "let us purify ourselves", "let us make every effort", "let us throw off everything that hinders" (Gal. 2:20; 1 Cor. 9:26, 27; 2 Cor. 7:1; Heb. 4:11, 12:1).'

Was it wise, Ryle asked, to make so little of the many practical exhortations to holiness in daily life which were found in the Sermon on the Mount, and in the latter part of most of Paul's letters?

Something more was needed than generalities about holy living which pricked no conscience and gave no offence. True holiness did not consist merely in believing and feeling, but in doing and bearing, and in practical exhibition of active and passive grace.

> When people talk of having received 'such a blessing', and of having found 'the higher life', after hearing some earnest advocate of 'holiness by faith and self-consecration', while their families and friends see no improvement in their daily tempers and behaviour, immense harm is done to the cause of Christ. True holiness . . . is much more than tears and sighs and bodily excitement and a quickened pulse and a passionate feeling of attachment to our favourite preachers and our own religious party and a readiness to quarrel with everyone who does not agree with us. It is something of 'the image of Christ', which can be seen and observed by others in our private life and habits and character and doings (Rom. 8:29).

Was it wise, Ryle asked, to teach believers that they ought not to think so much of fighting and struggling against sin, but ought rather to 'yield themselves to God', and be passive in the hands of Christ? Did this reflect the balance of Scripture? He did not think so. Scripture spoke of a holy violence, a conflict, a warfare, a fight, a soldier's life, a wrestling as characteristics of the true Christian.

The marks of practical holiness

Bishop Ryle listed the following as features of practical holiness:

- The habit of being of one mind with God: hating what he hates, loving what he loves. The most holy person is the one who agrees most with God.
- *Endeavouring* to shun every known sin, and keeping every known commandment. A mind set towards God, a desire to do his will, a greater fear of displeasing him than of displeasing the world (Rom. 7:22; Ps. 119:128).

- *Striving* to be like our Lord Jesus Christ. Learning to make Christ 'all' both for salvation and example.
- Following after meekness, long-suffering, gentleness, patience, control of the tongue.
- *Striving* after self-denial; *putting to death* the desires of the body; *crucifying* the flesh with its lusts, curbing passion.
- Following after Christian love and brotherly kindness (1 Cor. 13). Shunning lying, slandering, backbiting, cheating and dishonesty, even in the smallest matters.
- Having a spirit of mercy.
- *Striving* for purity of heart.
- Seeking to fear God. Fearing God because we love him as a child loves his father.
- Seeking to be humble. Viewing others as better than oneself. Ryle quoted 'dear Mr Grimshaw's' last words, 'Here goes an unprofitable servant.'
- Being faithful in all of life's duties (Col. 3:23; Rom. 12:11). Aiming to do everything well. *Striving* to be good husbands and good wives, good parents and good children, good neighbours, good friends, good in the place of business and good by the fireside.
- *Striving* after spiritual-mindedness. Setting our affections entirely on things above and holding things on earth with a very loose hand.

Ryle concluded his book *Holiness* by quoting the words of Colossians 3:11, 'Christ is all.'

These words are the essence of Christianity. A right knowledge of Christ is essential to right knowledge of sanctification as well as justification. Those who follow after holiness will make no progress unless they give to Christ his rightful place ... Let us live on Christ. Let us live in Christ. Let us live with Christ. Let us live to Christ. So doing, we shall prove that we fully realise that Christ is all. So doing we shall feel great peace, and attain more of that holiness without which no-one will see the Lord (Heb. 12:14).[13]

Ryle's emphasis on allowing something of the beauty of Jesus to be seen in individual Christian lives is perhaps an approach which can draw together the Evangelical and more Catholic versions of holiness, which competed against each other in the nineteenth century, just as they have so often done since the Reformation.

PART FIVE

Church on fire in twentieth-century England

Consider what a great forest is set on fire by a small spark.
(James 3:5b)

STRONG AND UNITED

Queen Victoria died in 1901 and was succeeded by her son Edward VII. Anglican Evangelicalism was as strong as at any previous period in its history. Despite the effect of the Oxford Movement, the influence of Evangelicalism had also spread to every diocese. Its missionary work continued to flourish and expand. Its societies and institutions were playing a notable part in the life of the Church.

At that time, too, Anglican Evangelicals were united in the central point of their witness: an acceptance of the scriptural testimony to Jesus Christ and of the doctrinal and liturgical principles of the Church of England.

As the twentieth century opened, the total number of clergy in England reached a peak of 25,235. The rest of the century has witnessed a steady decline in numbers. The First World War was a critical time for the Church of England. It was a period of abrupt change when many social conventions which had previously sustained church attendance (notably the 'English Sunday') were eroded. The clergy became aware of the competition of other leisure activities.[1]

Following the end of the war, relations between Church and state were altered when, in 1919, Parliament passed a measure which gave the three houses of the Church Assembly – bishops, clergy and laity – powers to prepare legislation on Church matters for Parliament to consider.[2]

Measures passed between 1919 and 1921 set up the whole system of Diocesan and Rural Deanery Conferences and Parochial Church Councils which brought lay people to manage Church affairs at all levels on a scale never seen before. In many parishes Church Councils had already existed, for the purpose of assisting the incumbent, but they possessed no standing or power, and were dependent entirely on the goodwill of the incumbent. Now lay members of the parish were given the right to make their voice heard in the affairs of their Church. In 1970 the Church Assembly was superseded by the General Synod. This set the seal on the whole process of bringing lay people into the running of the Church of England.[3]

Although Evangelicals have always been committed to a thoroughgoing belief in the priesthood of all believers, they were for some reason slow to make use of the opportunities offered by the changes introduced in the 1920s.

Prayer Book Revision

The modifications to Church government worked well until, in 1927 and 1928, the House of Commons twice rejected a project for revision of the Prayer Book, creating a deadlock in relations between the Assembly and Parliament.

The measure aroused considerable controversy in the country at large. Evangelicals, as so often, were not all of one mind, but the majority were strongly opposed to some of the proposed innovations, particularly a change which would have permitted the Reservation of the Sacrament, and an (Alternative) Eucharistic rite which was closer to the medieval services than the 1662 book. The second and final rejection of the Revised Book by the Commons came as a relief to many Evangelicals in the Church of England.

Evangelical theological colleges and schools

Three new theological colleges were founded in the 1920s and 1930s: the Bible Churchmen's College, Bristol (1925), Clifton Theological College, Bristol (1932) and Oak Hill College, Southgate, London (1932). St Aidan's College, Birkenhead, celebrated its centenary in 1947, and Wycliffe Hall, Oxford, and Ridley Hall, Cambridge, continued to be known as Evangelical colleges.

Monkton Combe School, near Bath, left its marks on many Anglican Evangelicals. It was a training ground for earnest, committed Evangelicals with a strong emphasis on Crusaders and the Christian Union, which were both more central to the life of the school than its chapel. The rather fundamentalist Christian teaching at the school was a basis upon which pupils could later build or depart. The young Graham Leonard arrived there in 1933 from an Evangelical family, and went on to become Balliol College representative at the Oxford Inter-Collegiate Christian Union (OICCU) – but that marked the end of his organised Evangelical commitment. Leonard later became a 'traditionalist' Bishop of London, opposing the ordination of women, and still later joined the Roman Catholic Church. He came in the 1990s to the view that the Church of England Synod 'could do exactly as it liked, ignoring the vast majority of Christendom'.

Monkton Combe produced real spiritual leaders such as W. J. Thompson (Bishop of Iran) and Maurice Wood (Principal of Oak Hill and Bishop of Norwich) as well as Graham Leonard. It also turned out people who later rejected Christianity altogether, drifted into other strands of Anglicanism, or joined other Christian denominations.[4]

Evangelical reaction to theological Liberalism

How would Evangelicals react to biblical criticism and theological Liberalism? One outcome was the formation of the Anglican Evangelical Group Movement, whose origin goes back to the beginning of the twentieth century. The group ran a journal called *The Liberal Evangelical*, was firmly Evangelical in its conception of church order, but adopted a 'Liberal' attitude to biblical interpretation. One of its primary aims was to 'apprehend by means of study the findings of modern scholarship in relation to the Bible and Christian doctrine'. As we shall see, the group eventually dissolved itself in 1967.

In the years immediately following the First World War the Church Missionary Society (as it then was) debated the issue of how it should respond to the findings of modern scholarship. After a protracted struggle the majority opted for a certain liberty of opinion, and this involved at least the possibility of a departure from the historic Evangelical tradition. A strong minority refused to accept this judgment, and in 1922 separated themselves from the parent body to form the Bible Churchmen's Missionary Society (BCMS). This move carried with it the bitterness which normally accompanies such division.

Missionary work

Notwithstanding the split in the ranks of the CMS, Evangelicals must be credited with giving their finest service to God in the twentieth century in the sphere of overseas mission. Their contribution has been out of all proportion to the influence of Evangelicals in Britain. The recognised Anglican Evangelical missionary societies have carried the main burden of the Church's missionary work and, certainly in the first half of the century, were the biggest single factor in the growth of the Anglican Communion overseas. All the time there has been an increasing emphasis on the need to build up strong indigenous churches with the CMS working in partnership with them.

In the 1990s the CMS has over two hundred mission partners in twenty-seven countries and an annual budget of over four million pounds. Since the fall of the Iron Curtain, the Society has been finding new opportunities for partnerships with the churches of Eastern Europe.

The Bible Society

By 1914 the British and Foreign Bible Society was to some extent active in every country in the world. In 1917 one-third of the Society's total circulation was in China and in that year three million Bibles were distributed.

In 1946 Bible Societies agreed to form the 'United Bible Societies', a fellowship of independent societies who co-operate to increase support for the worldwide work and channel it to needy people. The title British and Foreign Bible Society has given way to 'Bible Society', as the Society no longer has direct responsibility for staff located outside England and Wales.

I was invited to join the General Committee (since renamed Board of Trustees) of the Society in 1985 and now serve on the Executive Committee as well. In recent years we have adjusted priorities so that more resources are committed to England and Wales, which are themselves a needy mission field. But the Society's foreign role is still vitally important, providing support for other Bible Societies in their own countries through the provision of funds and services such as help with translation work and the purchase of Bibles. In September 1997 we heard from Moscow that visitors to the Kremlin could see a range of Christian Scriptures, published by the Russian Bible Society, on display and available for sale as they lined up to buy their tickets to visit this historic seat of power.

The Bible Society approaches its two-hundredth anniversary aware that it has unique expertise and authority in important fields: understanding the Bible's role in mission; developing Bible study material; Bible production; and research into how the Bible is used. It has a good record of working with churches internationally, nationally and locally, and with Christian agencies of many kinds. The Society's Board of Trustees now includes two Roman Catholics. Campaigning activities include the Open Book project, a major initiative being pursued by the Society in conjunction with Churches Together in England (CTE), aimed at developing creative, relevant and meaningful new ways to make the significance of the Bible more widely known – using the slogan 'Telling the Story to Shape Tomorrow' (see page 436).

MAX WARREN

Later to become a distinguished General Secretary of the CMS, Max Warren (1904–77) was Vicar of Holy Trinity, Cambridge, from 1936 to 1942 and felt a deep sense of responsibility towards the Evangelical cause between the two world wars. He had been placed in charge of the church where a famous Anglican Evangelical had made a real impact in Cambridge early in the nineteenth century and whose influence was still in evidence a hundred years later.

Max was in his element planning the commemoration of the

centenary of Charles Simeon's death in November 1936. Not content with the promise of just a single sermon from the Archbishop of Canterbury, Cosmo Gordon Lang, on the Sunday nearest the actual date, he set to work organising a whole week of addresses. His aim was that the talks would interpret Simeon and his significance for Cambridge and the Church at large in the twentieth century. Warren succeeded in gaining the enthusiastic help of distinguished speakers and helped to raised the profile of Evangelicalism generally.

In 1942 Warren established the Evangelical Fellowship for Theological Literature (EFTL). The Fellowship's founding document spoke of 'the dearth of theological writing inspired by Evangelical insights, and the consequent failure of Evangelicalism to make its proper contribution to the Church of England as one of the schools of thought within the church'.

Evangelicals, especially in the nineteenth century, had concerned themselves above all with action – giving themselves unstintingly to philanthropic, evangelistic and missionary activities. Warren saw that Evangelicals were somewhat deficient in ideas and intellectual research, and realised that alongside the activity of laymen like Wilberforce and Shaftesbury must be set the strand of preaching and doctrine represented by Simeon.

Reversing the 'anti' complex

Because they had concentrated on action, Warren thought that Evangelicals had been ill-prepared for the controversies which accompanied the Oxford Movement, with its emphasis on the authority of the Church, and badly equipped to respond to the findings of biblical criticism. From the 1850s Evangelicals had been thrown on the defensive and had developed an 'anti' complex: anti-Rome, anti-ritual, anti-biblical criticism, anti-Darwin, anti-worldliness. To a degree this promoted unity, for there are few things which so unite as opposition to a common foe, but it tended to obscure the unity which is to be found in devotion to Christ.

Being concerned with practical matters and the need for action, Evangelicals often felt the need for a clear-cut manual of faith and discipline. They found this in the Bible and the worship book which was based so clearly on it, the *Book of Common Prayer*. Anyone who tampered with these, or suggested inaccuracies, or proposed varieties of interpretation, was attacking the sure foundation on which both spiritual security and evangelistic motivation was based.

These tensions explain the splits among Evangelicals in the CMS in 1922 and over the revision of the Prayer Book in 1928. The vague term 'Liberal' was attached to those who were anxious to welcome the results of historical criticism and of scientific research. The term 'Conservative' was applied to those who clung to a literal interpretation of the Bible and, to some extent, the 1662 Prayer Book and the Thirty-nine Articles.

In the universities and in many parishes, the period between the wars was one of suspicion and controversy among Evangelicals, of attempted consolidation of the old traditions rather than of advancing into new insights. It went with a dearth of constructive theological writing. The danger (as so often) was that Evangelicals would cut themselves off from new understandings which were being developed by those engaged in historical, scientific and theological research.

Already, there were some who regarded Max Warren as 'unsound', 'too intellectual', ready to compromise on fundamentals. Actually, no one loved the Bible more or lived it more faithfully than he. And he was convinced that the Evangelical tradition had a valuable role to play within the Church of England. He believed that this contribution included a *theological* one. His insight was to realise that this could best be done by gathering together a group of his own contemporaries for mutual illumination and encouragement and by stimulating individuals to publish good quality work which would make an Evangelical contribution to theological understanding.

Warren's EFTL proved to be an admirable means of drawing and holding together a community of research and writing which, by 1952, had 150 members consisting of parochial clergy, missionaries and university or college teachers. In 1971 the EFTL ceased to exist as a formal body, but by then groups such as the Tyndale Fellowship were doing a similar job.[5]

Max Warren went on to serve as General Secretary of the CMS from 1942 until 1963, and as Canon and Subdean of Westminster from 1963 to 1973.

G. T. Manley

Max Warren first met the Rev. G. T. Manley, then the CMS Secretary for Africa, early in the 1920s. Manley, a Fellow of Christ's College, Cambridge, who went on to become an elder statesman of the Inter-Varsity Fellowship (IVF, now UCCF), had in 1893 gained the coveted distinction of the Senior Wranglership in the University of Cambridge; he headed the list of honours graduates in Mathematics, beating Bertrand Russell whose name appeared lower down in the same list. Manley had been converted through a Cambridge Inter-Collegiate Christian Union (CICCU) sermon and many years later, in August 1955, he recalled in *The Times* that when he became a Christian as an undergraduate, he 'felt a new responsibility for thinking out the foundations upon which the Christian faith rested' and found that 'a true conversion is rather a stimulus to study than a check upon it'.[6]

G. T. Manley was the distinguished editor of *The New Bible Handbook*, published in 1948, one of the books which established the IVF as a major Evangelical publisher.

JOHN STOTT

The son of a cardiologist at Westminster Hospital, John Stott was born in 1921. His mother taught him and his three sisters to read the Bible and pray, but his father remained a secular humanist. Some say that as a child John would sit in the gallery of All Souls and drop rolled-up bus tickets on the hats of the fashionable ladies below (though when I met him to talk about this book I did not check the accuracy of this allegation).

Stott became a Christian at the age of seventeen at Rugby School, gained a first in Modern Languages at Trinity College, Cambridge, and studied Theology at Ridley Hall. He was ordained as Curate of All Souls, Langham Place, London, in 1945. In 1950 he was made Rector of the same church, which became under his leadership a well-known centre of Evangelicalism. Stott remains Rector Emeritus of the church, still preaching there regularly.

In 1959 he was appointed Honorary Chaplain to the Queen. He has conducted teaching missions all over the world and is the author of more than thirty-five books – one of which, *Basic Christianity*, has sold over two-and-a-half million copies and been translated into fifty languages. He has been active either as president or chairman of Evangelical organisations ranging from the relief agency Tear Fund to the Universities and Colleges Christian Fellowship (UCCF). On his 'retirement' in 1975 he set about establishing the Institute for Contemporary Christianity which aims in a variety of ways to relate biblical faith to every aspect of life. He was the first director and is now president.

All his life Stott has been an avid bird-watcher and, in June 1997, at the age of seventy-six, he spent a week bird-watching in Siberia. His memory for names as he stands at the door of All Souls on a Sunday evening appears undimmed. He rises at 5 a.m. every morning and spends two-and-a-half hours in study and prayer. He does not accept second helpings at meals out of respect for hungry people in the Third World.

Stott has never married. One rumour that does the rounds is that at an early age he vowed never to allow himself to fall in love with a woman in order to devote himself to the ministry. The truth is rather different:

I've never taken a vow of celibacy. In fact, when I was in my twenties and thirties, I was expecting to marry. There were two particular people who attracted me, although not simultaneously! It's difficult to explain what happened. All I can really say is that when I made up my mind whether to go forward to commitment, I lacked assurance that this was God's will for me. So I drew back. Having done it twice, I realised it was probably God calling me to be single. Looking back over my life, I think I know why God has called me to be single – because I could never have travelled or written as I have done if I had had the responsibilities of family. It has been very lonely in some ways, but I'm grateful for a very large circle of friends.[7]

All Souls years

When I asked him to look back on the All Souls years, Stott recalled that in 1940 the congregation had moved to St Peter's, Vere Street. 'St Peter's was a little church seating five to six hundred people at the very most, and for six years after my ordination we continued to worship there. When we moved back to All Souls in April '51 after the restoration from bomb damage, the church immediately grew from a congregation of five or six hundred to one of a thousand. That was very thrilling to see. I can remember very well the opening service on, I think, 29 April 1951, when Bishop John Wand came to officiate at the service. Everything had been very carefully prepared and rehearsed – except that it hadn't occurred to us that the alms dish might be too small! I can still remember holding the alms dish while all the sidesmen put their offertory bags on it and the money cascaded off on to the marble steps. So we got hold of a second alms dish which has remained ever since!'

He told me that another highlight of the All Souls years was the arrival of Michael Baughen in 1970. 'What a marvellous thing that was for the church! He came with a fresh broom and brushed things clean.' With characteristic modesty, Stott had omitted to dwell on those years in the 1950s and 1960s when the church achieved international fame under his own leadership.

The Cross of Christ

Stott says that more of his heart and mind went into the writing of *The Cross of Christ* than into any other book. For him, the cross is the centre of Christian faith and life. 'I could not believe in God at all if it were not for the cross.' First published in 1986, some would argue that it is his best book, taking his readers to the heart of Evangelical theology – or, as Stott sees it, orthodox Christian theology. If we are looking for a definition of love, he says, we should look not in a dictionary but at Calvary.

One line of thought which he stresses in *The Cross of Christ* is important in the light of a recurring criticism of popular Evangelical theology, with its emphasis on the grace of God, that it makes too few demands on the believer: it neglects the cost of discipleship and encourages the notion of 'cheap grace'. Against this background, Stott makes it plain that before we can begin to see the cross as something done *for us* (leading us to faith and worship), we have to see it as something done *by us* (leading us to repentance). He quotes the Lutheran pastor Dietrich Bonhoeffer (1906–45) who said, 'When Christ calls a man, he bids him come and die.' And so, says Stott, the cross we are called to carry is not 'an irritable husband or a cantankerous wife'. It is the symbol of death to the self.

Confusion arises if we fail to distinguish between two different deaths and resurrections which are part and parcel of our Christian experience. First, there is the death to sin and subsequent life to God which happens to all Christians by virtue of their union with Christ in his death and resurrection. By this Christians share in the benefits both of Christ's death (forgiveness) and his resurrection (power) which are inherent in their conversion/baptism. Second, there is death to self which is known variously as carrying the cross, denying, crucifying or (in Catholic spirituality) mortifying oneself. This death is not something which has happened to us, but something that we deliberately do ourselves – through the power of the Spirit, putting our old nature to death.[8]

Created in the image of God

In the same book Stott deals with a strand in Scripture which he had hinted at in his earlier books, but which has come across more strongly in his writing over the last fifteen years. Alongside the explicit call of Christ to self-denial is his implicit call to 'self-affirmation'. This is the teaching of Jesus about the value of human beings in the sight of God: they are much more valuable than birds or beasts. Here is John Stott giving his blessing to a strand of teaching which has often been ignored in Evangelical theology (with its emphasis on sin and the fall) – the doctrine of creation. This tells us that human beings are the crown of God's creative activity and that he has made male and female in his own image. The divine image we bear gives us our distinctive value.

Nothing indicates more clearly the great value Jesus placed on people than his determination to suffer and die for them. Stott quotes William Temple: 'My worth is what I am worth to God; and that is a marvellous great deal, for Christ died for me.'[9]

Our 'self', says Stott, is a complex mixture of good and evil, glory and shame. The self we are to deny, disown and crucify is our fallen self; the self we are to affirm and value is the created self, everything in us which is compatible with Jesus – hence the remark of Jesus that when we lose ourselves (by self-denial) we find ourselves.

What is it that we are by creation which we must affirm? John Stott's answer is that it is our rationality; our sense of moral obligation; our sexuality; our family life; our gifts of aesthetic appreciation and artistic creativity; our stewardship of the earth; our hunger for love and experience of community; our awareness of the transcendent majesty of God; our 'inbuilt urge to fall down and worship him'. All this and more is part of our created humanness. It is a long way from the Calvinist doctrine of the 'total depravity of man'. John Stott grants that all these aspects of our personalities have been, as he puts it, 'tainted and twisted by sin'; but he argues that as Christ came to redeem this side of us, and not destroy it, 'we must gratefully and positively affirm it'.

What is it about ourselves that we are to deny? We must repudiate whatever we are by the fall: our irrationality; our moral perversity, including – and this puts him on collision course with much Liberal opinion – our 'blurring of sexual distinctiveness'; our lack of sexual control; the selfishness which spoils our family life; our fascination with the ugly; our lazy refusal to develop God's gifts; our pollution of the environment; our anti-social tendencies; our pride; and our idolatrous refusal to worship the living and true God.

Stott admits that all this oversimplifies the contrast between our createdness and fallenness. For one thing, the situation is not that Christians should think of themselves as 'created and fallen' but actually as 'created, fallen and redeemed'. We have not only been created in God's image: we are being recreated in it. 'Do not lie to each another,' the Apostle Paul tells the Colossians, 'since you have taken off your old self with its practices and have put on the new self, which is being renewed in knowledge in the image of its Creator' (Col. 3:9–10). Everyone who is in Christ is a new creation.[10]

The atonement

An emphasis on the atonement – how we are reconciled with God through Christ's death, 'at-one-ment' – is generally thought of as a distinctive feature of Evangelical theology. Theories of the atonement have proved controversial. St Anselm maintained that sin, being an infinite offence against God, required a satisfaction which was equally infinite. As no finite being could offer such satisfaction, it was necessary that an infinite being, that is God himself, should take our place and, by his death, make complete satisfaction to divine justice. Martin Luther taught that Christ, in bearing by voluntary substitution the punishment due to us, was reckoned by God a sinner in our place.

Many people in the twentieth century have objected that it is unjust and immoral knowingly to punish an innocent victim instead of the guilty party. And to suggest that God punished Christ instead of us can lead to a disturbing view of God, the danger being that good, moral people are put off Christianity because it seems to present to them an immoral God.

In *The Cross of Christ* Stott accepts that the words 'satisfaction' and 'substitution' need to be carefully defined and safeguarded. However, he vigorously defends a theory which is close to Anselm's and writes: 'We strongly reject, therefore, every explanation of the death of Christ which does not have at its centre the principle of "satisfaction through substitution", indeed divine self-satisfaction through divine self-substitution.'[11] He stuck to this view in his debate with the Liberal writer David Edwards when he said: 'I am not saying that substitution is the one and only meaning of the cross, for the cross speaks also of victory over evil, the revelation of love and glory through suffering. But if you are talking of atonement, the means by which we sinners can be reconciled to the God of holy love, why then, yes, I don't think we can escape the truth of the divine substitution.'[12]

The resurrection of Jesus

Taking issue with the former Bishop of Durham David Jenkins, who called the resurrection 'not an event, but a series of experiences', Stott insists that the resurrection was an *objective, historical event.* It was datable – it happened 'on the third day'; it became a series of experiences only because it was first an event. The words 'on the third day' witness to the historicity of the resurrection, just as the words 'under Pontius Pilate' in the Apostles' Creed witness to the historicity of our Lord's sufferings and death.[13]

John Stott gives three reasons for his conviction that 'resurrection' means 'bodily resurrection': first, because of the evangelists' testimony that the tomb was empty; second, because apostolic tradition affirmed that Jesus died, was buried, was raised and was seen (1 Cor. 15:3–5) in the sense that 'what was raised was what had been buried, i.e. his body'; and third, because the resurrected body of Jesus was and is the first portion of the material universe which has been redeemed, and is therefore the beginning and pledge of God's new creation.[14]

The need for ethical teaching

In 1978 Stott wrote: 'We Evangelical Christians, by making much of grace, sometimes thereby make light of sin. There is not enough sorrow for sin among us.'[15] In 1991 he wrote:

There is an urgent need for us, as pluralism and relativism spread worldwide, to follow Paul's example and give people plain, practical, ethical teaching. Christian parents must teach God's moral law to their children at home, Sunday school and day school teachers must ensure that their pupils know at least the Ten Commandments. Pastors must not be afraid to expound biblical standards of behaviour from the pulpit, so that the congregation grasps the relationship between the gospel and the law. And right from the beginning converts must be told that the new life in Christ is a holy life, a life bent on pleasing God by obeying his commandments.[16]

These passages about the need for people to take care to be good are not typical of much Evangelical writing. The leaders of the Oxford Movement asserted that Evangelicals rarely spoke or wrote in these terms. I asked John Stott if he would have been likely to write in this way in the 1960s, or whether the emphasis of his writing had changed. He replied that he was not conscious of any fundamental change, although he agreed that he might very well have spelled the point out in a more practical and direct way. He had always seen that repentance needs to be emphasised. 'If there's been a change it's been much more in my recognition of our social responsibility, and my concern to bring evangelism and social responsibility together under the rubric of mission. That's been a major change of emphasis.'

Stott argues that an insistence on holiness is an old Evangelical emphasis which is in danger of being lost today. 'I suspect it has been replaced by an emphasis on experience. Now experience is good, but holiness is better. For holiness is Christlikeness, and Christlikeness is God's eternal purpose for his children.'

Producing holiness is God's work *and* ours. 'Holiness is a harvest. True it is "the fruit (or 'harvest') of the Spirit", in that the Spirit is the chief farmer who produces a good crop of Christian qualities in the believer's life. But we have our part to play... We are to "walk by the Spirit" and "sow to the Spirit" (Gal. 5:16, 6:8), following his promptings and disciplining ourselves, if we would reap the harvest of holiness.'[17]

Why Evangelicals split

The constant tendency of Evangelicals to fragment makes Stott sad. Canon Colin Craston said some years ago that the Evangelical movement in Britain was now no longer a party but a coalition. 'There's no doubt', Stott told me, 'that, in spite of the influence Evangelicals have had under God, we haven't been able to exercise the influence we could have done if we'd been more united.' He thought that fragmentation was a spin-off from the Evangelical emphasis on the right of private judgment and the rugged individualism which has always characterised Evangelicalism. The Evangelical movement spawned a man (Luther) who said, 'Here I stand. I can do no other.' Since then Evangelicalism has attracted people of that ilk.

JIM PACKER

Jim Packer was born in Gloucester, England, in 1926, and educated at Corpus Christi College, Oxford, where two other famous West Country Anglicans – John Jewel and Richard Hooker – had studied. Between 1948 and 1979 he held a series of clerical and academic appointments in England. In the early part of that period, in 1952, he wrote to John Stott enquiring about the possibility of becoming a curate at All Souls. Stott's reply was polite but negative.

Packer has been one of the most influential Anglican Evangelicals of the twentieth century. By 1997 his books had sold almost three million copies worldwide, inspiring younger scholars with the intellectual coherence of Christianity itself, Anglicanism and Evangelicalism. He has been much influenced by Puritan thought. His writing combines clarity and insight with warmth of heart.

Why Packer left England

The account later in this book of Nottingham '77 (see page 304) refers to Packer's growing sense of isolation from Anglican Evangelicalism at that time. Alister McGrath also speaks of the Nottingham Congress seeming to have little place for the type of Puritan theology that Packer had worked hard to foster. In addition, the Charismatic movement, with its strong emphasis on experience, ran counter to Packer's emphasis on 'the mind grasping truth'. While he had held the post of Warden of Latimer House, Oxford (1961–

70), Packer had become a major figure on the Evangelical wing of the Church of England, but after he left Latimer, his influence within Evangelical groups such as The Church of England Evangelical Council (CEEC) diminished.

McGrath suggests that the emerging emphasis within Evangelical scholarship on hermeneutics may have been another factor in his disenchantment with the direction English Evangelicalism was taking. While Packer has never doubted the importance of hermeneutical questions, he feared that the new approach risked generating relativistic modes of thinking which could invade every aspect of theological thought. McGrath also hints that, from Packer's perspective, things were becoming increasingly centralised in certain Evangelical figures (like Stott) and organisations (like CEEC) which in the 1970s no longer seemed to have a place for him.

Eventually, a telephone call from James Houston of Regent College, Vancouver, taken by Packer at his desk at Trinity College, Bristol, one morning in 1976, started the process which eventually led to Jim and his wife Kit moving to Canada and to Jim becoming Professor of Historical and Systematic Theology at Regent College nearly three years later.

Packer's influence on Evangelical life

England's loss was North America's gain. Mark Noll of Wheaton College has done some useful work on Jim Packer's influence on the landscape of American Evangelical culture. His conclusions also have relevance for the English Evangelical scene. Noll believes that American Evangelicals have underemphasised (to their detriment) historical, contemplative and complex expressions of faith.

Against this background, Noll argues, Packer has exerted a wholly positive influence on American Evangelicalism by combining characteristics that have only rarely been combined in America. Packer's combination of his education, his Calvinism and his Anglicanism have kept him from 'the excesses that a largely unhistorical, mostly antitraditional and often anti-intellectual Evangelicalism has suffered in the course of American history'.

Months after he emigrated from England, in November 1979,

Jim Packer was asked to take part in a conference at Wheaton College on 'The Bible in America'. During the course of the conference, Packer spoke of the need for Evangelicals to 'sharpen their wits, even as they guarded their hearts'. He warned of the blinkers that Evangelicals are inclined to wear.

'We are victims,' Packer told the Wheaton academics and students, 'because we are children of the Protestant tradition, of the Evangelical tradition, of our own denominational tradition . . . all of these traditions have brought us strengths and we ought to be grateful for them, but . . . all of them can serve as blinkers, narrowing our vision for things which folks from other traditions can see. Again, we are children and therefore victims of reactions, negative reactionary attitudes which are there in our own tradition.

'Reactions I mean against the sacramentalism of Rome, which has made us distrust the sacraments; against the liturgical formalism of Rome, which has made us distrust all set prayers; against the beauty and dignity of worship which is characteristic of Rome and on which our traditions have tended to turn their back. We are victims of reaction against the heavy theology of earlier generations, which has made us an untheological lot opposing head knowledge to heart knowledge and treating head knowledge as if it did not matter.

'We are victims of reaction against love of the past. History, we say in our hearts, is bunk . . . The Psalmist prays, "Give me understanding that I may keep thy law." One of the things that is needed for understanding is that we should find the way to freedom from cultural prejudice.'

When Jim Packer told his Wheaton audience what they should be reading to help them understand Scripture, he recommended Luther, Calvin, Augustine, Jonathan Edwards, and the Puritans – but did not forget to include Catholic writers, 'John of the Cross and folk like that', as he put it.

Packer said that Evangelicals need to be liberated from 'the tyranny of being tied to our own thoughts . . . from the tyranny of being tied to our own time . . . from the tyranny of being tied to our own heritage . . . The Christian ought to practise fellowship across those traditions. The Holy Spirit has been with all God's people in all traditions in all centuries. You can expect to find wisdom and truth and vitamins in those traditions as well as finding mistakes.'

Packer and Roman Catholics

The German theologian Wolfhart Pannenberg is reported to have predicted that the next century will have room for only three major Christian groups: Roman Catholicism, Eastern Orthodoxy and Evangelicalism. Evangelicalism shares with Roman Catholicism alarm at the growth in secularism and materialism in Western society and the dangers posed to Christians throughout the world by the rise of Islamic fundamentalism. Both are concerned about the growth of what seems like moral chaos in the West.

Packer, like John Stott, has little patience with Evangelical approaches to Roman Catholics which amount to little more than 'papering over cracks'. Rather he believes we must acknowledge differences honestly and openly while rejoicing in what is held in common. Packer has publicly endorsed the major document *Evangelicals and Catholics Together* (ECT) which was first published in May 1994.

Packer sees the ECT statement as building on a platform on which Evangelicals and Catholics who share a common faith in the Trinity, the incarnation, the atonement and the new birth can unite and work together in reaching out to an increasingly secular world. He has insisted that he could never be a Roman Catholic on account of a number of that Church's beliefs, such as on the papacy and the infallibility of the Church's teaching. But he sees the joint course of action advocated by the ECT statement as 'not churchly but parachurchly' – in other words, collaboration among Christians who unite for specific purposes across traditional denominational divides, such as mission agencies, student ministry organisations, and educational initiatives. Bodies like this are not churches, but they have important roles to perform. When Evangelicals and Catholics work together like this they are not making any statements about the nature of the true Church, but they are recognising the importance of collaboration among Christians in pursuit of specified goals.

Packer and Anglicanism

Jim Packer told a conference of Reform (see page 331) in June 1995 that he thinks of himself as a 'heritage Anglican' or a 'mainstream Anglican'. He said that Anglicanism is the following:

- Biblical and Protestant in its stance.
- Evangelical and Reformed in its doctrine. 'That's a particular nuance within the Protestant constituency to which the Anglican church is committed. The Thirty-nine Articles show that.'
- Liturgical and traditional in its worship. 'If people say, "Well, I was fraternising with the Charismatics last Sunday and there wasn't much that was traditional about their worship," I smile and I say, "They are administering certain correctives to a formalism which edified nobody." But the main stream of Anglican worship is in line with the historic tradition of Christian worship and when everything settles down, I'm sure that they'll be back there just as all right-minded Anglicans always have been back there.'
- A form of Christianity which is pastoral and evangelistic in its style. 'I point out that ever since the Ordinal and the Prayer Book required the clergy to catechise children, Anglicanism has been evangelistic though the form of the evangelism has not been that of the travelling big tent. The form of the evangelism has been rather institutional and settled. The evangelism was part of the regular work of the parish clergyman and the community around him. But let nobody say that institutional parochial Anglicanism isn't evangelistic and today I know the wisest folk here in England are recovering parochial evangelism in a significant way and thank God they are.'
- A form of Christianity that is both Episcopal and parochial in its organisation.
- A form of Christianity that is rational and reflective in its temper. 'I say that in Anglican circles any question can be asked and the Anglican ethic is to take the question seriously and discuss it responsibly. There are of course Protestant churches which are always running scared and as soon as a question of this kind, a real puzzle about Christian truth and the ways of God is raised in

their circles, they bring out the big stick and say, "Now you mustn't talk like that. Just stay with the ABC of the Gospel and Bible truth." Theological reflection is discouraged rather than helped on its way. That makes for real immaturity. I think that there's no path to maturity except the path of serious thought which faces all the questions and works its way through them.'

- A form of Christianity that is ecumenical and humble in spirit. 'Unlike some denominations, we do not claim that Anglicanism is self-sufficient ... Anglicans have always rejoiced to receive wisdom from outside their own circles: being Anglican of course all the ideas that come from other quarters are tested by Scripture, but when that's done, Anglicans are happy to be enriched by wisdom from other parts of Christendom.'

In Packer's view, 'Anglicanism embodies the richest, truest, wisest heritage in all Christendom. When people say, "Well, those are fine words, but Anglicanism is sinking in the west everywhere isn't it?" In Canada: yes; in Britain, yes; in the States, yes; in Australasia, sure – I say, yes that's true, but we still may stay our hearts by reminding ourselves what is going on under Anglican auspices in black Africa, where the church grows and the Gospel advances by leaps and bounds.'

Packer and the atonement

Evangelicalism once regarded the doctrine of penal substitution as the only valid way to interpret the cross of Christ. Many Evangelicals still take this view, especially in America. However, the final statement produced by the Nottingham Congress in 1977 indicated that British Anglican Evangelicals were increasingly reluctant to commit themselves to understanding the atonement *exclusively* in this way. 'Some see the truth that Christ died in our place as the central explanation of the cross,' the statement said, 'while others, who also give this truth a position of great importance, lay greater stress on the relative significance of other biblical pictures.'

Packer, however, has continued to argue that 'all our sins, past, present and even future, have been covered by Calvary ... Our sins have already been judged and punished, however strange that statement may sound, in the person and death of another.' This, for Packer, is the essential meaning of Paul's testimony that Christ 'loved me, and gave himself for me' (Gal. 2:20).

Eternal punishment or annihilation?

The two leading Anglican Evangelicals of the twentieth century, John Stott and Jim Packer, apparently disagree on the question as to whether a loving God would eternally punish any of his creatures in hell. Since 1988 the idea of 'conditional immortality' has found favour among some Evangelicals. Conditional immortality is the belief that God created men and women with the *potential* to be immortal. The possibility of living for ever is a gift conveyed by grace through faith when the believer receives eternal life and becomes a partaker of the divine nature. As for those who do not receive this gift, John Stott has said, very tentatively, that he is inclined to believe in the final annihilation of the wicked rather than their eternal punishment. Stott stresses that he holds the view with some hesitation because of his 'great respect for long-standing tradition which claims to be a true interpretation of Scripture' and because he is concerned for the unity of the 'worldwide Evangelical constituency'.

Jim Packer disagrees with the view now held by Stott and others. He argues that the doctrine of eternal punishment was an integral aspect of the Christianity taught by the Lord Jesus Christ and his apostles and of major theologians through Christian history. He believes that the notion of 'conditional immortality' misses the 'awesome dignity of our having been made to last for eternity'. He is also concerned about the effect of conditionalist teaching on evangelism. If there is no everlasting punishment from which a sinner is to be delivered, there is little reason to preach a gospel of deliverance.

Certainly, in the nineteenth century, Hudson Taylor left home and family for China because he could not bear the thought of the most populous people on earth facing eternal punishment without Christ. But the 'conditional immortality' view of our eternal destiny deserves consideration on the basis of its intrinsic merit, not simply in the context of its alleged implications for evangelism.

Packer on holiness

Jim Packer's *Rediscovering Holiness*, which has not yet (as I write this) been published in the United Kingdom, is one of his most important books. It reflects his belief that we need to call a halt to what he calls 'the sidelining of personal holiness which has been a general trend among Bible-centred Western Christians during my years of ministry'.

This trend to neglect personal holiness has surprised Packer, since Scripture insists strongly that Christians are called to holiness, that God is pleased with holiness and outraged by unholiness, and that without holiness none will see the Lord. This reference by Packer to a text often quoted by Cardinal Newman and the leaders of the Oxford Movement – 'Make every effort to live in peace with all men and to be holy; without holiness no-one will see the Lord' (Heb. 12:14) – absolves him from the Tractarians' specific criticism of Evangelicals that they have a poor view of the heights of sanctity to which God's creatures, redeemed and renewed, can rise.

Packer states his case with characteristic vigour. 'The shift of Christian interest away from the pursuit of holiness to focus on fun and fulfilment, ego-massage and techniques for present success, and public issues that carry no challenge to one's personal morals, is a fact. To my mind it is a sad and scandalous fact, and one that needs to be reversed.'[18]

In his book, Packer develops the theme that he has touched upon from the earliest days of his ministry in the context of his criticism of the passivity which is inherent, for example, in the Keswick version of holiness and in some Charismatic circles. He stresses that holiness, like prayer, is something which, though Christians have an instinct for it through their new birth, they have to learn in and through experience:

As Jesus 'learned obedience from what he suffered' (Hebrews 5:8) – learned what obedience requires, costs, and involves through the experience of actually doing his Father's will up to and in his passion – so Christians must, and do, learn prayer from their struggles to pray, and holiness from their battles for purity of heart and righteousness of life . . . We must be clear in our minds that whatever further reasons there may be why God exposes us to the joys and sorrows, fulfilments and frustrations, delights and disappointments, happinesses and hurts, that make up the emotional reality of our lives, all these experiences are part of his curriculum for us in the school of holiness, which is his spiritual gymnasium for our reshaping and rebuilding in the moral likeness of Jesus Christ.[19]

Holiness, says Packer, has to do with the heart. A holy person's passion is to please God, by what he or she does and avoids doing. You practise good works and cut out evil ones.

The problem with poor human relationships is 'a self that has not learned to die'. True surrender to Christ shrinks our inflated egos. Holiness involves balancing a number of things: both action and motivation, conduct and character, God's grace and human effort, obedience and creativity, submission and initiative, consecration to God and commitment to people, self-discipline and self-giving, righteousness and love. 'It is a matter of Spirit-led law-keeping, a walk, or course of life, in the Spirit that displays the fruit of the Spirit (Christ-likeness of attitude and disposition).'

Holiness, and here again Packer is in agreement with Cardinal Newman, is the demonstration of faith working by love.

Holiness, repentance and happiness

While Evangelical Christians stress faith in Christ, they often touch rather lightly on repentance – that is, binding the believer's conscience to God's moral law, confessing and forsaking sin, making restitution for past wrongs, grieving over the effect of sins and developing a personal strategy for holy living. 'The post-Christian culture of the West', says Packer, 'doubts whether there are many moral absolutes.' But if we play down or ignore the importance of holiness we are absolutely wrong.

Holiness, for Packer, is the substance of which happiness is the spin-off. 'Those who chase happiness miss it, while to those who pursue holiness through the grace of Christ, happiness of spirit comes unasked.' *Rediscovering Holiness* is something of a classic in which Packer draws not only on Evangelical writers, but Roman Catholic and Orthodox wisdom through the centuries.

Praise and criticism of Packer

On the occasion of Jim Packer's seventieth birthday in 1996, Donald Lewis and Alister McGrath brought out a volume entitled *Doing Theology for the People of God: Studies in Honour of J. I. Packer.* John Stott set the tone of the volume by saying that his own contribution was 'like the shrimp paying homage to the whale'. A review of the volume in the May 1997 edition of SCM's *Reviews in Religion and Theology* (RRT) is, however, less complimentary.

The reviewer, Dr Martyn Percy, Director of the Lincoln Theological Institute for the Study of Religion and Society at the University of Sheffield, calls in aid none other than Mark Noll in suggesting that 'Evangelical scholarship is in its own ghetto.' While the volume in tribute to Packer gives a good deal of space to Packer's contribution to the inerrancy debate, the reviewer says that this is a debate which is only carried on in Evangelical circles and that in university theology departments the subject is more likely to occur in courses on recent church history or as a phenomenon in religious studies.

Second, Percy asserts that 'there seems to be little consciousness that the general Reformed agenda has ceased to be one of pilgrimage and challenge, and has slipped into the form of solidified tradition. Theology is no longer systematic but dogmatic. It is largely assumed that the Bible and the original Reformers were mostly right and there is little else to say about anything . . .'

Third, he says,

It seems barely credible that theology can be done any more in the way that Packer and friends imagine. The sheer narrowness of the perspective, coupled with the self-serving dogmatism that guarantees the same old principles to be exposited from the same old selection of biblical passages, is deeply alarming. Here is a theology which produces nothing new, practically prides itself on its social abrogation, and is in dialogue with no one but itself. Packer may well have deepened many Conservative Evangelicals' self-understanding, and he may well have helped keep Anglicans within this tradition as part of the established church by rebutting Martyn Lloyd-Jones in 1966. But he has not led Evangelicals into the heart of mainstream theology.[20]

In a Liberal journal, Martyn Percy wrote a vigorously anti-Evangelical piece. What he failed to tell his readers was that Mark Noll, whom he quoted in his support, remains an Evangelical and an admirer of Packer.

MARTYN LLOYD-JONES AND ANGLICAN EVANGELICALS

In 1926 Martyn Lloyd-Jones (1899–1981) abandoned a career in medicine to become minister in a small Presbyterian church in Wales. In 1939 he went to Westminster Chapel in London to be co-pastor with Campbell Morgan. From 1943, when he became sole pastor, he preached there almost every Sunday night until 1968 when ill-health forced him to retire.

Lloyd-Jones had no formal theological training but he read widely, especially on the Puritans, and kept himself up to date on current affairs. He was above all an expository preacher with a rich knowledge of the Bible.

At a meeting of the Westminster Fellowship on 16 June 1965 Lloyd-Jones argued that theologically orthodox Anglicans and others should consider leaving their denominations. Instead of trying to 'infiltrate' the various bodies to which they belonged, Evangelicals should stand together.

Two years before retiring from Westminster Chapel, Martyn Lloyd-Jones returned to the theme when he addressed the National Assembly of Evangelicals on the evening of 18 October 1966. The meeting had been organised by the Evangelical Alliance, a body which had been formed in 1846 to ensure that Evangelicalism remained a vital presence in Britain following the rise of Tractarianism. The 1966 Assembly was the first major gathering of British Evangelicals since 1846 to be organised by the Alliance. It aimed to foster Evangelical unity, but ended up damaging it.

John Stott chaired the meeting. During the course of his opening address, Martyn Lloyd-Jones called on Evangelicals to leave their denominations and form a national Evangelical church.

'Ecumenical people put fellowship before doctrine,' the doctor said. 'We, as Evangelicals, put doctrine before fellowship . . . I make this appeal to you Evangelical people this evening, what reasons have we for not coming together? Some will say we will miss evangelistic opportunities if we leave our denominations, but I say "Where is the Holy Spirit?" . . . You cannot justify your decision to remain in your denomination by saying that you maintain your independence. You cannot disassociate yourself from the church to which you belong. This is a very contradictory position, and one that the man on the street must find very hard to understand. Don't we feel the call to come together, not occasionally, but always?'

Those who were present at the meeting have spoken of the 'electric' atmosphere Lloyd-Jones's talk created. John Stott, in the chair, was already recognised as the leader of Anglican Evangelicals. What happened next was one of the most dramatic moments in the history of the movement. Stott rose to his feet.

'I hope that no one will make a precipitate decision after this moving address,' he said, going on to abandon a chairman's neutrality. 'We are here to debate this subject and I believe history is against Dr Jones in that others have tried to do this very thing. I believe that Scripture is against him in that the remnant was within the Church and not outside it.'

The *Church of England Newspaper* labelled Lloyd-Jones's proposition as 'barmy . . . nothing short of hare-brained'. Others wondered whether the doctor had the organisational skills to get his idea off the ground.

Looking back on the incident after thirty years, Jim Packer told Reform in June 1995: 'I lived, as some of you lived, through the era in which the late great Martyn Lloyd-Jones was telling us Anglicans from where he stood that we all of us ought to leave the Church of England. He had two bad arguments. He was a great man, but great men can be enmeshed in bad arguments. Bad argument number one was that if we stay in the Church of England we're guilty by association of all the theological errors that any Anglican may be propagating anywhere at all. To which of course the answer is rubbish: on that basis Paul would have been guilty of all the errors that were abroad in Corinth, in Colossae, in the Galatian churches and the Thessalonian church and elsewhere – and of course he wasn't guilty of any of that, and why not? Simply because he entered into the discipline of debate and wrote pastoral letters to them to put them straight. As long as we are free to raise our voices against the errors and seek to correct them from within we are not guilty of them. We are negating and refusing the error, we are not acquiescing in it, we are not guilty of it. It was a sad thing that a great mind like that of the late Dr Martyn Lloyd-Jones should ever have toyed with an argument as bad as this one.

'Secondly he said, "Don't you see that the times call us to leave all the doctrinally mixed congregations and form a pure new one." And I and others looked around and couldn't see that the times called us to do any such thing. We asked what do the times call us to do? And it seemed clear that the times called us to stay put and work for Reformation, renewal and fresh life in the church that has this rich heritage. So when people used to ask me why are you in the Church of England when the Church of England is in such a mess today I used to reply, "I'm in the Church of England today for the sake of what under God it might be tomorrow."'

KEELE 1967

Six months after Lloyd-Jones's controversial appeal, Anglican Evangelicals met on the windy campus of the University of Keele in April 1967 for their National Evangelical Anglican Congress. Whether Keele was a success is still debated today. Alister McGrath's description of the Congress as 'the most important event in twentieth-century English church history' is surely an overstatement.[21] One thing is certain, however: the decisions taken were almost totally contrary to what Dr Jones had pleaded with Anglican Evangelicals to do.

At Keele Anglican Evangelicals committed themselves to full engagement with the structures of the Church of England working constructively 'from the inside'. They affirmed ecumenism and serious engagement with social issues.

One of the young student delegates to attend Keele was John Gladwin. In 1995, by then Bishop of Guildford, he recalled:

Present at Keele were the historic elements of the Evangelical movement. Let no one think it has ever been a uniform movement! There were the Puritans and Anabaptists who sat uncomfortably in a comprehensive Church. There were the Pietists who thought the Church of England was the best boat to fish from. There were young Charismatics seeking renewal and revival. There were the radicals who wanted to embrace most things modern. In the midst were a group of leaders, young and old, lay and ordained, who held together this disparate and sometimes disorderly movement – in the best tradition of Cranmer, Hooker, Baxter and Simeon.[22]

Keele was certainly a turning point for Anglican Evangelicals, even if Charles Yeats revealed a shaky grasp of history when he wrote in 1995: 'Before Keele, Anglican Evangelicals lived in a kind of Christian ghetto; they concentrated on the parish church and shunned involvement in national and diocesan church structures. After Keele, having repented of their sectarian attitudes, many have moved out into an impressive engagement with the wider Church and the world.'[23] The members of the Clapham Sect would be justifiably aggrieved to learn that pre-Keele Anglican Evangelicals did not engage with the wider world!

Michael Saward, Canon Treasurer of St Paul's Cathedral, was personally involved as a young man in drafting the Keele Statement. He believes that there have been four main results of Keele which are evident thirty years later.

Numerical growth

First the Anglican Evangelical movement has grown numerically. The percentage of ordinands in Evangelical theological colleges has grown, passing the 50 per cent level in the late 1980s. In 1993, 56 per cent of ordinands were training in Evangelical colleges, 27 per cent in 'Central' colleges, and 17 per cent in Anglo-Catholic colleges. In 1967 only a very small number of Evangelicals occupied senior positions in the Church of England hierarchy. By 1993 there were thirteen Evangelical diocesan bishops, thirteen suffragans, eight deans and twenty archdeacons, although the interpretation of the word 'Evangelical' had by this time become less clear-cut.

By 1995 the *Church Times* was labelling Anglican Evangelicals under three headings: Evangelical (Liberal), Evangelical (Conservative) and Evangelical (Charismatic). The newspaper conducted a study of the election manifestos of successful candidates for seats in the House of Clergy and Laity of the General Synod. The most frequently mentioned overall priority was mission.

The table below shows the church traditions to which the 1995 Synod members belonged according to the *Church Times* designations. Percentages refer only to those who could be categorised.

DESCRIPTION	TOTAL	% OF WHOLE
'Central'	46	12.1
Affirming Catholic	45	11.8
Catholic (traditional)	39	10.2
Evangelical (Liberal)	33	8.7
Evangelical (Conservative)	23	6.0
Open Synod Group	11	2.9
Evangelical (Charismatic)	6	1.5

Evangelical scholarship

The second main result of Keele, according to Michael Saward, is that the quality of Evangelical scholarship has improved. This he sees in the number of Evangelicals occupying academic posts in the theological departments of British universities, in publications, in

General Synod speeches and in the number of doctoral students identifying with the Evangelical movement.

Liturgical developments

The third result, argues Saward, is that Anglican Evangelicals have developed liturgically:

> Evangelicals in the years before Keele were, for the most part, not even vaguely interested in liturgy. They used the *Book of Common Prayer*, often in a very wooden and unimaginative manner and knew little or nothing about the history and development of liturgy... They had a far higher view of extempore prayer meetings than of services of Holy Communion. This situation changed rapidly in the 1960s and 1970s. Keele cautiously welcomed modern liturgies and by the late 1970s half the members of the Revision Committee which presented Rite A to the General Synod were Evangelicals and they succeeded in creating a widely accepted eucharistic rite which they did not regard as having compromised the Evangelical position at any of the essential tension points.[24]

To Michael Saward's dismay, 'The popular desire for immediacy in worship undermined much of this development in the late 1980s.'

Structural developments

In 1960 John Stott created the Church of England Evangelical Council (CEEC). But the Council rather limped along, underfunded and with only qualified support from other influential organisations in the Evangelical constituency. In due course it became the English branch of the Evangelical Fellowship of the Anglican Communion (EFAC) and in the early 1980s created the Anglican Evangelical Assembly to be an annual focus for Anglican Evangelicals.

Although 'structural developments' is the fourth of Michael Saward's main results of Keele, he notes that the CEEC, which is currently chaired by Richard Bewes (John Stott's successor but one at All Souls), has never been able to gain the trust of the whole range of Anglican Evangelicals. 'Hard right' members of the Church Society view it with extreme caution while Charismatics are indifferent to it. 'It remains the voice-piece of the mainstream but, sadly, has gradually lost credibility due to its unwillingness, or inability, to make public statements on subjects concerning which the constituency has expected at least an opinion from it. The ordination of women was the supreme example of this failure.'[25]

McGrath on Keele

Alister McGrath looks back on Keele as a 'powerful stimulant to Evangelicalism within the Church of England'. He cites the Anglican Evangelical Group Movement (AEGM) as an example of a Liberal Evangelical organisation which found itself threatened by the resurgence of the more conservative forms of Evangelicalism. For bodies like this, Keele was the last straw and the AEGM dissolved itself in July 1967. 'Liberal Evangelicalism', McGrath concludes, 'had ceased to be a meaningful organised presence within the church. Conservative Evangelicalism had, quite simply, eclipsed it.'[26]

DONALD COGGAN

Born in London in 1909, educated at Merchant Taylors' School and St John's College, Cambridge, Donald Coggan trained for ordination at the Evangelical college Wycliffe Hall, Oxford. After a curacy at St Mary's Church, Islington, and academic appointments in England and Canada, he became Principal of the London College of Divinity in 1944, Bishop of Bradford in 1956 and served as Archbishop of York for fourteen years from 1961. In 1974 he became the 101st Archbishop of Canterbury.

The importance Donald Coggan attached to evangelism emerged in his 'Call to the Nation' in 1975 and in his strong support for the

Nationwide Initiative in Evangelism which emerged at the close of his archiepiscopate in 1979. For him, the way to a renewed social order would be through personal evangelism. Confident in his faith and full of hope himself, Coggan believed that the Church should be confident, faithful and hopeful too.

Evangelicals from all denominations were encouraged by his appointment, especially when, in 1978, a book from the Archbishop's pen was published which presented with directness and warmth some themes at the heart of the Christian faith, clearly written by a man with a deep knowledge of the Bible. In this book Dr Coggan quoted in full a Sankey hymn ('The Ninety and Nine'); spoke of Jesus not only as our teacher and example but as 'the Word of God, the Son of God, the Saviour'; referred to the Bible as the book by which the Spirit of the living God speaks to men and women today; and told his readers that 'if the room where you live becomes a place of prayer, it may be more powerful for good than the council chambers of the nations' potentates'.[27]

During 1997, in his late eighties, Lord Coggan was still able to lend his active support to Christian initiatives which captured his imagination.

THE CHARISMATIC MOVEMENT

In the early 1960s Michael Harper, one of John Stott's curates at All Souls and chaplain to the Oxford Street stores, was – in his words – 'baptised in the Holy Spirit' together with two other All Souls curates. The story of the phenomenal growth of a worldwide renewal movement of the 1970s, 1980s and 1990s is well known. But the Charismatic movement could not hold Harper.

In a twist in the tale, over thirty years later in 1995, Michael Harper and his wife, Jeanne, left the Church of England to join the Orthodox Church. Harper is now Dean of the British Antiochian Orthodox deanery. He has told the story of his spiritual journey in *The True Light*, published in 1997.

In the 1960s, when the modern Charismatic movement began,

divisions and tensions began in local congregations within Anglicanism and way beyond. Many Evangelicals thought the Charismatics were shaky in their biblical exegesis, but the movement spread rapidly. On 7 January 1964 John Stott addressed the Islington Conference of Evangelical clergy on the subject of 'The Baptism and Fullness of the Holy Spirit'. He subsequently expanded his talk and the Inter-Varsity Fellowship (now UCCF) published it in the form of a booklet.

Stott's *Baptism and Fullness* was typical of all his publications – written with clarity, carefully setting out his view of biblical orthodoxy on the Holy Spirit and applying it firmly but courteously to the new situation which was disturbing the peace of an increasing number of churches.

First, he argued, the fullness of the Holy Spirit was one of the distinctive blessings of the new age. Just as the ministry of John the Baptist was to baptise with water, so the characteristic of the ministry of Jesus would be to baptise with the Holy Spirit. When we repent and believe, Jesus not only takes away our sins, but also baptises us with the Holy Spirit. It is this 'baptism' or 'gift' of the Spirit which makes our experience of the fullness of the Spirit possible.

Second, the fullness of the Holy Spirit is the universal blessing for all who repent and believe. Since Pentecost, the Spirit has come to indwell all believers. The general teaching of the New Testament is that baptism, including baptism in the Spirit, is an initial experience. True, there are a few narrative passages in Acts which may suggest a special experience subsequent to conversion, but they occurred in special circumstances and are not normal for us today. The norm of Christian experience is a cluster of four things: repentance, faith in Jesus, water baptism and the gift of the Spirit. Though the perceived order may vary a little, the four belong together and are universal in Christian initiation. The laying-on of apostolic hands, together with tongue-speaking and prophesying, were special to Ephesus and to Samaria (as described in Acts), in order to demonstrate visibly and publicly that particular groups were incorporated into Christ by the Spirit. The New Testament does not suggest that these specific episodes would be the normal experience of Christians. The emphasis of the New Testament is not to urge on Christians some new and distinct blessing, but to remind them of what by grace they are, and to recall them to it.

Third, the fullness of the Holy Spirit is a continuous blessing to be continuously and increasingly appropriated. In response to the invitation of Jesus recorded in John 7, we are to keep coming, to keep believing and to keep drinking of the living water he offers.

As for the supernatural signs associated with Pentecost, they are no more typical of every baptism of the Spirit than those on the Damascus road are of every conversion. What is the evidence of the Spirit's indwelling and fullness? As with baptism, so with fullness, the chief evidence is moral not miraculous. The chief mark of a person filled with the Spirit of God will be seen in the Spirit's fruit (love, joy, peace . . .), not the Spirit's gifts. It is wrong to think of being filled with the Spirit as a sort of spiritual inebriation in which we lose control of ourselves. Under the influence of the Spirit we gain control of ourselves.

Stott ended his booklet with a plea to his readers constantly to seek to be filled with the Spirit, to be led by the Spirit, to walk in the Spirit. 'Can we not gladly occupy this common ground together,' he asked, 'so that there be no division among us?' The main condition of being filled is to be hungry. In this life we can never be filled to hunger no more. Jesus said, 'Blessed are those who hunger and thirst for righteousness' (Matt. 5:6), implying that hungering and thirsting after righteousness is as much a permanent state of the Christian as being 'poor in spirit' or 'meek' or 'merciful'. 'So let neither those who have had unusual experiences, nor those who have not, imagine that they have "attained" and that God cannot fill them any further with himself!'

What the apostles urge on us

In the mid-1970s John Stott revised his *Baptism and Fullness* book and made a point which would have won him the approval of the leaders of the Oxford Movement. He noted that in their epistles the apostles urge upon us ethical conduct, often in considerable detail, appealing to us to live out in the concrete realities of daily life what God has already done for us in Christ. They command us to grow in faith, love, knowledge and holiness. They beg us not to grieve the

Spirit, but to walk in the Spirit and to go on being filled with the Spirit. But never anywhere do they exhort and instruct us to 'be baptised with the Spirit'. Why? Because they are writing to Christians, and Christians have already been baptised with the Holy Spirit.

The fruit of the Spirit

Another subject Stott expanded on in his revision of *Baptism and Fullness* was the fruit of the Spirit, listed in Galatians 5:22–3 as love, joy, peace, patience, kindness, goodness, faithfulness, gentleness and self-control. He says that the mere recital of these Christian graces should be enough to make the mouth water and the heart beat faster. 'For this is a portrait of Jesus Christ. No man or woman has ever exhibited these qualities in such balance or to such perfection as the man Christ Jesus. Yet this is the kind of person that every Christian longs to be.' The Spirit gives different Christians different gifts, but he works to produce the same fruit in us all. He is not content if we show love for others, but have no control of ourselves. There is a wholeness, a roundness, a fullness of Christian character which only the Spirit-filled Christian ever exhibits.

The gifts of the Spirit

When John Stott compares the list of spiritual gifts given in Romans 12 with those given in 1 Corinthians 12 and Ephesians 4, he observes that while students of the 1 Corinthians list tend to focus on the supernatural (tongues, prophecy, healing and miracles), in Romans 12 all the gifts apart from prophecy are either general and practical (service, teaching, encouragement and leadership) or even prosaic (giving money and doing acts of mercy). He suggests that we need to broaden our understanding of the gifts.[28]

Charismatic 'renewal' and the Church of England

Michael Saward has observed that those not caught up in the Charismatic or 'renewal' movement were mildly offended by the label 'renewal', since they believed they had made some contribution to the renewal of the Church in different ways. He points out that the movement affected a wide range of churches far beyond Evangelicalism and manages to find some positive things to say about it: it brought a new vitality to countless congregations and individuals, and much of the old starchiness went out of church life. 'The recognition of widespread "giftedness" was to release many from the clergy-centred concepts that had gone before.'

Having thus cleared the way, Michael Saward wades in with a characteristically outspoken assessment:

> When the history comes to be written it may well be seen that the Charismatic influence was at least as damaging as it was beneficial within the Evangelical Anglican movement. For the most part, those involved, while seeing numerical growth in their congregations, became increasingly isolated from the actual renewal of the Church of England at almost every level outside parish life. 'Renewal' people generally were not prepared to bother with deaneries, dioceses, synods, indeed with the institutional life of the church . . . Charismatic leaders were noticeably missing from the Church of England Evangelical Council and rarely seen at the annual Anglican Evangelical Assemblies.[29]

Canon Saward also turned his fire on Charismatic worship music, arguing that mainstream Evangelicals have been the source and proving ground for a spate of hymns, psalm paraphrases, carols, canticles and prayers emanating from Jubilate Hymns, a group who worked together in the 1970s and 1980s to provide material that was largely geared to worship of a liturgical or semi-liturgical kind. Much of this material, says Saward,

> was ignored by Charismatic groups and churches who preferred to use songs and choruses of a repetitive kind. Some of these were excellent 'worship songs', well able to be used to enhance

Anglican worship. The vast majority were poorly written, set to banal music, and in Charismatic churches were often the spearhead used to push liturgy into the background or even out of the building altogether. As the 1980s moved into the 1990s so the number of Charismatic churches in the Evangelical tradition which had ditched coherent liturgy for 'chorus-sandwiches' grew and grew.[30]

Michael Saward's view is typical of that held by those Anglican Evangelicals who treasure their liturgical heritage as much as their Evangelicalism. There are many signs, as we approach the end of the 1990s, of a widespread desire to enrich worship with music from a variety of styles and traditions including songs from the Taizé Community, Iona music, liturgically sung Psalms, and Gregorian chants.

Packer on the Charismatic movement

Jim Packer's starting point is that the Holy Spirit comes to make us holy. All through the New Testament he sees (like John Stott) the ethical taking priority over the Charismatic. Christlikeness (not in gifts, but in love, humility, submission to the providence of God, and sensitiveness to the claims of people) is seen as what really matters. Any mindset which treats the Spirit's gifts (ability and willingness to run around and do things) as more important than his fruit (Christlike character in personal life) is spiritually wrongheaded and needs correcting.

He notes the positive aspects of Charismatic renewal: Christ-centredness; Spirit-empowered living; emotion finding expression; prayerfulness; joyfulness; every heart involvement in the worship of God; every member ministry; evangelistic zeal; small group ministry; impatience with church structures and traditions which quench the work of the Spirit; and generous giving.

Packer has also noted the negative aspects of Charismatic renewal. Many Charismatic Christians will agree with some or all of his points:

- Elitism: despite denials of this phenomenon by some Charismatics, Packer observes that when you have gone out on a limb in order to seek and find something that you now think everyone should be seeking, it is hard not to feel superior.

- Sectarianism: Charismatics tend to limit themselves to reading Charismatic books, hearing Charismatic speakers, enjoying fellowship with other Charismatics and backing Charismatic causes. This is the 'thin end of the sectarian wedge'.
- Emotionalism: the warmth and liveliness of Charismatic worship attracts highly emotional and disturbed people; others find the emotionalism a relief from the stresses and strains of work or of difficult marriages. Self-indulgent, escapist 'trips' are damaging in the long run and usually do not address deeper problems.
- Anti-intellectualism: Charismatic preoccupation with experience inhibits the long, hard theological and ethical reflection for which the New Testament letters call. The result is naïveté or imbalance.
- Illuminism: with its stress on the Spirit's personal leading, the Charismatic movement is vulnerable to sincere but deluded claims of direct divine intervention.
- 'Charismania': measuring spiritual health, growth and maturity by the number and impressiveness of people's gifts and spiritual power by (spectacular) Charismatic manifestations. Real growth and maturity will be retarded.
- 'Super-supernaturalism': this is Packer's word for that way of affirming the supernatural which exaggerates its discontinuity with the natural – constantly expecting miracles at every turn. It is often evidence of a misunderstanding of the call to patient, cross-bearing self-denial which is at the heart of following Christ.
- 'Eudaemonism': this is Packer's word for the belief that God means us to spend our time in a state of euphoria. It makes supernatural divine healing a constant expectation whereas the New Testament indicates that good health at all times is not God's will for all believers. It forgets that good can come in the form of wisdom, patience and the acceptance of reality without bitterness when Christians are exposed to the discipline of pain and re- maining unhealed. 'Eudaemonism' is also seen in the insistence by some Charismatics that if you honour God he will prosper your business and ensure a life of comfort.
- Demon obsession: when all life is seen as a battle with demons

so that Satan and his hosts get blamed for bad health, bad thoughts and bad behaviour without prayerful reflection on possibly reversible personal shortcomings, then spiritual immaturity will result.

• Conformism: group pressure to raise hands, clap, use approved phraseology, adopt facial expressions, see pictures, prophesy, speak in tongues, share experiences and emotions. But, Packer acknowledges, no type of Christian spirituality, including traditional Evangelicalism, is free from the danger of conformism.[31]

Packer on healing

Jim Packer suggests that the healing gifts referred to in 1 Corinthians 12:28–30 cannot convincingly be equated with Charismatic healing ministries today. He argues that in apostolic times the gift of healing was much more than Charismatics appear to have now. The most he is prepared to say of Charismatic healers is that 'at some moments and in some respects they are enabled to perform like the gifted healers of New Testament times, and every such occasion confirms that God's touch still has its ancient power. But that is much less than saying that in the ministry of these folks the New Testament gift of healing reappears.'[32]

Some would argue that Packer's analysis tends to underestimate the power of the God with whom nothing is impossible, and who is not limited by precedent.

The Charismatic movement and the cross

Tom Smail's experience is an interesting episode in the history of Anglican Evangelicalism on both sides of the Atlantic. Now an Anglican Evangelical, but brought up in Scottish Presbyterianism, Smail's experience of renewal came about as a result of a visit to England in 1965 by Denis Bennett, an American Episcopalian. Five years earlier, Bennett had had an experience of the Holy Spirit in California that marked the beginning of the Episcopal Charismatic movement and to some extent the mainstream Charismatic movement in the States.

Smail went on to work at the heart of the Charismatic movement as director of the Fountain Trust. He was for some years Vice-Principal of St John's College, Nottingham. Smail now has deep reservations about the Charismatic movement, though acknowledging his previous indebtedness to it. He argues that the basic structure of Pentecostal theology makes it difficult to recognise the close and intimate relationship between the renewing and empowering work of the Spirit and the centre of the gospel in the incarnation, death and resurrection of Jesus Christ.

'We are', says Smail, 'indeed rejuvenated and empowered at Pentecost, but we are judged, corrected and matured at the cross, and for these two processes to be brought into right relationship with each other, we must, I believe, understand the relation between cross and Spirit in a way that is quite different from the way it is understood by the Pentecostal theology that has shaped the renewal until now.' The way to Pentecost, says Smail, is Calvary. 'A spirit who diverts us from the cross into a triumphant world in which the cross does not hold sway may turn out to be a very *unholy* spirit.' He goes on:

What heals is not esoteric techniques, or even special supernatural endowment as such; what heals is Calvary love. The Charismatic renewal strays furthest from its own best insights and becomes most nearly Gnostic in its seemingly endless search for the effective technique, the method, the panacea that will release the power of God to deal with all the ills of his people. The sesame key to wholeness is not speaking in tongues, or the healing of the memories, thanking God for everything or asking him for anything; it is not having your demons cast out, still less being 'slain' in the Spirit or reliving your traumatic birth experience, or any other of the fashions that have followed one another in quite fast succession over the past twenty-five years. All these can at best offer subsidiary assistance to some people in some situations, but the ultimate key to the wholeness that God purposes for his people and his world is far more central to the Gospel than any of these; it is Calvary love . . .

If some of us who have been Charismatic leaders had been as set on being filled with the love of God as we have been on being filled with the power of God, the Charismatic renewal would be a more unambiguously wholesome affair than it has sometimes been.[33]

DAVID WATSON

The name of David Watson (1933–84) was closely associated with the Charismatic movement through the 1970s and early 1980s. David went up to St John's College, Cambridge, to read Moral Sciences in 1954. During his first year there he was converted and became an enthusiastic member of CICCU. He decided to offer himself for the ministry and from 1957 spent two years at Ridley Hall.

Watson served his first curacy at St Mark's, Gillingham, a tough, working-class parish, and his second at the Round Church, Cambridge. Back in Cambridge, he sought a deeper quality of Christian life and found it in a Charismatic experience which transformed his life. At this time too, he began to suffer acutely from the asthma which was to plague him for the rest of his life. In 1964 he married Anne MacEwan Smith, a partnership which was at times difficult, though rewarding for them both.

In the year that he married, David accepted a curacy in the parish of Holy Trinity, York, which also gave him responsibility for St Cuthbert's, a church with just a few parishioners but well located for a ministry to students at the new University of York. He and Anne worked immensely hard in developing a strategy based on long hours in prayer, careful teaching of Christian basics, family worship and a great stress on relationships, including living in an extended family which tested their marriage.

Growth accelerated and in 1973 the diocesan authorities agreed to David taking over as Vicar of the church where Guy Fawkes had been baptised – St Michael-le-Belfrey, close to York Minster. In the 1970s my wife and I used to visit 'St Mikes' while staying with friends who were members of the congregation. We watched as Watson built up a pattern of worship which combined teaching, music, dance, drama and the display of colourful banners. Much of this is commonplace now, but in the 1970s it was innovative. Congregational participation, Area Groups meeting all over York, the appointment of elders, prayer and Charismatic experiences were all features of life at St Michael's. Although the pastoral life of the large congregation could not have been sustained without delegation, and there were spiritual gains, Watson's desire to share leadership responsibility eventually contributed to a split in the church.

A report on the work stated: 'What comes across is the sheer weight of testimony upholding the word preached by the word received, believed in and being lived by so many happy but ordinary people who are part of proclaiming in themselves.'[34]

Watson also carried on an extensive ministry outside his parish. He became one of the Church of England's most effective evangelists during the 1970s and early 1980s, building up a team to accompany and support him. The asthma which continued to plague him, coupled with bouts of depression and a sense of failure, gave a depth to his preaching with which people could identify. I remember hearing him tell us, during a sermon at St Michael's, what he had learned at three o'clock that morning while quite unable to sleep.

David Watson came to abandon narrowly Evangelical attitudes and became widely acceptable to Christians in traditions other than his own, including Roman Catholics. He decided in 1982 to devote himself entirely to evangelism. Early in 1983, however, shortly after moving to London, he was diagnosed as having cancer.

He was surrounded by prayer and attended by key figures in the Christian healing ministry. There were some remissions, but they were very brief. The disease seemed to be taking its course. David reflected deeply on what was happening to him; his own awareness and that of his hearers changed. The fact that he was dying gave his ministry a special power and significance for some, but dismayed others whose expectations of healing had been raised. When he preached at St Michael's for the last time, he stood for an hour and a half after the service had ended, greeting individually the huge congregation who had come to say goodbye.

His much-read book *Fear No Evil* tells the story of his last months almost to the end. It is a remarkable book with a great deal of confession of weakness and dereliction. His last journey, as Michael Hinton has commented, 'gave the lie to the facile attitudes not uncommon among his followers and to which he had perhaps sometimes succumbed himself'.[35] The last paragraph of the book surely approaches the heart of any solution there may be to the problem of unanswered prayer: '"Father, not my will but yours be done." In this position of security I have experienced once again his perfect love, a love that casts out fear.'[36]

David Watson died in faith but not without a struggle in 1984. His innovative approach to worship lives on in many churches which adopted his ideas: simple worship songs accompanied by a range of orchestral instruments, thought-provoking dramatic presentations and colourful banners which have breathed new life into Anglican services and beyond.

NOTTINGHAM 1977: WHAT IS AN EVANGELICAL?

Two thousand delegates met at the University of Nottingham in April 1977 for the second National Evangelical Anglican Congress. They were visited and addressed by both Archbishops. The *Church Times* wrote in its editorial that the Congress 'demonstrates the vitality of the Evangelical movement. Probably no other section of the Church of England has the strength to organise such an assembly.'

According to Alister McGrath, preparations for the Congress, which had begun in 1974, involved disagreement between John Stott and Jim Packer over what the Congress should aim to achieve. Packer in the first instance doubted whether such a get-together was needed; and having lost this argument suggested that the conference should focus on a specific theme of importance, such as ethics. Stott, on the other hand, felt that the conference would only have significant appeal if it addressed as wide a range of issues as possible. McGrath's version has it that, when Stott's view prevailed, Packer felt increasingly isolated.[37]

Eventually the five main aims were announced as follows: to bring the 'centre' and the 'constituency' together, thus increasing mutual understanding and trust; to develop a common vision of where Evangelicals were going; to take stock ten years on from Keele; to look in depth at the theme of social ethics on which Keele had been weak; and to concentrate on renewal, mission and evangelism.

Forty-one per cent of the delegates at Nottingham were laymen, 26 per cent laywomen and 33 per cent clergy. The number of lay people present had been deliberately planned and was one of the main differences from Keele. A high proportion of the delegates were young.

One significant question at the start of the Congress was whether there was still a definable Evangelical party, or whether the Congress would reveal such divisions as to make it impossible for Evangelicals to act together any longer.

At the beginning of that April, John King had put the question thus in an article in the *Church of England Newspaper*: 'The delegates . . . will have to decide which they want: an Evangelical unity which is preserved by tucking inconvenient questions under the mattress or a unity of some Evangelicals behind an agreed policy which bears some relation to the days in which we live.'[38]

'What tensions do you think will arise?' journalists asked John Stott at the opening press conference.

'It won't be the Charismatic movement,' he replied. 'I guess that the publication of *Gospel and Spirit* has defused the issue before the Congress.' *Gospel and Spirit* had been published in April 1977 jointly by the Fountain Trust and *The Churchman*. The joint statement by a group nominated by CEEC and the Fountain Trust suggested a wide area of agreement and understanding over Charismatic issues which had been thought to divide. The group included John Stott, Jim Packer, Michael Harper and David Watson. Only four of its seventeen signatories were not involved in planning or speaking at the Nottingham Congress.

Far from marking either the beginning of a new 'party' discipline or the end of Evangelical coherence within the Church of England, the Congress seemed determined to show clear adherence to Evangelical essentials while allowing for the widest possible expression of belief on other matters. Packer had argued that there was little point in the Congress producing a report, since it would cover a wide range of issues and therefore inevitably lack depth. This, he thought, might create a negative impression of Anglican Evangelicalism among critical readers.

Nevertheless, a Statement Steering Committee pressed ahead, meeting for several hours from ten thirty each night in the 'comfortable dungeons' below Cavendish Hall. 'The reason we've been up so many hours', said John Stott, 'is because of our desire for integrity, so that the Statement accurately represents what was discussed.'

This accounts for the rather wishy-washy tone of *The Nottingham Statement* which emerged from the Congress: 'some of us think . . . and some think . . .' (representing a fifty-fifty division of opinion) and 'we believe . . . but also a substantial majority say . . .' (representing a sixty-forty division).

The call from the *Church of England Newspaper* (among others) for clear, unequivocal statements on matters such as the ordination of women, support for the Programme to Combat Racism, patronage, and so on, was not answered. To have produced resolutions on such subjects would have meant voting them through, perhaps by only small majorities.

But the question remained, 'What were the fundamental convictions which united Evangelicals?'

'What is an Evangelical?' one reporter asked at a press conference.

Next morning, John King headlined this question in the *Church of England Newspaper* daily bulletin and wrote: 'Hundreds of delegates would go home happier if they knew the answer without having it wrapped up in incomprehensible jargonese. The question of identity should be at the top of the list at NEAC. How can we know where we are going if we do not know who we are? What is an Evangelical?'

There was force in John King's criticism of the Nottingham Statement for its 'incomprehensible jargonese'. The drafters had a penchant for the trendy word or phrase and the statement has rather too many disconcerting references to 'the need for a costly identification with people in their alienation', and confessions that 'we have not always incarnated the joyful liberty, love and hope of the Gospel', as well as displaying touching faith in the value of 'ongoing discussions'. Nottingham was also the Congress when the word 'hermeneutics' was launched on its dazzling career.

John King had to wait until the very end of the Congress for something of an answer to his question about Evangelical identity. The answer came from the chairman of the Congress.

'Evangelicals are Gospel people'

'I am aware that some of you are suggesting we drop the epithet Evangelical,' said John Stott in his closing address, 'and it is time we merged in the main stream of church life. Certainly we shouldn't retain the word because we are cussed or obstinate, or to make us feel comfortable or more secure, or because we live in the past. We retain the designation because we have convictions: we Evangelicals are Bible people . . . and we Evangelicals are Gospel people . . .' We deplore the cavalier and sometimes arrogant attitudes to Scripture which are flaunted in the church today . . . We see it as part of our responsibility to remind our own church of its stance.'

He also stressed the need to be 'more conscientious in our study of the word. If Scripture is supreme over traditions, that includes our Anglican traditions and our Evangelical traditions . . . Nothing is sacrosanct to the radical Conservative Evangelical Christian except Scripture itself.'

This clear note from John Stott encouraged many, not least non-Anglican Evangelicals who were observing at Nottingham and who had to some extent felt estranged by the total commitment to the Church of England expressed at Keele.

'Particularly heartening to Free Church Evangelicals', said Michael Hews of the Scripture Union, 'was John Stott's reaffirmation in his closing talk that Anglican Evangelicals were "Bible people" and "Gospel people".'

'I don't like to think of Evangelicalism as a party,' Sir Norman Anderson had said in his closing address, 'but as a tradition with certain fundamental convictions.'

Trevor Lloyd, now Archdeacon of Barnstaple, was in 1977 Curate at Christ Church, Barnet, where my wife and I were confirmed and our two sons baptised. In his commentary on Nottingham '77, he observed that John Stott's remarks in his closing address about nothing being sacrosanct except Scripture itself highlighted two significant developments among Evangelicals between Keele and

Nottingham and at Nottingham itself: 'the growth of a more mature method of biblical interpretation and theological method, and the comparative freedom from past slogans in the radical application of Scripture to life today'.

Certainly, Nottingham continued to raise the profile of Evangelicalism within the Church of England and the British media. But whether the Congress achieved anything of genuine long-term significance continues to be debated. Most would agree that it lacked Keele's strategic significance. Jim Packer's view was that the Nottingham Statement consisted only of 'a series of virtuous statements, amounting to nothing in particular'. While Keele was a landmark, Nottingham was, for Packer, something of a dud. In his biography of Packer, McGrath cites the Nottingham Congress as one of the factors persuading a disappointed man to leave England for Canada.

JAMES BARR: EVANGELICALISM UNDER ATTACK AGAIN

In 1976 Professor James Barr, a successor to Edward Pusey as Regius Professor of Hebrew at the University of Oxford, launched a major attack on Conservative Evangelicalism. In his book *Fundamentalism* Barr argued that the core of Conservative Evangelicalism lay not in the Bible but in a particular kind of religion. Evangelicals supposed that this kind of religion was theirs because it followed as a necessary consequence from the acceptance of biblical authority. But actually the reverse was true: a particular type of religious experience, which in the past was believed to arise from the Bible, had come to be itself dominant.

According to Barr, the dominant tradition which has formed Conservative Evangelicalism is the religious experience of the Evangelical revivals. The characteristic experience of the revivals involved a series of related perspectives: the sense of a Church that was cold and dead, but where the introduction of a warm, living and biblical gospel brought about for many a personal conversion to a living faith; the understanding that personal salvation came not simply through belonging to the Church, but through the hearing and acceptance of a particular kind of message or gospel which was not necessarily or universally preached in the churches; the sense that salvation is not to be found in just belonging to the Church or going to church. The characteristic experience, therefore, is that of the person brought up as a member of the Church, who nevertheless comes to realise that his or her previous Christianity has been merely 'nominal'.

Barr held that striving to lead a good life, though widely taken outside Conservative Evangelical circles to be obvious natural ethics, was seen and felt in the experience of the revivals to be the worst of sins: it built up pride and increased self-satisfaction, leading people to reject the help of divine grace and ignore their dependence upon it, and therefore came near to making salvation impossible. This sense that people *within the Church* by their own religiosity and their own goodness, encouraged and abetted by the Church, became alienated from God and thus ripe for conversion through the hearing of the gospel, was a major strand of Evangelical thinking.

Conservative Evangelicalism believed that the true gospel was not being preached: false, 'Liberal' or 'modernist' ideas had taken its place. The blame for the enormous incidence of nominal Christianity in the churches lay in false teaching. This false teaching encouraged people in their self-assurance, and instead of making clear to them their sinful state, gave them an impression of being well set in the ways of good. Rather than basing itself squarely upon the Bible, Liberal Christianity was wishy-washy about the authority of the Bible, used it only vaguely and intermittently, and felt free to look elsewhere for its sources of authority.

Barr argued that the contrast between the 'nominal Christian' and the 'true Christian' was a distinction basic to all Conservative Evangelical thought and action. Distrust of the existing Church was carried to the point of cynicism; failures of the Church were diagnosed as failure to preserve something that had been there all the time, a gospel message that was given in the Bible and understood by the revivals. This gospel message had been thrown away because clergy and theologians wanted to say something more modern, more up to date, more in tune with the spirit of the age. You will not, said Barr, make a great impression on a convinced

Conservative Evangelical by pointing to the noble life, the good deeds, the saintly character of this or that non-Evangelical Christian. The Conservative Evangelical's interest is that we are saved by grace through faith, and not by the goodness of human works.

Barr made much of the fact that Conservative Evangelicalism had its own special forms of organisation. Though undenominational, they were commonly very exclusive and unco-operative towards non-Conservative-Evangelical organisations. In Britain the UCCF, the body which runs university Christian Unions, published a substantial amount of literature which was seen as 'sound'. Thus Conservative Evangelicals had an organisational base which came close to being a Conservative Evangelical denomination. The assurance that on platforms approved by the Evangelical establishment no false doctrine would be preached was a major reason for the moral hold of Conservative Evangelical leaders on their members.

Evangelical doctrine and approach to Scripture

In Barr's view, Evangelicalism picked out from the mass of biblical material certain themes, passages, contexts and emphases and said, 'This is the material that expresses the core of the Christian message.' He argued, however, that the Bible alone and taken as a whole, does not lead to the Evangelical position. If openness of interpretation is permitted it leads equally well in other directions.

Barr asserted that though many Evangelicals and Evangelical groups dissociated themselves from the term 'fundamentalism' and were anxious not to be confused with it, much of their language remained very often only a diluted and milder version of fundamentalist ways of thinking.

He acknowledged a certain improvement in the quality of Evangelical scholarship, but argued that this had to be balanced by the enormous influence in the Evangelical world of 'pseudo-intellectual gurus like Francis Schaeffer, of semi-educated evangelists and leaders of all kinds, and of rubbishy partisan literature'.

Barr argues that the Bible cannot and does not make claims for its own inspiration. Certainly, within the sixty-six books of the Bible, verses or passages such as in 2 Timothy or 2 Peter make statements suggesting that certain Scriptures are in some way inspired. The New Testament, however, makes no 'claims' about its infallibility. What Jesus said about Scripture referred to the Old Testament, and this is also true of most of the passages in the New Testament: when they talk about 'Scriptures' or 'as it is written' and the like, they are talking about the Old Testament. Whether 'Scripture' in 2 Timothy 3:16 or 'prophecy of Scripture' in 2 Peter 1:20 refer only to Old Testament writings, or whether they also include some New Testament material, is open to debate. But it is impossible to show that these passages refer expressly and uniquely to exactly the group of books which now constitute our New Testament canon, or our total biblical canon.

Barr on justification by faith

Certain biblical passages, maintained Barr, suggested very different ways of 'being saved' (for example Acts 16:30ff and Mark 10:17–22). Few in the Conservative Evangelical tradition of Christianity would be asked if they had kept the Ten Commandments, as if that would answer the question of the means of salvation. Even fewer in Conservative Evangelical society were likely to be told that they might inherit eternal life through selling their goods and giving to the poor. Although this was the very teaching of Jesus himself, it was commonly downgraded. The teaching of Jesus in Mark 10:17–22 (the story of the rich man who asked what he might do to inherit eternal life) was a complete contradiction of the idea of justification by faith.

Not all the Pauline letters mentioned the doctrine or insisted upon its binding character. Parts of the New Testament other than the Pauline letters did not mention it at all. Thus the New Testament might be read in a fashion in which justification by faith was much less central than Protestant and Evangelical tradition had led us to believe; the New Testament could be read equally well in a fashion in which other emphases – for instance more 'catholic' emphases – were dominant. These other emphases were just as well supported by the total text of the New Testament as the Evangelical approach.

Barr on Anglican Evangelicalism today

When, on a snowy day in January 1995, I visited James Barr in his home in Oxford, he told me that his assessment of Evangelicalism had changed little since he wrote his book twenty years earlier. He thought that the notion of Evangelicals strongly identifying themselves with, and seeking to sustain, one particular wing of Anglicanism was unhealthy. He believes that loyalty to a section of a Church is necessary for some people, but once it is made into a principle by which you guide your existence then it becomes a bad thing.

Barr recognises that there are many varieties of Evangelicals and that some escape almost entirely the criticisms which he made in his book. He spoke to me about some Anglican Evangelicals who he would acquit of most of the charges he made in his book. Canon F. W. Dillistone, a friend of Barr's when Dillistone was a Fellow of Oriel College, Oxford, had been Chancellor and then Dean of Liverpool Cathedral. He was the author of biographies of Charles Raven, C. H. Dodd and Max Warren. Dillistone was a near neighbour of the Barrs in Oxford, had come from an Evangelical background, and spent many hours discussing Conservative Evangelicalism with Barr. The two men found they had much in common.

Of living Anglican Evangelicals, Barr referred warmly to the Rev. Dr N. T. Wright, Dean of Lichfield. 'Tom Wright', Barr told me, 'is an Evangelical, but he is a man of his own mind. Nobody tells Tom Wright what he's got to think. I don't necessarily agree with everything he says, but I respect his ideas and alignments.'

Barr believes that the Church of England has a large number of people who have strong religious commitment but who are not aligned in a partisan way. Those who hold senior positions in the Church of England cannot remain partisan.

Barr and Liberalism

Some Evangelicals may be surprised to learn that Professor Barr does not regard his own position as a Liberal one. After retiring from his Oxford chair, he taught at the School of Divinity at

Vanderbilt University, Tennessee. The orientation of the Vanderbilt school is Liberal, though some of the students are Conservative . 'I have a bad conscience on their behalf,' Barr told me, 'because I feel that the school is so Liberal as to have become a dogmatic Liberal institution. The poor Conservative students feel that they're being pushed and bullied by the extreme Liberalism which a lot of the students and teachers espouse.'

John Stott takes the view that Barr was at his strongest when he attacked the Evangelical lack of theology. He concedes that Barr's criticism that Evangelicalism was a 'theologyless movement' contained an uncomfortable degree of truth. 'The resurgent Evangelical movement', admits Stott, 'has produced biblical scholars rather than creative thinkers.'

ANOTHER VIEW FROM THE SAME STABLE

Professor Hugh Williamson is the present holder of the Regius Chair of Hebrew at the University of Oxford. Pusey and Barr are two of his illustrious predecessors. He was brought up in the Church of England and currently attends an Anglican church in Suffolk where he lives. Williamson told me that he comes from a Conservative Evangelical background and still calls himself an Evangelical. He has difficulty, however, with the extreme Conservative approach on a number of familiar critical issues such as the unity of Isaiah and the Mosaic authorship of the Pentateuch.

I asked Professor Williamson for his reaction to James Barr's assertion that we cannot use expressions like 'what the Bible teaches' – i.e. that although sixty-six books were recognised as authoritative and given the status of canon by the Church in the fourth century, we should not necessarily expect them to speak with one consistent voice. In Williamson's view, this position is both right and wrong. It is right in so far as we have to be sensitive to the variety and diversity of Scripture. In his academic work he spends more time 'pulling things apart than putting them together'. Academic Evangelicals have been more aware of the diversity element of Scripture in recent years. They discuss it more readily and no longer rush to harmonise. Williamson concedes that, in one sense, it is a short-cut to say 'the Bible teaches this or that'.

At the same time, however, it is possible to exaggerate the consequences of diversity. 'There do seem to me', he said, 'to be some central emphases which unite the Scriptures. There's a unity as well as a diversity.' Therefore to acknowledge the authority of the Bible does not solve all the problems because sometimes the biblical books do speak with discordant voices. They certainly give us parameters within which to operate: a circle of ideas out of which we would not wish to move. Most people's reading of the Bible would suggest to them that some of the books which are more obviously difficult are 'gadflies within Scripture': raising questions about the central core. In other words, there are some boundaries, but a certain flexibility within that. To some extent the variety we see in the Church reflects that flexibility.

Conservative Evangelicals, in common with other strands within the Church, come to Scripture with some sort of prior system or set of beliefs. The natural tendency is to try to confirm this agenda from the Bible. It is very difficult, if not impossible, actually to start from the Bible pure and simple. If we did, it is reasonable to question whether we would arrive either at the classic Christian creeds or the Conservative Evangelical system. We all attach special importance to certain parts of the Bible while sitting loose to other parts. What causes us to say that this passage is central and other beliefs must be brought into harmony with it? What would happen if we began with some of the parables and tried to arrange everything around them? Things might turn out with a different emphasis.

Conservative Evangelicalism today is not as unified as it was when Professor Barr wrote his book *Fundamentalism*. Barr takes Howard Marshall to task for trying to harmonise the accounts of the ascension at the end of Luke's Gospel with the beginning of Acts. Williamson thinks Barr's criticism of Marshall is unfair and points out that it does not arise out of anything to do with Conservative Evangelicalism. On the normal assumption, Luke and Acts were written by the same writer, so the text itself obliges us to read the two books together, since Luke apparently intended them to be read as two sequential volumes. Therefore, quite apart from Conservative Evangelical expectations about harmony, anyone examining the text would expect it to be consistent and some attempt to consider whether the two accounts may be harmonised is a reasonable exercise.

Barr does tend to lump together Fundamentalists, with whom Williamson would disagree himself, with other reputable Conservative scholars.

Academic Evangelicals, such as members of the Tyndale Fellowship, represent a wide range of scholars: there are academics such as John Goldingay of Nottingham, who, like Williamson, would take a critical position on Old Testament literature, and then a complete spectrum across to those who take a very Conservative view. At the academic level, the rigid Fundamentalist view does not prevail. In Hugh Williamson's judgment, however, American academics tend to be more stereotyped – though some institutions, such as Fuller Theological Seminary, attempt to hold to the middle ground.

Professor Williamson's impression, based on his experience of visiting and preaching in English churches, is that people are either unaware of these issues or rather impatient of them. They would rather get on with the business of Christian living.

Many Conservative Evangelicals lead thoroughly admirable Christian lives. Within the Evangelical camp there are those who are involved in evangelism, Bible teaching, social action, the discussion of ethical issues and the response to them. Today, these things are taken very seriously by Evangelicals. If you examine the Evangelical scene across the range of its activities in Britain, you find a good balance of concerns: there is the strong Church dimension, and also Tear Fund, *Third Way*, and the Jubilee Centre in Cambridge. People are exploring a whole number of issues on which they want to set out a Christian position. Evangelicals are involved in most areas of the Christian life and mission.

Sadly, however, some – particularly among the more academic Conservative Evangelicals – tend to make a defence of the Conservative position an overriding concern in such a way that their tone and approach sounds positively un-Christian.

Most Anglo-Catholics and most Evangelicals are reasonably happy with their labels. Many Evangelicals are indeed proud of theirs. Most people who are given the label 'Liberal' probably would not call themselves that. There are some who are committed

Liberals, and who take a pride in the title, but there is a large group who might be called Liberal by Evangelicals but who really are not Liberal 'in the full-blown sense'. There is plenty of room in the Church for a variety of schools of thought. Some find one style of worship, for example, more meaningful and helpful than another.

Professor Williamson has an interesting perspective on authority, and the debate about the relative roles of the Bible and the Church. Individual Christians, he says, read Scripture in the context of the local congregation. It may be that the Scriptures challenge a previously held position and therefore the Christian adjusts his or her thinking to take account of this. Next time that Christian reads the Scriptures he or she is not quite the same person: he or she has changed. Then that person continues to read Scripture and talk to Christian friends, and listen to a preacher, and it becomes a process of continuous adaptation and change.

In as much as that process occurs in individual lives, causing Christians to grow, by dint of the fact that the Church is made up of a collection of individuals, so the Church itself progresses. This may be seen in Church history or in the life of individual congregations: different issues come into focus or prominence, and churches realise they have neglected one thing or overemphasised another. Therefore, of the three things – the individual, the Bible and the Church – two are in a state of change: the individual probably rather faster than the Church. Some individuals may move ahead particularly quickly and may move the Church forward somewhat; others may lag behind and hold the Church back. But the Church does not stay static.

Williamson finds it difficult to imagine a Church in which anything is completely fixed. The only thing that *does not* change in itself is the Bible. But because we are reading it, and because the Church is reading it, with different eyes it *appears* to change because different aspects become prominent for us. There is this constant state of flux and he does not think that there is a fixed point which can be regarded as 'a correct position for the Christian'. He believes that Scripture is the nearest we can get to it: but our appreciation of Scripture is changing all the time.

He cites the example of the 'testimony meeting'. He has heard many testimonies and often remembers hearing young people describe how they have come to faith. They would say: 'Before I was converted, I thought the Bible was a boring, dusty old book. But now I read it every day and it is a vital and exciting part of my life.' Now, he points out, the Bible has not changed: they have changed. In principle, that experience of change ought to be an ongoing experience in the life of every Christian. If the Bible can appear to change from being a boring book to becoming the source of life, are we saying a great deal when we hammer away at formulating a doctrinal understanding of it which implies something static?

Hugh Williamson was secretary of the (broadly Evangelical) Tyndale Fellowship twenty-five years ago. In those days they used to record in the committee when a member of the Fellowship got a university appointment. 'There was great rejoicing when we passed the figure of twenty-five,' he remembers. 'Since then, the number of Tyndale Fellowship members in university posts has grown enormously. Nowadays I could name people in the Tyndale Fellowship who are theologically considerably to the left of people in university positions who are not in the Tyndale Fellowship. If I'm allowed to be an Evangelical, there are many more Evangelicals teaching at all levels than there were a quarter of a century ago. And it so happens that the two Regius chairs of Hebrew at Oxford and Cambridge are occupied by men who feel quite at home among the Christian Brethren. But neither of us would be called "fundamentalist". In the theology departments of British universities today there's a complete range of academics from Conservatives to those who are very radical indeed. In the Old Testament field, some wouldn't consider themselves as Christians but as students of ancient literature or history. And then there are a great many who take a position somewhere between those extremes.'

Twenty-five years ago, to come across an Evangelical in a university department of Theology or Biblical Studies was still unusual. Now there is a much broader spread.

Why the Church of England needs Evangelicals

I asked Professor Williamson how healthy he thought it was for a powerful group of Anglicans to wish to preserve within Anglicanism an 'Evangelical heritage'. He replied that it was very important for the Church at large that there should be a lively Evangelical party. First, because Evangelicals are by far the best at recruiting. Certainly, other strands talk about evangelism, and although of course people come to faith in different ways, in terms of going out and getting people into the kingdom of God the Evangelicals win hands down. It is true that some come into the Church as a result of Evangelical witness and then move into another tradition, but it was the Evangelicals who performed the vital role of recruitment.

Second, it is very good that the Church should have a wing which continues to stress the authority of the Bible. 'I want to do that myself,' he told me, 'the difficulty is knowing what it is teaching. It's not always as straightforward as the Evangelicals make out and therefore what it is authoritatively telling me is not always easy to grasp. But the Bible is the ultimate source of authority for me. It doesn't solve the problems, but it puts the emphasis in the right place. I see alternative sources of authority as part of the "bouncing-off process": we have to bounce off Church tradition; we've got to use our reason. It's not one at the exclusion of the other. But if there's a pecking order, I hope my reason is informed by Scripture rather than the other way round. Similarly with the life and tradition of the Church: the Church has evolved over the centuries. But to be reminded forcefully that the Scripture is primary in the hierarchy seems to me important as an anchor.'

Third, although he is happy to see a diversity of liturgy and styles of worship, he ultimately thinks there is no preaching like the best Evangelical preaching. Certainly there is some *bad* Evangelical preaching, but people who can take the Scriptures and expound them with relevance and power are much needed. The best Evangelical preachers are doing what is needed and find a response among their congregations.

'Although the gospel has many expressions,' Professor Williamson told me, 'I still think that sin and salvation through the cross are at the heart of it all. I welcome that Evangelical emphasis as I do the insistence on the role of the Bible in the Church.'

ARE 'LIBERALS' THE ENEMY?

At their conferences and as individuals, Anglican Evangelicals, like all Evangelicals, are inclined to see Liberals as 'the enemy'. In North America, where they also use the term 'revisionist', the invective is even fiercer than in Britain. But on both sides of the Atlantic, Evangelical hostility to Liberalism is commonplace. To what extent is this attitude justifiable?

John Habgood, Archbishop of York from 1983 until 1995, doubts whether 'the Liberal position' exists as such, or whether there is any set of ideas or attitudes on which those who value the word 'Liberal' would agree. 'The notion', he wrote in 1991, 'frequently canvassed these days, that there is a cohort of Liberals within the Church of England who share certain definite aims and assumptions, and who constantly foster what has been called "the Liberal ascendancy" seems to me to reveal a deep misunderstanding of the Liberal phenomenon.'

However, Habgood sees a constant feature of Liberalism as the wish to take seriously the intellectual climate in which the Christian faith has to be lived. That is not the same as following intellectual fashion. 'Serious Liberalism does not start reconstructing its theology at the first hint of secular change . . . But it needs to take seriously the questions posed by fundamental sea-changes, and to be ready to live with loose ends, partial insights, and a measure of agnosticism, without losing its grip on the essentials of faith.'

For Habgood, the readiness to receive new truth itself belongs to the essence of faith:

The search for truth . . . through rational critical understanding (which needs of course to be self-critical as well) has theological roots no less significant than the theological basis of revelation. Both are from God: in different modes and degrees, maybe, but both originating and finding their fulfilment in him. It is this kind of faith, I believe, which undergirds the best Liberal approaches to theology. I want to emphasise that it is a theological undergirding, not an absence of faith in God, but a conviction that is to be found wherever the human mind can reach. That is why the equation of Liberalism with lack of faith is frequently so wide of the mark . . . From my perspective an intoxication with the greatness and mystery of God lies at the heart of it all.[39]

Habgood on the Evangelical resurgence

A few months before he retired in 1995, Habgood said that he had noticed the growth of a hardline Evangelicalism which believed in ways which he thought irrational, and which created an image of Christianity which actually made it harder for the people he was concerned to reach to take Christianity seriously.

When it was put to Habgood that Evangelicals had always been thought of as making up 'the sales department of the Church', he responded that they had been selling a kind of certainty which he did not think you could have: a certainty which was very attractive but, for that reason, dangerous. Uncertainty is not easy to sell, but you can sell honesty.

I think the honest search for a truth that transcends us, an honest exploration of mystery: these are what I find most attractive; and an approach which brings a wholeness to life. I think I've always begun with the sense that life is surrounded by mystery, and what is peculiar about human beings is the possibility that we might become aware of this . . .

We are witnessing a very strong Evangelical resurgence, and that contains many excellent elements: evangelism, taking the Bible seriously, and that sense of personal commitment which I think is terribly important. But again, one observes some elements who are feeling that mainstream, traditional Evangelicalism is not enough, and they're calling for a tighter and more exclusive form of Christianity.

I think we've suffered from a confusion in the middle between what one might call radicalism and the traditional centre: both are called 'Liberal', which has, alas, become a rather dirty word. But I think there is a very strong tradition at the centre of ordinary Anglican people who don't care very much for the extremes.'[40]

He himself was brought up High Church, became a member of the Evangelical Christian Union at Cambridge, deliberately went to Cuddesdon Theological College in order to learn what Catholicism was all about from that perspective, and has consistently tried to combine all those elements. Therefore he sees himself as an archetypal Anglican.

John Saxbee, the Bishop of Ludlow, is anxious to bridge the gap between Liberalism and evangelism. In his view, Liberalism must have an evangelistic thrust if it is to be credible; and the openness, honesty and respect for diversity that are the marks of the Liberal spirit should also characterise evangelism[41] (see also pages 451–2).

Fundamentalists, Liberals and Evangelicals

In his *Essentials* debate with David Edwards, John Stott said that the *Fundamentalist* seemed to him to resemble a caged bird, which possessed the capacity for flight, but lacked the freedom to use it. The Fundamentalist mind is imprisoned by an overliteral interpretation of Scripture, and by the strict traditions and conventions to which this has led. The Fundamentalist is not at liberty to question these, or to explore alternative, equally faithful ways of applying Scripture to the modern world, being unable to escape the cage.

The *Liberal* seemed to Stott (in 1988 – and he claimed to mean no offence!) 'to resemble a gas-filled balloon, which takes off and rises into the air, buoyant, free, directed only by its own built-in navigational responses to wind and pressure, but entirely unrestrained from earth. For the Liberal mind has no anchorage; it's accountable only to itself.'

The *Evangelical* seemed 'to resemble a kite, which can also take off, fly great distances and soar to great heights, while all the time being tethered to earth. For the Evangelical mind is held by revelation. Without doubt it often needs a longer string, for we are not renowned for creative thinking.' Nevertheless, at least in the ideal, he saw Evangelicals as finding true freedom under the authority of revealed truth, and combining a radical mindset and lifestyle with a conservative commitment to Scripture.[42]

McGrath on Liberalism

Alister McGrath, who went through a 'Liberal phase' himself, has spoken (like James Barr) of a reaction against Liberalism. McGrath claims that 'the sustained Evangelical critique of Liberalism at both the pragmatic and theoretical level has now been supplemented by other voices outside Evangelicalism, reinforcing the general consensus within Christian churches that Liberalism is intellectually flawed and tainted'.

McGrath argues that Liberalism has, in the view of many observers, 'degenerated from a commitment to openness and toleration into an intolerant and dogmatic world-view, which refuses to recognise the validity of any views save its own'. He quotes the British theologian John Macquarrie: 'What is meant by "Liberal" theology? If it means only that the theologian to whom the adjective is applied has an openness to other points of view, then Liberal theologians are found in all schools of thought. But if "Liberal" becomes a party label, then it usually turns out to be extremely illiberal.'[43]

As we shall see in Part Seven, which looks at the storm which rages over human sexuality, Liberalism (such as it exists) has tended too easily to accommodate itself to contemporary Western culture and has all too often uncritically abandoned much that is of vital importance for Christianity. When that happens, Evangelicals are surely right to see the phenomenon as an enemy of true faith in Christ.

Packer on Liberalism

For his part, Jim Packer has no doubt that Anglican Evangelicals should 'seek deliverance from the Liberal mindset in all its forms'. He believes that it does 'infect' unwary Evangelicals:

> It seeps into the church in all sorts of disguises. But the essence of it is this, and can be focused in a phrase: the Liberal mind-set is that the world has the wisdom and the Church must play catch-up. The Liberal mindset has been infecting the Church of

England for nearly two centuries so that Anglicans have constantly been playing back to a secular agenda. Let the Bible set the agenda in terms of giving us the vision of spiritual life and renewal that we long to see; let the Bible establish priorities for the Church and people of God; let the Bible establish priorities for the individual Christian.[44]

CAISTER 1988 AND THE DOCTRINE OF THE CHURCH

The last National Evangelical Anglican Congress (NEAC) was held in Caister, Norfolk, in 1988. Twice as many people turned up at Caister as at Nottingham eleven years earlier. Billed as a 'Celebration', some say that it failed to confront real differences within Anglican Evangelicalism. One moment which has been remembered is that the (then) Archbishop of Canterbury, Robert Runcie, addressing the Celebration, challenged his Evangelical audience to take the doctrine of the Church more seriously by producing a 'developed Evangelical ecclesiology'.

John Stott responded by affirming Evangelicals' loyalty to the Church of England but recognising that their tendency had been to focus on 'the concepts of an invisible and mystical body' and 'local, independent congregations' at 'the expense of an organised and visible society united by baptism and Eucharist'.

Following Caister, Tim Bradshaw's book *The Olive Branch* (1992) surveyed Anglo-Catholic, radical and Anglican Evangelical ecclesiologies, clarifying areas of agreement and debate and restating an Evangelical view. The Church's ministry, said Bradshaw,

> *as a whole people of God*, is firstly to face her Lord, her centre, to stand upon her living foundation stone. Into the olive tree of Christological faith she now has to graft the hundreds of thousands who have strayed or never heard this good news, never experienced the love and care of Christ, himself the true vine. Because her structures are so bonded into society and claim such historic pedigree, she needs repeatedly, as Barth says, to

consecrate herself to the gospel. If this Catholic and Evangelical consecration can happen, she stands well placed to proclaim and serve the gospel to all who are near and far off.[45]

Lord Runcie welcomed Tim Bradshaw's book, saying that it illustrated how our doctrine of the Church both shapes and reflects our attitude to authority, ministry and salvation. Nevertheless, by 1995 Anglican Evangelicals were divided between those who saw the doctrine of the Church as a primary, credal doctrine and those whose interdenominational sympathies reduced it to a second level of importance.

Michael Saward's view is blunt. He believes that the doctrines of Church, ministry and sacraments which Evangelical Anglicans (his preferred designation) and the free churches (he calls them 'Independents') hold are radically different. To Saward, Independent ecclesiology is wrong and largely responsible for the creation of something like twenty-five thousand sects and denominations worldwide. He sees himself as a credal man, welcoming the fact that, since Keele, mainstream Evangelical Anglicans have rediscovered their Anglican roots. For him, Independency is basically sectarian in spirit and history, and he worries that Evangelical Anglicans are recreating the 'sect' mentality.

ARCHBISHOP CAREY

George Carey was born in Dagenham, Essex, in 1935, left school at fifteen and became an office boy. Although he was baptised in a London parish, he was not brought up as a churchgoer. His younger brother Bob was the first member of the Carey family to start attending the local Anglican church in Dagenham regularly and invited George to go along with him. The church was thoroughly Evangelical, though at first the young Carey had no idea what the word meant. Preaching in the church focused on an appeal to respond to Christ, whilst its teaching was rooted in seeking to make the Bible relevant to everyday life. The vicar instilled in him the sense that Christianity was not something to be taken lightly.

At the age of seventeen, Carey responded to his vicar's appeal and became a Christian. Both he and the other members of the church youth group were left in no doubt that the call from Jesus was one to wholehearted discipleship.

After doing his national service as a radio operator in the Royal Air Force, Carey studied at the London College of Divinity and gained a BD at the University of London. He served a curacy at St Mary's, Islington, and after further study he lectured at the Evangelical Oak Hill Theological College in north London and St John's College, Nottingham, where he also gained a PhD. In 1975 he returned to parish work as Vicar of St Nicholas, Durham, a church with a busy work among students which he radically reconstructed, as he recorded in his book *The Church in the Market Place*. In 1982 Dr Carey became Principal of Trinity College, Bristol.

After four years at Trinity, Carey heard a rumour that his name was in the running for Bishop of Bath and Wells. He could not believe it at first. 'I am not interested,' he thought. 'I am happy in this job. I was very distressed when the letter came from Margaret Thatcher offering me Bath and Wells.'

He was consecrated bishop in 1987. When, two-and-a-half years later, he received another letter from Mrs Thatcher inviting him to become Archbishop of Canterbury, Carey and his wife only decided that he should accept after a period of agonised prayer and reflection.

To the surprise of many, on 19 April 1991 George Carey was enthroned as 103rd Archbishop of Canterbury in succession to St Augustine. 'From Augustine's chair', he said, 'I ask that we set above our divisions the urgency of witnessing to our nation that there is a God who cares and loves all people.'

The question in the minds of Evangelicals in the Anglican Communion, and in other denominations throughout the world, had often been asked before when members thought to be of their constituency achieved high office: *Would George Carey turn out to be a good, sound gospel man or would he go soft and become a figure of the middle-of-the-road Church establishment?* His credentials in both the Evangelical and Charismatic worlds seemed impeccable.

Quinquennial verdicts

Answers to that question have been mixed. After Carey's first five years in the job, the Rev. Tony Higton, an often outspoken Evangelical campaigner, said, 'Dr Carey has brought great strengths to Canterbury, particularly an ability to convey the gospel clearly, and a deep concern that the Church should give priority to mission and social justice. He speaks out strongly in favour of the traditional family as the basic unit of society . . . He could be one of the best Archbishops.'

Canon Stephen Trott gave a less enthusiastic verdict on Carey. 'I think he's been something of a disappointment. We expected a more traditional Evangelical, but as Archbishop he's been Evangelical in no obvious way . . . I like him best when he's not being the official Archbishop but speaking from the heart, as he did at the November ('95) Synod in the debate on the family. That was the real George Carey.'

Richard Holloway, Primus of the Scottish Episcopal Church, gave a fairly typical reaction from among Liberals: 'I think of him as a Jim Callaghan Archbishop – unflappable. He's had a steadying influence on all sorts of people and issues; he reassures people. My own difference with him would be that I think he hammers certain kinds of moral issues too simplistically – but, of course, that's what people want.'

From the headquarters of English Catholicism, Cardinal Basil Hume provided the press with a characteristically generous and judicious quote: 'In the five years that Dr Carey has been Archbishop I have seen a good deal of him, and have appreciated these contacts very much. He is very much a leader on the ecumenical scene, and I am grateful for his insistence on spiritual values, and his outspokenness on a number of important social issues.'[46]

Carey's churchmanship

Were those Evangelicals who thought of Carey as one of themselves correct? A few years into his primacy, he acknowledged his debt to the Evangelical church where he found Christ. 'My own spirituality is still grounded in the regular personal Bible study we were encouraged to make central to our Christian discipleship,' he said. 'Indeed, for me, one of the long-term attractions of the Anglican way has been the fact that it is rooted in Scripture as the foundation for our understanding of the faith.'

In those early years when he moved among Evangelicals, however, he also encountered a narrow biblicism which he thought failed to do justice to the rich diversity of the biblical record. 'I have always wanted to ask questions of anything I read, and I became increasingly dissatisfied with those who seemed to be avoiding some of the obvious difficulties in the biblical text. Words like inerrancy have never really appealed to me and certainly my own belief in the Bible's authority with regard to its revelation of God does not depend on having a text free from minor contradictions.'

Carey has said that he treasures Anglicanism's Liberal tradition with what he calls 'its stress on taking the world in which we are set very seriously indeed and using our reason to try to discern the mind of God'. Within mainstream Anglicanism he thinks (optimistically) that the word 'Liberal' is best understood as 'a commitment to orthodoxy which is open to new thought, new knowledge and to the challenges of our culture'. He is proud of a tradition within Anglicanism which is broad enough to include great diversity and the questioning spirit which is not content with narrowness of thought.

His encounters with the Catholic tradition within Anglicanism have taught him that two thousand years of Christian history should never be overlooked in seeking to understand the ways of God. Moreover, 'The importance of the sacrament of the Holy Communion, the use of silence, the practice of making retreats all of these I came to appreciate more fully and they now provide a richness to my life which I would be loath to be without.' Travelling in Africa as Archbishop, he was impressed with the way that Anglo-Catholic churches combined a depth of Catholic devotion with an Evangelical zeal for the gospel.

A Charismatic Archbishop?

'Whilst I have never been what some would call a "card-carrying Charismatic",' says Carey, 'I have greatly benefited from many of its insights. In particular its theology of the Spirit as active in the church and a power for living changed my perspective on the way God works in the world ... The contribution of this movement to lay ministry and its yearning for greater freedom in worship have proved to be formative in the Church as well as in my own spiritual development. My time as Vicar of St Nicholas, Durham, was a very exciting one indeed, not least because of the ways in which the Charismatic movement affected us during those years.'[47]

Speaking to John Humphries, on BBC Radio 4 in June 1997, Dr Carey said that he did not think the Archbishop of Canterbury was the top job, in the Christian sense. 'I think the best job in the Church is to be an ordinary, humble parish priest in a community getting on with the job. I am often saying that.'

The strengths of Evangelicalism . . .

I asked Dr Carey what was the most valuable input Evangelicals could make to the life of the Anglican Communion in the period leading up to the 1998 Lambeth Conference and beyond. He began his reply by reminding me that the Reformation represented the discovery of the Evangelical heart of the Christian faith. 'Such doctrines as the all-sufficient work of Christ on the cross, that salvation proceeds from grace and faith and the primacy of Scripture over all other forms of authority continues to this day to be the heartbeat of Evangelicalism. This is something I wholeheartedly endorse and which remains at the heart of all I stand for.

'Among the great strengths of Evangelicalism which I applaud are a commitment to mission, based on the uniqueness of Christ and the finality of his revelation. This has always been the driving force and passion of the Evangelical gospel. Also relevant is the Evangelical commitment to the possibility of people knowing God through a personal conversion. In short, Evangelicalism is a "heart" religion and delights in a love relationship with a personal Lord who calls people into a firm obedience to his laws and his ways.'

... and its weaknesses

'Where some Evangelicals have been traditionally weak', Dr Carey told me, 'has been their doctrines of the Church and the sacraments and in a tendency towards individualism, though this was never true of people like Cranmer, Luther or Calvin at the time of the Reformation. One impact of the Charismatic movement in the '70s and '80s on Anglican Evangelicals has been to help people rediscover the importance of the Church and sacraments. I have been thrilled, personally, by the growth of greater awareness among many Evangelicals of the importance of the Body and a greater desire to get involved in the structures of the Church. The greater strength of Evangelicalism now in the Church of England owes much to this trend.

'My own unwillingness to use the label "Evangelical" of myself (though others tend to be overgenerous in applying it to me!) is because I owe so much to other traditions in the Church that a simple designation does not do justice now to my theology. *I am a Christian before I am an Anglican, and I am an Anglican before I am an Evangelical.* That is to say, I have not left behind any of the great truths of an Evangelical faith but I am comfortable with "Catholic" worship and practice (as long as it doesn't stray into non-biblical categories) and I owe much to the "Liberal" tradition for its commitment and passion for truth.'

Evangelicals, holiness and social justice

I asked the Archbishop whether he thought that the tendency of some Evangelicals to concentrate on salvation rather than morality blunted the support he might expect to receive from them on what others have called his 'moral crusade'. He replied that he did not think he had lacked support from Evangelicals in his challenge to the nation for a rediscovery of a Christian morality. 'But there has always been a danger', he said, 'that the Evangelical emphasis on justification by faith can lead it to have a weak doctrine of social witness. Although the Evangelical tradition may be rightly proud of such giants as Wilberforce, Shaftesbury and others, it has not been as outstanding as Anglo-Catholic Christianity in standing firm for social justice, human dignity and suffering humanity.

'I am glad to say that this has changed over the last two decades and modern Anglican Evangelicalism is much more committed to the social witness of the Church in many different forms. The National Evangelical Anglican Congress at Keele in 1967 was instrumental in refocusing the vision of Evangelicalism away from a predominantly individualistic model to one which included the whole of humankind.'

THE ORDINATION OF WOMEN

The ordination of women was opposed by some Evangelicals and many Anglo-Catholics on different grounds. Nevertheless, the Deacons (Ordination of Women) Measure 1986 led to women being admitted to the diaconate and was followed by pressure for them to be made priests. This issue proved very divisive. In 1992, by a small margin, the General Synod passed the Priests (Ordination of Women) Measure. The Measure allowed for parishes to refuse to have a woman as incumbent and accompanying legislation authorised financial compensation for most full-time stipendiary clergy who felt bound in conscience to resign in consequence of the ordination of women. In 1993 an Act of Synod (the Episcopal Ministry Act) provided for three provincial ('flying') bishops who would, under the jurisdiction of the diocesan bishop, minister in those parishes which were unwilling to accept the ministrations of bishops who had been involved in the ordination of women.

By May 1997 a survey reported that a tenth of the Church of England's clergy were women. Nearly four hundred women were in charge of parishes. By the end of July 1996 there were 1,957 women in licensed ministry in the forty-three dioceses. Almost half of them were paid a full stipend. Most were middle-aged, with relatively few below forty or over sixty years old. More than two hundred of these women were in 'sector' ministries, working as chaplains in hospitals, prisons, universities, colleges and in industry. Six out of ten were married, 306 of them to clergymen. The diocese with the largest number of women was Oxford with 101, followed by Southwark and St Albans. The Bishop of Ely, whose diocese had the highest number of women in charge of parishes, said:

> I am happy to bear testimony to the warmth of the welcome given by many different types of parishes to the ministry of women priests. It is very encouraging to note that in such a short time, there are so many ordained women serving the Church of God and in relatively significant posts. As anticipated, there is a marked enrichment of the life of the Church of England through these developments at every level. I do not ignore continuing conflict, of course, but we pray for one another and seek to know and do God's will.[48]

REFORM

Reform was launched following a meeting on 22 February 1993, soon after the Church of England made its decision to ordain women to the priesthood. According to the body's own literature, the issues which concerned the founding members were as follows: the authority and sufficiency of Scripture; the uniqueness and finality of Christ; the priority of the local church; and the 'complementarity of men and women'. Reform has always denied that it is a limited-issue organisation concerned only with women's ordination, human sexuality or quota capping.

In the week that Reform was launched, by clergy from about twenty large Conservative Evangelical parishes, the Rev. David Holloway, Vicar of Jesmond, Newcastle, circulated a memo spelling out the case for capping the quotas that individual parishes pay to their dioceses. He argued that the Church of England penalised success and ensured the support of parishes which were ineffective or that proclaimed views that were contrary to the traditional doctrines of the Church.

Listing the key influences in his spiritual pilgrimage, David Holloway includes his own chaplain at University College, Oxford, T. M. Parker, 'an Anglo-Catholic, a polymath, but with a profound distaste for theological Liberalism'. Parker taught Holloway that thoughtfulness and Liberalism were not synonymous. David Holloway went on to study at Fuller Seminary in the USA. He believes we need to reform the Church for the effective preaching of the gospel because the gospel is true. Hence Reform's literature proclaims, 'Our overall aim is to win the nation for Christ.'

We desperately need, says Holloway, 'those three "R"s of evangelical religion – *ruin, redemption and regeneration*.' He quotes Pannenberg, saying that 'individual freedom cannot be unbridled licence'. Secularism's greatest success, he believes, is in the widespread demoralisation in the ranks of the clergy. He is sure that theologians delude themselves when they think that they are achieving their purpose by adapting Christian faith and life to the demands of secularism.

Just as Britain is adrift spiritually and in need of evangelising, so Holloway and Reform believe that the Church of England is adrift doctrinally, morally and in terms of social significance. It is adrift in part because its leadership has adapted the Christian faith and life to these demands of secularism. He asserts that in their official report, *The Nature of Christian Belief: A Statement and Exposition by the House of Bishops of the General Synod of the Church of England* (1986), the bishops made it clear that to deny the empty tomb of Jesus was acceptable. The empty tomb was an expression of the doctrine of the Church of England. 'The logic (and undoubted intention) of their statement', says Holloway, 'was to allow the denial of the empty tomb also as a legitimate expression of the Church's belief.'

David Holloway speaks of the 'lowest common denominator theology' at the centre of the Church of England. 'There is no plot,' he says. 'It is simply the fruit of synodical government, its proportional representation and its voting systems (together with the devil and human sinfulness).'

For Holloway and Reform, the Church of England is not only

adrift in terms of doctrine but also morally adrift. The House of Bishops must bear much of the blame and, not least, in the matter of homosexual behaviour. In 1991 the bishops 'virtually validated homosexual sex for lay people'. This was in their report *Issues in Human Sexuality*. Holloway agrees that parts of the report are good, for example its summary of biblical teaching:

> There is, therefore, in Scripture an evolving convergence on the ideal of lifelong, monogamous, heterosexual union as the setting intended by God for the proper development of men and women as sexual beings. Sexual activity of any kind outside marriage comes to be seen as sinful, and homosexual practice as especially dishonourable. It is also recognised that God may call some to celibacy for particular service in his cause. Only by living within these boundaries are Christians to achieve that holiness which is pleasing to God.[49]

However the section of the report which deals with the responsibility of the local congregation offended David Holloway and Reform:

> It is ... only right that there should be an open and welcoming place in the Christian community both for those homophiles who follow the way of abstinence, giving themselves to friendship for many rather than intimacy with one, and also for those who are *conscientiously convinced that a faithful, sexually active relationship with one other person, aimed at helping both partners to grow in discipleship, is the way of life God wills for them.*[50]

Holloway is relieved that so far the bishops have excluded clergy from what he describes as this 'openness to homosexual sex'.[51] He says that the bishops are saying that homosexual genital acts are wrong from the perspective of the Church, and contrary to God's law, but right for a person who conscientiously thinks they are right. Actually, I do not think he is quite fair to the bishops: what the report says is that, in certain specified circumstances, homophiles in a faithful, sexually active relationship with one person should be given an open and welcoming place in the Christian community. The report appears (at this point) to be neutral on whether their behaviour is right or wrong. I do not see how a group of redeemed sinners can do any other than, as the bishops suggest, welcome into their community other sinners who may wish to join them.

David Holloway dismisses this part of the bishops' report as no more than conventional moral relativism. He is critical of the attitude which he sees in the wider world (and often in the Church) which can only say that certain behaviours and beliefs are 'right for me'. He thinks that history offers few examples of institutions which reform themselves. Usually that is brought about by a minority movement within the body itself. Since Keele, 'Evangelicals have had a larger and larger share of the Anglican cake; but many of them appear to have "gone native" – not least those appointed to high office. They often seem to end up as ineffective as those they seek to reform.'[52]

Against this background, David Holloway sees Reform as a network of Anglican individuals and parishes committed on the one hand to the biblical gospel of Jesus Christ and on the other hand to principled action to evangelise the nation and to make the parishes of this land once again the heart of the Church of England.[53]

Packer addresses Reform on the ordination of women

In June 1995 Jim Packer referred to the ordination of women at the Reform conference. He said that he thought it 'absolutely scandalous that the whole Church should be required to change course on a matter like this because of just a whisker in debate. Just – what was it? – two people in the House of Laity who changed sides and so ensured the passage of the measure. Nothing that has no moral consensus behind it can really do any community much good.'

He took the line that the way the measure was passed had ensured that having women presbyters would not do the Church of England much good. 'I remember the days when we had two orders of women serving full-time in the Church: we had deaconesses, we had women workers, the pattern worked well: the women did a magnificent job. I suspect that making them presbyters, women presbyters, rather than holding on to the old pattern of deaconesses and women workers will prove over a generation to have been much more trouble than it was worth. It was in other words very unwise to proceed in the way in which action was taken. That's not a comment on the issue; that's a comment on procedures.'

On other occasions, Packer has not been so reticent in commenting on the issue. He believes that five factors underlie the trend to ordain women: the feminist movement heightening demands for equal opportunity; the trend since the Second World War for women to move towards positions of equality with men throughout society; the tendency to argue that Paul's prohibitions on women's ministry only applied to his local situation; God appearing to have blessed the ministry of women; and Christian professional women denied ordination feeling they lack full job satisfaction.

Packer was concerned that secular, pragmatic and social factors were dominating the ordination debate and that authentically biblical considerations were being given less than their deserved attention. For him, 'the creation pattern, as biblically set forth, is: man to lead, woman to support; man to initiate, woman to enable; man to take responsibility for the well-being of woman, woman to take responsibility for helping man.' Presbyters are set apart for a role of authoritative pastoral leadership, which is reserved for 'manly men rather than womanly women, according to the creation pattern which redemption restores'.

Critics of Packer would argue that he omits to take sufficient account of the sense of call to the priesthood felt by many women.

Saward on Reform

From Michael Saward's perspective, the decision to ordain women as priests was 'welcomed by the majority of Evangelical Anglicans', but led to the foundation of Reform whose chief goals he sees as opposition to women priests, existing Church structures and the House of Bishops.

A somewhat mixed group, they played the traditional Evangelical hand of claiming the moral and theological high ground and ignoring the arguments of the mainstream. Since the greatest weakness historically of the whole Evangelical movement has been its tendency to tear itself apart into conflicting groups and to distrust 'them' (whoever they are) in positions of institutional responsibility, combined with unreal expectations of what can be achieved in a national Church, the danger of serious collapse in the movement in the last five years of the century cannot be ignored.[54]

THE 1995 ANGLICAN EVANGELICAL ASSEMBLY

I attended the Anglican Evangelical Assembly at High Leigh, Hertfordshire, in the spring of 1995. Five working groups had done a great deal of work prior to the Assembly in the areas of the Church, Ministry, Mission, Truth, and Worship and Learning. The five subjects were known at the Assembly as 'tracks'.

Another answer to Runcie

When he presented the findings of the Church track, Mark Birchall recalled Caister and Archbishop Runcie's call to Evangelicals to work out a proper Evangelical ecclesiology.

'I think we want to tell him that Evangelicals do have an ecclesiology,' said Birchall, 'and it's one which we wish the rest of the Church would recognise a bit more. We hold as Evangelicals to a high view of two basic biblical aspects of Church: on the one hand, the local congregation, those whom God has called to serve him in each place; on the other the universal body of Christ, the blessed company of all faithful people. We wish that our fellow Anglicans would recognise all faithful people as fully and equally members of the one body: Baptists and Brethren, Pentecostals and New Church people, all part of the one Church of Christ.

'As Evangelicals we don't have such a high view of any particular denomination including our own, much as we love it and much as we sometimes despair of it. So we were glad later on when the same Archbishop Runcie wrote: "All denominations are transitional." I don't think he was talking eschatological language – we all know there will be no Catholics in heaven, as David Watson said once in Dublin, and there will be no Protestants either! I understood the Archbishop to be saying that denominations are transitional in terms of our experience in this world: they can merge, they can even die.

'So surely the real ecclesiological question we face', Mark Birchall continued, 'is in fact a practical one. What intermediate structures do we need – intermediate between the local church and the universal Church? We see no such clear structures in the New Testament. What we do see is a very clear grasp of the inter-relatedness of all Christian people and Christian bodies.'

At High Leigh that spring, Anglican Evangelicals said they wanted to affirm the Church of England. 'We groan about it sometimes but there is much to thank God for,' Mark Birchall said. 'We suggest in that, that our theology and our practice of "episcopal leadership in synodical Government" needs to be reformed in the light of experience and for more effective mission.'

The Assembly urged the General Synod, and especially the diocesan bishops, to act in such a way that the Church of England's structure, belief and behaviour would be more unambiguously rooted in Holy Scripture. Recognising the dangers of fragmentation, the assembly urged Anglican Evangelicals to work for greater trust and better communication among themselves even when disagreeing, and to be actively committed to and involved in their own organisational structures as well as the structures of the Church of England.

The Archbishop of Canterbury's response

'If there's one thing that came through this morning,' Dr Carey told High Leigh as he responded 'off the cuff' to the track presentations, 'and it's very heartening, it's that of Evangelical diversity – not disunity, diversity. And long may this continue. People are talking to one another and listening to one another.'

Responding to the findings of the Church working group, Dr Carey said: 'I used to get so fed up when I heard Anglican theologians talking about "the one thing that was provisional was the Church of England" as if no other Church was provisional. I'm glad you made the point that we are all provisional in terms of the end time when there'll be one Church.

'The first thing that is needed from all the Churches is generosity of spirit. I think that's a secular word for salvation. Generosity is recognising that God may be at work in that fellowship as well as in our fellowship . . .

'If there's one thing that I thought was missing – it was the importance of history. The importance that as Evangelicals we must not jump from the first century to this century as if nothing's happened in between.'

On mission, Dr Carey spoke of the 'the hermeneutic of the local church living, celebrating, worshipping Christ' as a 'gospel dynamic that leads to conversion'.

'I'm so pleased', he said, 'that in this Decade of Evangelism we are recognising that evangelism is not merely the prerogative of gifted people who are evangelists, but belongs to the work of the whole people of God, and it's done corporately.'

He stressed the importance of making sure that churches are accessible to the widest variety of people. 'Church is not just for us but for the person who's terrified of church and of making that timid first step towards us.'

The Archbishop confessed that he was troubled by the word 'post-modernism'. 'What comes after postmodernism?' he asked. 'Post-postmodernism? . . . What essentially it's recognising is the collapse of truth and that everything is up for grabs. A marketplace of ideas, no overarching metaphysical or ontological understanding of truth itself. And so truth is what you make it. It leads to collapse of morality, collapse at every level. That's why of course as Christians we've got to emphasise the truth of Scripture.'

Dr Carey said he had been sad to hear stories at the conference of people who felt Anglicanism had failed to offer them something at a very important part of their lives, but he went on to make a vital point. 'The other side of this is the worry I have that we're now moving into a kind of marketplace. If I'm not satisfied with this church there then I'll search around and see if I find something that's going to meet me and my need. So we need to bear in mind the problem there . . .

'How can we provide a ministry for those who want prayer book worship only or who are content with it and those who want more than that? I've long been a believer in adult education in church life; but actually offering something for the entire family is so difficult to work out. Maybe the fact that our nation is drifting more and more into a secular nation offers us a very profound challenge to provide a seven-day-a-week ministry. I don't think therefore all is lost by the loss of Sunday, although I regret it enormously. But now at last we can actually do something that the early Church did – which is to provide worship and ministry on a Monday to Saturday.'

Sir Fred Catherwood's plea to Anglican Evangelicals

Sir Fred Catherwood delivered a powerful address to Anglican Evangelicals at High Leigh, 1995. A former Director General of the National Economic Development Office and Member of the European Parliament, Sir Fred is not himself an Anglican. Thirty years earlier his father-in-law, Dr Martyn Lloyd-Jones, had made a dramatic call to Evangelicals which had been snubbed. For his part Sir Fred was gushing in his praise, taking the line that the future of a country in moral and social crisis depended uniquely on Anglican Evangelicals.

'Our neighbours in our confused society are in desperate need,' Sir Fred said. 'They need our help and much hangs on you. Your Church has the duty of leadership that goes with its role in the nation. And in your Church, as I see it, only the Evangelicals have the resources. So there is a duty of leadership which falls on your Church and within your Church on you. And if you do not pick up that duty of leadership, then I don't see where that leadership is going to come from . . .

'You are not only therefore important to your own Church, as the largest Church in the country, you are very important to all the Evangelical churches in England in this unprecedented moral and social crisis in our country . . .

'You are a national Church with a duty to the entire nation and the entire parish. This is built into your constitution. There has seldom been such a need as there is today. The Church is surrounded by all the misery of a society that has totally lost its bearings. Churches should be – where you are – a haven of sanity and stability for stressed and broken people . . .

'Practical, sacrificial Christian love is a power to which people will respond. It is a sure rock in the swampy morass of our society to which people will cling and it is the only power that will change our country. That power comes from God in answer to our constant prayer and, as we see from our Lord's example, it comes from self-giving to others. It is the greatest power in the world and that is the power through God's strength which we wield.'

Carey on being a missionary Church

In his main address to the conference, Dr Carey told Anglican Evangelicals, 'We must engage seriously with the culture of which we are but part.' He welcomed the way the five tracks grappled with the shift from the Enlightenment way of thinking to so-called post-modernist ways of thinking, even though he remained troubled about the definition of postmodernism.

He advised his audience not to equate the decline in church attendance with a lack of interest in spiritual things. 'At times that has been a valid inference to make. But today there's a great deal of evidence to show that this is no longer the case. As much as anything, we seem in the churches to be suffering from a much wider reluctance of people to commit themselves to membership of groups and institutions of any kind. Political parties, trade unions have seen their membership decline since the war. People have not wanted to commit themselves to formal institutions and have opted for a more informal approach.'

'We must', said Dr Carey, 'embrace with joy our vocation to be a missionary Church.' People go to cathedrals and leave requests for prayer, or they light a candle, or they request baptism for their children, 'but we cannot claim to be a Christian nation whose first instinct is to honour and obey God'. We have the ministry of the Servant. We 'must re-examine our ceremonies, our traditions, our bureaucracy, our legalities, our administration, not in order to jettison them mindlessly but in order to be more effective in our mission and ministry. We must seek ways of being a Church which travels light, a Church which is unafraid to focus on its work of mission and evangelism. We have much to learn from the Celtic tradition. We mustn't neglect the two thousand years of history we have inherited.'

We are not, said the Archbishop, good at using the talents of lay people and recognising and affirming their ministry in the world as well as the Church. He was glad the Assembly was wrestling seriously with the theology of ordination. This was a long overdue debate, particularly in Evangelical circles. He welcomed the growth of family and 'seeker' services which were of vital importance for the mission of the Church.

'Structures', said Dr Carey, 'are very important but only in so far as they support the ministry and mission of the Church and a Church which preaches Christ – which has been the *raison d'être* from Pentecost onwards. This is central to Evangelical faith, but historically it has been at the heart of Anglicanism. It continues to be so.

'Let me deny the description of an Anglican as "someone who is free to believe anything he likes as long as he doesn't do so very firmly". We have to rebut that very fiercely. We are Reformed and Catholic, we are a biblical Church, our Articles enshrine truths of the gospel that no true Anglican would wish to see lost. No one knows what lies ahead for our Church in the year 2000 and beyond. But I long for it to be confident in its faith, bold in its witness, and responsive to all the concerns and questions which our confused world asks of us. To prepare our Church for that task Evangelical Anglicanism has much to contribute . . .

'The value of being a national Church should not be underestimated. At the local level also the clergy are often the only professionals still living in some parts of our cities . . . At the moment we are heard and reported in a way which we shouldn't be if we were simply a grouping of churches. Let me remind you of some of the prophetic utterances from within the Church of England in recent years: on the needs of the inner cities, on Sunday trading, on education, on third-world debt, overseas debt, the National Lottery, prisons, euthanasia, and many other moral and ethical issues – not only by bishops and clergy but also from distinctive and able lay people . . .

'One of my great desires for the Church is that we shall see a new generation of apologists raised who can argue for and communicate the gospel at every level of our national life.'

Carey on the call to be holy

'Central to Evangelical theology,' Dr Carey reminded the Assembly, 'but by no means limited to our tradition, is the appeal to all people to know Christ and to know his benefits. Conversion is a journey of transformation by which we are changed into the image of God's dear Son. The journey across the deserts of this world takes us towards that kingdom where we shall see the glory of the Lord. As St Paul reminded the Thessalonians, 'God did not call us to impurity, but to live a holy life' (1 Thess. 4:7). That calling is both personal and corporate. Holy living and holy dying – as that great Anglican Jeremy Taylor reminded us – is something to seek both by worship and action, both individually and together.

'In its corporate aspect, holiness is not distinct from mission but indivisibly one with it. Holiness is one of the traditional marks of the doctrine of the Church. But it's also a feature of the Church's evangelism. That holiness not only takes the form of the distinctive lifestyle which is a mark of the witness of faith but is an aspect of the holistic mission which we desire to see embraced by all humankind . . . Now such attractive witness has long been a mark of Evangelical lifestyle. I believe that one particular mark of that Evangelical contribution to the life of our Church has been to bear witness to the power of the gospel to transform the lives of individuals, of communities and nations . . .

'But no effective movement for God simply looks back. I remind you of my analogy: the journey which lies ahead. We of all people believe in the Holy Spirit who moves in our world as the Spirit of revelation. There are new things to learn. New adventures to be found. New discoveries to be made. New initiatives to take for the glory of God. The significance of Evangelicalism in the future will not be charted by how many Evangelical bishops we have; how many senior Evangelical clergy there are; nor simply by what percentage of ordinands are Evangelical. But more significantly, how effective are we as a Church, a sign and sacrament of the gospel in bringing its power and gladness to succeeding generations . . .

'These are exciting days to be living in. Historians I believe will see this decade and the next as very significant ones in reshaping the life of the Church of England to fulfil its missionary role. Evangelicals, as the evidence of the Assembly shows, can play a vital role in that reshaping. Furthermore, it's vital for the health of our Church and our nation that they should continue to do so. It's a voice that we cannot afford to be without. The desperate need remains for all people everywhere to hear the gospel and to know its life-changing power. That's at the very heart of my ministry, my spirituality, my future. Our call and responsibility together is to bring the gospel to this nation, to make the rough places plain, to play our part in enabling our Lord to enter into his inheritance – the inheritance he won through his victory on the cross.'

All Anglicans will wish to pray that Archbishop Carey is given wisdom as he handles the deep divisions over human sexuality which threaten the unity of their Communion in the months leading up to the 1998 Lambeth Conference (see Part Seven).

PART SIX

Church on fire in twentieth-century America

When you walk through the fire, you will not be burned;
the flames will not set you ablaze.
(Isaiah 43:2)

SIXTY YEARS WITHOUT EVANGELICAL EPISCOPALIANS

By the beginning of the twentieth century Evangelical Episcopalianism (in the sense in which Jarratt, McIlvaine or Eastburn had understood it) had virtually died out in America. After 1900 the American Church went Liberal in two directions: Liberal Catholic and Liberal Evangelical. The Liberal Catholics were in the majority but there were also large pockets of low-church Liberalism, for example in Virginia around VTS, with varying degrees of orthodoxy. Some were more modernist than others. No classical Evangelical party existed from 1900 until the 1960s.

Then, in the 1960s and 1970s, a new burst of Evangelical enthusiasm made its way into America's mainstream Protestant denominations including the Episcopal Church – to the surprise of many in that Church itself. In these decades Charismatic and Evangelical renewal organisations proliferated, and 'renewed' parishes multiplied. These developments occurred at a time when the Episcopal Church as a whole suffered one of the most dramatic membership declines in its history.

In spite of its having brought new people into the Church, not all Episcopalians have welcomed Evangelical enthusiasm. 'There is an attempt', wrote one Episcopal theologian worried about contemporary Anglican Evangelicalism, 'to bring to this country a brand of English Evangelicalism which has never really found much acceptance here before.'[1]

The major thrust of renewal in the Episcopal Church came through Charismatics, many of whom had been grounded in High-Churchmanship of some sort: people like Graham Pulkingham and Dennis Bennett. Bennett was an Episcopalian who had an experience in California in 1960 which he described as 'baptism in the Holy Spirit', accompanied by speaking in tongues. This marked the beginning of the Episcopal Charismatic movement and to some extent the mainstream Charismatic movement in the States. Bennett

347

was not actually a High-Churchman, but he was not a classical Evangelical either. He was a powerful leader with some Evangelical roots.

Classic Anglican Evangelicalism in America began with isolated individuals in the 1950s, 1960s and 1970s, most of whom either came from or were influenced by English Evangelicals. Peter Moore, the current Dean of the Trinity Episcopal School for Ministry (TESM) – the story of which I tell below – studied in England as did leaders such as Philip Hughes and John Guest. There were very few 'American-grown' Evangelicals at this time.

Dr John Rodgers, who served for some years as Dean of TESM, is an unusual example of someone whose primary influence was not the English Evangelical movement. He came more through neo-Orthodoxy and the theology of Barth, with an Evangelical input.

In the 1970s there were some 'bridging people' such as John Howe, the present Bishop of Central Florida, who was trained in Evangelicalism by John Guest. Howe was Curate at St Stephen's, Sewickley, when Guest was Rector there. He played a part in moulding together the two emphases, becoming a leader in Charismatic renewal while retaining much of his Evangelical grounding.

THE STORY OF TRINITY EPISCOPAL SCHOOL FOR MINISTRY

When I embarked on the task of telling the story of Anglican Evangelicalism, I had not expected to come across a dramatic tale of one man's infectious faith in the power of God to answer prayer. Such an episode seemed somehow rather 'un-Anglican'. Here, however, is just such a story. It begins in Australia where Alf Stanway was born on 9 September 1908. When he was a child, his family worshipped at a Methodist church, but when they moved to Melbourne they joined an Anglican one. Alf was converted at the age of nineteen in St Paul's, Fairfield, Melbourne. He read biographies of George Müller and Hudson Taylor and decided to act by faith himself. Some remarkable incidents of answers to prayer strengthened his faith in God.

Stanway experienced a call to Africa which led him to offer himself for service with the CMS. After a training in accountancy, he spent three years at Ridley Theological College in Melbourne and developed the habit of regular study and quiet times with God. He began work in Kenya in 1937 and the following year announced his engagement to Marjory, whom he eventually married.

Geoffrey Fisher (Archbishop of Canterbury from 1945 to 1961) invited Alf to become a bishop, on condition that he and Marjory came to England for three months to learn how ecclesiastical and civil authorities work. In England in 1950, they heard John Stott preach in St Peter's, Vere Street, the first of many meetings. The following year Alf was consecrated bishop of Central Tanganyika (now Tanzania), at that time a diocese which covered half the country.

After sixteen years of his Tanganyikan episcopate, the number of people in Stanway's diocese had quadrupled. He preached personal surrender to Jesus Christ, putting strong emphasis on giving responsibility to local Christians. African bishops were consecrated and new dioceses created. He advanced medical, educational and Christian literature work and began to develop a network of Bible schools.

The Stanways' circle of friends and contacts was never narrowly Evangelical and, during one stay in England, they visited the widow of William Temple, the famous wartime Archbishop. During the same English interlude, they heard John Stott lead Bible studies at Oak Hill Theological College and they were inspired on hearing Archbishop Michael Ramsey preach.

In 1970 Alf Stanway decided to accept the invitation of Dr Leon Morris and join his old college, Ridley. He became for a few years Deputy Principal of Ridley College.

In November 1974 Alf received a letter that came as a great surprise. It came from John Guest, on behalf of a group of Evangelical clergy in the American Episcopal Church and some concerned lay people.

As these Evangelicals saw it, during the twentieth century many seminaries and clergy had abandoned the authority of Scripture as the supreme guide for life and doctrine and were placing less emphasis on the core of the gospel. In 1963 a small American branch of the Evangelical Fellowship of the Anglican Church (EFAC) had been set up. Founded by Dr Philip Hughes and Peter Moore, the main purpose of the American branch of EFAC, also known as the Fellowship of Witness (FOW), was education in parallel with evangelism. The origins of EFAC go back to England in the late 1950s, since when the Fellowship had arranged conferences throughout the world and provided bursaries for advanced theological studies by young Evangelicals from Third World countries.

Stott's advice sought

John Guest had found the atmosphere in the Episcopal Church hostile to renewal and during the 1960s and 1970s many Episcopalians left for other denominations. Peter Moore had been forced to steer individual students towards England. Guest had a vision for a place where men and women could be trained in the USA in an Evangelical seminary. With colleagues, he had begun to search for a Dean/President to head up such a seminary. John Stott had suggested Alf Stanway. And so the letter arrived at Ridley, inviting Alf to accept the role of Dean/President of the new seminary, to be called Trinity Episcopal School for Ministry.

Stanway, now sixty-six, wrote to ask John Stott for advice – not knowing it was he who had suggested his name in the first place – and also to Australian Archbishop Marcus Loane. Stanway's letters to Stott and Loane frankly noted, 'I have no academic qualifications of any significance.'

Both Loane and Stott replied, encouraging him to accept the invitation. A board of trustees was being formed in the USA and they discussed with the Bishop of Pittsburgh, Bishop Robert Appleyard, the possibility of locating the new college in the Pittsburgh area of Pennsylvania. Stanway developed a sense that God was calling him to the States to do a job for which he felt the Ridley experience had fitted him. He and Marjory decided to accept the invitation to establish the new seminary.

John Guest was at that time Rector of St Stephen's, Sewickley, an influential Evangelical parish a few miles north-west of Pittsburgh along the Ohio River. John Yates was Associate Rector, as was the

Rev. (later Bishop) John Howe. It was in Sewickley that they found a home for Alf and Marjory. Alf set up an office and used his garage as a library. The Stanways were overwhelmed by the warmth of the welcome they received.

Stanway constantly stressed the need to keep money from being either the major anxiety or the limit to what the School could do: 'It's a very good thing, whenever you're praying for money, to get it quite clear in your mind that God is not short of money. He's got it all. Bankers think they have it. Rich men think they have it. In actual fact, "the silver is mine, saith the Lord of hosts". And he can have it all, all he wants, when he requires it. He can meet every need. So have faith that God will provide, because with him there is no shortage. And avoid all extravagance. The right use of money given is the best guarantee of a fresh supply. Money will always be available if we are in the will of God.'

The required qualification for a potential student was that he or she be a graduate. The degrees awarded by Trinity – once the college received its charter – would be Master's Degrees in Divinity, after the successful conclusion of the three-year course. Students would be required to take the General Ordination Examination (GOE). A library would need to be set up and approved, as well as an Endowment Fund of half a million dollars set aside in reserve.

Enquiries from hopeful students-to-be came in steadily from all over the States and they came to Stanway to be interviewed. At that stage no bishop was willing to send anyone to the proposed TESM, so that meant that any students would come without backing. They had to trust that if they gave their lives to Christ, he would open up the ministry for them.

On 15 April 1976 the Trustees announced that the 'new School for educating men and women for ministry in the Protestant Episcopal Church' had made its first appointments to the faculty. The Rev. Dr John Rodgers would be Senior Professor, and the Rev. Peter Davids would be Assistant Professor of Biblical Studies. Davids came from the *Bibelschule Wiedenest* in Germany. Rodgers had qualifications from the US Naval Academy, VTS and the University of Basle. Stanway had persuaded him to give up his position as Professor of Systematic Theology, Chaplain and Associate Dean for Student Affairs at VTS to teach at TESM.

Stanway announced that a panel of visiting professor-lecturers would be employed, including John Stott, Jim Packer and Michael Green from St Aldate's, Oxford.

As for prospective students, Bishop Stanway asked them to write up an account of their personal relationship with Christ. He stressed to them that the School would be rigorous academically in order to meet the Episcopal Church's requirements. He interviewed married men along with their wives, believing it crucial that both partners agreed about the step they were taking.

Half of the first class of students at Trinity were Charismatic. In the subsequent history of Trinity, there has always been interaction between the Evangelical and Charismatic strands. Trinity has tended to speak of itself more as serving the renewal movement than serving the Evangelical movement, though its statement of faith was worked out with the assistance of Jim Packer and John Stott.

The Board decided to open the School in rooms at the Robert Morris College in Coraopolis at the beginning of the 1976 academic year. They set a date for the opening: Saturday 25 September 1976.

The school opens

When the day came, it dawned warm and sunny and coincided exactly with the first anniversary of Stanway's arrival in the States. Two hundred and fifty people travelled from all over the USA for the formal opening in the Hale Hall on the Campus of the Robert Morris College. The ceremony was presided over by the Chairman of the Board of Trustees, Peter Moore.

'As Episcopalians', Peter Moore said in his opening address, 'we need the vitality and vision of evangelism. When Anglicans have that they are often at their very best. Worship comes alive; churches grow; people give; the Bible becomes a living book with great personal authority for the believer; people begin to love each other in the Spirit and long to share their faith with others ... As Evangelicals we need the Episcopal Church. Without it we feel rootless, cut off from centuries of devotion, theology and practical wisdom. We need the Church's corporate concern for the needy and downtrodden. We need the Church's seriousness over liturgical worship;

the Church's witness to the sacraments as a means of grace, the Episcopate as a God-given blessing for the guidance and oversight of his Church.

'When Evangelicals have embodied these qualities they have often been at their best – saved from a narrow parochialism, sectarianism and a myopic concern for their own special emphasis to the neglect of the broader and deeper dimensions of Christian experience.'

John Rodgers gave the principal academic address, entitled 'Education for Ministry in the Anglican Evangelical Perspective'.

'TESM', he said, 'stands deeply, thankfully, and loyally in the Anglican tradition. Because Anglican Evangelicals do not make Church tradition normative and do not place it on the level of Holy Scripture, it is sometimes thought that we are lacking in appreciation for tradition. This is not so . . . There is first the blessing and teaching and practice of the early Church fathers . . . Then there is God's gift to the Church through the great sixteenth century reformers . . . Luther, Calvin, Bullinger, Cranmer, Latimer, Ridley, and later the judicious Hooker . . . They are one of God's richest gifts to his church . . . we have not excelled the Reformers on a single point and in much we have fallen sadly behind them . . .

'There is the rich understanding of the work of the Holy Spirit and the inner devotional life which arises from the work of the Puritans and the Evangelical revivals of the eighteenth and subsequent centuries, personal conversion to Christ, commitment to walk in holiness, mutual conversation to build one another up in Christ, a desire to be useful in personal evangelism . . . this too is part of the Anglican Evangelical tradition in which this school stands.

'Lastly there is the tradition of love of truth, the utter conviction that God's word in Christ is compatible with his truth wherever it may be found, and that all truth needs to be put to Christian use . . . no nervous hiding, no obscurantism, but a relaxed confidence that Christ alone is the proper interpreter of any discoveries of any age rightly and humbly held . . . We want to get students to appreciate the richness of this tradition. It is a tradition which is conserving, radical and liberating.'

Making Christ's name ring across the USA

In the closing address of the day, Alf Stanway described the sort of men and women they wanted to see at Trinity:

- Those who were unashamed of the Gospel of Christ.
- Men and women of prayer.
- Liberated persons: Jesus said, 'You shall know the truth and the truth shall set you free.' This meant being set free from the deadness of self-interest; from the love of money and possessions; from the tyranny of the love of the world.
- Seekers after holiness: 'When a Christian and minister gives up the battle for holiness', Stanway said, 'he is already a backslider at heart.'
- Those who have compassion for the poor and needy: The most needy are those without the gospel of Christ. It is a mark of the Christian to have compassion.
- Those who are alive with the life of the Spirit of God: with the '*imprimatur* of the Spirit of God himself'. 'What's the good', he asked, 'in being able to speak well, to be sound in doctrine, and know the way you ought to live if the whole of your life is not made alive with the Spirit of God?'
- Those gripped with a deep sense of gratitude for the privilege of being called to be Christ's servant: 'My dream', Stanway concluded, 'is that from the first batch of students, there will come such a development of God's Spirit on some of them that they will be those who will go out and make Christ's name known and ring across the United States of America.'

What was the School's attitude to the study of the Scriptures? John Rodgers summed it up in the early days by saying that critical scholarship was legitimate but had increasingly married itself to false assumptions and presuppositions. The result was that the Church was left with a Bible which had been reduced to the 'interesting speculations and curious thoughts of men and women of an earlier age'.

Challenging his students to be disciplined in keeping a daily quiet time of prayer and Bible study, Alf Stanway told them once that he had never missed his daily quiet time in forty years. In his class on prayer he used to say, 'The prayer you should pray most in your life is this: "Teach us to pray." If you think you've learned, then you'll never be a person of prayer. There's always more to learn, more to discover about prayer.'

The move to Ambridge

In time, an empty Presbyterian church and a supermarket came on the market up the Ohio River at Ambridge; and a gift was received which would enable the Board to buy it and make alterations. They decided to leave the rooms at the Robert Morris College and move to the new, self-contained site. Ambridge, Pennsylvania, was once the home of the American Bridge Company (hence the name) and had produced steel bridges for erection all over the United States. The company had gone into liquidation and the town had declined since the post-Second-World-War boom in the steel industry.

Today Ambridge has begun to experience some economic revival as light industries have moved in and since the nearby Pittsburgh international airport has been completed. When students first arrived at TESM in Ambridge, however, it was almost a symbol that they had given up the affluent American dream. The town has people from a wide variety of ethnic backgrounds – the children and grandchildren of immigrants who had settled there specifically to work in the steel mills. This provides a richness and diversity to the town, but the setting bears no resemblance to the 'Anglican ethos' of gentle scholarship and cloistered calm. Ambridge has featured in the *Guinness Book of Records* as having more bars and churches *per capita* than anywhere else in America.

'Nobody comes here', John Rodgers said at one stage, 'because of the beauty of the buildings or the campus!'

During 1976 Alf Stanway began to show the early symptoms of Parkinson's disease. He decided that the Board should set about the task of finding a successor for him. Eventually they chose John Rodgers as Dean/President to succeed Stanway. He took over on 1 November 1978. Stanway kept well enough to preach at a farewell service in Pittsburgh Cathedral.

Reflecting on their years on the banks of the Ohio River, Marjory Stanway recalled, 'We found American Christians to be very caring people, openly showing their feelings and most helpful in all kinds of situations. There is a softness in their natures which we Australians seem to lack. We seem to have a "toughness" which prevents us from showing the degree of love and care shown by our American counterparts.'[2]

TESM accredited

Support among the bishops gradually increased and they began to visit the school. Some were impressed with the sense of 'calling' at Trinity; others continued to be hostile and refused to send any postulants. However, when Presiding Bishop Allin spoke at Trinity's graduation in 1983, he praised the school for its '"dedication and perseverance which comes from faithfulness" and the humility and faith with which Trinity has nourished and encouraged the Church'.

In 1985 Trinity became the eleventh and newest accredited seminary in the Episcopal Church. In the same year the Community of Celebration and its music team the Fisherfolk, led by the Rev. Graham Pulkingham, returned to the United States after a decade in Scotland.

The Community of Celebration leaders decided that the small town of Aliquippa, across the Ohio River from Ambridge, would be an ideal location for them. Both Trinity and the Community would benefit from being near neighbours. So the Community came to settle in Aliquippa. With a base in the United States, the Fisherfolk could travel more easily to American parishes for concerts. Composer Mimi Farra eventually became Trinity's Music Director and Betty Pulkingham began to teach at the school. These two internationally known figures helped Trinity students become more aware of the role of music in liturgy and use their musical resources for the renewal movement.

In 1988 the newly installed Presiding Bishop Edmund Browning visited Trinity. 'I was very grateful to have been asked to come,' he said. 'You get all sorts of impressions about places from their reputation. I try to go with an open spirit about everything, and I was very moved by the work that Dean Rodgers has done, and by the kind of spirit, not only in the Board, but in the student body.

'I think the things the school is working with speak well about perseverance and dedication, and a real pursuit of things that are right for the Church.'

Alf Stanway died on 27 June 1989. They sang Newman's 'Praise to the holiest in the height' at a thanksgiving service at St Paul's Cathedral, Melbourne.

William Frey

In 1989 the trustees elected William Frey, then Bishop of Colorado, as Trinity's third Dean and President. The memory of Frey which I carry with me from a brief conversation during my visit to TESM is of his deep, resonant voice. He put this to good use in the 1940s during an early career as a disc jockey and later as a missionary preacher. After his call to the Episcopal priesthood, and serving parishes in America and Costa Rica, he became the youngest member of the House of Bishops when he was made Bishop of Guatemala in 1967, aged thirty-seven. He was expelled by the military government four years later for urging an end to the activities of paramilitary death squads and guerrilla forces.

Following a charismatic experience, he was elected Bishop of Colorado in 1972 and soon became a leader of the renewal movement in the Episcopal Church. I saw the impressive array of new buildings which were put up on the Trinity campus during the Frey years. As well as being an administrator, Frey was also a gifted teacher. 'Part of what I do in teaching', he says, 'is inductive, in trying to discover what God has already taught my students. My teaching is also experiential, in the sense that I want students to experience in their own lives the reality and power of the materials taught. I also want to teach people to have what Phillips Brooks called "a generous mind", one that grasps each new truth with a view to communicating it to other people.'

Frey had no doubt what sort of people he wanted Trinity to produce. 'Our graduates should be Evangelical, Catholic and Charismatic,' he said. 'They should be Evangelical in the sense of knowing the content of the *evangel* and the saving power of Jesus Christ, and should have a heart on fire to proclaim it. They should be Catholic, in the sense of seeking the fullness of God's revelation throughout history and the incarnational and sacramental ways which undergird that revelation. And they should be Charismatic, in the sense of knowing the power of God's Spirit and be enabled by the Spirit for mission.'

Peter Moore

Frey's successor as Dean, Peter Moore, has been associated with TESM from the beginning. He grew up in New York City, graduated from Yale University, has an Oxford MA and degrees from the Episcopal Theological School and Fuller. He was the first chairman of the TESM Board. Prior to becoming the fourth Dean, he spent ten years as Rector of Little Trinity Church in Toronto.

'I came to Trinity', Moore says, 'to be part of an Episcopal community dedicated to "live orthodoxy". I mean by that, one that adores God with minds as well as hearts, and hearts as well as minds. This requires the kind of discipline possible only in a worshipping community where scholarship is consciously cultivated in submission to the Word of God, and where people are lovingly held accountable to one another.

'My vision for Trinity is that we not only participate in the renewal that God is pouring out upon the Church, but help put a solid theological foundation underneath it. I want Trinity to continue to be a handmaid of the Holy Spirit, *commending* the Word of God in our life and ministry and *showing* the gifts of the Spirit in our life together . . .

'It's the combination of heart and head that I'm really stressing. The separation of heart from mind, of devotion from doctrine, is a very unhealthy thing for the Church. We need to combine head and heart if we want to reach others for the gospel.

'The first fruit of this combination is that we are able to confess Christ with our *whole* being and not with the tentativeness that has characterised so much of mainstream church life. So the combination of head and heart leads to holiness of life, it leads to

compassion, consistency, a biblical social and personal ethic. It also leads to the joy of serving him whose service is perfect freedom.'
Peter Moore has said this about the heritage of TESM:

Alf Stanway brought the best tradition of Anglican Evangelicalism to America. But our own Evangelical heritage in the Episcopal Church had been dormant for many years, we hardly knew what it would look like when it was Americanised. Our debt to leading Evangelicals like Alf Stanway and John Stott, and J. I. Packer, and Michael Green, and Festo Kivengere, and a host of others, was immense. But over the last decade, a genuinely American article has been reborn: radically Biblical in theological emphasis, gently charismatic in worship, strongly mission-and-evangelism-oriented, integrating clergy and laity in joint ministry, and fuelled by a desire to expound Scripture and proclaim the gospel.[3]

By the mid-1990s Trinity had grown to approximately a hundred and forty students and a faculty of ten teaching staff. Adjunct professors include experienced missionaries, youth ministers, a historian of Christian art and the renewal music composer, Mimi Farra.

In the autumn of 1995, over two hundred ordained Trinity graduates served parishes in seventy-three American dioceses and over twenty overseas dioceses, and over two hundred and fourteen lay graduates served in full-time Christian ministries or were working to spread the gospel in secular jobs. Two faculty members and one graduate had been elected bishops.

Stephen Noll

Stephen Noll is Trinity's Dean for Academic Affairs and Professor of Biblical Studies. After spending five years in parish ministry, he went to England to do a PhD on the Dead Sea Scrolls under F. F. Bruce at the University of Manchester. He has been teaching at Trinity since 1979.

Stephen told me that he was a convert to Christianity and baptised in the Episcopal Church as an adult. Some of his early Christian influences were neo-Orthodoxy – Barth, Bonhoeffer – and he did not look to the English Evangelical scene particularly.

Noll has become a leading spokesman in the American Episcopal Church (ECUSA) for the authority of Scripture. In the autumn of 1992 the American House of Bishops met to reflect on the role of Scripture in the life of the Episcopal Church. Noll was invited to contribute one of the papers which served as a starting point for the bishops' reflections. Taken together, the papers make up a good snapshot of the diverse views of the Bible's authority in America in the 1990s.

Noll's paper was the only Conservative contribution to the collection. In it he argues that understanding Scripture in its 'literal sense' is of fundamental importance for Christian life and teaching. He defines literal sense as 'that meaning appropriate to the nature of the Bible as the Word of God in the words of men'. Noll's paper allows for metaphorical meaning, but does not allow the link between verbal signs and what they signify to be dissolved. Though both experience and reason are involved in the process of under-standing and interpreting Scripture, neither may usurp the authority that the literal sense of the text has exercised, in Noll's view, throughout the Anglican tradition. The paper grants that there is diversity within the literal sense of Scripture, but opposes the tendency towards dissecting and fragmenting the Bible. Instead, Noll advocates a way of reading that honours Scripture's canonical wholeness.

Three dimensions of the literal sense are, first, the poetic or *literary* dimension; second, the *truth* dimension including pro-positional expressions of truth such as exhortation and command; and third, there is the *eschatological* dimension. 'What happened?' must never be separated from 'Where is all this going?' The consequence of interpreting Scripture according to the literal sense, as defined, is that the Christian community submits to the authority of the Word of God in human words and is transformed by that Word. Scripture should be read meditatively.

Noll challenges the Liberal view of homosexuality. Throughout its history, he argues, the Christian Church held that homosexuality was a sign of a disordered soul and society and that homosexual practice was sinful. The Church based this moral stance on specific passages of Scripture which we will examine in Part Seven and which were based on the more general creation principle that God intended sexual love for male and female partners in the context of marriage and children.

Certainly God's love redeems a fallen moral order, but biblical interpreters have never conceived an *agapē* principle that contradicted the will of the Creator or the specific teaching of Jesus. Jesus said, 'If you love me, keep my commandments.' Any love which violates God's express laws and purposes is a false love.

Noll believes that the Liberal position is vintage situation ethics. Moreover, he argues that the Liberal approach to Scripture raises a dilemma for ordinary Christians. They read the Bible and think they know what it says: it seems to condemn homosexual behaviour in very strong language. But along comes 'an expert' who tells them they are hermeneutically naïve – in other words they do not have the latest techniques of biblical interpretation. With the use of these modern techniques, the Bible is made to allow practices that believers always thought it forbade.[4]

Noll is committed to the primacy of Scripture and sees tradition as a guide: the Church's wisdom leading the interpretation of Scripture but not having an absolute authority. He is committed to the right use of reason and argues that the Hooker branch of Anglicanism has something to offer to the wider Evangelical movement – a confidence that the God who inspired the Scriptures is the same God who created the world and built his order.

What American Evangelicals can teach the English

Given that Liberalism in the American Church has tended to polarise into a very virulent form of revisionism, sometimes even involving elements of paganism and witchcraft, Noll believes that Evangelicals in the States may be able to offer a warning to some English Evangelicals. As the majority party in the Church of England and with the access to the universities which they have (American Evangelicals are isolated from the universities), English Evangelicals may be too enamoured with the lure of acceptability within the intellectual establishment. Noll wants to see Evangelical scholars fully engage with the highest level of learning, but at the same time he sees that this can be a seduction. To that extent he has some sympathy with Reform. The American experience serves as a warning that Liberalism can degenerate into something which has little to do with Christianity.

People who accept the homosexual agenda in the USA often also deny the essence of the Trinity, the deity of Christ, the authority of Scripture, any doctrine of eschatology, any idea of transcendence or revelation. They have reinterpreted Christianity. According to Noll, the battle of homosexuality is just the tip of an iceberg of a war which is going on in the States. Evangelicals are in a position to see this clearly. In the American Episcopal Church there is a weakness in the middle. Middle-of-the-road clergy and congregations tend to accept many of the presuppositions of the Liberal and radical left.

Noll believes it is quite possible that at some point after 1997 the Episcopal Church will approve trial rites for 'gay marriages'. They will refer to them as 'same-sex blessings'. 'Twenty years ago,' Noll told me (in 1996), 'if someone had said it was possible that a majority at the General Convention would approve homosexual practice, they would have been thought absurd. Now it's quite possible that the General Convention will vote in the gay agenda. Of the American theological colleges, Trinity and perhaps Nashotah House, the high church seminary, are the only colleges with overt policies which say they will not accept practising homosexuals. VTS has recently made its policy more Liberal.'

Evangelical hopes for Lambeth

'We are fighting an unscrupulous opposition,' Stephen Noll told me. 'One of my hopes would be that we can put an Evangelical testimony before the Lambeth Conference. That will be a test as to whether the Anglican Communion as a whole is willing to draw a line anywhere – or whether "Anglican" is simply a label that anyone can apply to themselves regardless of what they believe or are. This would be a test of Anglican unity and identity. I would expect stronger support outside of England.'

ECUSA TODAY

The former Dean of TESM, John Rodgers, recalls attending the first conference of the American branch of EFAC-USA in Leesburg, Virginia, in the 1960s at which John Stott spoke. As an ex-VTS man himself, Rodgers looks back to the seminary in those days as the most orthodox and Evangelical Anglican theological college in the States, yet as 'uncertain, divided and too polite'.

Thirty years ago, Evangelicals in the Episcopal Church were defensive and survival-minded, immature, scattered, barely beginning to go public, and with no strategy to make an impact on ECUSA.

Thirty years later, TESM has come on the scene. However, most bishops do not allow evangelically-oriented students to attend the School and Rodgers is afraid that even godly bishops are 'sending students to ungodly places'.

No Episcopal diocese in the USA is without three or more lively orthodox congregations of various types. In some dioceses they predominate. There is an increasingly aware group of 'biblically informed, orthodox, Evangelical and often Charismatic folk in the Church'.

Nonetheless, Evangelicals in ECUSA are, says Rodgers, 'alarmed and frustrated. Some are leaving. Many are waiting "on edge and on the edge".' As he sees it, Evangelicals are energetic but rather uncoordinated, even isolated. They are not always patient with one another and hence, as in the United Kingdom, there is the constant danger of fragmentation. Funds are often tight. Evangelical education in the seminaries is largely restricted to TESM, 'though some Professors at Yale and VTS and Nashotah House [Catholic] are solid'. VTS, though, is in danger of further departing from orthodoxy.

Evangelicals are seen by 'corporatists' and 'revisionists' within ECUSA as being defensive and reactive, with no positive plan or strategy. Evangelicals feel, and probably are, relatively powerless in the wider structures of the Episcopal Church, in many dioceses, in General Convention, and in the committees and staff of ECUSA generally. In this, the American situation is very different from the

English one. However, Evangelicals are gaining some ground at the congregational level, slowly but genuinely, though this progress is weakened when congregations leave ECUSA for the Charismatic Episcopal Church, the Reformed Episcopal Church or the Antiochian Orthodox Church.

From Rodgers' perspective, there are four types of leaders in the Episcopal Church today. First *revisionists*, i.e. old Liberals or Broad-Churchmen who have gone radical as a result of the drift of American culture; second *orthodox*, including Evangelical, Anglo-Catholic, Charismatic and combinations of all three ('combos'); third *corporatist*, i.e. those who place the peace and institutional unity of the Church above all else, especially over the truth of Scripture and tradition; and fourth *slumbering traditional*, i.e. those who do not want to change anything, do not want their peace disturbed, and who are usually not engaged in mission at all.

Liberals and revisionists are in charge of most dioceses, seminaries, General Convention, the House of Bishops, National Church committees and staff. 'We tend', says Rodgers, 'to pay for their ministries and get marginalised and suppressed for the effort. I see no way that this can be reversed in the near future. Orthodox (Evangelicals, Anglo-Catholics, Charismatics and combos) are tolerated because the canons don't yet exclude us, and for our money. We are growing and we tithe.'

John Rodgers believes that since the revisionists take their cue from the culture, things are going to get worse. 'This is true unless the Lord bestows a major revival.' He does not think the Anglican Communion will rescue orthodox Episcopalians, since the same problems are appearing throughout. 'At present Anglicanism doesn't have any structures designed to hold national churches accountable.'

A strategy for the future

The first thing Evangelicals need to do, says Rodgers, is to pray for revival. The second is 'to teach everyone and without equivocation that the Christian faith is radically related to the Word of God and that God's Word matters'. Christian love does not consist of doctrinal permissiveness.

American Anglican Congress

Rodgers refers to the work of the American Anglican Congress (AAC). The AAC was launched in 1996 when the Bishop of Pittsburgh, Alden Hathaway, wrote on behalf of a group of twenty bishops, priests and lay people to every rector and senior warden in the Episcopal Church. The purpose of the letter was to establish a network of Conservative Episcopalians. Many of the signatories, who met in Briarwood, Texas, in December 1995, would identify themselves as Evangelicals: in addition to Hathaway were Fitz Allison, formerly Bishop of South Carolina, Peter Moore, Rodgers himself and David Scott, a 'Liberal Evangelical' from VTS.

This emerging network of orthodox members of the Episcopal Church is known as 'The Briarwood Consultation' after the location of the group's first meeting. They plan to hold their first national convention in 1998 as 'the outward and visible sign of the merging church, the true and authentic Anglican presence in 21st century America'. Parishes aligning themselves with the AAC (sometimes known as the Briarwood Alliance) are encouraged to display the AAC logo on their letterhead and signs.

Rodgers sees the AAC as a place of orthodox and moral integrity in the midst of 'an increasingly apostate and immoral institution'; as a place of safety and negotiating power in a majority-driven institution; a place of mutual encouragement in mission, growth and discipleship.

Raising an issue which has been controversial in the Church of England, John Rodgers argues that Evangelical Episcopalians should put the parish at the centre in their hearts and minds. 'It is there', he says, 'that the people congregate around Word and Table, and ensure that the parish is balanced, deep and growing.'

Roger Boltz, administrative director of AAC, stresses that the AAC is more concerned with obeying Christ's Great Commission to preach the gospel than with seizing political power. 'We have seen that there is nothing wrong with the Episcopal Church that a million new believers in Jesus Christ cannot fix,' Boltz says. He believes that the AAC needs 'to stop arguing with those who don't believe the gospel and begin to gather together with those who do'.

A Place to Stand

The AAC adopted 'A Place to Stand' on 7 August 1996 and addressed it to individuals, congregations and specialised ministries. It calls on addressees to 'join together in common confession of the Gospel and in a radical commitment to support one another in accordance with classical Anglican orthodoxy'.

The document says that the AAC affirms the faith of the Church as it is set forth in the Nicene and Apostles' Creeds and in the 'classical Prayer Book tradition'. It expresses support for 'the principles of the Chicago-Lambeth Quadrilateral as an expression of the normative authority of Holy Scripture and as a basis for our present unity with brothers and sisters in the Anglican Communion and for the future reunion of all the divided branches of Christ's one holy, Catholic and apostolic church'.

On the *uniqueness of Christ*, the document says that 'while religions and philosophies of the world are not without elements of truth, Jesus Christ alone is the full revelation of God' and that it is only through the name of Christ that we may be saved (Acts 4:12).

On *sanctity of life*, it says that 'all human life is a sacred gift from God and is to be protected and defended from conception to natural death'. Therefore the AAC promises to 'uphold the sanctity of life and bring the grace and compassion of Christ to those who face the realities of previous abortion, unwanted pregnancy, and end-of-life illness'.

On *human sexuality and marriage*, the authors of the document promise to 'extend the welcome of the Church to every person, regardless of race, sex, social or economic status, sexual orientation, or past behaviour' and also to 'oppose prejudice in ourselves and others'. However, they 'renounce any false notion of inclusivity that denies that all are sinners who need to repent'.

The document recalls that God instituted marriage to be a lifelong union of husband and wife, 'intended for their mutual joy, help, and comfort, and, when it is God's will, for the procreation and nurture of children'. Divorce is seen as 'always contrary to God's original intention, though in a fallen world it is sometimes a tragic necessity'. The roles of father and mother are 'God-given and profoundly important since they are the chief providers of moral instruction and godly living'. The single life, either by call or by circumstance, is honoured by God. 'It is therefore important for unmarried persons to embrace and be embraced by the Christian family.'

Sexuality is 'inherent in God's creation of every human person in his image as male and female'. All Christians are 'called to chastity: husbands and wives by exclusive sexual fidelity to one another and single persons by abstinence from sexual intercourse. God intends and enables all people to live within these boundaries, with the help and in the fellowship of the Church.'

On the question of *support for the Episcopal Church*, the framers of the document say:

> We desire to be supportive of congregations, dioceses, provinces, and the national structures of the Episcopal Church and the worldwide Anglican Communion. However, when there arise within the Church at any level tendencies, pronouncements, and practices contrary to biblical, classical Anglican doctrinal and moral standards, we must not and will not support them. Councils can err and have erred, and the Church has no authority to ordain anything contrary to God's Word written (Articles of Religion XIX, XX). When teachings and practices contrary to Scripture and to this orthodox Anglican perspective are permitted within the Church *or even authorised by the General Convention* in obedience to God we will disassociate ourselves from those specific teachings and practices and will resist them in every way possible.

The document ends by inviting 'all members of the Episcopal Church who concur in this classical Anglican perspective, to stand with us for mutual enlightenment, encouragement, mission, and ministry, and, where necessary, for protection of the right to live and minister in obedience to Scripture, Anglican tradition, and conscience'.

WHITE HORSE TAVERN TODAY

Some Evangelical Episcopalians are members of an Internet mailing list known as 'White Horse Tavern'. The 'Innkeeper' is Stephen Noll from TESM and it is his job to try to ensure that the vigorous discussion is carried on within the bounds of reasonable courtesy and decorum. He describes the Tavern as a 'convivial cyber meeting place of biblically-minded Episcopalians/Anglicans' and recalls that the original White Horse Tavern in Cambridge in the 1520s was a place for vigorous debate about the gospel, theology, politics and Church affairs. The primary focus of the Internet mailing list of the late 1990s is the state of the Episcopal Church, the Anglican tradition and Communion, and the wider Church and society. Members of the list bring Catholic, Evangelical and Charismatic outlooks to bear on the reform and renewal of the Church.

White Horse Taverners today are Anglican Christians who share a common confession of faith: acceptance of the primary authority of Scripture, the historic doctrines of the Creeds and Thirty-nine Articles, and 'A Place to Stand'.

White Horse Tavern discussions

Many Taverners believe that the dividing line between orthodoxy and revisionist Liberalism has been changed in favour of Liberalism continually over the last fifty years. Some of the key changes are seen as beginning in 1946 when the General Convention in Philadelphia allowed divorced people to remarry in church and divorced clergy to be ordained. By 1996 one-third of the American clergy were divorced and remarried. This dilution of Christian marriage has, some think, opened the door to the claim by homosexuals to have their partnerships blessed and to talk of 'homosexual marriages'.

One view held by Taverners is that 'since the push for women's ordination was done in response to a secularist, cultural mandate the same secularist wind has continued to blow into the Church'. However, not all Taverners take this view and the AAC has agreed not to take a line on the ordination of women. Views both for and against are held by White Horse Taverners and at TESM.

Another example of 'dilution' discussed by Taverners dates back to 1979 with the bringing in of a new-style prayer book rather than (as originally intended) a modest revision of the *Book of Common Prayer* of 1928. Some Taverners argue that the new prayer book contains translations of psalms and canticles which the biblically faithful cannot use because they are politically correct and do not honour Christ. It is alleged that it also contains doubtful renderings of the Creeds and the creation of new formulae for the Holy Trinity and for Jesus Christ.

One Taverner believes that 'ECUSA is profoundly sick and many bishops are responsible for that sickness and until they repent they are enemies of Jesus! Is not sharing with them in what they call Eucharist a denying of Christ?'

Taverners often refer to the Episcopal Church as 'apostate'. Some believe that they belong to a denomination which is actively opposed to the gospel. One woman contributor to the discussions who worked for an Evangelical bishop told the forum that she had 'tried running once'. She had become a Roman Catholic for over twenty years, but had discovered that Rome had its problems and divisions too. So she had returned to the Episcopal Church. She urged: 'Let's not get so tied up in battles over approach and ecclesiology that we become isolated from each other and lose the war to win souls for Christ, the head of the Church and the author of our salvation!'

MARK NOLL

For more than half of the twentieth century, Inter-Varsity Press has been one of the leading UK Evangelical book publishers. It was therefore something of a surprise when, in 1994, IVP published (jointly with Eerdmans of Michigan) a book which began, 'The scandal of the Evangelical mind is that there is not much of an Evangelical mind.' Equally surprising is that the book's author, Mark Noll, is the McManis Professor of Christian Thought at a bastion of

American Evangelicalism, Wheaton College. His book, *The Scandal of the Evangelical Mind*, argues that the Evangelical Protestant mind has never relished complexity; it tends to oversimplify issues and substitute inspiration and zeal for critical analysis and serious reflection.

Noll directs his fire on a broad front. While most of his criticism is directed at the American scene, some of his general criticisms of Evangelicalism have relevance to the UK. During the twentieth century, he says, the intellectual component in the Evangelical press has shrivelled nearly to vanishing point. He alleges that *Christianity Today*, for example, which once aspired to intellectual leadership, has been transformed into 'a journal of news and middle-brow religious commentary in order simply to stay in business'.

He speaks of 'diffused educational energies' in America, with influential Evangelical figures such as Bill Bright, Oral Roberts, Jerry Falwell and Pat Robertson all deciding that no previously existing educational enterprise is capable of meeting the demands of the hour. 'Despite the absence of formal educational credentials, each man presumes to establish a Christian university. Small wonder that Evangelical thinking so often appears naive, inept or tendentious.' Nothing exists for Evangelicals in the United States like the universities of Britain and Europe, where the most serious work on the Bible and theology is carried on next to serious work in other academic disciplines. The US system does not enjoy the benefit gained in British universities of cross-fertilisation between work in the departments of theology and that in arts and science. 'Attempts to think – both profoundly and as Christians – about history, nature, the arts, and society have been frustrated by the very success of an institutional arrangement that maintains several mutually distinct forms of academic endeavour.' Noll speaks of 'the generations-long failure of the Evangelical community to nurture the life of the mind'.

He refers to Jonathan Edwards as 'the greatest Evangelical mind in American history and one of the truly seminal thinkers in Christian history of the last few centuries'. But he asserts that Edwards has had no intellectual successors. He says that 'fundamentalism, dispensational premillennialism, the Higher Life movement, and Pentecostalism were all Evangelical strategies of survival in response

370

to the religious crises of the late nineteenth century. In different ways each preserved something essential of the Christian faith. But together they were a disaster for the life of the mind.'[5]

Whitefield's continuing influence

Mark Noll is not an Anglican, but he argues that it was an English Anglican Evangelical who was the defining figure in the history of American Evangelicalism: George Whitefield.

> Whitefield's style – popular preaching aimed at emotional response – has continued to shape American Evangelicalism long after Whitefield's specific theology (he was a Calvinist), his denominational origins (he was an Anglican), and his rank (he was a clergyman) are long since forgotten . . . Almost every one of Whitefield's sermons is marked by a fundamentally democratic determination to simplify the essentials of religion in a way that gives them the widest possible mass appeal.
>
> And as it was in the days of Whitefield, so it has been in the two centuries since. The most visible Evangelicals, with the broadest popular influence, have been public speakers whose influence rested on their ability to communicate a simple message to a broad audience.[6]

It seems rather hard to blame the Oxford-educated George Whitefield for the excesses of Jimmy Swaggart and Jerry Falwell. Nevertheless, the weaknesses of an Evangelicalism born in revivalism cited by Noll are very similar to those cited by James Barr (see Part Five, pages 308–13), although Noll was not influenced by Barr's work. Noll maintains:

> The problem of revivalism for the life of the mind, however, lay precisely in its antitraditionalism. Revivals called people to Christ as a way of escaping tradition, including traditional learning. They called upon individuals to take the step of faith for themselves. In so doing they often left the impression that individual believers could accept nothing from others. Everything of value

in the Christian life had to come from the individual's own choice – not just personal faith but every scrap of wisdom, understanding and conviction about the faith.[7]

Noll argues that with its scorn for tradition, its concentration on individual competence, its suspicion of formal education, American revivalism did much to hamstring the life of the mind.

Mark Noll believes that Evangelicals who come into the Episcopal Church are usually veterans of church squabbles which they never want to see again. They do not want to abandon the sense of Christ as Saviour and King, but they are usually disillusioned with individualistic forms of Evangelicalism which are often dominated by powerful personalities. The discovery of the Thirty-nine Articles, of written prayers, of a liturgy which is still, even in its revisions, basically biblical, are to them like oases in the desert. But in time they discover that the American Episcopal Church is the most theologically Liberal of any branch of the worldwide Anglican Communion.

Evangelicals on the Canterbury Trail

A colleague of Noll's, Robert Webber, is the son of a Baptist minister, a graduate of Bob Jones University and Concordia Seminary, and now Professor of Theology at Wheaton College. In November 1972 he forsook his orders as an ordained minister in the Reformed Presbyterian Church and became an Episcopalian. In the book *Evangelicals on the Canterbury Trail*, Webber and six other Evangelicals described why they joined the Episcopal Church.

As a child and a teenager, Webber had been taught that 'the best Christians were fundamentalists. And the best fundamentalists were Baptists. Catholics were pagan. Episcopalianism was a social club. Lutherans had departed from the faith. Presbyterians were formalistic. And Pentecostals were off-centre.' He describes in the book a spiritual journey in 'six areas of orthodoxy' which took him into the Episcopal Church.

For Webber Anglicanism preserves in its worship and sacraments the *sense of mystery* that rationalistic Christianity of either the

Liberal or Evangelical sort seems to deny. He found himself longing for an experience of worship that went beyond either emotionalism or intellectualism. He believes he has found that in the Anglican tradition. He also felt a need for visible and tangible symbols which he could touch, feel and experience with his senses. This need is now met for him in the experience of Christ presented through the sacraments. He also feels that he has discovered a 'spiritual identity with all God's people throughout history, by embracing the church universal'.[8]

Evangelicals within the Episcopal Church who value the Reformed tradition within Anglicanism have been mixed in their reaction to the arrival in ECUSA of former non-Anglican Evangelicals of the Webber variety. Some of them argue that for Webber and others like him, liturgy actually means Anglo-Catholic liturgy. They accuse the Webber brand of Episcopalian of abandoning the classic Evangelical understanding of justification by faith and of coming to value a particular style of piety or religious observance.

GENERAL CONVENTION 1997

At the General Convention in Philadelphia in July 1997, the Rt Rev. Frank Griswold was elected twenty-fifth Presiding Bishop of the American Episcopal Church in succession to Ed Browning. The election took place in Christ Church, Philadelphia, where the first Presiding Bishop had been chosen in 1789. He took office on 1 January 1998. In his acceptance speech, Bishop Griswold described himself as 'an orthodox theologian' and emphasised the need for conversation between different constituencies in the Episcopal Church. Evangelicals in ECUSA see Griswold as a Liberal who has supported gay clergy and whose appointment was welcomed by homosexuals.

At a press conference, Griswold tried to reassure Conservatives that he would 'stand at the centre' of the Church which was 'destined always to contain diametrically opposing views'. He saw himself as 'an Anglican . . . with the breadth to live with ambiguity and contradicting perspectives and stay grounded'. On human sexuality, the Bishop suggested that opposing sides might 'enrich and transform one another'.

At the Convention, the Bishops decided that theological and liturgical debate about same-sex relationships should continue, although the nine hundred lay and clerical delegates of the House of Deputies defeated a resolution authorising 'same-sex blessings'. It was recommended that the Standing Liturgical Commission study the issue. The Bishops expressed their wish that the document be considered at the 1998 Lambeth Conference. The Convention as a whole approved a resolution apologising to gay and lesbian members of ECUSA for 'years of rejection and maltreatment by the church'. Both Houses agreed to the apology, which acknowledged the diversity of opinion on the morality of gay and lesbian relationships.

Evangelical reaction

On the last morning of the General Convention, James Stanton, Bishop of Dallas and President of the AAC, told the House of Bishops that many people were alarmed by continuing divisions in the Episcopal Church. Bishop Stanton raised two issues which seemed serious enough to constitute an impaired communion within the Episcopal Church and between it and other provinces of the Anglican Communion: coercion of women's ordination and affirmation of homosexual unions.

At the same time, AAC leaders claimed that 'one of the thrills of the General Convention was to watch dozens and dozens of Episcopalians testifying on behalf of biblical values in all the major committees on most of the major issues'.

The AAC took the view that the most positive thing to come out of the Convention was a definition of doctrine. For the first time, the convention inserted into the canons (Church law) a definition of the 'core doctrine' of the Episcopal Church. The new canon defined doctrine as 'the basic and essential teachings of the Church . . . found in the canons of Holy Scripture, as understood in the Apostles' and Nicene creeds, and in the sacramental rites, ordinal and catechism in the *Book of Common Prayer*'.

For the AAC, this effectively repudiated the vague definition of 'core doctrine' used by the Court in the trial to dismiss heresy charges in 1995 against the Rt Rev. Walter Righter (who had ordained a practising homosexual). In its decision, that court had asked the 1997 General Convention to clarify the meaning of 'doctrine' in order to avoid such ambiguity in the future.

The AAC issued a press notice which said:

> In a stunning defeat of the homosexual agenda, the House of Deputies voted down the most closely watched resolution of the Convention, one which called for the development of rites for the blessing of same sex unions. It had been widely predicted that this measure would easily pass in the House of Deputies. Its rejection marked a decisive reversal of the trend toward endorsement of homosexual practice.

The AAC commented on the election of Frank Griswold, by what it pointed out was a narrow 110–96 vote, as the new Presiding Bishop. Griswold, the AAC said, 'has ordained non-celibate homosexuals and encourages the blessing of their unions. Many parishes consider their communion with their own diocesan bishop to be impaired over this issue.'

Bishop Stanton said that the AAC would stand by 'the many faithful congregations, clergy and laity', who were 'anguished by the apparent willingness of some in the leadership of this church to bless, condone and promote sexual practices clearly at odds with the whole of the biblical pattern, and with historic Christian teaching – a teaching which is still the norm, be it noted, of this Church and of other provinces of the Anglican Communion'. The AAC Board agreed to establish an orderly process by which it would assist parishes which found themselves unable to receive ministry from a 'doctrinally compromised bishop'.

The AAC Board also addressed the question of financial stewardship. Parishes and their vestries were encouraged to fund 'faithful ministry and mission, both domestic and foreign, of the Episcopal Church'. Speaking on behalf of the Board, Roger Boltz said, 'We encourage enthusiastic funding of dioceses and agencies of the national church that are pursuing such godly ministry. At the same time, we support those who seek ways to direct their tithes away from projects and purposes that are clearly contradictory to Holy Scripture.'

In the next part we look in more detail at the fire which is blazing over human sexuality in the UK as well as the USA and the wider Anglican Communion; and consider the biblical basis for the stand Evangelicals are taking.

PECUSA INC.

In December 1997 news broke of the incorporation of a body within ECUSA known as PECUSA Inc. The background to this is the growing conviction that ECUSA has been departing from the historic Christian faith. In the last twenty years, a third of Episcopalians have left the Church and some dioceses have seen declines of 40 per cent. At least five dioceses have agreed to the blessing of same-sex unions. More have been ordaining practising homosexuals.

Many have left the Church to form other bodies, such as the Anglican Catholic Church, United Episcopal Church, American Episcopal Church, Anglican Church in America, and others. In addition to clergy and laity leaving the Episcopal Church for the 'Continuing Church', a number of clergy and laity have joined the Roman Catholic or Orthodox Churches.

Towards the end of 1995 several clergy and laity had discussed how they might keep a place in the Episcopal Church for those who were feeling 'disenfranchised'. They noted that the National Church had begun to remove from the Church Constitution and the American *Book of Common Prayer* all references to the old title 'The Protestant Episcopal Church in the United States of America', substituting instead the new name 'The Episcopal Church'. They discovered that the official incorporation of the Church had been under the name of 'The Domestic and Foreign Missionary Society of the Protestant Episcopal Church in the United States of America'.

The group of clergy and laity had decided to incorporate that name, 'The Protestant Episcopal Church in the United States of

America', so it could be preserved for those who embraced the historic faith. Trustees were chosen to hold the ancient faith 'in trust'. They drew up a Declaration of Faith during 1996. Towards the end of 1997 the Presiding Bishop became aware of what they were doing. They had not told him directly, but maintained that this was already a matter of public record, and that the process was becoming more public as time went on.

The outgoing Presiding Bishop, Ed Browning, called one of the Trustees, Bishop Wantland of the Diocese of Eau Claire, Wisconsin, to see him on 10 December 1997. According to Bishop Wantland's account it was an angry meeting. Bishop Browning alleged that the Trustees were planning schism, and were trying to steal the name of the Church. Bishop Wantland's account continues: 'He threatened publicity to "destroy our ministry", and possible suits, as well. He demanded that the corporate structure, just then in place to be used, be dissolved within 48 hours. I tried to explain to him that I could not make any unilateral decision for the Trustees, and that even if I could, or if the Trustees were willing to do so, it could not be accomplished that quickly. Legal action could take up to 60 days.'

Wantland told Browning that the Trustees did not intend to leave the Church or split it. 'This was made clear to him, but he would not hear of it. We have been concerned, however, with the recent threats by Primates of Anglican Churches in Africa, Asia and elsewhere to seek [to remove] the American Church from the Anglican Communion. In view of these very real threats, we were concerned to be sure that there remained in this country an Anglican Church still associated with the rest of the Anglican Communion. When it became obvious that we could not get the Trustees together within the time given, the Presiding Bishop did agree to allow a meeting to take place the next week to consider his demands.'

The Trustees met on 17 December 1997, and considered what the Presiding Bishop had said. They expressed a willingness to amend the Articles of Incorporation to make it clear that they were not laying claim to the programmes or funds of the central organisation of ECUSA in New York. However, since thousands had already accepted the umbrella organisation, it would be impossible to comply with the demand to dismantle it.

The Trustees are adamant they are not leaving the Church and that it is not their intention to split it, but to give a solid place for orthodox Episcopalians to stand together. They claim that it is not their intention either to confuse the new structure with the National structure of ECUSA, with the Presiding Bishop's office, or the Episcopal Church Centre in New York. Those associated with PECUSA Inc., include Bishops John-David Schofield and Alex Dickson, as well as Bishop Wantland, plus Father Larry Hall, Rector of St John the Divine in Houston (one of the largest parishes in the American Church) and Dr John Rodgers, retired Dean of TESM.

Despite claims that the new body is a movement to divide the Church over the ordination of women, a majority of the Trustees actually favour the ordination of women and that is not an issue. Bishop Wantland expressed his sorrow that controversy had arisen over the initiative and hoped that the matter could be resolved amicably. 'Nonetheless,' he said, 'having received literally hundreds of letters and calls from people throughout the Church in deep pain over the drift of the Episcopal Church further and further away from biblical truth, I have felt compelled to join with others in carving out a place for them to stand together, with some assurance that the Church they have known and served will not be taken away from them.

'Some of you will applaud this effort, and some will be dismayed by it. I regret this division and pain. However, it is a matter of conscience, arrived at by much prayer and deliberation . . . I ask your prayers . . . I am not infallible, I do not know everything, and I am certainly not all-wise. I am striving simply to do that which seems the right, but difficult, thing to do in this time of crisis of faith.'

That is how the matter stood at the end of 1997.

Institutional change or inner transformation?

The incorporation of PECUSA Inc. is a recent example of action by some Anglicans who feel so dismayed by what they see as a Church which has grown 'revisionist', even 'apostate', that they are either contemplating leaving or spending a great deal of energy in complicated political battles within the Church. These battles develop their own momentum and attraction.

Jim Packer has this advice for those who contemplate leaving Anglicanism altogether. 'In a divided Christendom we are always free to move from one denomination to another. We oughtn't to think that guilt attaches to such a move. But I do want to say "Weigh the loss before you go". You think only of the gain of not having to live with these particular troubles . . . that would be at least ease – if ease is a gain, although I think the New Testament is ambiguous on that. But see what you'd lose. You would lose a heritage and I think that the loss would far outweigh the gain.'

Some, including Packer, prefer the option of what the Norwegian Lutheran Church calls *the inner mission*. The Evangelicals get together within the Church, establish their own links of fellowship and joint action: they come together for the renewal and invigorating of the Church. 'And in Norway', said Packer in an address to Reform in London, 'the Evangelicals always have their eyes on tomorrow. They raise funds, they pray, they work, they confer with a view to renewal in the Lutheran Church tomorrow. That, it seems to me frankly, is how we as Evangelicals in the Church of England would be wisest to seek to understand our own calling and to proceed. We are the inner mission. I think it's clarifying to say it in that way.'

Probably no single Christian book in the last six hundred years has had more impact than Thomas à Kempis's *The Imitation of Christ*. Thomas More, Ignatius Loyola, Samuel Johnson, John Wesley and John Newton are among those who have been profoundly influenced by it. À Kempis, a member of the Congregation of the Common Life, represents a group of early advocates of reform in the fourteenth century who were convinced that what mattered supremely in the Christian life was not fine-spun speculation but holy living. They doubted whether the Lord was pleased to save his people by means of subtle points of theology.

'Of what use is it to discourse learnedly on the Trinity', asked à Kempis, 'if you lack humility and therefore displease the Trinity? Lofty words do not make a man just or holy; but a good life makes him dear to God. I would far rather feel contrition than be able to define it. If you knew the whole Bible by heart, and all the teachings of the philosophers, how would this help you without the grace and love of God?' Although à Kempis and the group around him were aware of the corruptions that infected the contemporary Roman Church, and were sometimes victims of the persecutions of that Church, they did not regard it as their primary duty to strive for institutional changes, but rather stressed the need for inner transformation of the believer's life.

Those concerned about revisionism or apostasy in the Church today have agonising decisions to take. It is helpful to consider the strategic options available to them in the context of the history of those who have faced similar dilemmas.

PART SEVEN

Church on fire over sexuality

'Is not my word like fire,' declares the LORD, *'and like a hammer that breaks a rock in pieces?'*
(Jeremiah 23:29)

In one sense it is sad to devote the final narrative part of a book which has told a generally positive and often inspiring story to an issue which is dividing the Anglican Communion and threatens to come to an explosive head at the 1998 Lambeth Conference. It may be that divisions over human sexuality are symptoms of a deeper malaise within our society and the Church. John Stott regards this whole issue as a crisis of faith. 'Who are we going to believe,' he asks, 'God or the world? Are we going to submit to the Lordship of Christ or give in to the pressures of our culture?'

Many people today have accepted the view, vigorously asserted by the gay community, that homosexuality is a normal form of sexual behaviour different from, but equal to, that of heterosexuality. Homosexuals demand equality of treatment with heterosexuals. They would resent the fact that I have expressed this as a 'demand' and state that, on the contrary, equality is something they should expect as a right. They insist that homosexuality is an alternative lifestyle, and many people these days accept that decisions about sex are a private matter.

The demand for equality of treatment between homosexuals and heterosexuals is made as strongly within as outside the Church. The fact that some bishops are ordaining practising homosexuals, openly in the States and more quietly in England, has caused great tension within Anglicanism.

Are homosexual partnerships a Christian option?

As far as the Bible is concerned, John Stott has adopted a position which has been widely accepted among Anglican Evangelicals and beyond. He notes that there are four main groups of passages which appear to refer to the homosexual question negatively:

- The story of Sodom (Gen.19:1–13) together with that of Gibeah (Judg.19).
- The Levitical texts (Lev. 18:22 and 20:13) which say: 'Do not lie with a man as one lies with a woman; that is detestable'; and 'If a man lies with a man as one lies with a woman, both of them have done what is detestable. They must be put to death; their blood will be on their own heads.'
- The apostle Paul's description of decadent pagan society in his day (Rom. 1:18–32) where he speaks of 'shameful lusts' in which 'women exchanged natural relations for unnatural ones', and 'men also abandoned natural relations with women and were inflamed with lust for one another', receiving 'in themselves the due penalty for their perversion'.
- Two Pauline lists of sinners (1 Cor. 6:9–10 and 1 Tim. 1:8–11) which include references to 'male prostitutes' and 'homosexual offenders', none of whom will inherit the kingdom of God because of their disobedience.

Reviewing these biblical references to homosexual behaviour, John Stott asks a number of questions. Is it right to conclude, as some have done, that the topic is marginal to the main thrust of the Bible? Do they constitute a flimsy basis on which to take a firm stand against a homosexual lifestyle? Are those gay Christians who claim that these biblical prohibitions are highly specific right when they say, for example, that the stories of Sodom and Gibeah are simply describing violations of hospitality; the Leviticus passages simply prohibiting religious practices which have long since ceased; the verses in Romans merely condemning shameless orgies; and the other Pauline references (in 1 Corinthians and 1 Timothy) simply warning against male prostitution and the corruption of the young? Is the homosexual lobby right to suggest that none of these passages refers to, let alone condemns, a loving partnership between a homosexual couple?

Stott argues that these apparent prohibitions of homosexual activity only make sense in the light of the *positive* teaching in Genesis 1 and 2 about human sexuality and heterosexual marriage.

Sex and marriage in the Bible

The account of creation in Genesis 2, says Stott, conveys three fundamental truths. First, *the human need for companionship* – 'it is not good for the man to be alone' (Gen. 2:18). God has created us social beings. Since he is love, and has made us in his likeness, he has given us the capacity to love and be loved. Second, *God provides for this human need.* Since no suitable helper can be found for Adam, a special creation is necessary. Adam awakes from a deep sleep and sees a reflection of himself, a complement to himself, indeed something created from a part of himself. God brings Eve to Adam, who breaks out into history's first love poem in Genesis 2:23:

> This is now bone of my bones
> and flesh of my flesh;
> she shall be called 'woman',
> for she was taken out of man.

The third fundamental truth of Genesis 2 is *the institution of marriage.* After Adam's love poem, the narrator adds: 'For this reason a man will leave his father and mother and be united to his wife, and they will become one flesh' (v. 24). This, says Stott, is deliberate. It tells us that heterosexual marriage is more than a union; it is a kind of reunion – the union of two persons who originally were one, were then separated from each other, and now in the sexual encounter of marriage come together again.

It is surely this which explains the profound mystery of heterosexual intimacy, which poets and philosophers have celebrated in every culture. Heterosexual intercourse is more than a union of bodies; it is a blending of complementary personalities through which, in the midst of prevailing alienation, the rich created oneness of human being is experienced again. And the complementarity of male and female sexual organs is only a symbol at the physical level of a much deeper spiritual complementarity.[1]

In the New Testament Jesus endorses this creation truth. He quotes

Genesis 2:24 and adds, 'Therefore what God has joined together, let man not separate' (Mark 10:9).

Scripture defines marriage as the union of one man with one woman; it has to be publicly acknowledged (the couple leave their parents); permanently sealed (the man is joined to his wife); and physically consummated ('one flesh'). The Bible envisages no other kind of marriage or sexual intercourse.

Therefore, says Stott, Christians should not single out homosexual intercourse for special condemnation. Every sexual relationship which deviates from God's revealed intention is displeasing to him and under his judgment. This includes polygamy, polyandry, clandestine unions, casual encounters, temporary liaisons, adultery and many divorces (which separate what God has joined), as well as homosexual partnerships (which violate the biblical principle that 'a man' is joined to 'his wife').

Stott accepts that if the only biblical teaching on homosexuality were found in the four groups of Scripture which have been traditionally taken to prohibit it, then it might be difficult to answer some contemporary arguments. The biblical authors, it is said, were addressing themselves to questions relevant to their own circumstances but very different from ours. In any case, they had never heard of 'the homosexual condition' and only knew about certain practices. The notion that two men or two women might fall in love and develop a stable relationship comparable to marriage never entered their heads.

Stott insists, however, that when we consider the prohibition texts in the context of the divine institution of marriage, we are talking about a principle of divine revelation which is universally applicable. Modern loving homosexual partnerships are wrong because they are incompatible with God's created order – heterosexual monogamy. Since that order was established by creation, not culture, its validity is both permanent and universal. There can be no liberation from God's created norms; true liberation is found only in accepting them.

Some advocates of gay liberation borrow from Scripture the truth that 'love is the greatest thing in the world' (which it is) and from the 'situation ethics' of the 1960s the notion that love is an adequate criterion by which to judge every relationship. Love needs law to guide it. When they emphasised love for God and neighbour as the two great commandments, Jesus and his apostles did not discard all other commandments. 'If you love me,' said Jesus, 'you will obey what I command' (John 14:15); and 'love', the apostle Paul wrote, 'is the fulfilment [not the breaking] of the law' (Rom. 13:10). Love is concerned for the highest welfare of the person we love. Our best purposes are served, our greatest joy is known, when we obey God's law, not when we rebel against him or ignore him.

It is often argued that the whole point of the Christian gospel is that 'God loves us and accepts us just as we are'. 'Just as I am,' wrote Charlotte Elliott, 'without one plea . . . O Lamb of God I come!' John Stott warns against the muddled thinking that this strand of Christian truth can encourage. God does accept us 'just as we are', and we do not have to make ourselves good first, indeed we cannot. But his 'acceptance' means that he fully and freely forgives all who repent and believe, not that he condones our continuance in sin. 'No acceptance, either by God or by the Church, is promised to us if we harden our hearts against God's Word and will. Only judgment.'

The only alternative to heterosexual marriage is sexual abstinence. In a moving and personal passage, writing as a lifelong bachelor, John Stott says: 'I think I know the implications of this. Nothing has helped me to understand the pain of homosexual celibacy more than Alex Davidson's moving book *The Returns of Love*. He writes of "this incessant tension between law and lust", "this monster that lurks in the depths", this "burning torment".'

The modern world tells us that 'sex is essential to human fulfilment'. The conventional wisdom is that to expect homosexual people to abstain from homosexual practice is to condemn them to frustration and to drive them to neurosis, despair and even suicide. But the message of the Bible and the best Christian teaching is different. Certainly sex is a good gift from God. The creation story and the institution of marriage underline this. But sexual experience is not essential to human fulfilment. God's commands are good, not burdensome. The yoke of Christ brings rest, not turmoil; unbearable conflict comes to those who resist it.

'The true "orientation" of Christians', says Stott, 'is not what we are by constitution (hormones), but what we are by choice (heart, mind and will).' All unmarried Christians experience the pain and struggle of loneliness. Can we call ourselves Christians and declare that chastity is impossible?

Having said all this, Stott admits that the Church has often failed to show love to gay people. He believes that many homosexuals have a natural human hunger for mutual love and friendship, are searching for identity, and are longing for completeness. 'If homosexual people', he writes, 'cannot find these things in the local "church family", we have no business to go on using that expression. The alternative is not between the warm physical relationship of homosexual intercourse and the pain of isolation in the cold. There is a third option, namely a Christian environment of love, understanding, acceptance and support.'

Encouraging and safeguarding same-sex friendships

Stott does not think there is any need to encourage homosexual people to disclose their sexual orientation to everybody; this is neither necessary nor helpful. But they need at least one confidant to whom they can unburden themselves, who will not despise or reject them, but will support them with friendship and prayer. There is no need to discourage same-sex friendships: the Bible tells us of Ruth and Naomi, David and Jonathan, Paul and Timothy. The narratives do not suggest that these were homosexual in the erotic sense: certainly they were affectionate and – in the case of David and Jonathan – demonstrative.

Of course safeguards are important. 'But in African and Asian cultures it is common to see two men walking down the street hand in hand, without embarrassment. It is sad that our western culture inhibits the development of rich same-sex friendships by engendering the fear of being ridiculed or rejected as a "queer",' says Stott.

The local church should be a warm, accepting and supportive community. 'Accepting' is not the same as 'acquiescing'; and in rejecting 'homophobia' Stott stresses that he is not rejecting a proper Christian disapproval of homosexual practice. There is a place of godly Christian discipline for those who refuse to repent and persist in homosexual relationships; but discipline, when necessary, must be exercised in love and humility. There must be no discrimination between men and women and between homosexual and heterosexual offences; and the necessary discipline in the case of public scandal should not become a witch hunt.[2]

Notwithstanding the painstaking and sensitive way in which John Stott has expressed his arguments, there will be those who will say either that he is setting impossibly high standards or that he has missed the point of the gay lobby's arguments about equality: homosexuality is a morally equal alternative to heterosexuality. Stott, however, is by no means alone in his views.

Sanitover

Jeffrey Sanitover is a psychiatrist and psychopharmacologist who practises in Connecticut, USA. He states that the problems associated with homosexuality include a decrease in life expectancy, inevitably fatal immune disease (AIDS) and associated cancers, chronic, potentially fatal, liver disease, a much higher than usual incidence of suicide, and a significantly decreased likelihood of establishing or preserving a successful marriage.

Sanitover has done a great deal of work which is intended to shed light on the issue of whether homosexuality is genetically or environmentally determined. Are homosexuals born to be gay, or do the people they meet and the places where they live and work encourage them to adopt the homosexual lifestyle? Is it nature or nurture? Sanitover has shown how complex the interaction is between genes and the environment.

He argues that there is essentially no dimension of behaviour which is not *both* environmentally and genetically influenced. He says 'there is absolutely no evidence whatsoever that the behaviour "homosexuality" is itself directly inherited.'[3] Observation of the lives of homosexuals reveals that at the point where homosexual activity becomes the central organising factor in their lives, they slowly acquire the habit of turning to it regularly – not just because of their original need for fatherly warmth and love, but to relieve anxiety of any sort.

Sanitover uses the word 'healing' to speak of the journey which some people do take away from the homosexual lifestyle. He describes the road as 'long and difficult – but extraordinarily fulfilling' and comments that 'the course to full restoration or heterosexuality typically lasts longer than the average American marriage – which should be understood as an index of how broken all relationships are today'.

Gay activists paint a picture of homosexual life, especially among men, that is the counterpart of heterosexual life. In spite of data which clearly indicates that homosexual standards of behaviour are strikingly different from the heterosexual norm, the general public impression has been created that gays are little different from heterosexuals. In describing, as he has done in some detail, the medical problems which accompany typical homosexual behaviour, Sanitover stresses that homosexual *desire* is no more intrinsically problematic than any other desire. Neither so-called 'homosexual orientation' nor 'homosexual identity' themselves cause medical problems; only homosexual behaviour can.

According to Sanitover, what is known as the 'gay lifestyle' is largely a way of life constructed around unconstrained sexuality. He argues that the gay lifestyle is more concerned with the many possible forms of sexual pleasure than the 'straight' lifestyle. He accepts that many heterosexuals seek unconstrained sexual expression but states that this is less common than among homosexuals.[4]

Sanitover knows well that, in the current atmosphere, the evidence he has assembled that homosexuality is dangerous is inflammatory. But, he asks, if the evidence of the increased risk of illness and death is correct, how could anyone with a concern for the sufferings of others stand by in silence? Given the risks, he believes that the only ethical approach to helping men and women who consider themselves homosexual – especially young people wrestling with their emerging sexual feelings – must include a willingness to help them change not only their behaviour but the homosexual 'orientation' itself. He refers to 'considerable evidence' that homosexuality (the 'condition') is no more difficult to change than the behaviour.

Pannenberg

The German theologian Wolfhart Pannenberg, who was born in 1928, studied under Karl Barth in the 1950s. He is now Professor Emeritus at the Institute of Fundamental Theology in the University of Munich. For Pannenberg, as for Stott, the words of Jesus constitute the foundation and the criterion for all Christian pronouncements on questions of sexuality. According to Jesus's teaching, human sexuality as male and as female is intended for the indissoluble fellowship of marriage.

The Bible's assessments of homosexual practice, says Pannenberg, are unambiguous in their more or less pointed rejection, and all its statements on this subject agree without exception. The New Testament does not contain a single passage which might indicate a more positive assessment of homosexual activity to counterbalance the Pauline statements. Thus the entire biblical witness includes practised homosexuality without exception among the kinds of behaviour which give particularly striking expression to humanity's turning away from God. This places very narrow boundaries around the view of homosexuality which any Church that is under the authority of Scripture may take. The biblical statements about homosexuality cannot be dismissed as the expressions of a cultural situation which today is simply outdated. This is because biblical references to homosexuality are explicitly opposed to the assumptions of the cultural environment in which they are set in the name of faith in the God of Israel, who in creation appointed men and women for a particular identity.

The Church has to live with the fact that, in this area of life as in others, departures from the norm are not exceptional but rather common and widespread. The Church must encounter all those concerned with tolerance and understanding, but must also call them to repentance. It cannot surrender the distinction between the norm and behaviour which departs from it. A Christian Church which knows itself to be bound by the authority of Scripture has to face up to this.

Those who urge the Church to change the norm of its teaching on this matter must know that they are promoting division. If a Church were to let itself be pushed to the point where it ceased to treat homosexual activity as a departure from the biblical norm, and recognised homosexual unions as a personal partnership of love equivalent to marriage, such a Church would no longer stand on biblical ground but would be acting against the unequivocal witness of Scripture.

Pannenberg concludes that a Church which took such a step would thereby have ceased to be one, holy, Catholic and apostolic.

THE ANGLICAN COMMUNION ON FIRE

Kuala Lumpur statement

At a conference in Kuala Lumpur, Malaysia, in February 1997, called 'Second Anglican Encounter in the South', representatives of tropical and southern-hemisphere churches unanimously agreed a 'Statement on Human Sexuality'. Subsequently the Standing Committee of the Province of South East Asia (an administrative collection of Anglican churches) unanimously adopted the Kuala Lumpur statement and declared itself 'in communion with that part of the Anglican Communion which accepts and endorses the principles aforesaid and not otherwise'.

The statement, which has often been quoted since, makes the following points:

- God's glory and loving purposes have been revealed in the creation of humankind (Rom. 1:18; Gen. 1:26, 27). Among the multiplicity of his gifts we are blessed with our sexuality.
- Since the Fall (Gen. 3), life has been impaired and God's purposes spoilt. Our fallen state has affected every sphere of our being, which includes our sexuality. Sexual deviation has existed in every time and in most cultures. Jesus's teaching about lust in the Sermon on the Mount (Matt. 5:27–30) makes it clear that sexual sin is a real danger and temptation to us all.
- It is, therefore, with an awareness of our own vulnerability to sexual sin that we express our profound concern about recent

developments relating to church discipline and moral teaching in some provinces in the North – specifically, the ordination of practising homosexuals and the blessing of same-sex unions.

- While acknowledging the complexities of our sexual nature and the strong drives it places within us, we are quite clear about God's will in this area which is expressed in the Bible.

- The Scripture bears witness to God's will regarding human sexuality which is to be expressed only within the lifelong union of a man and a woman in (holy) matrimony.

- The Holy Scriptures are clear in teaching that all sexual promiscuity is sin. We are convinced that this includes homosexual practices between men or women, as well as heterosexual relationships outside marriage.

- We believe that the clear and unambiguous teaching of the Holy Scriptures about human sexuality is of great help to Christians as it provides clear boundaries.

- We find no conflict between clear biblical teaching and sensitive pastoral care. Repentance precedes forgiveness and is part of the healing process. To heal spiritual wounds in God's name we need his wisdom and truth. We see this in the ministry of Jesus, for example his response to the adulterous woman, '. . . neither do I condemn you. Go and sin no more' (John 8:11).

- We encourage the Church to care for all those who are trapped in their sexual brokenness and to become the channel of Christ's compassion and love towards them. We wish to stand alongside and welcome them into a process of being whole and restored within our communities of faith. We would also affirm and resource those who exercise a pastoral ministry in this area.

- We are deeply concerned that the setting aside of biblical teaching in such actions as the ordination of practising homosexuals and the blessing of same-sex unions calls into question the authority of the Holy Scriptures. This is totally unacceptable to us.

- This leads us to express concern about mutual accountability and interdependence within our Anglican Communion. As provinces and dioceses, we need to learn how to seek each other's counsel and wisdom in a spirit of true unity, and to reach a common mind before embarking on radical changes to church discipline and moral teaching.

• We live in a global village and must be more aware that the way we act in one part of the world can radically affect the mission and witness of the Church in another.

In May 1997 the Episcopal Synod of America (not to be confused with ECUSA's General Convention, the official decision-making body), claiming to represent 'thousands of orthodox Episcopalians', strongly backed the Asian Anglicans. On 1 May six bishops of the Episcopal Synod signed a letter to Archbishop Moses Tay of Singapore, commending the South East Asian action and promising solidarity with efforts to uphold the traditional Christian understanding of sexual responsibility. The letter affirmed the Kuala Lumpur statement and celebrated 'our continued communion with the Province of South East Asia and other like-minded Provinces'. The letter expressed confidence that other orthodox American bishops would affirm the statement.

The Archbishop of Nigeria, the Most Rev. Joseph Adetiloye, who chaired the meeting in Kuala Lumpur in February 1997, said he and others would fight against any attempt to change the Church's teaching on homosexuality. 'If we start making the Bible fit our prevailing culture then Christianity will cease to have any impact on the world.'

Not all leading African Anglicans have taken the same line. In February 1996, Archbishop Desmond Tutu declared that he supported homosexual rights in the Church. Tutu's successor, however, takes the traditional view.

A history of tensions in England

Back in 1987, the General Synod of the Church of England voted overwhelmingly in favour of a motion which said, 'Homosexual acts fall short of the [biblical] ideal, and are to be met by a call to repentance and the exercise of compassion.'

As we saw in Part Five (pages 333–4), the 1991 House of Bishops report *Issues in Human Sexuality* took the line that the Church should welcome into its fellowship lay people in conscientious and committed homosexual relationships while keeping a ban on ordaining active homosexuals and ruling out same-sex 'marriages'.

In May 1995 the Archbishop of Canterbury told the Anglican Evangelical Assembly that it had been a disappointment to him that *Issues in Human Sexuality* had been so little discussed in the first three years after it had been published.

'It's only now', he said, 'that people seem to be addressing it seriously and the questions which it raises. Now that they are I hope that people will look at the report as a whole and reflect on it in its totality rather than taking small sections out of context. I very much welcome the news that a working party has been set up . . . to consider the subject of our sexuality and I look forward to reading the conclusions in due course.

'Let me say this: that all of us, whatever our sexuality, are valued by God. But with regard to the question of sexual practice, let me make it quite clear that *Issues in Human Sexuality* only recognises two options as being in full accord with the Bible and the Church's tradition, namely heterosexual marriage and celibacy. It underlines that there's a particular requirement on the clergy to follow these patterns as examples to their flocks but it does not thereby judge them to be matters which can be treated with indifference by the laity. Far from it, all of us, clergy and laity alike are called to live lives of holiness. And here let me affirm particularly the contribution to the life of the Church made by those whose vocation has been and is to the celibate life.

'The House of Bishops will reflect thoughtfully and prayerfully on the responses to the statement in due course. But it will not be stampeded into changing either its theological position or its pastoral practice. It suits some groups to talk up the story that the Bishops are preparing to accept parity between marriage and long-term same-sex relationships, or to allow the ordination of practising homosexuals. That is simply not so. Such speculation is misleading and causes unwarranted suspicion and anxiety and prompts a flood of letters to Lambeth Palace. Moreover, even within the realm of sexuality the significance of homosexuality should not be overstated.

'Leaders of all churches as well as all businesses know all too well that heterosexual misconduct is a much more frequent threat to holy living than homosexual practice. Indeed let me repeat again that holiness of life is related to a whole lifestyle which is focused on Christ and which seeks to live life in the power of his Holy Spirit. How we relate to our families and our friends, how we act in business relationships, how we treat the poor and disadvantaged, all these too are part of the holy living and the holy dying.'

In May 1996 Lord Runcie, the former Archbishop of Canterbury, admitted he had ordained homosexuals. In October the only openly homosexual Anglican bishop in England, the Rt Rev. Derek Rawcliffe, was sacked as Assistant Bishop in Ripon, North Yorkshire, for conducting homosexual 'marriages'.

In November 1996 a controversial service to celebrate the twenty-fifth anniversary of the Lesbian and Gay Christian Movement was held in Southwark Cathedral. The sermon was preached by the Bishop of Guildford, John Gladwin, who many years earlier had been a young delegate at Keele '67. He spoke of the obligation on Christians to 'hear the Word of God as revealed in the Scriptures and interpreted in the historic teaching of the Church down the ages' but referred to the 'tension – even a conflict – between the Church's understanding of the tradition and what gay and lesbian people find to be good and creative in their lives'.

Bishop Gladwin spoke bluntly in his sermon about marriage, reminding the members of the Lesbian and Gay Christian Movement that it was 'a God-given building block of a loving and ordered community'. He said that 'marriage is not something which we create for our own convenience. We live in a culture in danger of privatising marriage by reducing it to a personal arrangement between two people. It is not surprising, if that is all it is, that people begin to think that any private arrangement between two people should be treated as if it were marriage. But that falls well short of the Christian tradition. We cannot solve our dilemma by turning cohabitation or same-sex relationships into marriage. That is the hard part and I know it is not easy to hear.'

In April 1997 members of Outrage!, the homosexual rights group, confronted the Archbishop of Canterbury in the grounds of Lambeth Palace during a meeting planning the 1998 Lambeth Conference.

In July 1997 Archbishop Carey told the General Synod meeting in York that the question of homosexual practice raised deeper questions about how we do our theology and how we live with differences of opinion. 'I also often remind myself that it is not merely a "matter", an "issue" or a "problem" that we are discussing but real people, loved by God, made in his image and likeness.'

Dr Carey said that human sexuality – not just homosexuality – would be discussed in one of the four Sections of the 1998 Lambeth Conference. He recognised that in the Anglican Communion a strand of opinion challenged the traditional understanding of the Church.

'Let me make clear my own starting point,' he said. 'I do not find any justification, from the Bible or the entire Christian tradition, for sexual activity outside marriage. Thus, same-sex relationships in my view cannot be on a par with marriage and the Church should resist any diminishing of the fundamental "sacramentum" of marriage. Clergy, especially, must model relationships that commend the faith of Christ. I know that this statement will distress some, and I understand the pastoral difficulties that come from working out the discipline of the Church in the personal life, but I could not commend any significant departure from the principles and conclusions set out in the *Issues* statement. Of course, that statement or its preface is not to be seen as Holy Writ and is there to be debated. In that sense it is not intended to be the last word, as if prayerful discussion should stop! But I do not believe any major change is likely in the foreseeable future and I do not myself share the assumption that it is only a matter of time before the Church will change its mind.'

TOWARDS LAMBETH 1998

The 1998 Lambeth Conference will meet at the University of Kent for three weeks from 19 July to 9 August and will be attended by nearly one thousand bishops.

John Stott told me, 'I have a great regard for George Carey. I like the way in which he has said quite clearly that, on the homosexual issue, there are only two possibilities – marriage and celibacy. I pray that he might have the courage to take this stand at Lambeth. Of course he will have all the African, Asian and Latin American bishops with him. It's the British, to some extent, but even more the Americans who will be his problem.'

Archbishop Carey's advice for Evangelicals

I asked Dr Carey (a) whether he thought that John Stott's perspective on the situation was accurate, and (b) what kind of support he would most value from Evangelicals on this issue. The Archbishop told me that John Stott was generally correct in his analysis.

'I have been consistent on this matter', he said, 'in saying that the two lifestyles for Christians should be marriage or celibacy. Evangelicals, however, should not fall into the trap of seeing this as a simple black/white issue. There are many complexities about homosexuality and in our compassion for people we must be willing to understand as much as possible about the dilemmas of homosexual people. I believe the House of Bishops' report gives a splendid theological approach which is at the same time very compassionate.

'As ever, I would hope that Evangelicals, in seeking the truth, would read that document carefully and reread the Scriptures in the light of all the evidence before us. There are good reasons for retaining a traditional understanding on this matter, but not if we reach our understanding by shutting our ears to the pain, fears and understanding of others.'

BISHOP SPONG

Jack Spong is the controversial Bishop of the Diocese of Newark, New Jersey, across the Hudson River from New York. He has publicly argued for the permissibility of sexual relations outside marriage both for heterosexuals and homosexuals, maintaining that 'sex outside marriage can be holy and life-giving in some circumstances'. He has written a book which denies that Jesus was born of a virgin and another which disputes the Church's traditional understanding of the resurrection of Jesus. He has campaigned for the ordination of practising homosexuals and lobbied hard for abortion rights on the grounds that abortion restrictions are oppressive to women.

By the early summer of 1997, Spong had ordained twenty-three homosexual clergy. On a visit to Britain, he said: 'England will deal with this in the way it always does, covertly. I could name a handful of gay Church of England bishops and dozens of gay clergy.'

Alister McGrath has referred to Spong's 'somewhat modest theological competence' as being 'vastly exceeded by his ability to obtain media attention'. McGrath says that Spong's *Rescuing the Bible from Fundamentalism* 'would probably have been dismissed as utterly inconsequential were its writer not a bishop'. Spong's book 'offers to liberate the Bible from a fundamentalist stranglehold. But it soon becomes clear that the Bible is to be "liberated" only to be enslaved to the latest cultural norms prevailing among the Greater New England Liberal élite. This work is as aggressive in its modernity as it is selective and superficial in its argumentation and intolerant and dismissive of the views of others.'[5]

Spong's message to the Anglican Communion

On 12 November 1997 Bishop Spong circulated 'A Message to the Anglican Communion on the Subject of Homosexuality' under cover of a letter to Anglican Primates. Sometimes known as Bishop Spong's 'White Paper', this is a remarkable document. It begins by asserting that 'our knowledge and understanding of homosexuality is changing' and continues:

Over the last fifty years dramatic new insights have been achieved in the studies of both human behaviour and the science of brain function and formation. These insights have forced the western world, led by medical and scientific people, to reject the wisdom of the past that viewed homosexuality as a choice rather than a given aspect of reality, as a mental illness rather than as part of the spectrum of human sexual activity, and as aberrant and evil behaviour engaged in by morally depraved people rather than a natural, albeit a minority, part of humanity.

He asserts that the 'constancy of the number of gay/lesbian people in the population of the world is also generally accepted' and that 'homosexuality is a part of the human and biological norm'. It is 'not an aberration or a sickness that needs to be overcome'. These 'new insights', Spong tells the Anglican Communion, which are 'overwhelmingly accepted by the medical and scientific community', continue to be rejected by 'uninformed religious people who buttress their attitude with appeals to a literal understanding of the Bible'. He complains that this 'same mentality has marked every debate about every new insight that has arisen in the western world over the last six hundred years'. The 'tired, threadbare argument' (of the uninformed religious people) has 'become one of embarrassment to the cause of Christ'.

Spong says that the Church's ministry of reconciliation is hurt by 'continuing religious prejudice toward homosexual persons'. What he calls the 'integrity of the gospel' is, he says, 'at risk unless we confront this killing prejudice in our midst and root it out from the body of Christ'.

Spong then launches into a series of attacks on groups and individuals (including personal insults) across the Anglican Communion. He begins at the top by launching a missile in the direction of the Archbishop of Canterbury, criticising him for endorsing the report of the English House of Bishops, *Issues in Human Sexuality*. This report, says Spong, was outside the moral tradition in Anglicanism when it suggested that something 'might be morally acceptable for the laity and not for the clergy'.

Archbishop Carey, says Spong, has 'disappointed those who expect more of his leadership role in the English Church' by refusing to conduct a dialogue with either 'the major church-related gay/lesbian organization in the United Kingdom, the Lesbian and Gay Christian Movement' or the founder of Integrity, the equivalent group in the United States. He notes that 'the white, apartheid-supporting government of South Africa also sought to act this way. They wanted to speak only with those representatives of black Africa with whom they were comfortable.' This, says Spong, is 'an unacceptable procedure for Christians in general to follow and it is not a becoming stance for one who wears the mantle of Christ'.

Curiously, Spong then directs his fire on the Bishop of Oxford,

Richard Harries, whom some Conservative Christians in England suspect is hopelessly Liberal. Spong attacks Harries for allegedly saying, 'Marriage and gay unions are not on a par.' This, says Spong, is said so often by English bishops that 'one suspects they have almost become the party line'. The problem, Spong announces, is that both Bishop Harries and the Archbishop are 'speaking out of their own heterosexual perspective'. For the Bishop of Newark, this is an example of the language of power, not the language of Christ.

White people defended slavery, segregation, apartheid, and anti-miscegenation laws with similar versions of that statement which maintained that black people were simply not on a par with white people. Males in previous generations have acted to keep females from voting, from achieving the ability to hold property in their own name, from getting adequate educations, from entering professions reserved for men only, from being ordained and even from getting divorces when they lived in abusive marriages. These conclusions were also justified by the claim that women were in fact not on a par with men.

Spong then attacks the Church of England for its handling of the ordination of women.

The Church of England rejected the ordination of women until that idea had achieved more than an 80 percent approval rating in the population at large and until the damage done to the institution of the Church by not ordaining women had become greater than the damage that would be done by ordaining women. Only then did they act. Surely we must recognize that there is no integrity and no leadership in this kind of pattern.

Having dealt with the Archbishop of Canterbury and the Church of England, Bishop Spong then accuses the Archbishop of the Southern Cone (South America), the Most Rev. Maurice Sinclair, of misusing the Bible. He prefaces his second attack on an Archbishop by reminding the Anglican Communion that the 'Bible is the book of life; it must not be used as a weapon of repression'. The Bible, says Spong,

[was] quoted in the 16th and 17th centuries to oppose Copernicus and Galileo. In the 18th and 19th centuries it was quoted to support the practice of slavery and to oppose both the use of vaccinations and the ideas of Charles Darwin. In the 20th century it has been quoted to undergird segregation, apartheid and the second class status of women. Now it is being quoted to condemn homosexual persons. The Bible must never be used to give moral justification to prejudice of any kind. Archbishop Sinclair needs to be confronted publicly.

Having now finished off two Archbishops and the Church of England, Bishop Spong turns on the bishops who signed the Kuala Lumpur statement. They are 'ill-informed and filled with the prejudice of propaganda'. Sadly, 'the overwhelming scientific data available today in the western world has simply not penetrated the minds of the signatories of this document'.

Perhaps they have never read those portions of scripture which validate polygamy and the treatment of women as property. Perhaps they want to go back to the time when homosexuals or suspected homosexuals were burned at the stake in conformity with the Levitical code that called for their execution (Lev. 20). Perhaps they have not read Romans 1 where Paul's argument is that those who do not worship God properly will have their sexual natures confused by God as punishment. Perhaps they have never seen monogamy lived out by loving, faithful gay or lesbian couples. I do not know what their reasoning was. I only know that their statement was an embarrassing misuse of the Bible and that it greatly confused moral categories.

Spong condemns the bishops who signed the Kuala Lumpur statement for their 'hint that homosexuality is a manifestation of a "brokenness" that when admitted and faced, could be "part of a healing process"'.

If one is going to prescribe for a segment of the human race, one has a responsibility to be informed. The possibility that homosexuals might be 'cured' by conversion, forgiveness, prayer, psychotherapy or 'spiritual counseling' is totally discredited in the scientific world today. A recent statement by the American Psychiatric Society referred to it as 'pastoral violence'. To quote from certain persons who claim to be 'cured homosexuals', who are today enriching themselves and their organizations by playing on the homophobic pain and fear that infects our society when there is no scientific basis or support for their claims is without honor and without integrity.

Reminding the rest of the world that the Anglican Province in the US has been 'debating the issues surrounding homosexuality for more than twenty years', Spong says, 'We are troubled by the arrogance that the Kuala Lumpur statement expresses, and we reject that arrogance forthwith as unbecoming to our partners in this Communion.'

Apparently unaware of any arrogance in himself, Spong then returns to his attack on English bishops.

Even those bishops in England, who know better on this issue of homosexuality, have, with a few rare exceptions, been muted by some strange commitment to institutional unity. That unity has come at the cost of sacrificing truth. If even a minority of bishops would speak out, it would allow gay and lesbian people to know that they are not alone and that someone, somewhere, in the body of Christ understands their plight.

Looking towards Lambeth, Bishop Spong is not squeamish about issuing at least two threats. First he states that: 'If the Lambeth Conference is forced to vote negatively on this issue, we will take to the public media to assure the gay and lesbian population of the world and most especially those gay and lesbian Christians we are privileged to serve, that they have not been abandoned by the leadership of their Church.'

Second, Spong supports the idea of a special commission to work on this issue during the next ten years, providing (a) that the body is advisory only; (b) that the membership reflects adequately 'those who are leaders in the struggle to make the Body of Christ whole by including God's gay and lesbian children'; and (c) that the commission is chaired by someone of whom he approves. Then says: 'Once again, if this commission is formed without full participation by the authorized bodies representing Anglican gay and lesbian Christians, it will be denounced immediately and its conclusions will be ignored.'

Assessing Spong's message

Bishop Spong's message to the Anglican Communion is remarkable for its confident tone and for the fearless way in which he discharges his volleys on a wide front. Thoughtful and sincere people who wish to take up the cause of gay and lesbian people may well wish that they could find a more measured spokesman to spearhead their force within the Anglican Communion.

Quite apart from its tone and tactlessness, however, Bishop Spong's 'White Paper' appears to be weakened by a series of flaws. These weaknesses may be summarised as follows:

- Spong refers a number of times to 'insights' which have 'forced the western world, led by medical and scientific people, to reject the wisdom of the past', but he never tells us either what these insights are or what they have to do with medicine and science. Even Liberal critics of Spong admit that there are as yet no solid conclusions coming from biological research in the areas which he is presumed to have in mind.
- Spong says that the wisdom of the past 'viewed homosexuality as a choice rather than as a given aspect of reality'. Here Spong appears to have confused two aspects of homosexuality which is normally agreed to cover (a) sexual desire for a person of one's own sex and (b) sexual activity with a person of one's own sex. Now it may be that the sexual *desire* under discussion is a 'given aspect of reality', although there is no agreement that science has yet shown this. However, sexual *activity* always begins with the decision (made by choice) to engage in the behaviour. It is true that the decision may be made in a situation of passion, but without this choice being made, the sexual behaviour will not

take place. So the 'wisdom of the past' was correct to refer to homosexual activity as a choice. As Spong goes on to say that the wisdom of the past viewed homosexuality as 'aberrant and evil behaviour engaged in by morally depraved people', it is clear that he is using the word homosexuality to refer to the behaviour and not the desire. It is certainly true that the wisdom of the past, not to say nearly two thousand years of Church tradition, viewed homosexual behaviour – homosexual intercourse – as evil and immoral. The question at issue is whether homosexual intercourse is actually moral or immoral and whether Christian tradition has been correct to see it as immoral.

- Spong characterises homosexuality as 'a natural, albeit a minority, part of humanity'. In contrast, traditional wisdom recognised that homosexual behaviour was found in nature, but said that such behaviour was against nature, something other than nature intended, or something other than that which God intended should occur in nature. The obvious implications of human physiology and the potential for procreation have traditionally been taken as suggesting a certain appropriateness about hetero-sexual behaviour. Spong, however, appears in his message to confuse the concept of what is natural – occurs in nature – with the concept of 'what is right'. Common sense tells us that much that occurs in nature is good, and much that occurs in nature is not so good. We do not take our morality from the way foxes are inclined to treat chickens.

- Spong makes much of the fact that in 1973 'the American Psychiatric Association removed homosexuality from its list of mental illnesses'. Now, quite apart from the inevitability of this decision in the cultural climate of America in the 1970s, homo-sexuality does not meet (and never has met) the medical criteria necessary to be designated a disease. Indeed, the Bible never uses disease terminology when referring to homosexuality. Medically it is correct to categorise homosexual behaviour as simply that, a behaviour. The issue of its rightness or wrongness is a separate matter.

- Spong asserts that today 'the debate centers on such things as the role of the hypothalamus, the level of the male hormone testos-terone in the pregnant female, the work of the Y chromosome in sexual development, neuro-chemical realities and other newly discovered physiological facts in the studies of brain formation and function'. Here it is not clear which debate he is talking about. Is he referring to the debate about whether there are anatomical and physiological items in an individual that correlate with homosexual behaviour, or to the debate over whether homosexual behaviour is right or wrong? Certainly there is some scientific research today which is looking at the phenomena Spong lists to see if there is a correlation between any of them and the presence of homosexual behaviour. However, no clear conclusions have yet come out of this work. But science is not even looking at the issue of whether homosexual behaviour is right or wrong. That is not a question science could ever answer.

- Spong says that it is now 'generally accepted' that the number of homosexual people remains constant in every generation and society. In fact, this is not generally accepted and current research findings are at variance with the results of research by Kinsey in the 1940s. It is curious that in his 'White Paper' Spong goes out of his way to suggest that research in this area supports his side of the argument, since the latest research findings are *not* helpful to him.

Carey's reply to Spong

On 24 November 1997 the Archbishop of Canterbury replied to Bishop Spong as follows:

> I acknowledge receipt of your letter addressed to Primates of the Anglican Communion and I am also copying this brief reply to them.
>
> I am saddened by the hectoring and intemperate tone of your Statement which appears to leave little room for the dialogue you demand. You claim the high ground of science and reason; you argue that the view of those who disagree is 'tired and threadbare' and their leadership lacks integrity. Furthermore, you attack personally those of us who disagree with your opinion and in doing so you distort the theologies and reasons why we are led to

conclude that there is no justification for sexual expression outside marriage.

I would invite you, Bishop, to reread my Christmas Letter in which I express my hope that bishops coming to Lambeth will come to 'give' and 'receive'. I assure you that there will be open and honest debate on all issues that concern our Communion. I expect that to characterise the discussion on the issue of homosexuality. I understand that you feel passionately about this and that you have the support of a significant number of bishops. However I would ask you in turn to recognise that a very large number of bishops from all over the world disagree with you with equal passion. You seem to be under the impression that the Kuala Lumpur Statement is the work of South Asian bishops.

This is not the case. It was agreed by a conference of some eighty participants representing the majority of Anglican provinces in the southern hemisphere. The most recent Dallas statement, which expresses similar sentiments on sexuality, also drew bishops from many parts of the world. I draw your attention to these facts because I want to be sure that everyone fully realises the divide potential of this, not just for the Communion, but for people more generally. If bishops come to Lambeth wanting a showdown on this issue, I am quite clear that there will follow a very negative and destructive conflict which will put even further back the cause of the people you represent. I have no wish to lay further burdens on any groups, but the tone of your paper, ironically, risks creating such a situation. If we each come to listen to others in the spirit of our Lord whom we all try to serve, then we shall all benefit from our common discussion.

I hope that the bishops will ask me to set up an International Commission to consider these issues. The Conference will be less inclined to do so, however, if you, or, indeed, others on the opposite side of the argument, intend to split the Conference open on this matter. Do come in peace, do come to learn, come to share – and leave behind any campaigning tactics which are so inappropriate and unproductive, whoever employs them. I urge you to come in a constructive spirit.

Spong's response

Two days later, on 26 November 1997, Bishop Spong replied to the Archbishop of Canterbury:

> Thank you for your letter received by facsimile and dated November 24th. Your response was quite helpful in that it illustrated more clearly than I could ever have hoped the nature of the problem faced by this Communion.
>
> You characterized my statement as 'intemperate' and as 'leaving little room for dialogue'. Yet I do not recall your issuing any criticism, much less similar harsh words, about the Kuala Lumpur Statement, the Dallas Statement, or the Statement by the Archbishop of the Southern Cone. Those statements made assertions about gay and lesbian people that were not just intemperate, but offensive, rude and hostile. Those statements went so far as to threaten schism if their point of view did not prevail or to break off communion with provinces of our Communion who disagreed with them. You do not appear to have suggested that they left 'little room for dialogue'. These statements also threatened to withdraw financial support from the work of the Church unless the Church's leadership endorses their point of view. That strikes me as a form of ecclesiastical blackmail. By your silence in the face of these affronts, you reveal quite clearly where your own convictions lie. That makes it quite difficult to have confidence in your willingness to handle this debate in an even-handed way. Gay and lesbian Christians are at great risk if these attitudes prevail at Lambeth.
>
> You suggest that the problem for our Communion lies in the fact that there are deep divisions among the bishops on the subject of homosexuality. May I respectfully disagree. We have had deep divisions before over important issues like slavery, segregation, apartheid and the full humanity of women and their right to pursue equality in both Church and society. The Church can live with divisions. The issue is not that these divisions exist, but who is right. Church unity is important to me, but it is not an ultimate value. Truth and justice are. A Church unified in racism, chauvinism or homophobia cannot be the Body of Christ. Our

task as God's Church is to discern truth and to proclaim justice, and if that disturbs the unity of the Church, then so be it. In our effort to discover truth, however, we cannot close our minds or ignore new insights that challenge even the literal truth we quote from holy Scripture. I am aware, as I am certain you are, that church people have used biblical quotations, as well as what you have called 'theologies and reasons' for centuries to justify attitudes that today are universally rejected.

Why do we not recognize that quoting an ancient text to try to solve a complex moral or scientific issue is as irrelevant today as it was when the book of Joshua was quoted to condemn the discoveries of Galileo? I am amazed that this is not clear. It certainly is to so many in the secular world who have rejected the Church as no longer viable for their lives.

How many more moral debates will we have to undergo in the Christian Church before people recognize that the literal Bible was wrong on the seven day creation story, wrong on epilepsy being demon possession, wrong on sickness resulting from sin, wrong on the sun rotating around the earth, wrong on slavery, wrong on defining women as inferior people, and is now wrong on the origins, causes and meaning of homosexuality? How many irrelevant rear guard battles must we Christians lose before we give up this tactic? How much longer will we pretend that this is about divisions in the Church?

Perhaps we need to remind ourselves that Anglicanism has never identified the word of God with the literal words of Scripture. The living word of God for us is rather found underneath the literal words of Scripture and in the person of Christ, whom we have called traditionally the 'Word of God Incarnate'. In the living word of God we hear it proclaimed that all persons are created in God's image, loved by God through Jesus Christ and called to the fullness of life inside God's Holy Spirit. Our task as Christian ethicists today is to apply that 'Living Word' to the complex moral issues of our day with minds informed by knowledge developed in the secular and scientific world. We cannot stop the world because it no longer affirms our prejudices. If we are uninformed by available scientific data, we have no business trying to prescribe for the lives of millions of people.

Finally, you seem to assume that my intention is to seek to impose a solution to this issue upon our Communion. Perhaps if you would reread my statement, you would discover that is absolutely not what I said or what I intend. I speak today as I do only because of the silence of leaders like yourself in the face of the abuse present in the public statements of the Southern Hemisphere bishops, the Archbishop of the Southern Cone and the Dallas signatories who do seek to impose their solution on the Church. They are the ones threatening the Church. I seek, and will continue to do so in the future, to stand between the gay and lesbian Christians I am privileged to serve and the negativity and abuse of one more insensitive statement issued on this subject by those who, while quite sincere, are not well-informed. I do not want our Church to be embarrassed yet again because we are so slow in embracing new knowledge and new ways of perceiving reality. Your leadership in this endeavor is crucial.

I will come to Lambeth guided by the motto of my theological seminary, 'to seek the truth of God come whence it may, cost what it will'. I hope you and all the other bishops of this Church will do likewise.

Clearly Bishop Spong is in a mood to oppose the views of a very wide section of Anglican opinion across the world. The Archbishop's reply to his 'White Paper' has not persuaded him to change his tone: his anger appears to be intensifying. I assume that he sincerely regards himself as engaged in a fight on behalf of the gay and lesbian Christians whom, as he puts it, he is 'privileged to serve'.

However, the fact remains that if those holding views contrary to his are to be painted as ignorant and likened to people fighting a rearguard action against Galileo, Bishop Spong owes it to the accused to be specific about the science he is referring to and provide some support for its supposed incontrovertible nature. Before the theological significance of the science can be assessed, it would help to know what the science is. Obviously we are all to some extent selective in what we take into account in informing our respective world-views. What credible, established scientific evidence have the bishops who signed the Kuala Lumpur and other statements not taken into account?

Certainly, scientists are looking at chromosomes, brain anatomy and neurochemicals in their investigation of homosexual behaviour. But they have reached no clear conclusions regarding correlation – much less cause – between homosexual behaviour and any of these biological entities. Scientists also look closely at chromosomes, brains and chemicals in connection with cancer, diabetes and suicide, but – whatever relationships science discovers – that will not have any bearing on whether we think cancer, diabetes and suicide are good or bad, right or wrong.

Spong rests much of his argument on the alleged findings of science, even though he is vague about what these findings are. He is dismissive of the Bible, theology and Church tradition. To rest so much on science is curious, for what he seems to be saying is: 'It makes no sense to claim that homosexuality is wrong because homosexuality is determined by genetics or brain chemistry.'

This argument is countered by saying that there are many types of behaviour towards which we might be inclined by our genes or our brain chemistry which we would not want to say are morally acceptable. For example, inclination to rage, which can be destructive to others, or depression, which can be destructive to ourselves, both probably have a biochemical basis but we do not argue that either of them are good things. We believe that they are conditions which it is good somehow to overcome and in some cases to treat medically. The logical conclusion of Spong's argument seems to put homosexuality in the same category as other conditions which are regarded as a handicap and which may benefit from professional help. Presumably many homosexuals would not wish their behaviour and lifestyle to be seen in this way. If, however, this is not what Spong is saying it would be very helpful if he would tell us.

Even if Bishop Spong is well-intentioned in his desire to take up the cause of homosexual Christians, his attitude to them and the categories into which the logic of his arguments places them sound patronising. If his arguments are flawed, he may be guilty of increasing their unhappiness – a consequence which few can believe he wishes.

Both in his original message to the Anglican Communion (his 'White Paper') and in his response to the Archbishop's reply to this, he accuses the signatories of the Kuala Lumpur statement, and indeed all who support the line on homosexuality which the Church has traditionally taken, of buttressing 'their attitude with appeals to a literal understanding of the Bible'. Actually, however, there is little or no indication in the Kuala Lumpur or similar statements that the authors are biblical literalists in the pejorative sense intended by Bishop Spong, or that they have an understanding of Scripture outside the range comprehended by Anglicanism. What does Spong mean when he accuses his opponents in the sexuality debate of taking the Bible literally? We are not discussing the edibility of Jonah or even the reference to a star stopping above the birthplace of Jesus. We are not talking about the use of isolated verses out of context to establish an argument. We are talking about the major biblical themes of the creation of males and females and their need for mutual companionship, the institution of marriage, the procreation of children and the value of the family.

A response to Spong from South Africa

An indication of how Spong's 'White Paper' was received in the southern hemisphere, and confirmation that bishops who do not share Spong's views are not mindless 'biblical literalists', came on 9 December 1997. On that date the Rt Rev. John Lee, Bishop of Christ the King in the Church of the Province of Southern Africa, writing from Sharpeville, addressed an open letter to Bishop Spong. Bishop Lee wrote: 'You may not realise how offensive your papers will be to a wide circle of Christian leadership outside your own setting in the "First World"; many of your episcopal colleagues had hoped that we would not be meeting this kind of attitude at the Lambeth Conference.'

Referring to Spong's categorisation of anyone who disagrees with his viewpoint as 'ignorant', 'out of touch with the knowledge revolution', and 'uninformed', Bishop Lee asks Spong, 'Have you any idea how that sounds outside the so-called "west"? Is there not some inconsistency in claiming to oppose racism, and then holding in contempt much of the Christian opinion of the southern hemisphere? You will inevitably be heard in the Two-Thirds World as patronising and racist.'

Lee tells Spong:

> I sit on the theological commission of the CPSA where we have
> spent many hours weighing the exegetical and theological com-
> plexities and the widely varying scientific and psychological
> understandings of homosexuality; we have also received
> testimony from homosexual clergy and lay people, and tried to
> engage the people of our Church in a serious and sensitive debate.
> We do not yet agree, but our debate is not uninformed.

Bishop Lee says that in his experience bishops in Africa, Asia, India,
Pakistan, the West Indies, South America, Australia and New
Zealand are also informed in these areas; they have read the
literature, listened to the debates, and formed careful theological
and pastoral views which defy Spong's characterisation of them as
unread and theologically incompetent.

'In fact,' Lee tells Spong, 'there is also no consensus in the
homosexual community, either on some of the issues on which you
claim to be so clear, or on what that community is asking of the
Church. If that could be clarified, we would be better able to find
our way towards understanding.' Bishop Lee recalls that he and his
colleagues have enjoyed 'rich and deep relationships with
individuals, parishes and dioceses all over' the American Church:

> We have received American generosity but have worked at
> creating relationships of mutuality and non-dependency. Many
> of our American friends have been sensitive to the feeling that
> their part of our Church has thrown its weight about in the past,
> not least at previous Lambeth conferences. They have worked
> hard to overcome these perceptions and ensure that they are not
> reinforced in the future.

Acknowledging that there are those in the Episcopal Church who
want to approach Lambeth with sensitivity and due humility, he
goes on to remind Spong that ECUSA is 'a relatively small church
with a top-heavy leadership which translates into a disproportionate
presence at Lambeth. That would not matter if the role of the
majority Churches is recognised and the Episcopal representation

behaves with the sensitivity we have come to expect of its bishops.'
Lee goes on:

> By contrast, your correspondence suggests that a few of you may
> be coming with an attitude of superiority and a will to dominate.
> Please let us not go that way, for it will surely set you against the
> greater part of the Communion and make it harder for your
> serious concerns to be heard . . .
>
> I have no further place in this process but to appeal to you and
> your 'Liberal' colleagues (I use quote marks because the appel-
> lation calls for debate) to meet with theological conservatives in
> the Episcopal Church and talk to each other seriously. It would
> be good to do this now, with an eye to the good of the Church at
> large, before you export your crisis to the rest of us. You can
> hardly call for 'room for dialogue' if there is no such room in
> your own jurisdiction.
>
> It would be hugely helpful if you could clear the ground and
> rebuild some bridges among yourselves before Lambeth begins.
> Surely we need a wider process too, but there does seem to be an
> immediate urgency at home in the US, which weighs heavily on
> the hearts of those who love you.

Can Lambeth make progress?

The story of Anglican Evangelicals, as would the story of any strand
within the Christian Church, demonstrates that people form their
beliefs in community. Bishop Spong allies himself with a particular
community, and tends to believe what they believe. No doubt the
Kuala Lumpur bishops tend to do likewise. In order for progress to
be made at the Lambeth Conference, Spong and the other bishops
ought first to prepare themselves for their meeting with much prayer.
Then they will need to to try to accept each other as members of the
same community. They will need to listen to the voice of God. They
will need to listen carefully to the deep reservations they have about
each other's positions.

They do not need me, or anyone else, to tell them that this will
require patience and self-sacrifice on all sides. One Liberal Christian

who broadly supports Spong's position admitted to me that the tone of Spong's 'White Paper' seemed calculated to raise hackles and impede the development of the atmosphere necessary if any progress is to be made at Lambeth. The same Liberal Christian granted that Carey's statement seemed to him to be an attempt to pour balm on a troubled situation, and that (especially given the Archbishiop's own stated view) he came across as more graciously disposed to the other side than did Spong.

The English Professor of Philosophy, Roger Scruton, has suggested that, in the politically correct atmosphere of America today, Liberalism has become an intolerant creed, which regards dissent as the voice of oppression and covers it with ridicule. He argues that traditional sexual morality was centred on marriage, conceived as the lifelong union of man and woman, from whom a family would grow. All other sexual activity was regarded with disfavour. Of course, it has always been recognised that some adults would misbehave, but the main goal of sexual conduct – marriage and family – was never seriously doubted. A large part of sexual morality consisted in the strictures required if young people were to make successful marriages.

Until encountering Liberals, Western societies endorsed the idea of normal sexual desire; they endorsed the distinction between normal and perverted conduct; and they regarded marriage as the difficult but necessary consummation of our sexual endeavours, to be enshrined in a vow of unending commitment. Then Liberals came on the scene:

> The vow became a contract between "consenting adults", who wrote the terms according to their own requirements. Children lost their special place in the sexual project and became by-products, to be avoided if possible until their cost could be met. Easy divorce, legalised abortion, and a growing acceptance of cohabitation without commitment effectively wrote the next generation out of the script.

Scruton fears we are bringing up children to regard sex as a commodity, and their sexual partners as interchangeable means to pleasure, rather than as objects of love and commitment. He believes that if we reject the Liberal conception of sex we must also reject the easy equation of homosexual and heterosexual intercourse.

Sexual possession is also a moral awakening, and a peculiar sense of responsibility comes from recognising that you have awakened feelings which could never be yours. The heterosexual therefore makes himself more vulnerable in the sexual act, and is in consequence more a suitor for love and understanding than the homosexual. Sex for him is a foreign country, which he enters safely only with a trusted guide.[6]

Many Evangelicals hold their position in the homosexuality debate with great certainty. They do not give the impression that their thinking is ever troubled by doubt and some are accused of expressing their views in strident tones. On this issue, Bishop Spong sounds equally certain that he is right to state in uncompromising terms his conviction that 'modern insights' have discredited the traditional Christian position on human sexuality.

Anglican Evangelicals will surely wish to pray that Dr Carey and the bishops are given humility and wisdom at Lambeth '98 as they handle an issue which has set the Church on fire in the wrong sense.

PART EIGHT

Gospel people for the twenty-first century?

Bend us, O Lord,
where we are hard and cold,
in Your refiner's fire;
come purify the gold:
though suffering comes,
and evil crouches near, still our Living God
is reigning, He is reigning here.
(Graham Kendrick)

WHAT ANGLICAN EVANGELICALS HAVE ACHIEVED

Archbishop George Carey told the 1995 Anglican Evangelical Assembly that he had recently read Canon Charles Smythe's comments on the first fifty years of the Evangelical revival: 'Within the incredibly brief space of a half century, the Evangelicals, although a minority, converted the Church of England to foreign missions, effected the abolition of the slave trade and of slavery, initiated factory legislation and humanitarian reform, healing the worst sores of the industrial revolution. Has any Church in Christendom accomplished so much in so short a time?'

Over a longer period too, I believe that the achievement of the men and women whose story I have told has been remarkable. Wycliffe and the Lollards protested against corruption in the late-medieval Church of Rome, which few Catholic historians today would deny. They sought to persuade their contemporaries that the Bible was the eternal 'exemplar' of Christianity and that inward religion – faith and practice which touched the heart – was more important than mere formalism. Christ was the author of salvation. Ordinary English people of all ages should have the opportunity to read the Scriptures in their own language. The work of translation begun by Wycliffe and his team of scholars was built on by Tyndale and Coverdale.

At a time of religious and political turmoil, when an English king had intensely personal reasons for wanting to rid himself of the Pope's jurisdiction, Cranmer ensured that the Church in England would worship God in a language, and using a liturgy, which was homely and biblical. Cranmer's latest major biographer, Diarmaid MacCulloch, believes that the word 'Evangelical' usefully describes the main ideas of the English reformers in Tudor England. Anglicans would address God using prayers in their own tongue which combined all that was best in the monastic tradition with phrases and images from the Scriptures. Having no doubt that God was good for

419

them, Parliament passed laws which required English people to attend church and approved Articles of Religion which had been drafted by men who were sympathetic to reformed and Evangelical ideas but which were crafted in an ingenious way, ensuring support from those with more Catholic inclinations for centuries to come.

Queen Elizabeth's Archbishop, Matthew Parker, exercised a wise, scholarly and tolerant leadership of the young Church of England, identifying himself with moderate reformers while preserving some links with the past. Two Devonians, John Jewel and Richard Hooker, thought deeply and prayerfully about what Anglicanism was all about, steering a course which distanced their Church from Roman Catholicism and Puritanism. In particular, Hooker (many of whose ideas remain popular with Evangelicals) well understood that in church life some form of authority has to be recognised and wrote down his thoughts on the relative roles of Scripture, reason, tradition and experience. It may be that the Hooker strand of Anglicanism has something to offer to the wider Evangelical movement – a confidence that the God who inspired the Scriptures is the same God who created the world and built his order.

Early in the seventeenth century, the Puritan President of an Oxford College persuaded a somewhat reluctant Bishop of London and a rather more enthusiastic King James I that there should be a new translation of the Bible which would be the sole one used in the Church of England. The resulting 'Authorised Version' achieved an immense popularity among Anglicans of all shades of churchmanship and with Evangelicals in all Christian denominations for about three hundred and fifty years, until it was eclipsed by a barrage of new translations in the second half of the twentieth century.

Later in the seventeenth century, Richard Baxter set the town of Kidderminster on fire with his energetic preaching of the gospel and infectious holiness. His writings set high standards of behaviour and commitment for generations of Christian ministers inside and outside the Church of England, even if some fellow Evangelicals then and more recently have thought him unsound in his teachings on justification.

In the eighteenth century the Wesleys and Whitefield sparked a religious revival which went way beyond the Church of England, although they themselves never left the denomination in which they had been reared and taught the things of God. Evangelicals working as Anglican clergymen who were caught up in this new movement of the Holy Spirit began to think of themselves in a new sense as members of an Evangelical 'party', but, more importantly, still worked within the Church of England as successful evangelists, pastors of their flocks and unselfconscious examples of holiness. In his hymns, Charles Wesley expressed the thinking and spirit of the revival in memorable verse, which was exuberant in the praise of God and his grace as well as understanding the nature of the response required in the lives of believers. His hymns are sung today throughout Anglicanism and Methodism and in many parts of the Christian world.

Newton and Cowper also wrote hymns which retain their popularity, and Scott created a Bible commentary which was to influence the early thinking of John Henry Newman. Selina, Countess of Huntingdon, devoted her life, fortune and formidable personality to ensuring that the Evangelical message was proclaimed from Anglican pulpits in many parts of England.

George Whitefield took the revival across the Atlantic to a new world which already had a good deal of religion. Devereux Jarratt earnestly and enthusiastically worked as an Evangelical priest within the Church of England in the colony of Virginia, preaching the gospel not only in his own parish but in almost thirty counties in Virginia and what is now the State of North Carolina. By the time the colonies achieved their independence, the gospel was also being preached in Jarratt's America by Methodists and Baptists – turning a convinced churchman into a sad and rather bitter old man.

Evangelical Christianity, however, sprang to life again in the newly formed American Episcopal Church (ECUSA), achieving something of a golden age in the middle years of the nineteenth century in New York, Kentucky, Philadelphia, New England, Ohio and Illinois as well as Virginia. In the 1840s and 1850s Evangelicals made up almost half of the American House of Bishops and approximately one-third of the clergy. Under the influence of an Evangelical chaplain (who later became a bishop), a revival broke out in the West Point Military Academy. Evangelical theological colleges were founded to train people for service in ECUSA, and powerful and effective preachers – some of whom were also attractive and colourful personalities – drew large congregations into America's Anglican churches.

Back in England, Charles Simeon gradually won the respect of both the town and University of Cambridge as Vicar of Holy Trinity for fifty-three years and supporter of many Evangelical causes. Lord Macaulay believed that Simeon's influence in the Church of England was greater than that of any Archbishop.

The members of the Clapham Sect devoted their wealth, time and energy to support many aspects of the Lord's work and a variety of needy causes. William Wilberforce, assisted by members of the sect, worked hard and patiently for nineteen years to bring about the abolition of the slave trade, and finally of slavery itself throughout the British Empire.

The Church Mission Society, founded by English Anglican Evangelicals in 1799, undertook pioneering missionary work in many parts of the world and in the 1990s is still at work in some thirty countries.

Members of the Clapham Sect were also intimately involved with the foundation of the British and Foreign Bible Society in 1804 and most of the early office holders were Anglican Evangelicals, even though they believed that the provision of Bibles for the world was a cause in which churchmen and nonconformists should work together.

Not all English Evangelical clergy in the nineteenth century were quite as successful as Daniel Wilson, who at his first Confirmation service as Vicar of Islington presented 780 candidates to his bishop! Most, however, worked long hours organising prayer meetings, preparing sermons and preaching the gospel, running Sunday schools and visiting their parishioners. Wilson himself went on to become Bishop of Calcutta in 1832, encouraging every clergyman in India to be a missionary, spending half days in prayer, reading the Bible right through every year, supervising the building of Calcutta's cathedral, and making Christ the theme of every sermon he preached.

The seventh Earl of Shaftesbury, who described himself as an Evangelical of the Evangelicals, became the most eminent social reformer of the nineteenth century, working tirelessly to improve the conditions of adults and children in factories, mines and homes, reforming the care of the mentally ill, and providing homes and schools for working people in London. He influenced the appointment of bishops from across the church spectrum, including seven Evangelicals. One Evangelical, John Bird Sumner, became Archbishop of Canterbury in 1848.

A group of Evangelical laymen from Islington founded the Church Pastoral Aid Society in 1836, with Shaftesbury as their first President and W. E. Gladstone as a member of their committee. CPAS remains the Church of England's major home mission agency, providing resources for parishes, encouraging and supporting work amongst young people, and administering the patronage of hundreds of churches.

Across the Atlantic, by the end of the nineteenth century all the Evangelicals in ECUSA had either joined the Reformed Episcopal Church or become Liberals. For the first sixty years of the twentieth century there were no Evangelicals in the traditional sense within the Episcopal Church. But from the 1960s a new wave of Evangelical enthusiasm, partly associated with Charismatic renewal, made its way into the Church. Following the initiative of a group of Evangelical clergy in 1974, and inspired by Alf Stanway's faith, an Evangelical theological college to train men and women for service in the Episcopal Church opened in 1976, now located and flourishing in Ambridge, Pennsylvania. By the mid-1990s, in the midst of an overwhelmingly 'Liberal' or 'revisionist' ECUSA, no diocese was without at least some lively orthodox congregations of various types. In some dioceses they predominated. This increasingly aware network of biblically informed, orthodox, often Charismatic people (with either Evangelical or Catholic inclinations) became increasingly frustrated by the path which a majority of their national Church leaders were apparently taking away from the historic Christian faith.

Under the banner of the American Anglican Congress (AAC), and its document 'A Place to Stand', this group of orthodox Episcopalians now find themselves in the position of inviting all members of ECUSA who acknowledge what they see as a classical Anglican perspective to join with them for mutual protection and in the task of mission and ministry.

In England in the twentieth century, Evangelicals in the Anglican Church have been strong but not always united. Books by John Stott,

Jim Packer, Michael Green, David Watson and, more recently Alister McGrath, came to be widely read by Christians from all denominations. All these men, and others like them, preached, conducted missions and lectured in many parts of the world. Their speaking and their writing encouraged young people to believe that Evangelicalism could hold its own in academic circles and that the Christian faith itself was something worth proclaiming and defending. Several generations of young people brought up in churches in the All Souls mould and studying at the feet of Evangelical teachers were inspired to live sacrificial lives in the service of Jesus, and in the power of the Spirit, at home or on the mission field.

The appointment of Donald Coggan as Archbishop of Canterbury in 1974 was a further encouragement for Evangelicals, and by the 1990s over half of all ordinands for the Church of England trained in Evangelical colleges, compared with rather less than 30 per cent in 'middle-of-the-road' colleges and less that 20 percent in Anglo-Catholic colleges (though by this time, individual and corporate holders of such labels had become less easy to categorise).

George Carey, who had found Christ in an Anglican Evangelical church in the early 1950s, on his appointment as Archbishop of Canterbury in 1991 spoke warmly of his debt to Evangelicalism and of its strengths as a 'heart religion' delighting in a love relationship with a personal Lord. He has also spoken of what he has learned from the Catholic, Charismatic and Liberal strands within the Church and how his own spirituality has been enriched by all three traditions in addition to the one through which he became a Christian.

The history of Anglican Evangelicalism constitutes a rich and inspiring heritage. But the story produces its healthiest effects when it is told and heard in a wider context. Just as we are enriched when we reflect on the lives and achievements of a succession of men and women from Wycliffe to Wilberforce and from Shaftesbury to Stott, so it is enriching to have our understanding broadened by the insights of William Law, Herbert Ferrar, George Herbert, Jeremy Taylor, John Henry Hobart, Phillips Brooks, James Barr and Michael Ramsey. Anglican Evangelicals are strong when they treasure the memory of their antecedents, but weak when they idolise them.

ANGLICAN EVANGELICALISM'S STRENGTHS . . .

Anglican Evangelicals have been attractive when they have been *devoted to Christ*. Max Warren pointed out that, from the 1850s, Evangelicals were often thrown on the defensive, developing an 'anti' complex: anti-Rome, anti-ritual, anti-biblical criticism, anti-Darwin, anti-worldliness. To a degree this promoted unity, for there are few things which so unite as opposition to a common foe. Warren also pointed out, however, that a much healthier unity was to be found in devotion to Christ.

They have also been attractive (as George Carey has reminded us) when they have followed a *religion of the heart*. From the start of the story told in this book, this was one of Wycliffe's greatest themes. Both he and the Lollards insisted that inward religion – faith and practice which touches the heart – was more important than mere formalism. Richard Baxter, like George Herbert, told preachers that their every word must be 'heart deep'.

Anglican Evangelicals have been even more attractive when they have combined this heart religion with a *readiness to think*. Well before James Barr, Mark Noll and Os Guinness rebuked Evangelicals for failing to use their minds, John Stott had argued vigorously that the great doctrines of creation, redemption and judgment all implied that we have an inescapable duty to think and act upon what we think and know: otherwise 'keen but clueless' Christians would multiply.[1]

Anglican Evangelicals have been attractive when they have *achieved a balance between 'orthodoxy' and 'fire'*. Peter Moore, the present Dean of the Trinity Episcopal School for Ministry in Ambridge, Pennsylvania, put this well when he spoke of adoring God 'with minds as well as hearts, and hearts as well as minds. This requires the kind of discipline possible only in a worshipping community where scholarship is consciously cultivated in submission to the Word of God, and where people are lovingly held accountable to one another.'

Bishop Charles McIlvaine had a point when, in 1836, he told the diocese of Ohio that if they were to 'promote the spirit of vital godliness in the world', they must do so 'by means of that only body

– the Church'. 'You may as well expect your minds to be in health while your bodies are diseased, as that the spirit of religion will flourish, while the body of religion, the visible Church is disordered,' he said.

In his *Apology for authorised and set Forms of Liturgy* (1646), Jeremy Taylor wrote thus of the Church of England:

> To the churches of the Roman communion we can say that ours is reformed; to the reformed churches we can say that ours is orderly and decent: for we were freed from the impositions and lasting errors of a tyrannical spirit, and yet from the extravagances of a popular spirit too: our reformation was done without tumult, and yet we saw it necessary to reform; we were zealous to cast away the old errors, but our zeal was balanced with consideration and the results of authority.[2]

This emphasis on the value of some order, authority and accountability in the Church is important at a time when there are said to be something like twenty-five thousand Christian sects and denominations worldwide. This is bound to be seen by many outside the Church as scandalous.

Anglican Evangelicals have been strong when they have *preached the gospel at home and abroad*. Examples have abounded, with Wesley riding 250,000 miles throughout Britain, defying opposition to preach over 40,000 sermons; or William Grimshaw mounting his horse to preach in barns and in the open moorland air in the north of England; or the nineteenth-century Evangelical Episcopalian Gregory Townsend Bedell, whom the residents of (and visitors to) Philadelphia crowded to hear; or the famous missionary Henry Martyn devoting his all-too-short life to taking the gospel to India; or, in this century, John Stott, David Watson and Michael Green leading missions all over the world.

Jim Packer has pointed out that ever since the Ordinal and the Prayer Book required clergy to catechise children, Anglicanism has been evangelistic, though the form of the evangelism has not always been that of the 'travelling big tent'. The evangelism has often been institutional and settled, part of the regular work of the parish clergy and the community around them.

Gospel people for the twenty-first century?

Anglican Evangelicals have been strong when they have *treated the Bible with the utmost seriousness*. This is another aspect of the heritage which goes back to Wycliffe's time. Many Anglicans agree with Evangelicals that Scripture is, under God, our foremost authority. The Bible is crucial. Apart from anything else, without the Scriptures we should have virtually no knowledge of the unfolding story of God's plan of salvation and the life, death and resurrection of Jesus. For centuries, on every continent, the Bible has touched hearts, illuminated minds and bent wills. Uniquely it has spoken to men and women whatever their race, language, intellectual ability and need.

Many Evangelicals recognise that the same Holy Spirit who inspired the authors of the Bible has also guided the Church through the centuries in forming its traditions. This tradition is not just a dead inheritance from the past: it is a living reality in the Church today (though not infallible). Furthermore, we use our minds to understand the Bible and tradition, and we have experience to guide us. It is unlikely that we would believe in God if we were without any experience of his presence.

Anglican Evangelicals have been strong when the *pursuit of holiness has been a part of their story*. John Wesley's first objective was to 'spread Scriptural holiness throughout the land'; unbelieving French author Voltaire, when challenged to name a character as beautiful as that of our Lord, pointed to his fellow countryman Fletcher of Madeley. A trend in recent years to neglect personal holiness has surprised Jim Packer, since Scripture insists strongly that Christians are called to holiness, that God is pleased with holiness and outraged by unholiness, and that without holiness no one will see the Lord (Heb. 12:14).

Anglican Evangelicals have been attractive when they have *demonstrated the love of Christ in compassion to others*. Thomas Scott abandoned his Unitarianism, not immediately on hearing John Newton's reasoned arguments, but when the older man visited dying members of his parish. Lord Shaftesbury made up his mind to 'found a policy upon the Bible, in public life observing the strictest justice, and not only cold justice, but active benevolence'. In the twentieth century, a young Anglican member of the staff of the Evangelical Alliance was given the job of co-ordinating the Alliance's then small

427

overseas relief fund. George Hoffman set to work with determination, prayer and vision. In little more than a decade, Tear Fund became one of Britain's major charities.[3]

John Stott acknowledges an increasing recognition in his own thinking of the Christian's social responsibility, and is concerned to bring evangelism and social responsibility together under the rubric of mission.

Anglican Evangelicals have been strong when they have *taken pains*. Again, this is a feature of the heritage which goes back to Wycliffe, the Balliol philosopher who combined a gift for popular preaching with the highest level of scholarship – using abilities which his country had recognised when it entrusted him with detailed international diplomacy. Think of the pains Cranmer took in pouring over Henry VIII's theological treatises, drafting the *Book of Common Prayer* and preparing Church of England homilies. Remember Wilberforce in his patient fight over many years to abolish the slave trade, or Shaftesbury, always determined to see everything for himself, taking nothing on trust or hearsay, so that he could speak of things needing reform from his own experience. None of these men was inclined to offer instant solutions to complex problems.

. . . AND WEAKNESSES

Anglican Evangelicals have been at their least attractive when they have acted in ways which have given credence to the sort of criticism made by Martyn Percy that they have *abandoned pilgrimage and challenge in favour of a solidified tradition* – approaching theological issues from a narrow perspective which produces nothing new and conducting a dialogue with no one but themselves.

Anglican Evangelicals need to accept that they are as culturally conditioned as Liberals, Catholics or Charismatics. They need to be aware of the criticism that they often operate in a 'tight interpretative community' which places boundaries on their exploration of Scripture and colours their perception of the wider Church. They need to listen, discuss and develop, to take the risk that in listening to someone of a different view, even a Liberal view, their own views may change or be modified.

Anglican Evangelicals are weak when they *expect theology to be logically neat and tied up*, or when they are *uncomfortable with fuzzy edges or partial answers*. They must allow room for what Tom Wright calls 'the Scriptural basis for residual untidiness'. Anglican Evangelicalism is unattractive when it assumes that to engage in new approaches to literary criticism and biblical interpretation is to sell out to the old enemy 'Liberalism'. Anglican Evangelicals on both sides of the Atlantic will be weak if they repudiate the spirit of Keele and Nottingham and form a group of churches whose walls become rigid and whose contribution to the mission to the modern world is irrelevant. Evangelicals need to be self-critical, in order to earn the authority to criticise the wider Church. They must always be ready to listen, not just to their own community, but also to the wider community of the Church and to the Church in history.

Anglican Evangelicals are weak when they *make ill-thought-out claims about the Scriptures*. John Stott has warned that 'to say "the Bible is the Word of God" is true, but it is only a half-truth, even a dangerous half-truth. For the Bible is also a human word and witness'. He argues that this is the account the Bible itself gives of its origins (e.g. 2 Pet. 1:21, 'men spoke from God'). God spoke and men spoke. Both statements are true, and neither contradicts the other. Stott cautions against speaking only of the divine origin of Scripture and forgetting that it was also written by human authors. This, he says, is the 'heresy of fundamentalism'.

Moreover, whatever view of the Bible they take, Anglican Evangelicals should remember that if they are to be obedient to the Bible they cannot make the book itself the focus of their attention. It points away from itself. The centre of attention can never be merely the Bible; it must always be Jesus of Nazareth, Messiah, Saviour and Lord.

Anglican Evangelicals have been unattractive when they have become *overcommitted to the idea of themselves as a party*. Just as when the term 'Liberal' becomes a party label, it usually turns out to be extremely illiberal, so Anglican Evangelicals get into difficulties when they grow too concerned to preserve the distinctiveness of their heritage. The notion of Evangelicals strongly identifying themselves with, and seeking to sustain, one particular wing of Anglicanism, or taking a partisan position as a guiding principle, is unhealthy.

Different strands within Anglicanism and Evangelicalism are often simply the result of differences in acquired information and opinion: people who have been born into particular families, attended certain schools and colleges, read particular books, heard a select group of preachers and moved in certain circles are said to believe particular things. But these 'beliefs' often owe more to the accident of background than the strength of genuine, informed conviction.

It certainly is possible to speak of a distinctive Evangelical heritage within Anglicanism, though beliefs have not been uniformly held. If you could arrange for a group of people drawn from All Souls, Langham Place, in London, and St Stephen's Church, Sewickley, Pennsylvania, to meet John Wycliffe and William Tyndale they would warm to much of what the two early reformers said; but the modern Anglican Evangelical group would probably be uncomfortable if the conversation wandered to the matter of justification by faith. Although Wycliffe rejected any concept of merit which implied that God rewarded a person's acts as if they were performed without the assistance of divine grace, he never applied his mind to an understanding of justification which resembled Luther's; and while Tyndale shared Luther's insistence on the authority of the Bible, in the course of his translation work he moved away from Luther's teaching on justification by faith alone.

One of the striking aspects of the story to emerge in this book is that if you could transport the group from the modern All Souls across the Atlantic and back through time to St George's Church, New York City, to arrive at any time during the rectorships of the Rev. Dr James Milnor (there from 1816 to 1845) or his successor Stephen Higginson Tyng (there from 1845 to 1879), they would feel very comfortable indeed (at least spiritually). And I suspect that a sermon from the current All Souls Rector, Richard Bewes, would have been well received at St George's throughout much of the nineteenth century.

Today, Anglican Evangelicals are not agreed on the ordination of women: a majority support it, despite opposition from Reform and

Gospel people for the twenty-first century?

Jim Packer's doubts. Stott and Packer have immense respect for one another, and no doubt enjoy warm fellowship when they meet, though Packer does not share Stott's inclination tentatively to believe in the final annihilation of the wicked rather than their eternal punishment. On issues of human sexuality there is a wide measure of agreement throughout the constituency, despite loud voices to the contrary.

Archbishop Carey, like John Stott, regards the traditional Evangelical tendency towards individualism as a weakness, although Stott has reminded us that it is a tendency which in some circumstances has been (and remains) a strength.

GOSPEL PEOPLE FOR A NEW MILLENNIUM

We saw in Part Five (page 307) how John Stott told the National Evangelical Anglican Congress in 1977 that Evangelicals were 'gospel people'. He told me that it is the rediscovery of the gospel in every generation or in every person which causes joy. Archbishop Carey believes that 'the desperate need remains for all people everywhere to hear the gospel and to know its life-changing power'. That, he says, is 'at the very heart of my ministry, my spirituality, my future'.[4]

If Anglican Evangelicals are to be gospel people in the twenty-first century, a number of questions need to be asked:

- What is the gospel?
- In what sense is it 'good news'?
- In what ways, if any, should the gospel's content differ from the message which Anglican Evangelicals have preached for much of their history?
- What attitude to contemporary culture should they adopt?

Stott also told the 1977 Congress that Evangelicals were 'Bible people' and it therefore seems right to begin to answer our questions from Scripture. The New Testament Greek word *euangelion* is translated in English Bibles as 'joyful tidings', 'good news' or 'gospel' (from the Old English word *godspel* which meant good news). Mark 1:15 gives us the first recorded words of Jesus in the years of his adult ministry: 'The time has come . . . The kingdom of God is near. Repent and believe the good news!'

The use of the words, 'The time has come' (or 'has been fulfilled') reminds us that the whole idea of the proclamation of good news has an Old Testament background, particularly in Isaiah chapters 40–66. Here Jerusalem's deliverance from bondage and a wider announcement of freedom for the oppressed is spoken of as 'good news'. It is a message of comfort (Isa. 40:1), peace and salvation brought by messengers (whose feet are beautiful) convinced that 'Your God reigns!' (Isa. 52:7). Paul quotes this passage in his letter to the Romans.

The first recorded words of the adult Jesus (Mark 1:15) not only remind us that he came as expected and promised, but also alerts us to the fact that the message of the coming kingdom has a stern and challenging element ('repent') as well as inviting a joyful, trusting response ('believe the good news'). Jesus often set out the content of his message in parables which he frequently prefaced with the words, 'The kingdom of heaven is like . . .' followed by a story. These stories, although told with vividness and warmth, contained the same blend of sternness and joy that we see in Mark 1:15. On the one hand there is the Father's loving offer of mercy and free forgiveness for the undeserving and outcasts (e.g. the parables of the lost son or the great banquet); and on the other hand there are stories with severe warnings, such as the ending to the parable of the unmerciful servant, who was turned over by his master to jailers to be tortured until he could pay back his debt. 'This', concludes Jesus, 'is how my heavenly Father will treat each of you unless you forgive your brother from your heart' (Matt. 18:35).

As Jesus went about proclaiming his message of good news, he issued a simple invitation which was itself a challenge, demanding a sacrificial response. The invitation was to 'follow him': Peter, Andrew, James and John responded instantly, gladly leaving their nets, their father (in the case of James and John) and their hired men behind them (Mark 1:16–20). Months later, Peter observed to Jesus, 'We have left everything to follow you!' In a perplexing reply Jesus said that the gospel made great demands but promised greater reward – mixed with persecution (Mark 10:29–31).

On a number of occasions, Jesus spelt out the nature of the response he was looking for, specifically telling his disciples and the people that the gospel (even though it was good news) demanded a commitment which might even mean loss of life:

> Then he called the crowd to him along with his disciples and said: 'If anyone would come after me, he must deny himself and take up his cross and follow me. For whoever wants to save his life will lose it, but whoever loses his life *for me and for the gospel* will save it. What good is it for a man to gain the whole world, yet forfeit his soul? Or what can a man give in exchange for his soul? If anyone is ashamed of me and my words in this adulterous and sinful generation, the Son of Man will be ashamed of him when he comes in his Father's glory with the holy angels' (Mark 8:34–38).

From these verses we see that the gospel (a) is closely interwoven with themes of cross and sacrifice; (b) is concerned with issues of vital importance, matters of life and death; and (c) paradoxically offers the prospect of the gain of personal identity (finding oneself) in this life and reward in the next for those prepared to take up the cross and live self-denying lives. The reference to an 'adulterous and sinful generation' reminds us that there were many features in the culture which Jesus was addressing which are also characteristic of our world today.

The cross shows us how seriously God takes sin, and that in his love he is prepared to forgive it. The word 'sin' is unfashionable in the secular world and even in some parts of the Anglican Church. For most of their history, Anglican Evangelicals have taken sin seriously, believing that they have good news to tell people even when speaking about this aspect of their lives.

Many hymn books today omit the second verse of Charles Wesley's hymn, 'Love Divine', which includes the lines:

> Take away the love of sinning,
> Alpha and Omega be;

433

End of faith as its beginning,
Set our hearts at liberty.

The omitted verse echoes of the theme of Romans 7 and 8 which speak of the 'glorious liberty' (Rom. 8:21 AV) experienced by those who struggle to conquer sin in the power of the Spirit.

The apostle Paul believed that Jesus had given him 'the task of testifying to the gospel of God's grace' (Acts 20:24). In his letters he reflected on the nature, content and power of the gospel. He told Christians in Rome that he had been 'set apart for the gospel of God' and that this was 'the gospel he promised beforehand through his prophets' (Rom. 1:1–4). Later in the same chapter, Paul tells us:

I am not ashamed of the gospel, because it is the power of God for the salvation of everyone who believes: first for the Jew, then for the Gentile. For in the gospel a righteousness from God is revealed, a righteousness that is by faith from first to last, just as it is written: 'The righteous will live by faith.' (Rom. 1:16–17)

Paul spoke of three secrets which gave the gospel power. The first was his message of the cross which was 'foolishness to those who are perishing, but to us who are being saved it is the power of God' (1 Cor. 1:18). The second secret was the Holy Spirit, and the third the conviction with which he spoke. 'Our gospel came to you', he told the Thessalonians, 'not simply with words, but also with power, with the Holy Spirit and with deep conviction' (1 Thess. 1:5).

Paul's words in all his letters reveal the same blend of kindness and severity which we saw in the words of Jesus. Indeed, he writes, 'Consider therefore the kindness and sternness of God' (Rom. 11:22). This sternness includes God's judgment as an integral part of his gospel message (Rom. 2:16).

Paul's understanding of salvation involves obedience: 'If you confess with your mouth, "Jesus is Lord," and believe in your heart that God raised him from the dead, you will be saved' (Rom. 10:9). In both Paul's and Peter's New Testament letters the themes of 'faith', 'obedience' and 'gospel' are inextricably linked (Rom. 1:5, 10:16 AV & NRSV; 16:25–7; 2 Cor. 9:13; 2 Thess. 1:8; 1 Pet. 4:17).

Gospel people for the twenty-first century?

In announcing the gospel of Jesus Christ as Lord, Paul challenged his listeners to submit in obedient faith to Christ as king. We recall Richard Baxter's emphasis that faith and obedience are not in opposition to one another (pages 88–9) and Jeremy Taylor's careful treatment of the nature of faith (pages 84–7).

If we speak of the gospel's challenge to obedience as an example of its severe side, we must add that God's intention is blessing, life and happiness. When Moses stood as an old man on the uplands of Moab and reminded the Israelites of the importance of loving God, walking in his ways and keeping his commands, he told them that the result would be that things would 'go well' with them (Deut. 4:40), with 'houses filled with all kinds of good things' (6:11), they would 'live and increase' and God would bless them (30:16). 'I delight in your commands because I love them,' said the Psalmist, 'they are the joy of my heart' (Ps. 119:47, 111). Thomas Wilson, Bishop of Sodor and Man for nearly sixty years from 1697 until his death in 1755, aged ninety-two, observed, 'The commands of God are all designed to make us more happy than we can possibly be without them.'

Although Paul described the gospel as 'treasure in jars of clay' (2 Cor. 4:7), he said it was important not to soften its demands in a world where the thinking of unbelievers was already distorted by the 'god of this age'. An honest presentation of the gospel would allow the God who said, 'Let light shine out of darkness,' to cause his light to shine 'in our hearts to give us the light of the knowledge of the glory of God in the face of Christ' (2 Cor. 4:2–6).

The source of all the blessings of the gospel is the grace of God; the purpose is that the followers of Jesus should lead holy lives (2 Tim. 1:8–9). Holiness is the substance of which happiness is the spin-off.

The gospel as story

Many Christians of all denominations have been pleased to discover that modern hymn books, including *Mission Praise*, still manage to find space within their covers for the well-loved hymn which begins:

Tell me the old, old story
Of unseen things above,
Of Jesus and his glory,
Of Jesus and his love.

'Story' is a fashionable term today in discussion both of evangelism and theology, along with words like 'narrative' and 'metanarrative'. Andrew Walker has usefully summarised the concept:

For there is a story, once widely known, that tells us who we are, where we came from, and where we are going. It is a story which was once the official ideology of many an emperor and government (although this in itself is no recommendation, and does not make the story legitimate in any way). More significantly, it is a story that was once celebrated in villages and towns throughout the western world, and gave meaning and hope to millions of ordinary men and women. This story is told by Christians and it is called the gospel. The gospel is good news of the kingdom of God which has been revealed to us by the birth, life, death and resurrection of Jesus of Nazareth.

In the modern world, this story is now either forgotten, half-remembered, distorted, fragmented, or misrepresented.[5]

The long-term 'Open Book' initiative, launched in 1997 by Churches Together in England and the Bible Society to stretch into the new millennium, takes as its starting point the thought that our society has been built on a story, the story of God's involvement and interaction with the whole of his creation.

For Andrew Walker, the Gospel and Culture movement, and 'Open Book', the gospel is the 'grand narrative' which Christians wish to recommend to the modern world as a story to live by. Setting out some suggestions as to how this might be done, Walker wrote in 1996: 'How would the British public react if the Archbishop of Cantebury spoke of national repentance with the imprimatur of a biblical "thus saith the Lord"? We can be certain that his remarks would not be understood as prophecy, but interpreted as idiocy.'[6] I believe that Dr Carey does speak from time to time with biblical authority (although such statements do not always receive media attention), and many people would welcome calls for repentance from national Church leaders.

ANGLICAN EVANGELICALS, THE GOSPEL AND JUSTIFICATION

The way we are to understand justification by faith is not an issue which is of interest only in the seminar rooms of theological colleges or in academic journals. How Anglican Evangelicals – and indeed all Christians – understand justification will affect the tone and emphasis of their gospel message, whether from the pulpit or in one-to-one conversation. One danger is that an unthinking presentation of 'justification by faith alone' can distort or soften the gospel's demanding note. The subject is important to Evangelicals, and many Evangelical organisations which have a 'statement of faith' make some reference to the doctrine in their list of fundamental beliefs.

Traditionally, justification has been thought of as the event or process by which men and women are made or declared to be righteous in the sight of God. If you read the New Testament in Latin you are likely to think of justification as something which *makes* you righteous, since the Latin verb *justificare* is derived from the words *justum facere*, 'to make righteous'. That indeed is what Augustine believed and his view established a tradition which remained unchallenged until the end of the Middle Ages. The sense of the original Hebrew term, however, tends to suggest that at justification God *declares* you to be righteous.

It is well known that during the Reformation there was great controversy about justification. The dispute concerned both the meaning of the term (what happened) and how you came to be justified (how it happened). Most Protestants came to believe that what happened at justification was that God declared you to be righteous (recovering the Hebrew sense) and distinguished the term from sanctification, by which you are 'made righteous'. As to how you were justified, both Luther and Calvin believed that justification was wholly an act of God and this emphasis was highlighted during the storms of the Reformation in phrases such as *sola fide* ('by faith alone') and *sola gratia* ('by grace alone').

Luther saw his view of justification as a theological breakthrough and it may be dated from 1514–15, when he came to a new understanding of the phrase 'the righteousness of God' in the apostle Paul's letter to the Romans (Rom. 1:17). He said that we are unable to respond to God without his grace, that we may be justified only through faith (*per solam fidem*) by the merits of Christ 'imputed' to us: works or religious observance are not relevant to our justification. Luther's understanding of justification has been widely accepted by Protestants and Evangelicals.

Thirty years after Luther made his discovery, the Roman Catholic Church, at the Council of Trent which began in 1545, attempted to agree on and then restate its position on a whole series of issues which had been disputed during the early years of the Reformation. In 1547 the Council addressed itself to justification and agreed a statement which stressed that in the process of justification God works a transformation within the believer. Trent defined the 'formal cause' of justification (which Protestants, following Luther, had seen as the 'imputed' righteousness of Christ) as the inherent or 'imparted' righteousness of Christ.

Although, as Alister McGrath has pointed out, the Council of Trent explicitly condemned the doctrine of justification by works, the Council also said that justification requires the believer's co-operation with God. More recently, the *Catechism of the Catholic Church*, published in 1994, specifically dismissed the idea that we are justified on the basis of works rather than the grace of God: 'Our justification comes from the grace of God. Grace is favour, the free and undeserved help that God gives us to respond to his call to become children of God, adoptive sons, partakers of the divine nature and of eternal life.'[7]

Despite the view taken in official Catholic documents from Trent to the present day, however, in practice there are different under-standings of justification held by Catholics and Evangelicals which still need to be explored. Although recent ecumenical discussions have suggested that many of these differences are to do with the use of words rather than points of substance, not everyone agrees that

Anglican and Roman Catholic theologians working in this area have resolved the issues.

The story told in this book helps us see how reflective people within and outside Evangelicalism have reacted to the doctrine of justification by faith alone. Critics of the doctrine have objected both to its scriptural basis and its practical effects in the lives of believers.

King Henry VIII, though a monster in some respects, took theology seriously and, as we saw in Part One, worked hard at it. He objected that the doctrine of justification by faith undermined the whole principle of human morality. By removing the value of good works, it endangered the peace of a godly commonwealth. Cranmer's argument that this fundamental worry was removed by a suitable doctrine of repentance did not convince him.

Richard Hooker (like Newman) argued that 'the faith of true believers cannot be divorced from hope and love'. Faith is certainly made perfect by good works, 'and yet no works of ours good without faith'. Paradoxically, said Hooker, 'we are justified by faith alone, and yet hold truly that without good works we are not justified' (see pages 63–6).

The value of Jeremy Taylor's writings is that they go in some depth into the *nature of faith* and I have set out his view on pages 84–7. Richard Baxter (pages 88–90), who thought of faith as 'obeying trust', argued that no one was justified unless they produced 'Evangelical works' which rendered them worthy of justification.

John Owen disagreed with Taylor and Baxter on justification and it was through his writings that William Grimshaw was converted, with such memorable results for the spread of the gospel in the north of England.

Some years after his Aldersgate experience, John Wesley came across some Lutheran and Calvinist authors, 'whose confused and undigested accounts magnified faith to such an amazing size, that it quite hid all the rest of the commandments'. This would never do for Wesley. 'Justifying faith cannot exist without previous repentance,' he said. 'Whoever desires to find favour with God should cease to do evil, and learn to do well'.[8] Even though many remember Wesley for the description of his Aldersgate experience as the time when he felt he 'did trust in Christ, Christ alone for salvation' (pages 123–4), the mature Wesley came to see faith as a moral and spiritual act of the will expressing itself in love – and in this his ideas more resembled those of Taylor and Baxter than of the Lutherans. Augustine also saw faith as an act of the will.

Generally, however, at the time of the eighteenth-century Evangelical revival it seems that whether preachers of the gospel were influenced by either the Taylor/Baxter emphasis or the Luther/Calvin approach to justification, the results were similar. Grimshaw had been converted through reading Owen, but was supported and admired by Wesley – the Arminian who was nearer to Baxter than Calvin. Both Wesley and Grimshaw had hearts which were full of Christ, were convinced of the vileness of sin, the need for repentance, the call to holiness and the life of the world to come. Wesley gladly said of Grimshaw: 'A few such as him would make a nation tremble. He carries fire wherever he goes!'

In colonial America, before the Calvinist Whitefield arrived, most Anglican clergy believed that through both faith and good works, people co-operated with God's grace in salvation. For them, conversion came about gradually as men and women co-operated with the Holy Spirit, who led them through a process which involved reason, faith, good works and habits of piety. They criticised Whitefield for implying that we are passive in the work of regeneration.

In nineteenth-century Oxford, the Tractarians believed that Evangelicals used only selected passages – especially parts of Paul's epistles – to support their version of Christianity. They accused them of paying too little attention to passages like the Sermon on the Mount, with its high standard of Christian righteousness and absence of obvious references to the atonement. Evangelicals, they said, thought of these passages as mere moralising – not the gospel (pages 241–2).

John Stott agrees with the leaders of the Oxford Movement where they draw attention to the dangerous effects that the Protestant doctrine of justification can have on behaviour – that it could lead to passivity or antinomianism (the view that Christians are set free by grace from the need to observe any moral law). He refers to Romans 6:1 as Paul's own rebuke of this error. He also agrees with

Newman when he spoke of the cross in two ways: as a place where Christ has done something for us, but also as a picture of what should happen in the life of the believer – being crucified with Christ and taking up the cross.

Newman believed that justification *was* wholly the work of God; it came from God to us; it was a power exerted on our souls by him, however, Christ's cross did not justify by being looked at but by being applied. Christ atoned by the offering of himself on the cross; and he justified by the mission of his Spirit.

Professor James Barr argues that the New Testament may be read in a fashion in which justification by faith is much less central than Protestant and Evangelical tradition has led us to believe; the New Testament can be read equally well in a fashion in which other emphases, including Catholic ones, are dominant.

Jim Packer's view is that it is not 'any theory about faith and justification' which brings salvation to people, but 'trusting Jesus himself as Lord, Master and divine Saviour'. He has drawn attention to the danger of holding a doctrine of 'justification, not by works, but by words – words, that is, of notional soundness and precision'. Packer has pointed out how 'it is the way of fundamentalists to follow the path of contentious orthodoxism, as if the mercy of God in Christ automatically rests on persons who are notionally correct and is just automatically withheld from those who fall short of notional correctness on any point of substance'.

Packer believes that many Catholics who would disagree with the Reformation teaching on 'justification by imputed righteousness, or who have never either heard or understood this doctrine, nevertheless love and trust Jesus. Isn't this what matters?' He argues that the teaching of both the Council of Trent and the *Catechism of the Catholic Church* is basically that of Augustine. Are some Evangelicals suggesting that Augustine was no Christian or that he had no gospel?[9]

Beyond the Reformation disputes

We have seen that Evangelicals have not always agreed among themselves on justification; that some of them have found the practical outworking of Luther's doctrine disturbing; and that their beliefs have been criticised by non-Evangelicals.

Critics of Evangelicals argue that they read the Bible through the 'lens of the Reformation' which subtly distorts the balance of scriptural teaching on justification. They suggest that there are other lenses which do more justice to the overall tone of Scripture than the slogans which were highlighted by the reformers. They say that Luther and the reformers were, like us all, people of their time, with ideas which required philosophical assumptions which simply did not exist at the time of the New Testament.

These critics question the fact that a large body of (Catholic) Christians found it possible to do theology prior to the Reformation without reference to a doctrine which many Evangelicals now regard as indispensable. At the very least they would argue that the doctrine of justification by faith was not as central for Paul as it was for Luther; and they point out that Luther's understanding made it difficult for him to accept the Book of James.

Some critics of Luther's view of justification argue that the 'forensic' view of justification is not a central New Testament metaphor (forensic means 'as used in lawcourts'). If righteousness is a forensic matter, they argue, then why does God not declare that we are all righteous, believers and unbelievers alike?

Some theologians believe that in the history of Western theology, legal imagery has come to dominate thinking about grace and forgiveness. They argue that grace, forgiveness and repentance are not legal matters, but are concerned with a transformation in the soul itself. Remitting someone's sins in a legal sense might relieve them of punishment, but it will not change them or do them good. Repentance is a requirement of forgiveness, not because that is the legal way of things, but because an unrepentant soul closes itself to the healing and forgiveness which is the gift of grace. They see this as a process, a working out of salvation (Phil. 2:12–13).

Tom Wright, Dean of Lichfield, has taught New Testament studies in British and American universities, and has been described as one of the world's foremost scholars on the apostle Paul. He appears on Evangelical platforms and is associated with Evangelical causes although he believes that labels can be confusing, even if offering a loose indicator of someone's background and tradition of spirituality.

His recent book *What Saint Paul Really Said* besides answering A. N. Wilson's argument that Paul, not Jesus, founded Christianity, also offers a major study of justification in Paul's thought and its place in the apostle's gospel. 'When people proclaim most loudly', he writes, 'that they are being Pauline, that the great apostle is their real guiding star, then we find often enough that they are elevating one aspect of his thinking above all the others, so much so that other aspects, for which he was equally concerned, are left to one side or even outrageously denied.'[10]

What does Paul mean by 'gospel'? Wright suggests that we should not think of Paul's gospel as a message about 'how one gets saved', but as an announcement about Jesus. Paul's gospel reveals God in all his grace and love supremely demonstrated at Calvary. But it does not just reveal all this so that 'people can admire it from a distance'. It reveals it precisely by putting it into action. Paul discovered on his missionary journeys that when he announced the lordship of Jesus Christ, the sovereignty of Jesus the king, this announcement was the means by which God reached out with his love and changed the hearts and lives of men and women, liberating them from the paganism which had held them captive, enabling them to become, for the first time, the truly human beings they were meant to be. 'The gospel, Paul would have said, is not just about God's power saving people. It is God's power at work to save people.'[11]

Paul's good news for pagans was not the sort of good news which told them they were more or less all right as they were, but the sort of good news which told them that, though they were at present going about things in a totally wrong way, the God who made them loved and longed to remake them. Paul stood out against the many gods with the news of the one true Creator God.

Paul's message to the pagan world was that God, through the fulfilment of his covenant with Israel, was reconciling the world to himself. The true God had revealed himself in his crucified and risen Son and summoned the whole world to repentance and a new allegiance.

The way you could tell who belonged to the people of God was quite simply by faith: faith in the God who sent his Son to die and rise again for the sake of the whole world. This was the point where the doctrine of 'justification by faith' became crucially relevant in Paul's mission to the pagan world. It was not the message he would announce on the street to the puzzled pagans of Corinth; it was not the main thrust of his evangelistic message. 'It was the thing his converts most needed to know in order to be assured that they really were part of God's people.'[12]

What does Paul mean by the phrase 'the righteousness of God' in the early chapters of Romans? Wright takes it to refer to God's own faithfulness to his promises, to the covenant. God's 'righteousness', especially in Isaiah chapters 40–55, is that aspect of God's character which causes him to save Israel, despite her repeated disobedience. The righteous God has made promises; Israel can trust these promises.

Tom Wright argues that 'righteousness', as used by Paul in the early chapters of Romans, *is* a forensic term, i.e. taken from the lawcourt. However, the background needs to be understood. In a Hebrew lawcourt a judge decided an issue between a plaintiff, bringing an accusation, and a defendant, who stood accused. The judge had to try the case according to the law; he had to be impartial; he had to punish sin as it deserved; he had to support and uphold those who were defenceless and had no one but him to plead their cause.

If and when the court upheld the plaintiff's accusations, he or she was 'righteous'. This did not necessarily mean that he or she was good, morally upright or virtuous; it simply meant that in this case the court had vindicated him or her in the charge they had brought. The same would have been true in the case of a defendant acquitted of a charge brought by an accuser. Using the language of the Hebrew lawcourt, it makes no sense to say that the judge either imputes or imparts his righteousness to either the plaintiff or the defendant. 'To imagine the defendant somehow receiving the judge's righteousness is simply a category mistake. This is not how the language works.'[13]

God's own righteousness is his covenant faithfulness, because of which he will vindicate Israel, and bestow on her the status of 'righteous', as the vindicated or acquitted defendant. But God's righteousness remains, so to speak, God's own property.

Tom Wright is convinced that this is the only understanding which does justice to the many Old Testament Scriptures to which Paul refers or alludes in Romans. For him, it is the key to understanding Paul on justification. What God has done in Christ was all along the meaning and intention behind the promises made to Abraham in Genesis 15.

Certainly, says Wright, Paul uses the metaphor of the lawcourt in Romans at a key stage of his argument. But it is not at the heart of his theology. If you do not go beyond the lawcourt metaphor, you are left with a God who is logical and correct, but hardly one you would want to worship. If, however, you understand God's righteousness in terms of the covenant faithfulness of God, you are led on to Paul's passages in Romans chapters 5 to 8, where he speaks of the cross of Jesus revealing supremely the *love* of God and his description of the new life in the Spirit. 'God's love is the driving force of his justice, so that it could never become a blind or arbitrary thing, a cold system which somehow God operates, or which operates God.'[14]

A series of groups and individuals whom we have met in our history of Anglican Evangelicals have either explicitly or implicitly had reservations about an understanding of the gospel which Wright summarises like this: 'People are always trying to pull themselves up by their own efforts; to make themselves good enough for God, or for heaven. This doesn't work; one can only be saved by the sheer unmerited grace of God, appropriated not by good works but by faith.'[15]

This view, says Wright, though not totally wrong, does not do justice to the 'richness and precision' of Paul's doctrine and distorts it at various points. He argues that Paul's polemic against the law in Galatians should not be interpreted as a rebuke directed either against straightforward self-help moralism or against the more subtle snare of 'legalism' as many have suggested. Paul does not regard God's moral law as a bad thing. 'Do we, then, nullify the law by this faith? Not at all! Rather, we uphold the law.' (Rom. 3:31). Paul regards the law as a vital stage in God's plan.

Pelagianism is the heresy which holds that you can take the initial and fundamental steps towards salvation by your own efforts, apart from the grace of God. Wright insists that Paul was not trying in

Romans to stop people being Pelagians 350 years before the error arose.

The gospel is preached when the message about Jesus and his cross and resurrection is announced to men and women. God works through his Spirit on their hearts. They come to believe the message. They join the Christian community through baptism and begin to share in its common life. That is how people come into a relationship with the living God.

The badge of membership of this community is faith, the confession that Jesus is Lord and the belief that God raised him from the dead (Rom. 10:9). 'Faith' should not be seen, as some Evangelicals have viewed it, as something which is opposed to 'moralism' or as a preference for a religion of inward feeling above that which is outward and formal. Faith 'is very precise and specific. It is faith in the gospel message, the announcement of the true God as defined in and through Jesus Christ'.[16] There have been times in the history of the Church when a half-understood doctrine of justification by faith has been used to add weight to an anti-moralism which is almost indistinguishable from secular culture.

Unlike Bishop Spong, who, as we saw in Part Seven, appears to believe that modern man has arrived at profound new insights into the human condition, Tom Wright believes that the Western world is moving rapidly towards new forms of paganism. If we want to address our own generation with the message of Jesus Christ, we need to rediscover the way in which the gospel really is good news for a pagan world.

If Jesus is Lord of the world, the goddess Aphrodite, the goddess of erotic love, is not. Paul confronted this goddess on the streets of every pagan city he visited, just as he would in most cities of the world today. 'Aphrodite's power,' writes Tom Wright, 'which holds millions in its iron grip, promising bliss and giving confusion and misery, must be challenged in Jesus' name.'[17] Charles Wesley expressed the true alternative to this confusion and misery with his usual economy of words:

A peace to sensual minds unknown,
A joy unspeakable.[18]

The gospel challenges people to give their allegiance to the true king and to discover through the process of death and rebirth the joy of genuine self-giving love.

Perhaps unwisely, I venture to make some observations and suggestions on the subject of justification against the background of the story I have told in this book and my prayerful reflections on it.

A check with my wife has confirmed that, as I suspected, I am a sinner standing in need of the grace of God. I am therefore relieved to discover from Scripture that we are justified by grace through faith (e.g. Rom. 5; Gal. 3; Eph. 2) and that 'there is now no condemnation for those who are in Christ Jesus' (Rom. 8:1). At the same time, my Evangelical roots remind me that I must take the whole of Scripture seriously. With this thought in mind, I notice that the first use of the word 'justified' in Romans tells me that it is 'the doers of the law who will be justified' (Rom. 2:13 AV, NRSV), and that Paul urged those who have died to sin not 'to live in it any longer' (Rom. 6:2). Moreover, if I turn to the book of James, I find, not in isolated verses but in a lengthy passage (Jas. 2:14–26), that the writer insists repeatedly and precisely that 'a person is justified by what he does and not by faith alone' (Jas. 2:24). I have read valiant efforts by Bible commentators to reconcile Paul and James (and Paul with himself), some more convincing than others. I do not think it will do, as Luther did, to refuse to regard James as on a par with the other Bible books because he thought it contradicted Paul and was therefore 'a right strawy Epistle'. The most successful attempts I have seen to reconcile Paul and James are along the lines developed by Peter Lombard in the twelfth century. Lombard distinguished between unformed faith (pure intellectual assent to a proposition) and 'faith expressing itself through love', which Paul himself says is 'the only thing that counts' (Gal. 5:6).

Luther was a giant of Church history. I do not disagree with the Evangelical assessment which holds that Luther's teachings, courageous stands and voluminous writings directed people to the centrality of Christ; drove him to seek to re-form what had become de-formed; corrected distortions in medieval theology and super-stitions in medieval practice; restored the doctrine of the priesthood of all believers; and modified the mysterious power and authority of the priesthood, removing the priest's almost magical powers to mediate between humankind and God. I have read that many Catholic scholars admit that 'it was Christendom's greatest mistake when she rejected the monk of Wittenberg' (where Luther taught theology and biblical exegesis).[19]

Luther always held to biblical standards of morality as he understood them and believed that the performance of 'evangelically motivated good works' in home, church and society was the essence of the holy life. 'Faith', he affirmed, 'engages tirelessly and endlessly in such works.'[20]

Having said this, the story which has emerged in this book – of disagreement over justification within Evangelicalism and criticism from without – suggests that Luther's interpretation of Pauline thought on justification (at least as popularly understood by many Protestants) may not have been entirely satisfactory. This suspicion is reinforced by the number of twentieth-century New Testament scholars who have cast doubts on Luther's account of the function of justification language in Pauline theology.

We cannot simply ignore the severe Tractarian assertion made in nineteenth-century Oxford that certain strands of Evangelical anti-moralism were actually more damaging than the secular morality followed by some respectable but godless people. Certainly I think that Evangelicals should beware of expressing the doctrine of justification by faith carelessly, for example, by implying that there is something rather distasteful in the pursuit of good works. For the Christian who has been called by God to be holy, good works must always be better than bad works.

Personally I have found it helpful to read Tom Wright's explanation of the sense in which Paul used lawcourt imagery, the place which this language occupied in his wider theology, and the implication all this has for the tone, emphasis and thrust of the gospel we must proclaim to a troubled world in the years ahead.

CHRIST TRANSFORMING CULTURE

When Anglican Evangelicals announce the lordship of Christ in the twenty-first century, they should make it clear that the one true God who has dealt with sin in Jesus now calls men and women to abandon the idols which hold them captive and to discover a new life. The gospel does not primarily offer a certain type of self-fulfilment or a certain style of religious experience. Neither is it a take-it-or-leave-it thing, or a hobby to add to a list of interests in a curriculum vitae. The gospel is a royal announcement. It offers a new way of life which ultimately will be the way of self-fulfilment. But first it offers the cross. New experiences may result from giving oneself to Jesus. But, as Bonhoeffer reminded us earlier in the twentieth century, the only experience guaranteed by Jesus's summons is that of carrying the cross. Following Jesus is costly; and any preaching which, in an attempt to be 'non-threatening', hides that fact is not the gospel. It is simply offering 'cheap grace'.

Many young people grow up in a spiritual void, without faith or hope. Scepticism has triumphed and the loss of serious faith has been devastating for our society. 'Culture' for the young is often a world of soundbites and images which may be violent or sexually explicit rather than truly beautiful and good. When people carry on their lives without worshipping their Creator, they live in a state of frustration, the origin of which is unknown to them, since nobody has effectively told them what is missing in their lives. If God has indeed made us for himself, there is no more human way of living than by following Jesus and living in the power of his Spirit. Archbishop Frederick Temple believed that the best proof of Christianity was to be found, not as Paley taught in external evidence, but in the correspondence of its teachings with the deepest things in human nature.

The temptation for the Church is to construct new forms of worship and evangelism from the debris of popular culture: to give people religion by making a religion of what they already have. This simply reinforces the idea that that there is nothing higher than the human and that no one stands in judgment over us. Roger Scruton believes that if the churches are to restore faith and hope to the young, 'they must find the means not only of attracting young people to church, but of making them uncomfortable when they get there ... The church has one overriding duty, which is to cease pandering to a popular culture rotten with idolatry, and to stand once again in judgment over it.'[21]

We smile at William Grimshaw's quaint behaviour in seeking to drive sin out of the moorland villages of eighteenth-century Yorkshire – but he packed his church with hundreds of communicants. We feel uneasy about Wesley's insistence that Christian perfection (as he carefully defined it, page 128) was achievable in this life – but he left hundreds of thousands of disciples behind him on both sides of the Atlantic and was a key human influence in producing a revival in the Church of England which changed the course of its history.

In the golden years of Evangelicalism in the American Episcopal Church in the middle of the nineteenth century, preaching was uncompromising. Anglican Evangelicals delivered the strong call of God to a careless and godless American people, awakening in each soul a sense of its accountability to God, its need of personal salvation, its obligation to lead a godly and consistent life in view of the judgment to come. The test of religion was a conscious personal experience of its power to change the heart and create newness of life. Those were the years of Evangelicalism's greatest success within the Episcopal Church. The American Church was on fire.

Edward Norman has drawn attention to the emergence of 'religion as therapy', which he calls a 'modern and probably baneful development'. He points out that 'in the past, religion was often seen as a set of terrifying obligations, an assent to awesome truths which preceded, not the nice feelings we expect, but privation and suffering'. But today, 'religion is ceasing to be a matter of doctrines and is becoming a way of sacralising individual emotional need'.[22]

Even some therapists themselves make a similar point. An American Christian psychotherapist asked recently:

When Christ asks us to take up our cross and follow him, is he not describing a road of sanctification that is not only made possible by God's grace, but also includes our own willingness to accept the suffering that is part of what it takes to follow him?

Those who come to me become most whole and holy when they are willing to face and accept the real pain that turns out to be a necessary part of becoming sanctified.

Jim Packer's advice to Anglican Evangelicals is unequivocal. 'Learn a counter-cultural approach to the dominant culture of the country and the dominant culture of the church ... That will mean quite specifically – because here I think is the most glaring point at which the Liberal mind-set seems to infect us all – restore the biblical understanding of sin, what it is and what it does, what it does for individuals, what it does for communities, what it does for the Church. Restore that biblical understanding of sin to your analysis of every human situation and every church problem. Don't forget sin. When Evangelicals become bishops, when Evangelicals become Archbishops, somehow they seem to forget about sin. And they make public utterances into which discussion of sin, and diagnosis of troubles in terms of sin, doesn't seem to enter.'

However much we may agree with this analysis of the short-comings of our modern world and the importance of the task facing the Church in being the channel by which Christ may transform that culture, Anglican Evangelicals will be wise to communicate their challenging, transforming message in ways which capture the attention and imagination of today's generation. Clear, uncompromising preaching is vital – but it must be heard.

Listening before speaking

John Saxbee, Bishop of Ludlow, believes that Liberal Christianity has a contribution to make in announcing the good news in this generation. He defines Liberalism in terms of openness, honesty and adaptability to differing cultural contexts. In his book *Liberal Evangelism*, Saxbee quotes with approval Alister McGrath, who has argued that the apologist for Christianity should listen before speaking. However, Saxbee is disappointed that McGrath apparently only wants to listen to his audience so that he may improve the *presentation* of the gospel message, rather than concede the possibility that he may need to adjust its *content* in the light of what he learns from his secular audience.

Saxbee believes that the people who are the products and representatives of our secular culture (Tom Wright and Roger Scruton's modern 'pagans') are also likely to have a grasp on truth, 'and it is in our being and belonging together that we shall move a little closer to that fullness of vision that is our modern goal'. Saxbee argues that he and other Liberal evangelists will need 'the self-confidence to express clearly the truth as we see it, but always in that spirit of humility that truly expects to be challenged and changed by the truth as perceived elsewhere'.[23]

Most Evangelicals would probably react to the Saxbee approach to evangelism by saying, as the Gospel and Culture movement has put it, that 'mission activity should be determined by the content of faith and not the context of culture. Too much attention to culture distorts the message, and Christianity becomes not inculturated but domesticated.'[24] Modern culture is itself based on certain often untested presuppositions, which themselves need to be tested and tried by the Church in the light of the gospel.

What does the gospel have to say to those taken up with post-modernist ideas? 'Postmodernism' and 'postmodernity' are notoriously slippery concepts to define and the literature is vast. The terms, however, tend to cover a range of approaches which regard all belief systems – including Christianity – as equally plausible: 'something is true for you if it is true for you'. Although he grapples with how these ideas should be defined, George Carey has little doubt that they lead to a collapse of morality and, indeed, to collapse at every level.

Tom Wright has a suggestion: 'Paul's view of truth, of reality, of the self, of the controlling story of the creator and the cosmos, of the covenant God and his covenant people – these can serve very well as the true and vital answer to postmodernity's attempt to deconstruct truth and reality, to destabilize and decentre the self, and to destroy all metanarratives.'[25] God is the source of all that is beautiful, good and true.

Jim Packer emphasises that the Anglican ethic is to be reflective and that there is 'no path to maturity except the path of serious thought which faces all the questions and works its way through them'. He believes that Anglican Evangelicals should 'cultivate a passion for truth and wisdom in the great tradition that is in the Anglican heritage – that rational, biblical, wise heritage which must now turn itself to standing against postmodernist irrationality and postmodernist experientialism. Postmodernity and experientialism are just two orchestrations of the anti-intellectualism of our time. But Christianity is a faith which calls upon us and teaches us first and foremost to think. "You shall love the Lord your God with all your mind." You can't be a faithful disciple of the Lord Jesus, you can't be an honest servant of God unless you learn to do that. So we have to stand for rationality in an increasingly irrational age.'

Living the message

Looking to the next century, Packer returns to one of his favourite themes. 'Let us seek in the Church and in our own lives a passion for holiness. No movement that claims to stand for truth – I mean in the Christian sense – will have credibility if it isn't backed by holiness of life. As we seek reconstruction of the Church in terms of truth and gospel, let us see to it that we don't fall victim to the secular idea that the truest path of human life is the path of self-discovery and self-expression . . . The gospel speaks differently: the gospel speaks of a Christ who renews sinful hearts and who by his Spirit engenders holiness in his followers . . .

'And so, let's distinguish between Christian holiness and the idea that Christians are called to be the nicest people in the society of which they're part according to the ideals which that society has set itself. We're called to be different and we're called to be wholly different with a 'wh' by being holy with a single 'h'. God give us a passion for holiness.'

Paul does not see holiness as an optional extra to which some Christians are called but not others. An important theme in his writings (as in the words of Jesus himself) is that genuine holiness is seen in terms of dying and rising with Christ (e.g. Rom. 6:1–10, 17; Eph. 2:1–10). The *agent* of holiness is the indwelling Holy Spirit; the *experience* of holiness is that it requires effort and conflict. The apostle Peter reminds us that growth in holiness demands effort in adding to faith a whole list of qualities culminating in love (2 Pet.

1:5–6). Holiness is the appropriate and right way by which those who find themselves, by grace, believing members of the family of God should live.

John Stott believes an insistence on holiness is an old Evangelical emphasis which is in danger of being lost today. He suspects it is being replaced by an emphasis on experience. 'Experience is good,' he says, 'but holiness is better. For holiness is Christlikeness, and Christlikeness is God's eternal purpose for his children.'

If Anglican Evangelicals are to preach the gospel, they cannot expect to be exempt from living the gospel. Paul's words to the Philippians remain true: 'Whatever happens, conduct yourselves in a manner worthy of the gospel of Christ' (Phil. 1:27).

I have found the history of Anglican Evangelicalism on both sides of the Atlantic an inspiring story to tell. The 650 years which have elapsed since Wycliffe preached a Bible-based, Christ-centred religion of the heart have produced saints, religious and social reformers, evangelists, missionaries and scholars, as well as some unedifying squabbles. The lives of many thousands of 'ordinary Christians' who have loved their Lord, his work and their Bibles have gone unrecorded in these pages. I have no doubt that in the new millennium, the Anglican Church will need a major representation of Evangelicals; and I understand the argument that Evangelical Christianity is, at its best, authentic Christianity. I also believe that Evangelicals have much to learn from all that is best in the diverse richness of the Anglican heritage. I pray that in the twenty-first century there will be many Evangelicals who feel they can serve God within the Anglican Communion.

I am happy to give almost the last word to the former Bishop of Thetford, John Stott's biographer. Tim Dudley-Smith has said that the essential marks of Evangelicalism are 'the search for holiness, the spread of the gospel, and the cross of Christ; underpinned of course in all true Evangelicalism by the word of the Scriptures and the work of the Spirit'. I trust that those qualities will continue to mark Anglican Evangelicals in the new century. The search for holiness and the spread of the gospel will go together – for all people of true holiness are living arguments for God.

NOTES

Introduction

1. Alister McGrath, *A Passion for Truth: The Intellectual Coherence of Evangelicalism* (Apollos, 1996), p. 22.

Part One: Church on fire with reforming zeal

1. Quoted by F. F. Bruce in *The English Bible* (Lutterworth Press, 1961), p. 29.
2. *Church Times*, 29 November 1996, p. 2.
3. Merle d'Aubigné, *History of the Reformation of the Sixteenth Century* (Religious Tract Society, 1846), p. 769.
4. Quoted in Procter and Frere, *A New History of the Book of Common Prayer* (Macmillan, 1908), p. 397.
5. Diarmaid MacCulloch, *Thomas Cranmer* (Yale University Press, 1996), p. 593.
6. Kenneth Hylson-Smith, *The Churches in England from Elizabeth I to Elizabeth II*, Vol. 1, 1558–1668 (SCM Press, 1996), p. 29.
7. Richard Hooker, *Of the Laws of Ecclesiastical Polity* (1594–97), (Keble's edition, Oxford University Press, 1836).
8. Anthony Russell, *The Country Parson* (SPCK, 1993).
9. Quoted by J. I. Packer in his introduction to the Banner of Truth edition of Baxter's *The Reformed Pastor* (Banner of Truth, 1974).
10. ibid., p. 12.
11. See, for example, C. F. Allison, *The Rise of Moralism: The Proclamation of the Gospel from Hooker to Baxter* (SPCK, 1966).

12. Jeremy Taylor, *Holy Living and Dying: with Prayers containing the whole duty of a Christian* (George Bell edition, 1897), pp. 162–3.
13. ibid., p. 165.
14. Packer's introduction to *The Reformed Pastor*, p. 14.
15. ibid., p.16.
16. ibid., p. 17.
17. ibid., p. 18.
18. ibid., pp. 64–5.
19. ibid., p. 53.
20. See, for example, Allison, *The Rise of Moralism*, p. 158.
21. Alister McGrath, *To Know and Serve God: A Biography of James Packer* (Hodder & Stoughton, 1997), pp. 47–9.
22. J. I. Packer, *Rediscovering Holiness* (Servant Publications, 1992), p. 109.

Part Two: Church on fire in revival

1. G. R. Balleine, *A History of the Evangelical Party in the Church of England* (Church Book Room Press, 1951), p. 18.
2. Arthur Warne, *Church and Society in Eighteenth-Century Devon* (David and Charles, 1969), p. 9, quoted in Michael Hinton, *The Anglican Parochial Clergy: A Celebration* (SCM Press, 1994), p. 9.
3. Quoted in Russell, *The Country Parson*, p. 100.
4. ibid., p. 106.
5. John Wesley, '*Scriptural Christianity*', a sermon before the University of Oxford, 1744.
6. Balleine, *A History of the Evangelical Party in the Church of England*, p. 2.
7. ibid.
8. ibid., p. 4.
9. Robert Backhouse (ed.), *The Journals of George Whitefield* (Hodder & Stoughton, 1993), p. 14.
10. Note added in 1771 to an entry in John Wesley's *Journal* for 29 February, 1738.
11. J. H. Overton, *John Wesley* (Methuen, 1891), p. 44.

12. Reginald Ward and Richard Heitzenrater, *The Works of John Wesley,* Vol. 18, Journals and Diaries I (1735–38) (Abingdon Press, 1988), p. 222.
13. Overton, *John Wesley*, p. 58.
14. Ward and Heitzenrater, *The Works of John Wesley*, Vol. 18, pp. 249–50.
15. ibid., p. 250.
16. Overton, *John Wesley*, pp. 71ff.
17. William Cowper, *The Task*, Book III.
18. Hinton, *The Anglican Parochial Clergy*, pp. 31–2.
19. Balleine, *A History of the Evangelical Party in the Church of England*, p. 90.
20. Hinton, *The Anglican Parochial Clergy*, p. 34.
21. Balleine, *A History of the Evangelical Party in the Church of England*, p. 104.
22. ibid., p. 103.

Part Three: Church on fire in the New World

1. Devereux Jarratt, *The Life of the Reverend Devereux Jarratt: An Autobiography* (The Pilgrim Press, 1995), p. 11.
2. ibid., p. 27.
3. ibid., p. 47.
4. ibid., pp. 47–8.
5. ibid., p. 48.
6. ibid., p. 50.
7. ibid., p. 53.
8. ibid., p. 59.
9. ibid., p. 61.
10. ibid., pp. 88–9.
11. ibid., pp. 86–7.
12. Clowes Chorley, *Men and Movements in the American Episcopal Church* (Charles Scribner's Sons, 1946), pp. 34–5.
13. ibid., pp. 35–6.
14. Robert Bruce Mullin, *Episcopal Vision/American Reality: High Church Theology and Social Thought in Evangelical America* (Yale University Press, 1986), pp. 30ff.

15. ibid., p. 54.
16. Chorley, *Men and Movements in the American Episcopal Church*, p. 29.
17. Diana Hochstedt Butler, *Standing Against the Whirlwind: Evangelical Episcopalians in Nineteenth-Century America* (Oxford University Press, 1995), p. viii.
18. ibid., pp. 67–8.
19. ibid., p. 70.
20. Roger Steer, *Dream of Reality: An Evangelical Encounters the Oxford Movement* (Hodder & Stoughton, 1993), pp. 106–46.
21. H. C. Potter, *Reminiscences of Bishops and Archbishops*, pp. 64–5. Quoted in Chorley, *Men and Movements in the American Episcopal Church*, p. 49.
22. Chorley, ibid., pp. 49–50.
23. ibid., p. 299.
24. ibid., p. 89.
25. James Arthur Muller, *The Episcopal Theological School 1867–1943* (The Episcopal Theological School, Cambridge, Massachusetts, 1943), p. 27.
26. *Historical Magazine of the Episcopal Church*, Vol 1, p. 63, quoted in Chorley, *Men and Movements in the American Episcopal Church*, p. 90.
27. Chorley, ibid., p. 92.
28. Butler, *Standing Against the Whirlwind*, p. 41.
29. ibid., p. 232.

Part Four: Church on fire in nineteenth-century England

1. Balleine, *A History of the Evangelical Party in the Church of England*, p. 119.
2. Eugene Stock, *The History of the Church Missionary Society* (CMS, 1899), Vol 1, p. 253.
3. G. Barnett Smith, *Eminent Christian Workers of the Nineteenth Century* (SPCK, 1893), p. 105.
4. ibid., pp. 110–11.
5. John Martin, *Gospel People? Evangelicals and the Future of Anglicanism* (SPCK, 1997), p. 204.

6. John Henry Newman, *Apologia pro Vita Sua* (Sheed and Ward, 1976), pp. 5–6.
7. Steer, *Dream of Reality*, pp. 48–55.
8. ibid., pp. 150–2.
9. ibid., pp. 171–4.
10. John Charles Ryle, 'Pastoral Address', printed in *Liverpool Diocesan Calendar* (1881), p. 109.
11. Balleine, *A History of the Evangelical Party in the Church of England*, pp. 220–2.
12. John Charles Ryle, *Knots Untied: being Plain Statements on disputed points in Religion from the Standpoint of an Evangelical Churchman* (Charles Murray, 1896), pp. 1–30.
13. John Charles Ryle, *Holiness* (abridged by Robert Backhouse, Hodder & Stoughton, 1996), pp. 9–64.

Part Five: Church on fire in twentieth-century England

1. Russell, *The Country Parson*, p. 117.
2. The Church of England National Assembly (Powers) Act.
3. Christine Hall and Robert Hannaford (eds.), *Order and Ministry* (Gracewing, 1996), p. 118.
4. John Peart-Binns, *Graham Leonard: Bishop of London* (Darton, Longman and Todd, 1988), pp. 3–5.
5. F. W. Dillistone, *Into all the World: A Biography of Max Warren*, (Hodder & Stoughton, 1980), pp. 57–60.
6. Quoted by F. F. Bruce, *Answers to Questions* (Paternoster Press, 1972), pp. 230–1.
7. *Church Times*, 13 October 1995, p. 10.
8. John Stott, *The Cross of Christ* (Inter-Varsity Press, 1986), pp. 279–80.
9. ibid., p. 282.
10. ibid., pp. 281–5.
11. ibid., p. 159.
12. John Stott in *Essentials* (with David L. Edwards, Hodder & Stoughton, 1988), p. 165.
13. John Stott, *The Contemporary Christian* (Inter-Varsity Press, 1992), p. 77.

14. John Stott, *Your Confirmation* (Hodder & Stoughton, 1991), p. 70.
15. John Stott, *Christian Counter-Culture* (Inter-Varsity Press, 1978), p. 42.
16. John Stott, *The Message of Thessalonians* (Inter-Varsity Press, 1991), p. 77.
17. John Stott, *The Message of 2 Timothy* (Inter-Varsity Press, 1973), p. 56.
18. Packer, *Rediscovering Holiness*, p. 9.
19. ibid., p. 15.
20. *Reviews in Religion and Theology* (SCM, May 1997), pp. 67–9.
21. McGrath, *To Know and Serve God*, p. 283.
22. Charles Yeats (ed.), *Has Keele Failed? Reform in the Church of England* (Hodder & Stoughton, 1995), pp. 3–4.
23. ibid., p. 7.
24. ibid., p. 35.
25. ibid., p. 36.
26. McGrath, *To Know and Serve God*, p. 132.
27. Donald Coggan, *The Heart of the Christian Faith* (Collins, 1978), p. 94.
28. John Stott, *The Message of Romans* (Inter-Varsity Press, 1994), p. 328.
29. Yeats (ed.), *Has Keele Failed?*, p. 37.
30. ibid., p. 38.
31. J. I. Packer, *Keep in Step with the Spirit* (IVP, 1984), pp. 94ff and 185–97.
32. ibid., p. 214.
33. Tom Smail, Andrew Walker and Nigel Wright, *Charismatic Renewal: The Search for a Theology* (SPCK, 1993), pp. 63–4.
34. Teddy Saunders and Hugh Sansom, *David Watson* (Hodder & Stoughton, 1992), p. 241, quoted in Hinton, *The Anglican Parochial Clergy*, p. 39.
35. Hinton, *The Anglican Parochial Clergy*, p. 364.
36. David Watson, *Fear No Evil* (Hodder & Stoughton, 1984), p. 171, quoted in Hinton, ibid., p. 364.
37. McGrath, *To Know and Serve God*, pp. 213–4.
38. Quoted in Trevor Lloyd, *Evangelicals, Obedience and Change:*

Notes

A Comment on NEAC (Nottingham 1977) and its Statement (Grove Books, 1977), p. 7.

39. John Habgood, *Making Sense* (SPCK, 1993), pp. 197–206.
40. *Church Times*, 26 May 1995, pp. 8–14.
41. John Saxbee, *Liberal Evangelism* (SPCK, 1994), p. 112.
42. Stott in *Essentials*, p. 106.
43. McGrath, *A Passion for Truth*, pp. 119–24.
44. Packer addressing a conference of Reform in June 1995.
45. Tim Bradshaw, *The Olive Branch: An Evangelical Anglican Doctrine of the Church* (Paternoster Press, 1992), p. 300.
46. *Church Times*, 12 April 1996, p. 5.
47. Ian Bunting (ed.), *Celebrating the Anglican Way* (Hodder & Stoughton, 1996), pp. 14–16.
48. Anglican Communion News Service.
49. *Issues in Human Sexuality* (Report of the House of Bishops, 1991), p. 18.
50. ibid., p. 47.
51. Yeats (ed.), *Has Keele Failed?*, p. 54.
52. ibid., p. 61.
53. ibid., pp. 45–63.
54. ibid., p. 40.

Part Six: Church on fire in twentieth-century America

1. Urban T. Homes, quoted in Butler, *Standing Against the Whirlwind*, p. viii.
2. Marjory Stanway, *Alfred Stanway* (Acorn Press, 1991), p. 230.
3. Janet Leighton, *Lift High the Cross: A History of the Trinity Episcopal School for Ministry* (Harold Shaw Publishers, 1995), p. 87.
4. Frederick Houk Borsch, *The Bible's Authority in Today's Church* (Trinity Press International, 1993), pp. 28–34 and 203–10.
5. Mark Noll, *The Scandal of the Evangelical Mind* (Inter-Varsity Press, 1994), pp. 21–4.
6. ibid., p. 61.
7. ibid., p. 63.
8. Robert E. Webber, *Evangelicals on the Canterbury Trail – Why*

Evangelicals are attracted to the Liturgical Church (Jarrell, 1985), pp. 15–16.

Part Seven: Church on fire over sexuality

1. John Stott, *Issues Facing Christians Today* (Marshall, Morgan and Scott, 1984), p. 311.
2. ibid., pp. 301–22.
3. Christl R. Vonholdt (ed.), *Striving for Gender Identity: Homosexuality and Christian Counselling. A Workbook for the Church* (The Reichenberg Fellowship, 1996), p. 141.
4. ibid., p. 178.
5. McGrath, *A Passion for Truth*, p. 64.
6. *The Times*, 15 July 1997.

Part Eight: Gospel people for the twenty-first century?

1. John Stott, *Your Mind Matters* (Inter-Varsity Press, 1972), pp. 13ff.
2. Reginald Heber, *The Whole Works of the Right Rev. Jeremy Taylor, DD,* Vol. 1 (Longman, Orme, Brown, Green and Longmans, 1839), p. cxci.
3. Martin, *Gospel People?*, p. 135.
4. Archbishop George Carey speaking at the 1995 Anglican Evangelical Assembly.
5. Andrew Walker, *Telling the Story* (SPCK, 1996), p. 2.
6. ibid., p. 119.
7. Quoted by McGrath in *To Know and Serve God*, p. 266.
8. J. H. Overton, *John Wesley*, p. 44.
9. McGrath, *To Know and Serve God*, p. 274.
10. Tom Wright, *What Saint Paul Really Said* (Lion, 1997), p. 11.
11. ibid., p. 61.
12. ibid., p. 94.
13. ibid., p. 98.
14. ibid., pp. 110–11.
15. ibid., p. 113.

16. ibid., p. 132.
17. ibid., p. 155.
18. Charles Wesley's hymn 'All praise to our redeeming Lord', verse 5, lines 3 and 4.
19. Article on Luther in *New Dictionary of Theology* (Inter-Varsity Press, 1988), p. 404.
20. Packer, *Rediscovering Holiness*, p. 105.
21. *The Times*, 15 February 1997.
22. *Church Times*, 11 April 1997, pull-out section, pp. xiii-xiv.
23. Saxbee, *Liberal Evangelism* (SPCK, 1994), pp. 22, 113–14.
24. Walker, *Telling the Story*, p. 6.
25. Wright, *What Saint Paul Really Said*, p. 165.

BIBLIOGRAPHY

Books

Allison, C. F., *The Rise of Moralism: The Proclamation of the Gospel from Hooker to Baxter*, SPCK, 1966

Backhouse, Robert (ed.), *The Journals of George Whitefield*, Hodder & Stoughton, 1993

Balleine, G. R., *A History of the Evangelical Party in the Church of England*, Church Book Room Press, 1951

Barnett Smith, G., *Eminent Christian Workers of the Nineteenth Century*, SPCK, 1893

Barr, James, *Fundamentalism*, SCM Press, 1981 (first published 1976)

Bateman, Rev. Josiah, *The Life of the Right Rev Daniel Wilson, DD, Late Lord Bishop of Calcutta and Metropolitan in India*, John Murray, 1861

Baxter, Richard, *The Reformed Pastor*, Banner of Truth, 1974

Baxter, Richard, *Reliquiae Baxterianae*, Everyman's Library, 1931

Bebbington, David, *Evangelicalism in Modern Britain, A History from the 1730s to the 1980s*, Unwin Hyman, 1989

Bettenson, Henry (ed.), *Documents of the Christian Church*, Oxford University Press, 1967

Borsch, Frederick Houk (ed.), *The Bible's Authority in Today's Church*, Trinity Press International, 1993

Bradshaw, Tim, *The Olive Branch: An Evangelical Anglican Doctrine of the Church*, Paternoster Press, 1992

Bruce, F. F., *Answers to Questions*, Paternoster Press, 1972

Bruce, F. F., *The English Bible: A History of Translations from the Earliest English Versions to the New English Bible*, Lutterworth Press, 1961

Bunting, Ian, *Celebrating the Anglican Way*, Hodder & Stoughton, 1996

Butler, Diana Hochstedt, *Standing Against the Whirlwind: Evangelical Episcopalians in Nineteenth-Century America*, Oxford University Press, 1995

Chorley, E. Clowes, *Men and Movements in the American Episcopal Church*, Charles Scribner's Sons, 1946

Coggan, Donald, *The Heart of the Christian Faith*, Collins, 1978

Cooke, Jean and Rowland-Entwistle, *Theodore, Factbook of British History*, Rainbow Books, 1984

Cross, F. L. and Livingstone, E. A., *The Oxford Dictionary of the Christian Church*, Third Edition, Oxford University Press, 1997

d'Aubigné, Merle, *History of the Reformation of the Sixteenth Century*, Religious Tract Society, 1846

Dillistone, F. W., *Into all the World: A Biography of Max Warren*, Hodder & Stoughton, 1980

Douglas, J. D. (ed.), *Twentieth-century Dictionary of Christian Biography*, Paternoster Press and Baker Books, 1995

Dudley-Smith, Timothy (ed.), *Authentic Christianity: From the Writings of John Stott*, Inter-Varsity Press, 1995

Eagle, Dorothy and Stephens, Meic (eds.), *The Oxford Literary Guide to Great Britain and Ireland*, Oxford University Press, 1993

Edwards, David L. and Stott, John, *Essentials*, Hodder & Stoughton, 1988

Eyre, Richard, *Faith in God?*, Churchman Publishing, 1990

Ferguson, Sinclair B. and Wright, David F. (eds.), *New Dictionary of Theology*, Inter-Varsity Press, 1988

Foxe, John, *Book of Martyrs*, Adam and Co., 1873 edition

Griffith Thomas, W. H., *The Principles of Theology*, Vine Books, 1930

Guinness, Os, *Fit Bodies, Fat Minds: Why Evangelicals Don't Think and What to Do About It*, Hodder & Stoughton, 1995

Habgood, John, *Making Sense*, SPCK, 1993

Hall, Christine and Hannaford, Robert (eds.), *Order and Ministry*, Gracewing, 1996

Harper, Michael, *The True Light: An Evangelical's Journey to Orthodoxy*, Hodder & Stoughton, 1997

Hastings, James (ed. et al.), *A Dictionary of the Bible*, Vol. 1, T & T Clark, 1906

Bibliography

Heber, Reginald, *The Whole Works of the Right Rev. Jeremy Taylor, DD*, Vol. 1, Longman, Orme, Brown, Green and Longmans, 1839

Hinton, Michael, *The Anglican Parochial Clergy: A Celebration*, SCM Press, 1994

Hooker, Richard, *Of the Laws of Ecclesiastical Polity (1594–97)*, Keble's edition, Oxford University Press, 1836

Hylson-Smith, Kenneth, *The Churches in England from Elizabeth I to Elizabeth II*, Vol. 1, 1558–1668, SCM Press, 1996

Hylson-Smith, Kenneth, *The Churches in England from Elizabeth I to Elizabeth II*, Vol. 2, 1689–1833, SCM Press, 1997

Jarratt, Devereux, *The Life of the Reverend Devereux Jarratt: An Autobiography*, The Pilgrim Press, Cleveland, Ohio, 1995 (new edition with a foreword by David L. Holmes)

Leighton, Janet, *Lift High the Cross: A History of the Trinity Episcopal School for Ministry*, Harold Shaw Publishers, 1995

Lewis, Donald and McGrath, Alister (eds.), *Doing Theology for the People of God: Studies in Honour of J. I. Packer*, Apollos, 1996

Lindsay, A. D., *The Nature of Religious Truth*, Hodder & Stoughton, 1927

Lloyd, Trevor, *Evangelicals, Obedience and Change, A Comment on NEAC (Nottingham 1977) and its Statement*, Grove Books, 1977

Loane, Marcus L., *Cambridge and the Evangelical Succession*, Lutterworth Press, 1952

MacCulloch, Diarmaid, *Thomas Cranmer*, Yale University Press, 1996

Magnusson, Magnus, *Chambers Biographical Dictionary*, Chambers, 1990

Martin, John, *Gospel People? Evangelicals and the Future of Anglicanism*, SPCK, 1997

McGrath, Alister, *Iustitia Dei: A history of the Christian doctrine of Justification*, Vol. 1, The Beginnings to the Reformation, Cambridge University Press, 1986

McGrath, Alister, *Iustitia Dei: A history of the Christian doctrine of Justification*, Vol. 2, From 1500 to the present day, Cambridge University Press, 1986

McGrath, Alister, *A Passion for Truth: The intellectual Coherence of Evangelicalism*, Apollos, 1996

McGrath, Alister, *To Know and Serve God: A Biography of James Packer*, Hodder & Stoughton, 1997

Montefiore, Hugh, *Reaffirming the Church of England*, Triangle, 1995

Muller, James Arthur, *The Episcopal Theological School 1867–1943*, The Episcopal Theological School, Cambridge, Massachusetts, 1943

Mullin, Robert Bruce, *Episcopal Vision/American Reality: High Church Theology and Social Thought in Evangelical America*, Yale University Press, 1986

Myers, A. R. (ed.), *English Historical Documents: 1327–1485*, Eyre and Spottiswoode, 1969

Newman, John Henry, *Apologia pro Vita Sua*, Sheed and Ward, 1976

Noll, Mark A. (et al.), *Christianity in America: A Handbook*, Lion Publishing, 1962

Noll, Mark A., *The Scandal of the Evangelical Mind*, Inter-Varsity Press, 1994

The Nottingham Statement, *The official statement of the second National Evangelical Anglican Congress held in April 1977*, Falcon, 1977

Overton, J. H., *John Wesley*, Methuen, 1891

Packer, J. I., *Knowing God*, Hodder & Stoughton, 1973

Packer, J. I., *Keep in Step with the Spirit*, Inter-Varsity Press, 1984

Packer, J. I., *Rediscovering Holiness*, Servant Publications, 1992

Peart-Binns, John, *Graham Leonard: Bishop of London*, Darton, Longman and Todd, 1988

Procter, Francis and Frere, Walter, *A New History of the Book of Common Prayer*, Macmillan, 1908

Ramsey, Michael, *Introducing the Christian Faith*, SCM Press, 1970 edition

Reid, Daniel G. (ed. et al.), *Concise Dictionary of Christianity in America*, Inter-Varsity Press, 1995

Reid, Gavin (ed.), *Hope for the Church of England?*, Kingsway, 1986

Russell, Anthony, *The Country Parson*, SPCK, 1993

Ryle, John Charles, *Knots Untied: being Plain Statements on disputed points in Religion from the Standpoint of an Evangelical Churchman*, Charles Murray, 1896

Bibliography

Ryle, John Charles, *Holiness,* abridged by Robert Backhouse, Hodder & Stoughton, 1996

Saxbee, John, *Liberal Evangelism*, SPCK, 1994

Smail, Tom, Walker, Andrew and Wright, Nigel, *Charismatic Renewal: The Search for a Theology*, SPCK, 1993

Smith, G. Barnett, *Eminent Christian Workers of the Nineteenth Century*, SPCK, 1893

Southey, Robert, *Life of Wesley*, Vol. 2, Longman, Orme, Brown, Green and Longmans, 1846

Spinka, Matthew (ed.), *Advocates of Reform from Wycliffe to Erasmus*, SCM Press, 1953

Stanway, Marjory, *Alfred Stanway*, Acorn Press (Australia), 1991

Steer, Roger, *Dream of Reality: An Evangelical Encounters the Oxford Movement*, Hodder & Stoughton, 1993

Stephen, Leslie and Lee, Sidney (eds.), *The Dictionary of National Biography*, Oxford University Press, 1917

Stock, Eugene, *The History of the Church Missionary Society*, Vols. 1–4, CMS, 1899–1916

Stott, John, *The Baptism and Fullness of the Holy Spirit*, Inter-Varsity Fellowship, 1964

Stott, John, *Christ the Controversialist*, Tyndale Press, 1970

Stott, John, *Your Mind Matters*, Inter-Varsity Press, 1972

Stott, John, *The Message of 2 Timothy*, Inter-Varsity Press, 1973

Stott, John, *Christian Counter-Culture*, Inter-Varsity Press, 1978

Stott, John, *Issues facing Christians Today*, Marshall, Morgan and Scott, 1984

Stott, John, *The Cross of Christ*, Inter-Varsity Press, 1986

Stott, John, *The Message of Thessalonians*, Inter-Varsity Press, 1991

Stott, John, *Your Confirmation*, Hodder & Stoughton, 1991, revised edition

Stott, John, *The Contemporary Christian*, Inter-Varsity Press, 1992

Stott, John, *The Message of Romans*, Inter-Varsity Press, 1994

Sykes, Stephen, *Unashamed Anglicanism*, Darton, Longman and Todd, 1995

Taylor, Jeremy, *Holy Living and Dying: with Prayers containing the whole duty of a Christian*, George Bell edition, 1897

Thompson, Jim, *Why God? Thinking Through Faith*, Mowbray, 1997

Varlow, Sally, *A Reader's Guide to Writers' Britain*, Prion Books, 1996

Vonholdt, Christl R. (ed.), *Striving for Gender Identity: Homosexuality and Christian Counseling. A Workbook for the Church*, The Reichenberg Fellowship, 1996

Walker, Andrew, *Telling the Story*, SPCK, 1996

Ward, W. Reginald and Heitzenrater, Richard P. (eds.), *The Works of John Wesley*, Vol. 18, Journals and Diaries I (1735–38), Abingdon Press, 1988

Ward, W. Reginald and Heitzenrater, Richard P. (eds.), *The Works of John Wesley*, Vol. 21, Journals and Diaries IV (1755–65), Abingdon Press, 1992

Webber, Robert E., *Evangelicals on the Canterbury Trail – Why Evangelicals are attracted to the Liturgical Church*, Jarrell, 1985

Welsby, Paul A., *A History of the Church of England 1945–1980*, Oxford University Press, 1984

White, Stephen Ross, *Authority and Anglicanism*, SCM Press, 1996

Wright, David and Jill, *30 Hymns of the Wesleys*, Paternoster Press, 1985.

Wright, Nigel, *The Radical Evangelical: Seeking a place to stand*, SPCK, 1996

Wright, Tom, *What Saint Paul Really Said*, Lion, 1997

Yeats, Charles (ed.), *Has Keele Failed? Reform in the Church of England*, Hodder & Stoughton, 1995

Articles and papers

'A bastion of the English nation', pull-out section in the *Church Times*, 11 April 1997, pp. xiii–xiv

'*Amor vincit omnia* – or does it?', translation of article by Wolfhart Pannenberg, *Church Times*, 21 June 1996

'Archbishop's quinquennial', the *Church Times*, 12 April 1996, p. 5

'Backing the basics', feature in the *Church Times*, 13 October 1995, p. 10

Casswell, Peter J., *The Parish Church of Lutterworth*, booklet available in the church, 1978

Chapman, Ian, 'Charles Simeon of Cambridge', article in *The Churchman*, February 1996

Bibliography

'Curators find new Tyndale Bible', articles in the *Church Times*, 29 November 1996, p. 2.

'Goodbye to York: "the best job in the Church"', feature in the *Church Times*, 26 May 1995, pp. 8–14

Harp, Gillis J., '"I don't believe as this my neighbour does . . .": Phillips Brooks and the Forging of Liberal Protestantism', draft article

Harp, Gillis J., ' "We cannot spare you": Phillips Brooks's break with the Evangelical party, 1860–1873', draft article

Levenson Jr, Russell, 'In Worship and Witness, John Stott talks about today's church', article in *The Living Church: The Magazine for Episcopalians*, 5 May 1996, pp. 8–9

'New Synod puts mission first', articles in the *Church Times*, 3 November 1995, p. 5

Noll, Mark A., 'J. I. Packer and the Shaping of American Evangelicalism', article in *Regent College – Don Lewis Project*, 1996

Noll, Stephen F., 'The Righter Trial and Christian Doctrine', article originally written January 1996, as supporting argumentation for the Presenters' counsel; revised and updated April 1996

Noll, Stephen F., 'The Righter Trial and Church Discipline', article April 1996

Percy, Martyn, review of *Doing Theology for the People of God* (Apollos, 1996) in *Reviews in Religion and Theology*, SCM Press, May 1997, pp. 67–9

'Righter case lost for lack of "full, clear authority"', the *Church Times*, 24 May 1996, p. 2

Rodgers, John, 'Anglican Evangelicalism, an essay in theological definition', paper delivered in St Stephen's Church, Sewickley, Pennsylvania, May 1996

Rodgers, John, 'The Present State and the Future of the Evangelical Movement in the Episcopal Church', paper delivered in St Stephen's Church, Sewickley, Pennsylvania, May 1996

Scruton, Roger, 'Golden idols won't fill Anglican pews', article in *The Times*, 15 February 1997

Scruton, Roger, 'Our sexual supermarket', article in *The Times*, 15 July 1997

White, William, 'Essay in High Church Principles', unpublished essay, original manuscript held at Episcopal Divinity School, Cambridge, Massachusetts

INDEX

Index

475

Cuddesdon Theological College 321
Cummins, George David 208, 220
culture 327, 383, 394, 433, 446; and
    Christ 449–54

Dallas Statement 407–9
Dartmouth, Earl of 149, 156
Dartmouth College, New Hampshire
    200
Davids, Peter 351
Davidson, Alex 387
Deacons (Ordination of Women)
    Measure (1986) 330
Decade of Evangelism 338
Declaration of Independence 187
Declaration of Indulgence (1687) 93
Delamotte, Charles 115, 121
Devon 52, 54, 66, 91, 104, 105
Dickens, Charles 236
Dillistone, F. W. 312
Dinwiddie County, Virginia 181
Directory of Public Worship 82–3
Disraeli, Benjamin 237
Dissenters 93, 96, 144, 155, 166, 245
divorce 366, 368
Doane, George Washington 202
Dodd, C. H. 312
Doddridge, Philip 175
Donne, John 74
Drake, Francis 54
Dublin, University of 87
Dudley-Smith, Timothy 454
Dykes, Thomas 166

early Church 58
East India Company 230
Eastburn, Manton 197, 208–11
Eastern Diocese 196
Eclectic Society 228
ecumenism 289
Edward VI 29–34
Edward VII 261
Edwards, David 273, 321
Edwards, Jonathan 174, 278, 370
election 49
Eliot, T. S. 73
elitism 298
Elizabeth I 45–66
Elizabeth II 1, 269
Elliot, Charlotte 203, 387
Emancipation Act (1833) 228
emotionalism 299
England in eighteenth century 101–7
enthusiasm 193, 200
Episcopal Church (ECUSA) 172; and
    'core doctrine' 374–5; dress in 216;
    and bishops (episcopacy) 353; end

of old-style Evangelicalism 221–2;
    and Episcopal Synod of America
    (ESA) 394; form and spirit 218–9;
    formation of 189; General
    Convention, 1977 373–6; golden
    age for Evangelicals 202; needed
    by Evangelicals 352; and other
    denominations 200, 372–3;
    PECUSA, Inc. 376–8; prayer
    meetings 217–8; preaching in 219–
    20; present state 363–9, 373–8,
    413–4; and revival 203, 218–9;
    Sundays 216; system of government
    190
Episcopal Ministry Act (1993) 330
Episcopal Theological School (ETS)
    214–6, 221, 358
Epworth, Lincs 108, 114
Erasmus 18
eternal punishment 221, 282–3
eternity 282
Eton College 165, 244, 249
Eucharist, see Holy Communion
Evangelical, use of the word 3
Evangelical Alliance 287, 427
Evangelical Fellowship of the Anglican
    Communion (EFAC) 291, 350, 363
Evangelical Fellowship for Theological
    Literature (EFTL) 266–7
Evangelicalism 86, 107–8, 131, 134,
    141, 149, 160, 161, 174, 192, 211,
    218, 221–2, 231, 249, 261, 266,
    269, 276, 277; Barr on 308–13; and
    Phillips Brooks 212–3; as a
    continuation of the English
    Reformed tradition 78; and
    Cranmer 22; definition 3–4, 304–8,
    321, 454; Pusey on 244–5; Ryle on
    250–4; Stott on 275–6; strengths
    328–9; under attack from Oxford
    Movement in England 239–46;
    under attack from Oxford
    Movement in America 206–7;
    weaknesses 329
Evangelicals and Catholics Together
    (ECT) 279
evangelism 275, 280, 282–3, 290, 292–
    3, 303, 315, 320, 321, 327, 332,
    338, 342, 350, 352, 359, 365, 449,
    452
Exeter, Devon 27, 54, 66, 229

Factory Act (1833) 236
Factory Act (1844) 237
faith 26, 122–3, 124, 173, 242, 247,
    254, 271, 282, 309, 348, 434, 438,
    440, 444–8, 453; Baxter on 89;

Index

Index

Index